SOUTHERN CRUCIBLE

D0061236

Oxford University Press is a department of the University of Oxford.
It furthers the University's objective of excellence in research,
scholarship, and education by publishing worldwide.

Oxford   New York
Auckland   Cape Town   Dar es Salaam   Hong Kong   Karachi
Kuala Lumpur   Madrid   Melbourne   Mexico City   Nairobi
New Delhi   Shanghai   Taipei   Toronto

With offices in
Argentina   Austria   Brazil   Chile   Czech Republic   France   Greece
Guatemala   Hungary   Italy   Japan   Poland   Portugal   Singapore
South Korea   Switzerland   Thailand   Turkey   Ukraine   Vietnam

Copyright © 2015 by Oxford University Press.

Published in the United States of America by
Oxford University Press
198 Madison Avenue, New York, NY 10016
http://www.oup.com

Oxford is a registered trade mark of Oxford University Press.

The CIP data is on-file at the Library of Congress.

ISBN: 978-0-19-976363-4

Printing number: 9 8 7 6 5 4 3 2 1

Printed in the United States of America
on acid-free paper

SOUTHERN CRUCIBLE

The Making of an American Region

VOLUME II

William A. Link

NEW YORK   OXFORD
OXFORD UNIVERSITY PRESS

Contents

List of Maps

Acknowledgments

This book presented me with the daunting task of digesting several generations of rich scholarship about the history of the American South. That scholarship has not let up; if anything, southern history continues to attract among the best thinking in US history. I have drawn on this body of work, new and old, and I must thank the larger community of historians of the South for their talent contributions, past and present. I am grateful to a number of people and institutions whose help made this book possible. Brian Wheel of Oxford University Press (OUP) first suggested the book; no doubt, it would not have been published without his advice, support, and encouragement. I also appreciate the assistance of Brian's coworkers at OUP, including Gina Bochetta, Taylor Pilkington, and Brianna Provenzano.

I have profited from various scholars who read and reread, affirmed and challenged, my mostly unformed ideas emerging from early drafts. I appreciate the anonymous readers from Oxford who provided trenchant and useful suggestions on a first draft. Michele Gillespie read the entire first volume, and I benefited from her sharp editorial and conceptual sense. Steven Lawson read the latter portion of the second volume with extreme care, and he spared readers omissions and errors. Jim Broomall, Pete Carmichael, Christine Flood, Matt Gallman, Watson Jennison, Aaron Sheehan-Dean, and Ben Wise were likewise helpful. Finally, I also relied on the support of my graduate assistants who worked on details, large and small, related to the book. Matt Hall helped with an early version, as did Brenden Kennedy, Allen Kent, and Chris Ruehlen. Allison Fredette assisted with many things and began the process of assembling illustrations and maps. Jenn Lyon did a superb job organizing these images and obtaining permissions. The book could not have been written without this substantial assistance.

I must also acknowledge the continued support of the University of Florida. I was afforded a substantial start on reading and writing while on sabbatical leave, and the Richard J. Milbauer Fund has supported travel to libraries and time for writing. I also profited from the warm collegiality of colleagues and library staff at the University of North Carolina at Chapel Hill (UNC). Harry Watson secured an appointment for me at the Center for the Study of the American South; Jocelyn Neal and Kenneth Janken have kept me on. The most important part of this appointment resulted in continued access to the magnificent libraries at UNC, including Davis Library, the Southern Historical Collection, and the North Carolina Collection. Appropriately, this part of the world is known as the center of the southern history universe.

My family has been a constant source of support. Snow Camp provided a wonderful location for writing without the interference of human beings and the Internet. My daughters listened to much about the book, with their usual sympathy and interest. My sister Peggy and brother-in-law Michael have been unfailingly hospitable, providing a home away from home in Chapel Hill. Susannah, as always, has been my best critic and editor.

William A. Link
Snow Camp, NC
August 2015

Preface

On the morning of July 10, 2015, a scorching hot day, the state of South Carolina lowered the Confederate battle flag that had been flying since 1961 at the state capitol grounds in Columbia. One hundred and fifty years after the end of the Civil War, spurred on by the murder, on June 17, of nine African Americans by a flag-waving white supremacist in the Emanuel African Methodist Episcopal Church in Charleston, public opinion had decisively turned against this symbol of a racist past. A crowd of eight thousand onlookers chanted "Take it down, Take it down" as the flag was lowered. An honor guard comprising seven state highway patrolmen—five white and two black—cranked the mechanism that controlled the flag, lowering it in about thirty seconds as the crowd erupted into a cry of "USA! USA!" once it reached the ground. Later that day, the flagpole was also removed, and the Confederate battle flag was taken to the Confederate Relic Room and Military Museum, a state-supported museum in Columbia.[1]

The Confederate battle flag flies over some southern government buildings—or is part of some state flags—and appears on vanity license plates across the South, while numerous other symbols of the Confederacy survive into the twenty-first century. Alabama recognizes three state holidays: Robert E. Lee's and Jefferson Davis's birthdays, along with Confederate Memorial Day. Four other southern states observe Confederate Memorial Day. Texas celebrates Confederate Heroes Day on Lee's birthday, January 19, which is also Martin Luther King's birthday. Many county courthouses across the South contain memorials to fallen southern soldiers. Icons such as Robert E. Lee, Jefferson Davis, and even former slave trader, Klansman, and Confederate cavalryman Nathan Bedford Forrest are memorialized by named

---

[1] Richard Fausset and Alan Blinder, "Era Ends as South Carolina Lowers Confederate Flag," *New York Times*, July 10, 2015.

buildings, schools, roads, and bridges. A number of federal military installations—Ft. A. P. Hill, Ft. Bragg, and Ft. Benning, along with seven other military bases—are named for Confederate heroes. The memory of the Civil War, and the strong sense of southern white nationalism, served as powerful, living symbols of the importance of the past. Supporters saw these symbols as part of a heritage of independence, bravery, and valor. Opponents saw them as vestiges of slavery and white supremacy.

During the past four centuries, the American South came into existence as the most distinctive region in the United States. How this occurred was a historical process and can be understood only as a result of the South's unique past. The creation of the distinctive South was, in other words, part of a "crucible" of historical processes and factors. Its "otherness" reflected a particular history that spawned often-conflicting forces of regionalism and nationalism; conditions that were uniquely southern became, to a large extent, American characteristics. The American Revolution, the advent of industrial capitalism and commercial agriculture, the Civil War, white supremacy, the New Deal and World War II, and the modern civil rights movement all played roles in defining the South. Binding the South together was (and is) race. Although most of British North America adopted slavery, the region south of the Potomac eventually embraced it to such an extent that the institution dominated all its political, economic, social, and cultural institutions. Owning the world's largest number of enslaved African Americans, the southern master class dominated political life in the growing American Republic, defining a way of life that eventually set it apart from the nation. Even after the Civil War proved a catastrophe for slaveholders, southern whites reimposed white supremacy by the end of the nineteenth century.

Southern Crucible presents the story of the American South in a form that can be understood by students and general readers. It explains, in twenty-four chapters, how and why the American South came into existence. Its coverage is comprehensive, from the first peoples and their contact with invading Europeans, to cultural and social changes affecting the South up until the early twenty-first century. It combines a general narrative with a thematic framework, combining the diversity within the South with the ways in which southerners, white and black, fashioned a strong regional identity. It combines an understanding of politics and power with cultural, social, and economic forces that shaped the lives of ordinary people.

As an organizing theme, the book charts the central role of race in the evolution of the powerful regional identity—and the clash of identities—over the course of southern history. The establishment of plantation slavery in the seventeenth century; its solidification in social, legal, constitutional, and political institutions by 1776; and its revitalization as a result of the cotton boom all made racial domination a prevailing feature of southern life by the time of the Civil War. The destruction of slavery as a result of the war, followed by emancipation, the uncertainties of freedom, and the harsh reimposition of white supremacy, defined the New South era. But slavery and emancipation cast a long shadow. The undoing of public segregation during the civil rights era made the problem of race a national, even international, challenge. As black scholar W. E. B. Du Bois declared in 1903: "The problem of the twentieth century is the problem of the color-line."[2]

Several features appearing in *Southern Crucible* should appeal to students and distinguish the book with a coverage that is inclusive and balanced. Along with an up-to-date coverage, *Southern Crucible* combines social, cultural, political, and economic history. Although I consider regionalism and the development of regional identity, I am sensitive to the variety and complexity of subregions that existed within the South. The book is richly illustrated, with images and maps that provide visual explanation. Chapters are also balanced chronologically, with twenty-four chapters that include full consideration of what the South became between the late fifteenth century and the early twenty-first century. I offer a full treatment of the development of the modern South, extending into the post–civil rights era.

It is my hope that this combination of characteristics in *Southern Crucible* successfully communicates the complexity and intrinsically interesting nature of the story I try to tell. For most of my career, I have been intrigued with the possibility of writing an integrated history that engages the ways the American South persists so powerfully in culture and self-identity and why the survival of a regional consciousness continues to attract keen students into the twenty-first century. I experienced this myself, in the context of growing up in the mid-twentieth century. My parents were native white southerners who lived most of their adult lives in the Midwest and North. Expatriates, they nonetheless communicated their very strong regional consciousness, with particular expectations about manners and language, religion and values, diet, and environment. My parents always had a critical eye about the South's failings, but they both loved the region. I spent my childhood in the Midwest and North, but there was never any question where "home" was. As an adult, I have had the experience of being in, but not completely of, the South.

Writing a comprehensive history of the South has proven a daunting task in other respects. Although I have been teaching, reading, researching, and writing about southern history for nearly four decades, the continuing quality of scholarship about the South produced in the past century or so remains impressive—and difficult for one person to absorb fully. That scholarship moves on, asking new questions and uncovering new sources, but also challenging those brave or foolhardy enough to try to construct a coherent narrative.

William A. Link
Snow Camp, North Carolina

---

[2] W. E. B. Du Bois, *The Souls of Black Folk: Essays and Sketches* (Chicago: A. C. McClurg, 1903), vii.

Introduction

How the South Was Made

In 1941, North Carolina journalist Wilbur J. Cash published his life's work. Titled *The Mind of the South*, it made the case that the American South—a vast and amorphous region—composed the most distinctive part of the United States, "sharply differentiated from the rest of the American nation, and exhibiting within itself a remarkable homogeneity."[1] Cash's conception of southern exceptionalism reduced to the abiding, persisting set of values that made the South the South—localism and resistance to governmental interference and "perhaps the most intense individualism the world has seen since the Italian Renaissance." The South was male dominated, with a patriarchal obsession with race and manhood. The social system was geared around "pure personal" and the "purely self-asserting," but the pressure of a "close-pressing throng of his fellow men, rigid class distinctions, and the yoke of law and government" became a "crushing weight." Individualism combined with intense localism, at every level of society, from planters to crackers, who were "as fiercely careful of their prerogatives of ownership, as jealous of their sway over their puny domains, as the grandest lord." Custom and political culture made the South "the most poorly policed section of the nation," bereft of much exercise of governmental power.[2]

An odd sort of democracy prevailed in the Old South, said Cash. Combined with the haughty aristocratic attitudes of a parvenu gentry, common whites, though scorned by their social superiors in a "land-and-slave pride and the snob spirit,"

[1] W. J. Cash, *The Mind of the South* (New York: Vintage, 1991), xlvii–xlviii. Originally published in 1941.
[2] Cash, *Mind of the South*, 31–34.

remained fiercely loyal to the social hierarchy. "If the common white ... was likely to carry a haughtiness like that of the Spanish peasant very well," Cash observed, "so far from challenging and trampling on that, his planter neighbors in effect allowed it, gave it boundless room—nay, even encouraged it and invited it on to growth."[3]

The mind of the South, concluded Cash, arose from the institution of slavery and the social, economic, and political conditions surrounding it. A "proto-Dorian" bond of racial unity among white males transcended class differences. Southerners' military prowess blended with patriarchy, male dominance, social class, exalted values of personal honor, and, above all, race. This "savage ideal" characterized the South historically as a region bound to defend its traditions of individualism, localism, and racial hierarchy against all outside intrusion.

What defines the South—and the extent to which it really was and is different from the American nation—lies at the nub of the widespread interest in southern history, literature, and culture. Southern particularity—in its economy, its system of racial hierarchy, its cooking, its climate, and its speech—seems to mean a sort of country within a country, at odds, perhaps, with the rest of the nation. "Certainly the South has been the region most often the exception to the American rule," writes sociologist John Shelton Reed, "and would-be generalizers have often run aground on its peculiarities." Reed finds an arresting particularity to southern attitudes about themselves. In particular, southerners seem "more likely than other Americans to think of their region, their states, and their communities possessively, as *theirs*, and as distinct from and preferable to other regions, states, and localities." Southerners, Reed concludes, continue to regard themselves "as others see them, as *different*— and, in some ways, they are different."[4]

Other scholars have pointed out that southerners' regional identity remained connected to their national identity. It might even be true, as Howard Zinn suggests, that characteristics of Americans were nothing more than watered-down versions of southern characteristics. The South, historian C. Vann Woodward writes, "was American a long time before it was Southern in any self-conscious or distinctive way," and it remained "more American by far than anything else, and has all along."[5] Southerners were truly American, says Carl Degler, because the South "has always contained persons and displayed attitudes that are similar to if not identical with those in the remainder of the nation."[6]

Southern Crucible argues that the American South came into existence as a result of a historical process in which shared experiences of slavery, geography, and ethnicity created a set of common interests and values. There was no such thing as "the

[3] Cash, *Mind of the South*, 41–42.
[4] John Shelton Reed, *The Enduring South: Subcultural Persistence in Mass Society* (Lexington, MA: Lexington Books, 1972), 1, 33, 90.
[5] C. Vann Woodward, "The Search for Southern Identity," in *The Burden of Southern History*, rev. ed. (Baton Rouge: Louisiana State University Press, 1968), 25.
[6] Carl N. Degler, "Thesis, Antithesis, Synthesis: The South, the North, and the Nation," *Journal of Southern History* 53, no. 1 (February 1987): 4–5.

South" until after the American Revolution. Before then, the region south of the Potomac River remained a collection of disparate colonies with differing cultures and political traditions, united mainly by the dominant influence of slavery and slaveholding. The birth of the American Republic paradoxically fanned feelings of state particularity and sectional difference, and, in the new federal constitutional system of 1787, the interests of slaveholding states diverged from those of nonslaveholding states. The South's regional consciousness accentuated a continuing debate about what the Republic meant.

The creation of the South as a self-conscious region occurred in the American Revolution's aftermath. This historical development related to the creation of the nation itself; southern identity grew in proportion to the emergence of an American nationality. That is, what made southerners self-consciously different is their history, but that history remains central to the story of the American nation. Nineteenth-century southerners remained ardent patriots who fervently believed in the American Republic. But the South was different, and the difference became most apparent in the prevalence of the institution of slavery. In most of the Western Hemisphere, during the first half of the nineteenth century racial slavery gradually passed out of existence. In contrast, in Cuba, Brazil, and the United States, the institution became revitalized because of the cotton boom and the expansion of slavery into the Gulf South and the Mississippi valley. Possessing the world's largest population of slaves and the most powerful slaveholding class, the South became a society in which racial slavery permeated the economic system, defined politics, and determined the social structure.

White southerners considered westward expansion essential to their survival. The attempt to limit slavery extension during the 1850s spurred a political crisis in heightened sectionalism, a growing sense of differentness, and, eventually, secession and Civil War. In 1860–1861, secession led to independence and the culmination of decades of southern nationalism. Confederate defeat, solidifying southern nationalism, became a shared memory, though with different meanings. The war left a heavy aftermath in political, economic, cultural, and ideological terms, while race and poverty distinguished southerners from Americans into the twentieth century.

The history of the South during the century and a half after the Civil War remains central to the story of the American nation. Ex-slaves became citizens, but during Reconstruction efforts to ensure civil rights for freed people failed in the face of unified and often-violent southern white opposition. A part of Reconstruction's failure lay in the unwillingness of northern whites to intervene strenuously in defense of black civil and political rights. Eventually, northern whites in Congress, the presidency, and the Supreme Court acknowledged that southern whites would determine their own racial affairs. The result was predictable. Eventually, a new system of white supremacy—in some respects, slavery by another name—came to dominate life in the postwar South. During and after Reconstruction, southern whites limited and eventually deprived black males of the franchise. The power of custom and new legislation solidified the institutionalized social, economic, and political inferiority of African Americans under white supremacy.

The system of southern apartheid and racial oppression eventually collapsed during the middle of the twentieth century, primarily because of African American resistance. During the six decades after World War I, millions of southern blacks voted with their feet, leaving their native region for cities in the Northeast, Midwest, and West. The Great Migration became the largest internal migration in American history, and it fundamentally destabilized white supremacy by undermining the coercive and racialized labor system and by creating new constituencies of black voters in the North.

Black people took on white supremacy, in addition, by organizing a massive social movement. That movement began with legal challenges to Jim Crow segregation, culminating in the NAACP's victory in the *Brown* v. *Board of Education* case in 1954. Thereafter, a mass movement emerged that succeeded in mobilizing ordinary black people in effective social protest against segregation. The victory of the "classic" civil rights movement, from 1954 to 1965, brought an end to segregated public education, transportation, and public accommodation. Although the movement had less impact on the long legacy of poverty and discrimination, it was truly revolutionary in its impact on the South. Moreover, the civil rights movement demonstrated that the problem of race was national rather than regional.

The Great Migration, and ensuing Southern Diaspora, left an important legacy for the nation as a whole. Southern culture became less exotic and more common as expatriates spread around the country. Southern sports such as stock-car racing developed into nationalized, highly developed industries. Southern religious traditions, especially evangelical fundamentalism, spread nationally, especially in areas with native-born expatriate southerners. Music provided another cultural vehicle expressing the experiences of displaced southerners, as southern white rural musicians built a country-and-western industry that was international in scope. Black musical traditions, rooted in the rural forms of the blues, also became commercialized and nationalized. The blues provided a basis for the rhythm-and-blues and rock-and-roll musical revolutions of the 1950s and 1960s.

Today, southerners speak differently, eat differently, live in a different climate, and regard themselves as apart from the rest of the United States. Still, what constitutes "the South" remains a contested concept that evolved over time. Some parts of the South were dominated by slavery; others were largely isolated from it. Most scholars agree that the eleven former states of the Confederate nation are southern, but so probably are the border states that did not secede—Maryland, Kentucky, and Missouri. Parts of Delaware historically are southern; much of the state in 1861 remained wedded to slaveholding and plantation agriculture.

Rather than a single "South" there were in fact many Souths, and the region exhibits remarkable geographical, economic, and demographic diversity. Within the South, there remains a physical diversity that includes mountains and highlands, coastal plains, towns and cities, piney woods, and river bottoms and swamps and wetlands. The South spread west, extending from Arkansas into Texas, while, to the north, it also included border regions in Virginia, West Virginia, Maryland, Kentucky, and Missouri.

The South's diversity was both geographical and historical. The particularity of the region is rooted in the physical differences extending across the South, from the marshy coastal areas on the Atlantic Seaboard, to the red-clay interior of the Piedmont, to the hill country and mountainous regions, and to the delta region that extends down the spine of the Mississippi River. Along the Gulf of Mexico, a Gulf South emerged whose original European influences were Spanish and French, not English. The unification of these diverse regions was historical, occurring over centuries between the colonial era and the Civil War. Ultimately, these Souths converged in the nineteenth century, with the spread of plantation agriculture and spectacular expansion of cotton culture across the Gulf region and the Mississippi valley.

Perhaps more useful is to regard the South as a highly diverse region, often at odds with itself, which shared a regional identity based on unique historical forces. Despite its diversity, the South, as an identifiable region, came into existence by the middle of the nineteenth century. Its identity lies in what Cash described as a "peculiar history" of the South, a history distinguishing it so much from national norms. And this "peculiar history" is tied to the rise and fall of racial slavery, its destruction during the Civil War, and the troubled aftermath of emancipation. Although "not quite a nation within a nation," Cash reminded us that the South was the "next thing to it."[7] But the story of the South charts, and helped define, the history of the United States.

---

7 Cash, *Mind of the South*, xlvii–xlviii.

12

THE CIVIL WAR AND THE DESTRUCTION OF SLAVERY

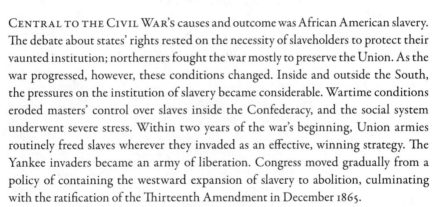

CENTRAL TO THE CIVIL WAR'S causes and outcome was African American slavery. The debate about states' rights rested on the necessity of slaveholders to protect their vaunted institution; northerners fought the war mostly to preserve the Union. As the war progressed, however, these conditions changed. Inside and outside the South, the pressures on the institution of slavery became considerable. Wartime conditions eroded masters' control over slaves inside the Confederacy, and the social system underwent severe stress. Within two years of the war's beginning, Union armies routinely freed slaves wherever they invaded as an effective, winning strategy. The Yankee invaders became an army of liberation. Congress moved gradually from a policy of containing the westward expansion of slavery to abolition, culminating with the ratification of the Thirteenth Amendment in December 1865.

Slaves, above all, took charge of their destiny in a process of self-liberation during wartime. They quickly recognized the potential that the war possessed for their liberation. Pressing for their freedom, again and again forcing the issue, slaves in countless instances engaged in acts of self-emancipation by running away, joining the Union army, undermining the Rebel war effort, or agitating for stronger federal antislavery policies. By transforming the war into a struggle to destroy slavery while relying on Union military power, African Americans exploited every opportunity to press for their liberation. Emancipation thus came as much from black people liberating themselves as from Northern soldiers freeing them. In a turning point of southern history, African Americans became the main actors in emancipation and its consequences.

SELF-EMANCIPATION

"Ever since the beginning of the war," former slave Louis Hughes remembered in his autobiography, *Thirty Years a Slave* (1897), black people realized that fighting during the Civil War might bring freedom. Hughes was enslaved in Mississippi; at the end of the war he absconded to Memphis. The very thought of their liberation, Hughes wrote, made slaves "unspeakably happy," though they rarely expressed their happiness in the presence of slaveholders. "They were afraid to let the masters know that they ever thought of such a thing," he recalled, "and they never dreamed of speaking about it except among themselves." Enslaved workers, Hughes later remembered, would often "laugh and chat about freedom in their cabins; and many a little rhyme about it originated among them, and was softly sung over their work." "There'll be no more talk about Monday, by and by," ran one such song, but "every day will be Sunday, by and by."[1]

Boston Blackwell, enslaved during the Civil War in Arkansas, recalled how in October 1863 he fled his master for Union lines. Interviewed by a Works Progress Administration oral historian in 1937, Blackwell described how, for two days and nights, he waded streams and hid out in the woods in "cold, frosty weather" in order to avert detection by the slave patrol. "When we gets to the Yankee camp all our troubles was over," he recalled, because of food and shelter. "Was they more runaways there? Oh, Lordy, yessum. Hundreds, I reckon." Blackwell became a teamster for the Quartermaster's Department, but he remained careful about staying in the Union camp for his own protection. "They told me I was free when I gets to the Yankee camp, but I couldn't go outside much. Yessum, iffen you could get to the Yankees' camp you was free right now."[2]

Slaves faced perilous conditions when they ran to Union lines, involving, if apprehended by Confederates, severe beatings or even summary execution. Hughes described two slaves from a nearby plantation who were caught attempting to run away and were hanged. Hughes's master summoned his slaves, told them "every detail of the runaway and capture of the poor creatures and their shocking murder," and then took them to see the bodies, rotting on the noose. "I never shall forget the horror of the scene," Hughes wrote later, "it was sickening." This "barbarous spectacle" demonstrated "what would be the fate of those caught in the attempt to escape, and to secure the circulation of the details of the awful affair among them throughout all the neighborhood."

Slaveholders were sorely aware that war undermined slavery's stability. In living memory, during the Revolutionary War and the War of 1812, British invaders liberated slaves in order to sow discord and weaken slaveholders' ability to fight. In Virginia, the rivers running through the state's eastern third provided a porous route for escape. At City Point, a port on the James River, Edmund Ruffin complained in his diary in May 1861 about how "ample facilities" for subverting slavery had long

---

[1] Available at http://nationalhumanitiescenter.org/pds/maai/emancipation/text5/hughes.pdf.
[2] Available at http://nationalhumanitiescenter.org/pds/maai/emancipation/text5/warslaveswpa.pdf.

existed because of trade with outsiders. Frequent contact with northerners fostered the "indoctrinating & deluding slaves with northern ideas." Aware of the prospect of northern invasion, Ruffin wrote, slaves possessed a "very general, if faint & false" impression that "Northerners were operating for Negro emancipation, or as friends, real or pretended, to the slaves."[3] Slave departures depended on the proximity of Union forces. In states suffering invasion, such as Virginia, masters experienced significant losses; according to some estimates, perhaps three-fifths of Virginia slaves left their plantations. By 1864, 400,000 slaves had fled their masters and crossed over to Union lines in search of freedom—a large number, though a tenth of the total enslaved population. Even among those who did not flee, the threat of flight forced masters to move slaves inland, further disrupting the slave system. Slaves seemed to exhibit a new spirit of restiveness and willingness to challenge the rules. "The negroes are going off in great numbers," a Virginia woman complained in 1862 as Yankee forces approached. Slaves had become "very independent and impudent," and she feared the "lawless Yankee soldiers" as well as the "negroes if they should rise against us."[4]

Slaveholders would not go easily into the night. Sixty years prior to the Civil War, a massive slave uprising in Haiti overthrew the French slaveholder class, killing them, sending them into exile, and establishing the world's first black republic. In contrast, the British Caribbean underwent emancipation in a mostly peaceful, legal process in which slaveholders were compensated after the emancipation of 700,000 slaves. Spanish America abolished slavery after Central and South America broke up into independent states. However, slavery survived in remaining Spanish colonies—Puerto Rico until 1873 and Cuba until 1886. The last nation in the Western Hemisphere to abolish slavery was Brazil in 1888.

The end of slavery in the South differed from other experiences of emancipation elsewhere. The national economy was deeply dependent on the institution of slavery; the cotton trade provided the most important source of export earnings and capital. Nowhere else in the world was the master class so strongly entrenched; nowhere did the social, political, and cultural systems protect them so effectively. The collapse of slavery resulting from the war violently and convulsively brought this social system crashing down.

The violent and sudden arrival of emancipation, occurring with Union victory in 1865, occurred traumatically both for slaves and masters. Probably many slaveholders believed that slavery would survive the end of the war and that, perhaps, freed slaves might be reenslaved. A Charleston slaveholder wrote that he had believed his slaves were "content, happy, and attached to their masters." The war seemed to undermine these assumptions. "If they were content, happy, and attached to their masters," he wrote, "why did they desert him in the moment of his need and flock to an enemy whom they did not know; and thus left their, perhaps, really good masters whom they had known from infancy?"[5]

[3] Diary of Edmund Ruffin, May 26, 1861, in *Diary of Edmund Ruffin*, vol. 2, *The Years of Hope, April 1861–June 1863*, ed. Scarborough (Baton Rouge: Louisiana State University Press, 1976), 35.
[4] Gallagher, *Confederate War*, 149.
[5] Oakes, *Freedom National*, 483.

Self-emancipation challenged slaveholders' assumptions about contented slaves. In addition, self-emancipation forced Union military policy to change. However they felt about black people, Yankee commanders came to realize that attacking the institution of slavery struck at the heart of the Confederacy's ability to survive. Almost as soon as Northern troops invaded and occupied the South, they faced a crucial question: How should they treat the thousands of slaves who fled their masters and crossed into Union lines? Before the Civil War began, Lincoln's posture toward an aroused and emboldened slave population remained unclear. During the early months of the war, federal authorities continued to enforce the Fugitive Slave Act and used their authority to return runaways to their masters in the Border states. Nonetheless, slaves pushed matters forward. A week after Lincoln's inauguration, a slave canoed out across Charleston Harbor to the federally controlled Fort Sumter, hoping that he could free himself. The fort's commander returned him to his owner. A day later, four slaves entered Fort Pickens, near Pensacola, Florida. As in Charleston, the Union army commander returned them to local authorities. These policies were not unusual. Maj. Gen. Henry Halleck, in November 1861, ordered that no slaves be admitted within Union lines.[6]

Despite these discouraging policies, slaves left their masters for Union lines. During the early weeks after the start of the war, as Yankee military units moved to Washington, slaves joined them en route in Maryland. Enslaved labor soon proved a valuable resource. Rebels and Yankees faced labor shortages, especially the Confederates. Early in the war, masters loaned or rented their slaves to help with the construction of fortifications. Slaves also worked in transportation, manufacturing, and distribution—all vital to the Rebel war effort. As time progressed, masters became

more reluctant to permit slaves to work for the Confederacy, as their departure created opportunities for freedom from white supervision. Slaves' labor for the Confederacy, complained one Virginia slaveholder in late 1861, had "delayed the threshing of the wheat crop, [and] has engendered some feeling of discontent."[7] Eventually, Rebel authorities impressed slaves and free blacks anyway, with the further effect of undermining slaveholder authority. Early on, however, Union commanders realized the strategic importance of enslaved workers, and their efforts to liberate slaves were often justified as a stroke against the Confederacy.

Benjamin Butler. *Library of Congress.*

In May 1861, Maj. Gen. Benjamin F. Butler arrived in eastern Virginia in command of Chesapeake Bay's

[6] Henry W. Halleck, General Orders, No. 3, November 20, 1861, "A War for the Union," in *Free at Last: A Documentary History of Slavery, Freedom, and the Civil War*, ed. Ira Berlin, Barbara J. Fields, Steven F. Miller, Joseph P. Reidy, and Leslie S. Rowland (New York: New Press, 1992), 17–18.

[7] Glenn David Brasher, *The Peninsula Campaign and the Necessity of Emancipation: African Americans and the Fight for Freedom* (Chapel Hill: University of North Carolina Press, 2012), 62.

Fort Monroe. Shortly after his arrival, three slaves, who had been workers on Confederate fortifications, crossed Union lines, seeking freedom. When Confederates demanded the three slaves' return, Butler refused. In a historic pronouncement, Butler declared runaway slaves as "contraband of war," a nebulous status that was neither slave nor free. The fleeing "contrabands" worked on Confederate fortifications; permitting them to stay, Butler reasoned, undermined the

Contrabands, Cumberland Landing, Virginia. *Library of Congress.*

Rebel war effort. Though he remained in "utmost doubt" about what to do, Butler saw his policy as "a measure of necessity" to deprive their masters of their services. More slaves poured into Butler's encampment: by July 1861, nine hundred had flocked to Union lines around Fort Monroe. Butler put the contrabands, who lived in a camp in nearby Hampton, to work, with males working on entrenchments and women working in washing and cleaning.[8]

The slaves' desire to free themselves, in this way, converged with the North's objectives of undermining the Confederacy's economic and political security. Self-emancipation was effective only because of the opportunities that Northern invasion presented. Butler's policies reflected an ad hoc attempt to deal with the enslaved people's overwhelming determination to use the war to end slavery. President Lincoln refused to reverse Butler; this meant that permitting self-emancipating slaves to cross lines became policy. Although these new rules about contrabands initially applied only to states that had seceded, they soon affected the loyal slaveholding states—indeed, wherever Union forces existed, slaves saw their lines as a safe haven. In Maryland, an army commander complained in September 1861 that his soldiers had "forgotten their duty as to excite and encourage insubordination among the colored servants in the neighborhood of their camps." A few months later, another officer in Kentucky described a "general Stampeed of slaves" who had "already become a source of annoyance to me."[9]

Union invaders soon became what one historian calls a "counter-state within the southern states, an alternative government inside the South but beyond the reach of the police powers of southern slave society."[10] Slaves embraced the opportunity.

---

[8] Butler to Winfield Scott, May 27, 1861, in *Freedom: A Documentary History of Emancipation, 1861–1867*, ser. 1, vol. 1, *The Destruction of Slavery*, ed. Ira Berlin, Barbara J. Fields, Thavolia Glymph, Joseph P. Reidy, and Leslie S. Rowland (New York: Cambridge University Press, 1985), 70–71.

[9] General Orders, No. 16, September 23, 1861; A. McD. McCook to William T. Sherman, November 5, 1861, in *Free at Last*, ed. Berlin et al., 12.

[10] Oakes, *Freedom National*, 89.

In occupied Tidewater Virginia, a visitor described the "universal desire among the slaves to be free." Their masters insisted that they preferred to remain slaves. "We do want to be free," they responded; "we want to be for ourselves." Even aged male and female slaves, "with crooked backs, who could hardly walk or see, shared the same feeling." Well-treated slaves—perhaps, well-treated slaves especially—wanted freedom. One slave described how his mistress had been kind to him, permitting him to hire himself and pocket a portion of his wages. But when she asked him to flee the Hampton area, he refused. "Still he hated to be a slave, and he talked like a philosopher about his rights. No captive in the galleys of Algiers, not Lafayette in an Austrian dungeon, ever pined more for free air."[11]

The military advance of Union forces undermined slavery near the front lines. A Virginia slaveholder described "heavy losses of Slaves" fleeing in the direction of the "Abolition army."[12] A Maryland slave who escaped to Union lines in Virginia wrote his wife in January 1862. "This Day," he noted proudly, "I can Adress you thank god as a free man. . . . As the lord led the Children of Isrel to the land . . . [of Canaan]. So he led me to a land Whare freedom Will rain in spite Of earth and Hell."[13] Wherever a Union military presence existed, slaveholders witnessed mass departures. In Liberty County, in coastal Georgia, slaveholders described the disintegration of slavery. The group estimated that 20,000 slaves had fled the county, and the "constant drain" was "immense." The result was an "insecurity of the property along our borders & the demoralization of the negroes that remain, which increases with the continuance of the evil & may finally result in perfect disorganization and rebellion."[14]

Northern invasion opened up new opportunities for slaves to free themselves. During the Peninsula Campaign in the spring and summer of 1862—the first major Union attempt to conquer Richmond—the Northern army found itself an army of liberation, despite commanding general George B. McClellan's distaste for emancipation. Slaves fleeing their masters "were ready to go anywhere except back to their old servitude," wrote one Northern officer. They eagerly took up work for the Northern army. "They profess themselves willing to work, fight, or do anything for us," noted a newspaper correspondent.[15]

Masters discovered slaves' new willingness to challenge the status quo. When a Union military officer "got at the feelings" of slaves, he said, "I found they were not afraid of the slaveholders." The slaves reported that there was "nobody on the plantations but women and they were not afraid of them." "Now they are getting their eyes open they are coming in." In general, they were not afraid anymore. Whites had lost their power over slaves; the "blood hounds are not there now to hunt them and they

[11] Edward L. Pierce, "The Contrabands at Fortress Monroe," *Atlantic Monthly* 8(November 1861): 626–641.

[12] James W. Cook to J. M. Mason, August 27, 1861, in *Destruction of Slavery*, ed. Berlin et al., 77.

[13] John Boston to his wife, January 12, 1862, in *Free at Last*, ed. Berlin et al., 29–30.

[14] R. Q. Mallard, T. W. Fleming, and E. Stacy to Gen. Hugh W. Mercer, August 1, 1862, in *Free at Last*, ed. Berlin et al., 62.

[15] Brasher, *Peninsula Campaign*, 146–148.

are not afraid." Numerous slaves abandoned their plantations, he reported, because they "had heard these stories, and wanted to come and see how it was."[16]

TOWARD THE EMANCIPATION PROCLAMATION

Lincoln largely acquiesced in—and to some extent even encouraged—the ad hoc policies of his field commanders. Northern occupiers in Virginia, North Carolina, South Carolina, and Louisiana defined their own policies toward thousands of fleeing slaves. In the Sea Islands of South Carolina, after Yankee invaders occupied the area in November 1861, slaveholders fled en masse. Although the Union command was initially instructed not to interfere with slavery, they discovered that contrabands were occupying deserted cotton plantations. Union gunboats navigating in the islands witnessed a flood of escaped slaves to their lines. Meanwhile, slaves from other Lowcountry plantations attempted to evade Confederate sentries posted to keep them from leaving. The Sea Islands witnessed a kind of experiment in freedom, as northern missionaries flocked to the area and established schools for the freed people. The Union forces, under the command of Gen. Rufus Saxton, also permitted the slaves to farm the abandoned lands.

The invasion of the Lowcountry was not without the usual mixture of responses from the Northern troops and commanders. Many northerners expressed little sympathy, and perhaps a great deal of suspicion, toward blacks, and in some instances they sympathized with slaveholders' attempt to keep their slaves. This was especially true in Florida, where many masters were Unionists and supported the capture and occupation of Fernandina Beach in March 1863. This was in contrast to the Sea Islands, where the sudden departure of masters left the occupiers with no choice but to deal with slaves as contrabands and perhaps even as freed.

In his inaugural address in March 1861, Lincoln told southern slaveholders that no basis existed for fear that "their property, and their peace, and personal security, are to be endangered." He had no intention, he said, of interfering with slavery in states where it existed.[17] In order to reassure white southerners and to persuade them not to secede, Lincoln even endorsed a constitutional amendment protecting slavery. He maintained that he would protect slavery in the nonseceding Border states of Maryland, Kentucky, Delaware, and Missouri, which did not join the Confederacy but contained 420,000 slaves. But events changed Lincoln's position. In August 1861, Congress enacted the First Confiscation Act, which permitted the seizure of slaves used by Rebel masters in the Confederate cause—what became an evolving notion of "military emancipation." The fourth section of the law declared that slaveholders with persons "held to labor or service under the law of any State" used in support of rebellion "shall forfeit his claim to such labor." Notably, the law described

---

[16] Capt. C. B. Wilder, testimony before American Freedman's Inquiry Commission, May 9, 1863, in *Destruction of Slavery*, ed. Berlin et al., 89–90.

[17] Michael Vorenberg, *The Emancipation Proclamation: A Brief History with Documents* (Boston: Bedford / St. Martin's, 2010), 37.

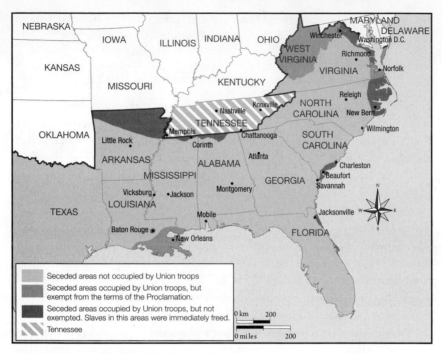

MAP 12.1 Impact of the Emancipation Proclamation

slaves not as property but as "persons," though the measure was limited.[18] In practice, the act provided authorization for freeing slaves if they ran to Union lines, though, at least at this point, the military generally would not "entice" slaves to freedom.

In March 1862, Lincoln proposed a plan for gradual emancipation and the compensation of slaveholders. Meanwhile, Republicans in Congress pressed Border states. When the new state of West Virginia applied for admission to the Union in March 1862, congressional leaders required the abolition of slavery. Also in March, the Senate ratified a treaty with Britain to suppress the illegal slave trade, while the State Department began issuing passports to African Americans (it had denied them since *Dred Scott* because they were not considered citizens). In April 1862, Congress ended slavery (but compensated loyal masters) in the District of Columbia, appropriating funds for the freed slaves' colonization in Haiti and Liberia. Ambassadors were exchanged with both of these black republics, something that previous administrations had opposed. In June 1862, in addition, Congress ended slavery in the territories.

The momentum toward emancipation had decisively shifted. In July 1862, Congress authorized the army to hire black workers and to emancipate them. The Second Confiscation Act, enacted on July 17, 1862, freed slaves owned by Confederates, declaring they should be "captives of war, and shall be forever free of their servitude,

[18] Oakes, *Freedom National*, 119.

and not again held as slaves." Despite opposition by congressmen and Democrats in the Border states and a six-month battle to enact the law, Congress effectively repealed the Fugitive Slave Act of 1850 by placing a new legal burden on masters to retrieve runaways in free states. Under terms of the law, Congress empowered the employment of "persons of African descent" in the war effort. Section 6 of the act also provided new authority for a presidential emancipation proclamation.

Lincoln moved more cautiously than Republican congressmen. In September 1861, when Gen. John C. Frémont ordered freedom for slaves owned by Confederates in Missouri, Lincoln reversed the order and removed Frémont. The impetus toward liberating slaves varied according to field commander. Until March 1862, Gen. Thomas W. Sherman, commanding the army invading the Lowcountry, pursued a cautious policy toward contrabands. Sherman's successor, David Hunter, who became commander of the Department of the South, with strongly antislavery views, used military power to hasten the slaves' liberation. Hunter's subordinate, Gen. Alfred H. Terry, who commanded Fort Pulaski, at the mouth of the Savannah River, exercised his authority to protect slaves and prohibited masters from physically abusing them. Public violence, Terry declared, was a "disturbance of . . . public order" that would be ended by military force.[19]

Eventually, Hunter went too far. In May 1862, Lincoln voided Hunter's order declaring the 900,000 slaves in his district "forever free" and empowering his subordinates to enlist black males in the Union army. Pressured by circumstances, antislavery advocates, and congressional Republicans, however, Lincoln changed his policies toward slaves. A year into the war, he sought to persuade the Border states to abolish slavery by state action, even obtaining congressional authorization to compensate them. But the Border states resisted these proposals. Meanwhile, Lincoln came to see emancipation as a military and political tool in the war against the Confederacy. By July 1862, after the passage of the Second Confiscation Act, the president pursued emancipation in the Rebel states by presidential proclamation. He wanted to make the announcement after a Union military victory. Those were rare in 1862; Lincoln settled for the bloody standoff at the Battle of Antietam in September.

On September 22, 1862, Lincoln announced the preliminary Emancipation Proclamation. It declared that, on January 1, 1863, all slaves in states "in rebellion against the United States shall be then, thenceforward, and forever free" and that the Union military would "recognize and maintain the freedom of such persons, and will do no act or acts to repress such persons, or any of them, in any efforts they may make for their actual freedom." Although the Proclamation did not affect loyal slave states, Lincoln encouraged them to abolish slavery by offering a compensation and colonization plan.[20] In his annual message to Congress in December 1862, Lincoln again proposed a gradual emancipation plan in which all slaves would be freed, with compensation, no later than January 1, 1900. Lincoln's message, though conservative and

[19] Berlin et al., eds., *Destruction of Slavery*, 109.
[20] Text of the Preliminary Emancipation Proclamation can be found at http://www.archives. gov/exhibits/americanoriginalsiv/sections/transcriptpreliminaryemancipation.html.

cautious, affirmed that the Civil War was really all about slavery. "Without slavery," Lincoln declared, "the rebellion could never have existed; without slavery it could not continue." His plan, he said, would avoid the "sudden derangement" of immediate emancipation. In order to provide for the restoration of wealth and property lost in emancipated slaves, Lincoln proposed that a "common charge" should be levied on all Americans in order to finance his plan. "In giving freedom to the slave," he said, "we assure freedom to the free—honorable alike in what we give and what we preserve."[21]

On January 1, 1863, Lincoln issued the final Emancipation Proclamation, which reaffirmed the emancipation of slaves in areas under Rebel control. Lincoln again declared that the Union military would "recognize and maintain the freedom of such persons." Under these proclamations, the Yankee military, previously restrained from enticing slaves to freedom, became an agent of liberation. Any freed person, the January proclamation added, could participate in military service.[22]

Although Lincoln did not emancipate any slaves immediately—the Emancipation Proclamation freed slaves outside Union military control—the document represented a new statement of Union war aims. Thereafter, wherever Northern armies appeared, they became an army of liberation. Thousands of slaves, understanding the meaning of Lincoln's Proclamation, deserted their masters and encamped with Northern soldiers. Lincoln realized that breaking the southern will to fight depended on the ability to bring the Confederacy to its knees, and destroying slavery went a long way toward accomplishing this goal.

AFRICAN AMERICANS AND THE MILITARY EXPERIENCE

Writing in February 1863 from coastal South Carolina, a Union officer described the recent arrival of black troops from the Fifty-Fourth Regiment Massachusetts Volunteer Infantry. "The negro soldiers," he wrote, "have surpassed the expectations even of most of their friends." He visited their camp and was "very much pleased . . . with their good appearance." Already their readiness for battle had been tested with skirmishes with Confederates, and "even those not friendly to them admit that they have fought bravely on those expeditions."[23]

The Massachusetts Fifty-Fourth became the first African American military unit to fight in the Civil War. It was composed of volunteers, most of them from the Massachusetts free-black community, who eagerly responded to the call to fight against slavery. The new unit, despite avid abolitionist support, evoked questions among some whites about whether African Americans could fight and lead and be led. The unit was created, but a political compromise associated with its creation was that all the officers would be white, with no blacks above the rank of noncommissioned officers. Massachusetts governor John A. Andrew commissioned abolitionist Robert Gould

---

[21] Lincoln, Second Annual Message, December 1, 1862; available at http://www.presidency.ucsb.edu/ws/index.php?pid=29503#axzz1tiffOPbK.

[22] Vorenberg, *Emancipation Proclamation*, 71–72.

[23] Edward Hooper to Henry W. Foote, February 23, 1863, folder 1a, Penn School Papers, Southern Historical Collection, University of North Carolina at Chapel Hill Library.

The Fifty-Fourth Massachusetts Regiment, assault on Fort Wagner, South Carolina, July 18, 1863. *Library of Congress.*

Shaw, a war veteran, as the regiment's colonel. The Fifty-Fourth became renowned for its courage, including combat in March 1863 in Union operations in Georgia and South Carolina. The unit participated in a murderous assault on Fort Wagner, outside Charleston, in July 1863, in which Shaw and more than three hundred Yankee soldiers were killed. Although a military disaster, the assault on Fort Wagner valorized black soldiers and helped persuade northern public opinion to accept African Americans in the military. More than a century after the Civil War, the event became the subject of an Academy Award–winning film, *Glory*, which appeared in 1989.

Not only were there pressures to increase recruitment to the Union army, black leaders realized that they would have a greater voice in determining war policies if black soldiers fought. By the end of the war, black men had enrolled en masse in the Union army, with a total of 186,000 serving. About 134,000 of them were from slave states. Many served in a support capacity, as teamsters, laborers, cooks, laundresses, scouts, guides, and spies. Blacks participating in the war effort paid a high price. About a third of black soldiers were killed or missing in action, or dead by disease, with the death rate among them three times what it was for whites. African American participation in the Union military helped them take part in the destruction of slavery. As a result of black military service, said one US senator, "the black man is henceforth to assume a new status among us." Although suffering from widespread racial discrimination in the military, black soldiers enjoyed new freedoms—the freedom to bear arms, to learn how to read and write, and to testify against whites in military courts.[24]

Emancipation Proclamation, lithograph. *Library of Congress.*

[24] Eric Foner, "Rights and the Constitution in Black Life during the Civil War and Reconstruction," *Journal of American History* 74, no. 3 (December 1987): 864.

Arlington, Virginia, Band of 107th US Colored Infantry. *Library of Congress.*

Gradually, the Union moved toward making black military participation possible. The Second Confiscation Act of July 1862 authorized the hiring of black people in the war effort, while the Militia Act of the same year provided for people of African descent to be enlisted in "any military or naval service for which they may be found competent." Slaves working in the war effort were emancipated.[25] Soon, black military participation followed on the heels of military-sponsored emancipation. As early as May 1862, Gen. David Hunter began recruiting freed slaves in South Carolina. Hunter's efforts continued unofficially until August, when Secretary of War Edwin Staunton authorized up to five thousand recruits but admonished Gen. Rufus Saxton that the policy was "so much in advance of public opinion."[26]

Lincoln's announcement of the Emancipation Proclamation greatly spurred the organization of black military units. The Proclamation provided that freed slaves of "suitable condition, will be received in the armed services of the United States"—a statement that transformed long-standing exclusion of African Americans in the military.[27] In March 1863, General in Chief Henry Halleck instructed Gen. Grant, in command of Union armies in the West, that black soldiers could be used as a "military force." Over thirty regiments of African Americans were organized; by December, there were 50,000 black troops. New black regiments were subsequently organized, and, in May 1863, Lincoln created a Bureau of Colored Troops, with 250 agents eventually spreading across the South to advertise the Emancipation Proclamation and recruit black soldiers. Black soldiers saw action during the summer of 1863 in Louisiana and South Carolina.[28] "This year has brought about many changes that at the beginning were or would have been thought impossible," wrote an enlistee, a free black from Baltimore in 1863. "The close of the year finds me a soldier for the cause of my race."[29]

[25] Berlin et al., eds., *Free at Last*, xxx.
[26] Eric Foner, *The Fiery Trial: Abraham Lincoln and American Slavery* (New York: W. W. Norton, 2010), 230.
[27] Oakes, *Freedom National*, 344.
[28] Oakes, *Freedom National*, 378–379.
[29] Leon F. Litwack, *Been in the Storm So Long: The Aftermath of Slavery* (New York: Vintage, 1979), 71.

The Bureau of Colored Troops fanned out into the occupied South, urging slaves to leave their masters and join the army of liberation. In Missouri, Tennessee, and Maryland, the War Department opened recruitment offices to enlist black troops. Although the Border states were exempt from the Emancipation Proclamation, they were not excluded from recruitment—indeed, quite the contrary. Although possessing a fifth of the total slave population, Border slave states provided two-fifths of black recruits. In Kentucky, recruitment reached a high level—57 percent of military-age black males—because the military offered freedom to slaves and their families with enlistment.[30]

The use of black soldiers remained controversial in Congress, where Border state congressmen worried about the implications of this policy. But antislavery field commanders such as Hunter exploited circumstances to promote the destruction of slavery. In June 1862, a congressional resolution directed Hunter to explain his policies of enlisting fugitive slaves. Hunter's response was forceful, if sarcastic. No regiment of fugitive slaves, he wrote, had been organized, only a "fine regiment of persons whose late masters are 'Fugitive Rebels.'" Slaveholders fled before the "appearance of the National Flag, leaving their servants behind them to shift as best they can for themselves." The abandoned slaves worked with "remarkable industry to place themselves in a position to go in full and effective pursuit of their fugacious and traitorous proprietors."[31]

The push for black troops came especially from abolitionists and their allies in the army. During the spring of 1863, Gen. Edward A. Wild organized an African Brigade, composed of North Carolina and Virginia escaped slaves. This unit began incursions into slaveholder territory designed to liberate slaves in areas where they had lived. Wild also led the ex-slaves in retributions against former masters, including, in one instance, having the freedmen whip their former masters. Wild enjoyed the support of Butler, who by 1863 had returned to Tidewater Virginia. Butler expanded Union raids into slaveholder territory, encouraging slaves to leave their masters and to join the military. Federal raids in Tidewater Virginia prompted panicked masters to "refugee" their slaves farther into the interior in order to prevent their liberation. In October 1863, a Virginia master plaintively wrote that "our slaves have nearly all left us."[32] As another Confederate commander wrote, Butler's depredations threaten to make that area "entirely denuded of slaves."[33]

Energetic Northern field commanders conducted regular raiding parties from occupied Tidewater Virginia and eastern North Carolina. In November 1863, in orders to a commander of a hundred-man black raiding brigade, the Union army issued clear instructions about their role in the slaveholding regions of southeastern Virginia. Soldiers were ordered to do no plundering, although foraging was permissible. Any slaves leaving their master were "not to be driven back, but are to be

[30] Oakes, *Freedom National*, 388.
[31] David Hunter, statement, June 23, 1862, in *Free at Last*, ed. Berlin et al., 57.
[32] Berlin et al., eds., *Destruction of Slavery*, 68.
[33] G. E. Pickett to Confederate adjutant and inspector general, December 15, 1863, in *Destruction of Slavery*, ed. Berlin et al., 93.

protected by you." Any property brought by the slaves should also be protected. If fired upon by "guerrillas," the troops were ordered to hang them and burn their houses. The party was further ordered to return recruits directly to the enlistment ranks.[34]

Border states, often the scenes of intense partisan warfare, saw a nearly complete disruption of the system of slavery. During the summer and fall of 1862, Confederate forces under the command of Gen. Braxton Bragg and Gen. Edmund Kirby Smith invaded Kentucky, and the ensuing fight provided an opening for slaves, many of whom were pressed into service by both sides. Once separated from their masters, Kentucky slaves inhabited a semifree world under the protection of Union forces. Although Lincoln delayed the recruitment of black soldiers in Kentucky until March 1864, scores joined up thereafter. Some masters even enlisted their slaves, claiming the bounty that the northern recruiters were offering. Others used their slaves' enlistment to evade conscription. By July, the Union army began an even more aggressive effort, announcing the enrollment and liberation of all slaves "regardless of the wishes of their owners." This new policy justified what amounted to a wholesale roundup of able black males. In March 1865, the military mobilization's association with liberation became complete with the army edict that all enslaved families of soldiers were free.[35]

White southerners were alarmed by black military participation. The very presence of blacks bearing arms and fighting for the northern cause seemed, to them, insulting. When two hundred black prisoners of war were marched through Columbia, South Carolina, in August 1864, local whites expressed their disgust. Black prisoners were brought in "barefoot, hatless and coatless and tied in a gang like common runaways," wrote a woman. The public appearance was "revolting to our feelings" and "injurious in its effects upon our negroes."[36] Masters redoubled their efforts to prevent a mass exodus, and many sent their slaves away from military zones. Slaveholders also increased patrols and instituted harsh measures against runaways.

Confederate authorities responded harshly to black troops. In December 1862, President Jefferson Davis announced that captured black soldiers would not be treated as prisoners of war but would be considered "slaves in arms," and those commanding them were treated as outlaws inciting servile insurrection. In some instances, surrendering black soldiers were summarily executed, while others were reenslaved. In July 1863, Lincoln responded to calls for retaliation against prisoner executions and reenslavements. For every Union soldier killed in "violation of the law of war," Lincoln announced, a Confederate prisoner would suffer the same fate. If any Union soldier was reenslaved, an equivalent number of Confederate prisoners would be put to work on hard labor on the public works. There was little evidence, however, that Lincoln's policy was implemented in the field. As one black editor put

[34] Hiram W. Allen to Col. A. G. Draper, November 17, 1863, in *Destruction of Slavery*, ed. Berlin et al., 92–93.

[35] Marion B. Lucas, *A History of Blacks in Kentucky: From Slavery to Segregation, 1760–1891* (Frankfort: Kentucky Historical Society, 2003), 154.

[36] Litwack, *Been in the Storm*, 87.

The Fort Pillow Massacre, April 12, 1864. *Library of Congress.*

it, "Northern sentiment, already weak on the subject, will revolt against the taking of the life of white men for 'Niggers.'"[37]

A number of atrocities involving massacres of black troops occurred on the field. On April 12, 1864, on the Mississippi south of Memphis, Confederate cavalry forces under the command of Nathan Bedford Forrest surrounded about six hundred defenders at Fort Pillow, about half of whom were African American members of the Sixth US Regiment Colored Heavy Artillery. Overwhelming the defenders, the Confederates shot or bayoneted most of the Union soldiers. "It appeared as if the rebels were possessed of demons," according to one account, "and nothing but blood would satiate their vengeance."[38] As Forrest put it, that the battlefield was "dyed with the blood of the slaughtered" offered conclusive proof that "negro soldiers cannot cope with Southerners."[39] In reality, the Fort Pillow massacre inspired black soldiers to fight hard and to refuse surrender.

There were a small number of African Americans serving in the Union navy, as well. Robert Smalls, who was born a slave in Beaufort, South Carolina, moved with his master to Charleston. During the war, he worked as a pilot, hired by the Confederacy. In a spectacular act in May 1862, he guided the Confederate transport steamer *Planter*, loaded with arms, out of Charleston Harbor and then successfully surrendered it to Union forces. While the *Planter*'s white crew went ashore, Smalls loaded up his wife and twelve other slaves and took the ship. Attracting national attention, he became a second lieutenant in the Northern navy, while Congress rewarded him with $1,500. Smalls became a celebrity, advocating greater use of blacks in the military.

Black troops participated in the final defeat of the Confederacy, and their presence reminded southern whites of their defeat. On April 2, 1865, four days before Robert E. Lee's surrender at Appomattox Court House, Lincoln steamed up the James River and visited Richmond. Basking in the Confederate surrender of the city only days before, Lincoln made the trip with a light military escort. As soon as

[37] Litwack, *Been in the Storm*, 90.
[38] "The Capture of Fort Pillow," *Milwaukee Daily Sentinel*, April 19, 1864.
[39] Litwack, *Been in the Storm*, 91.

Lincoln left USS *Malvern*, he began to walk up the hill from Rocketts Landing on the James to Jefferson Davis's residence, a two-and-a-half-mile trip. Enthusiastic African Americans mobbed the president, in what an observer later called the "wildest excitement, bursting into all sorts of characteristic ejaculations, throwing up their hands and dancing about, as if the Savior of mankind Himself had made his second advent on earth."[40] "No electric wire could have carried the news of the President's arrival sooner than it was circulated through Richmond," according to one account. "As far as the eye could see the streets were alive with negroes and poor whites rushing in our direction, and the crowd increased so fast that I had to surround the President with the sailors with fixed bayonets to keep them off." The crowd encircled Lincoln, all wanting to "shake hands with Mr. Lincoln or his coat tail or even to kneel down and kiss his boots." Later, in April 1865, when U. S. Grant occupied the defeated Confederate capital at Richmond, black troops participated in the parade and local African Americans celebrated in the streets.[41]

One of the soldiers, Garland H. White, a former Virginia slave who had escaped to Ohio, served as an army chaplain when black troops marched through Richmond. He described a "vast multitude" greeting the black troops on Broad Street, one of the city's main thoroughfares. Asked to speak, White was "aroused amid the shout of ten thousands voices, and proclaimed for the first time in that city freedom to all mankind." The African American soldiers broke up the jails of a well-known slave dealer, freeing slaves who weeks earlier would have gone on the auction block. "I became so overcome with tears," White wrote, "that I could not stand up under the pressure of such fullness of joy in my own heart." A few hours later, White was reunited with his mother, from whom he had been separated for twenty years.[42]

Union victories elicited similar responses by African Americans everywhere. When Sherman's troops—which included the Fifty-Fourth Massachusetts—entered Charleston in February 1865, they sang the Union's army anthem, "John Brown's Body," to a celebrating black community. A little more than a month later, a large gathering of four thousand Charleston blacks, which included soldiers and local African Americans, paraded through town. The parade carried a hearse with a sign proclaiming: "Slavery is Dead." Black women, dressed in mourning but exhibiting "joyous faces," participated in a general "jubilee" celebrating black freedom from slavery.[43]

THE CONFEDERACY AND SLAVERY

Although the war began primarily as an effort to defend slavery and slaveholders, Confederate policies, geared toward military victory, undermined the institution. Acute shortages of labor and resources forced Confederates to impress slaves for use

---

[40] Hiram T. Peck, "The Fall of Richmond: Personal Recollections of the Triumphal Entry of Union Troops into the Rebel Capital," *National Tribune,* October 4, 1900.

[41] Lincoln's Visit to Richmond; available at http://www.nps.gov/rich/historyculture/lincvisit.htm.

[42] Litwack, *Been in the Storm,* 169.

[43] Carole Emberton, *Beyond Redemption: Race, Violence, and the American South after the Civil War* (Chicago: University of Chicago Press, 2013), 15–16.

in labor to construct fortifications and military facilities. Yankee forces used contraband labor, partly as a way to undermine the Confederate labor system. The war effort required the use of slave labor, but on the Confederate home front, slaves found that they could exploit their position to their advantage. Ultimately, as well, the Confederacy, in repudiation of the notion of the war as an effort to defend slavery, considered using black soldiers.

With three-quarters of the white male population serving in the Rebel army, the war created a severe labor shortage. On the military front, the importance of defensive fortifications became a vital strategic consideration, and black laborers provided much of the arduous and dangerous labor. At the same time, manufacturing weapons and materiel and operating and maintaining the railroad system also depended on slave labor. Interior towns such as Lynchburg, Virginia, and Atlanta, Georgia, served as arsenals and depots supplying and feeding the army, and these centers depended on slave workers. In Upper South states such as Virginia, there already existed a large pool of hired slaves available for labor. That source of labor dried up as the Confederacy turned to coercive measures that impressed slaves and even took them from their masters. By the end of the war, Gen. Robert E. Lee favored the establishment of a permanent corps of black laborers impressed from slaveholders.

The Confederate army, like the Union army, faced a chaotic situation in which runaways sometimes joined their units. In May 1862, a Virginia slaveholder complained that masters were "injured by a practice which has become habitual and extensive among the soldiers of our own army." Confederate soldiers, he wrote, hired runaways as manual laborers, and, as a result, slaves were encouraged to leave their masters for a "safe harbor" in the army camps.[44] Masters who took their slaves with them to the military also discovered that this undermined slaves' willingness to submit to discipline. Returning home, slaves working with Confederates often told other slaves of the chaotic conditions prevailing, further undermining the authority of the slaveholder regime.

The Rebel army, whose manpower resources became badly depleted during the last year of the war, was desperate for troops. A month after the Southern defeat at the Battle of Missionary Ridge, Tennessee, on December 29, 1863, officers from the Army of Tennessee sent a memorial to the Confederate Congress calling for an expanded conscription program. The soldiers also requested the elimination of exemptions from conscription, especially those excusing people who owned more than twenty slaves. Without saying that they should be made soldiers, the petitioners urged that blacks be included in the draft.

In January 1864, Maj. Gen. Patrick R. Cleburne expanded on these ideas to the Confederate general staff. The time had come, Cleburne argued, for a change in manpower policies. Slavery, which had been a source of strength, was now of "great and increasing worth to the enemy." Given the choice between nationhood and the loss of slavery, Cleburne argued, southerners should "give up the negro slave rather than be a slave himself." Proposing emancipation, Cleburne maintained that freeing

[44] L. H. Minor, letter, May 2, 1862, in *Free at Last*, ed. Berlin et al., 43.

the slaves could provide a way to win the war and "remove forever all selfish taint from our cause and place independence above every question of property." A contentious discussion followed among Confederate military and political leaders. The commander of the Army of Tennessee, Joseph Johnston, said that Cleburne's ideas would jeopardize popular "unity and harmony." Albert Sidney Johnston, Confederate chief of staff, described it as a "monstrous proposition." President Jefferson Davis quashed Cleburne's proposals and prevented them from seeing the light of day.[45]

The success of the Confederacy required the recognition that slaves were people as well as property. "The relation of person predominates so far as to render it doubtful whether the private right of property can consistently and beneficially be continued," Jefferson Davis declared in his annual message to the Confederate Congress in November 1864. "The subject is to be viewed by us, therefore, solely in light of the policy and our social economy." In other words, Davis and other Confederate nationalists increasingly reached the conclusion that nationhood and the goal of winning the war trumped everything else, even the sanctity of slaveholding. A further step in this process occurred in February 1864, when the Confederate Congress enacted a measuring providing for even-wider conscriptions of slaves.[46]

During 1864, the Confederate military situation so deteriorated that Davis did an about-face. In November 1864, he sent a message to the Confederate Congress outlining a "radical modification" in the status of slavery. In order to more fully engage slaves' participation in the war, white southerners must be prepared to "liberate the negro . . . after service faithfully rendered." Davis's proposals sparked bitter debate. Southern whites, warned the *Charleston Mercury*, were "not dependent on slaves," and Davis had raised the prospect of whites becoming "slaves of their slaves." The proposals to arm slaves, the *Mercury* later said, were "mad," reflecting the ideas of "panic-stricken men" who were "desperate, destructive, utterly hopeless."

Robert E. Lee endorsed the proposals in March 1865, a month before his army surrendered at Appomattox. In a public letter, Lee announced that militarizing the slaves was "not only expedient but necessary." Slaves made good soldiers, Lee said, describing their physical capabilities and "habits of obedience." Lee preferred a voluntary slave force rather than a conscript force. If using slaves as soldiers subverted slavery, Lee wrote in another, unpublished letter in January 1865, "it will be accomplished by ourselves, and we can devise the means of alleviating the evil consequences to both races." The decision facing the Confederacy was whether "slavery shall be extinguished by our enemies and the slaves used against us, or use them ourselves at the risk of the effects which may be produced upon our social institutions."

When the Confederate Congress enacted Davis's proposals in March 1865, they proved too little and too late. Only one black Confederate unit was organized, and

[45] Armstead L. Robinson, *Bitter Fruits of Bondage: The Demise of Slavery and the Collapse of the Confederacy, 1861–1865* (Charlottesville: University Press of Virginia, 2005), 274–278; Anne Sarah Rubin, *A Shattered Nation: The Rise and Fall of the Confederacy, 1861–1868* (Chapel Hill: University of North Carolina Press, 2005), 105.

[46] Lynda J. Morgan, *Emancipation in Virginia's Tobacco Belt, 1850–1870* (Athens: University of Georgia Press, 1992), 91.

Freedman's Village, Arlington, Va. *Library of Congress.*

it quickly surrendered to Northern forces after the surrender of Richmond in April. Given the erosion of slaveholder authority, it seems dubious whether the Confederates could have maintained the loyalty of enslaved soldiers with a promise of postwar emancipation. In no instance, however, were the basic contradictions of the Confederacy itself displayed more clearly than in the debate about black soldiers.[47]

NORTHERN MISSIONARIES AND THE ABOLITIONIST LEGACY

Northern abolitionists, eagerly welcoming the collapse of slavery, became deeply involved in the shaping of Union policies toward freed people. In portions of the occupied South, northern missionary relief workers and educators worked to improve the lot of ex-slaves. Across the region, abolitionists established the first black schools during the war, and these provided the basis for a permanent system of black education thereafter. Various freedmen's-aid organizations, composed of northern abolitionists eager to become involved with freed slaves, were formed. Many of them early on worked in the contraband camps, where they administered relief and began missionary work with the freed people. Northern missionaries saw a larger opportunity to transform ex-slaves out of what they believed was the immorality and degradation of slavery.

The most important northern missionary organization, the American Missionary Association (AMA), was founded as an interdenominational (though Protestant) evangelical organization. The AMA became especially active in the one hundred or so contraband camps existing in the Union-occupied South. In Roanoke Island, North Carolina, under Northern occupation starting in early 1862, the AMA established a colony under the supervision of Horace James, a Congregational minister and chaplain. James oversaw activities for freed people under Union occupation in eastern North Carolina. Although established as a self-sufficient colony of freed people at Roanoke Island, the colony had difficulty sustaining itself. The AMA also established schools, which formed an essential part of the colony.

[47] Robinson, *Bitter Fruits of Bondage*, 277–283; Rubin, *Shattered Nation*, 107–108.

The semi-independent Roanoke Colony survived until 1865, when President Andrew Johnson returned the property to white owners.

Another setting for northern missionary activity occurred in the coastal Sea Islands of South Carolina and Georgia. Union military forces occupied the area for most of the war, in the region stretching from Charleston to Savannah. Characterized by large and wealthy plantations growing highly valued long-staple cotton, the Sea Islands had a population that was about four-fifths enslaved. Operating under a gang system of labor on their plantations, slaves enjoyed some autonomy despite the arduous working and environmental conditions. Slaves greeted the Union invasion in the autumn of 1861 enthusiastically. One young slave, Sam Mitchell, told his mother that Union cannon fire was thunder. "Son," she responded, "dat ain't no t'under, dat Yankee come to gib you Freedom."[48]

The Sea Island with the most plantations, Port Royal Island, saw a general panic among planters with the arrival of the Yankees. Many of them fled, abandoning their plantations and about 11,000 slaves. In their absence, slaves established a semi-independent social, economic, and political system. The Union occupiers, faced with the issue of what to do with the abandoned slaves and plantations, were on uncertain ground this early in the war. Were the slaves free, or were they contrabands? What was the status of the abandoned plantations? The running of the Port Royal contrabands soon came under control of Secretary of the Treasury Salmon P. Chase. In December 1861, Chase dispatched Col. William H. Reynolds to investigate, seize abandoned cotton, and assess what to do with the deserted plantations and slaves. Chase also sent Edward L. Pierce, who had worked with contrabands at Fort Monroe. Pierce organized labor to harvest the cotton and made plans to feed the liberated slaves at Port Royal. In April 1862, about fifty male and female northern teachers and missionaries began what became known as the Port Royal Experiment. From Boston, New York, and Philadelphia, many of the northern missionaries were Harvard and Yale graduates. The missionaries coming to Port Royal called themselves Gideon's Band, or Giddeonites.

Notably, many of the Giddeonites were women. Laura M. Towne, a Philadelphia Quaker associated with the Pennsylvania Freedmen's Aid Society, was an abolitionist who early in the war became involved in freedmen's relief and educational efforts. She moved to Saint Helena Island, remaining for the rest of the nineteenth century. Along with other women such as Towne's associate Ellen Murray, the Saint Helena Giddeonites worked primarily in black education. Founding the William Penn School in June 1862, Towne and Murray established an abolitionist education presence in the occupied South. The Penn School's main building, completed in 1865 in sections in the North and then shipped to Saint Helena, enjoyed financial backing from northern supporters until the school closed in 1948.

Northern idealism competed with the profit motive, as army and Treasury officials sought to employ former slaves as wage laborers to cultivate cotton. Treasury officials sold the Sea Island plantations for tax delinquency, yet little of the land went

---

[48] Oakes, *Freedom National*, 198.

to freed people. The largest investors were led by two Massachusetts entrepreneurs, Edward Atkinson and Edward S. Philbrick. Believing in the moral and spiritual value of free labor, the investors sought to create a new model for plantation labor. Despite the investors' plans, black people were reluctant to farm cotton—which they regarded as a vestige of slavery—rather than other crops. The Atkinson-Philbrick experiment had failed by 1865.

The Northern army adopted its own approach regarding freed people. During the fall of 1862, Grant appointed John Eaton Jr. as superintendent of contrabands, in an effort to employ freed slaves in the western theater. Eaton, an advocate of the virtue of free labor but no abolitionist, emphasized habits of work and thrift among freed people. He envisioned a network of independent black landholders occupying former slaveholder lands, which would enable a "quickening of their enterprise."[49] He oversaw labor contracts between contrabands and planters, but Eaton also established "home farms," which were self-run black farms.

The Davis Bend plantation became the primary example of Eaton's experiment in freedom. Jefferson Davis's oldest brother, Joseph Emory Davis, had founded the plantation, located twenty-five miles south of Vicksburg, Mississippi. Lying on a twenty-eight-mile-long and twelve-mile-wide peninsula in the Mississippi River, Davis Bend was founded as an experimental, "model" system of slave management. Davis provided autonomy to the 350 slaves on the plantation, operating it as a communal enterprise and awarding considerable authority to Benjamin Thornton Montgomery, a literate slave who was a mechanic, machinist, and civil engineer. Handling Davis's account and cotton transactions, Montgomery operated a dry-goods store and was able to purchase a home. When Union troops invaded the area in the summer of 1862, Davis fled and left the plantation in the hands of the slaves. With Yankee troops in control in the fall of 1863, the slaves remained, and the plantation attracted about three thousand contrabands. Gen. U. S. Grant turned the plantation over to African American control, declaring it a "negro paradise." Joseph Davis eventually sold the plantation to Montgomery for $300,000, and during the post–Civil War years it became a model of communal enterprise and self-government.[50]

When the guns were silenced in 1865, of the four million slaves in the South, about 525,000, or 13 percent of the total, were free. Wartime emancipation came slowly. Lincoln and congressional Republicans based early hopes on the willingness of reconstructed southern governments to abolish slavery. Lincoln believed that emancipation by congressional enactment was unconstitutional. As he put it in his annual message to Congress in December 1862, "the general government had no lawful power to effect emancipation in any State."[51] Among white southerners, there was limited support, to say the least, to abolish slavery. In 1864, reconstructed governments in Arkansas and Louisiana issued emancipation decrees, and in the next

[49] Steven Joseph Ross, "Freed Soil, Freed Labor, Freed Men: John Eaton and the Davis Bend Experiment," *Journal of Southern History* 44, no. 2 (May 1978): 216.

[50] Eric Foner, *A Short History of Reconstruction, 1863–1877* (New York: Harper Collins, 1990), 27.

[51] Oakes, *Freedom National*, 457.

year, Maryland, West Virginia, Missouri, and Tennessee followed suit. Despite the abolition of slavery in Maryland in November 1864, the state legislature excluded former slaves from state-supported schools and legalized measures to compel them to work for former masters. On the other hand, Border states such as Kentucky and Delaware stubbornly tried to maintain slavery until the end of the war.

What solidified the end of slavery was the Thirteenth Amendment, adopted by Congress in January 1865 and ratified by the states in December. Using the language of the Northwest Ordinance of 1787, which banned slavery in the Northwest territories, the amendment stated that "neither slavery, nor involuntary servitude," except for criminal punishment, "shall exist in the United States, or any place subject to their jurisdiction." The second section of the amendment authorized Congress to enforce the amendment. Even though emancipation took place with invading armies throughout the war, and freedom occurring in the immediate aftermath of Confederate defeat, the Thirteenth Amendment solidified the reality that slavery had ended.

Slaves greeted freedom enthusiastically, often to the shock of their masters. African Americans fervently supported the Union cause, silently cheering about Northern victories. After Lee's surrender at Appomattox in April 1865, word gradually reached slaves during the spring and summer about their freedom. For many, that meant leaving the plantation and the supervision of their masters—and the assertion of their physical freedom. In actual fact, with the great majority of slaves still in bondage, much remained before true freedom would come to the black masses of the South. Nonetheless, the Civil War had resulted in the permanent destruction of slavery. With the Thirteenth Amendment, the wartime liberation of slaves became irreversible, and the remainder of the enslaved population became theoretically free. In addition, the process of reconciliation, and particularly Congress's insistence that Reconstruction depended on emancipation, finalized the end of slavery.

PART FOUR

RECONSTRUCTION AND ITS AFTERMATH

13

RECONSTRUCTION

WHEN THE CIVIL WAR ended in the spring of 1865, those portions of the South experiencing the heaviest fighting lay devastated. Although much of the rural South outside the battle zones escaped damage, cities such as Charleston, Columbia, and Atlanta suffered considerable destruction. A visitor found Charleston as having the "most picturesque" ruins of any he had seen in the South. Broad marble steps now led to ruins. "Over their cracked and calcined slabs, to the level of high foundations swept of everything," all that remained were the "crushed fragments of their former superstructures."[1] Northern invaders took and destroyed livestock, burned crops and buildings, pulled up iron rails, and damaged canals and levees. This was a "desolated land," commented an observer of postwar Georgia, in which crossroads towns and railroad stops "presented an array of ruined walls and chimneys standing useless and solitary." Untold wealth disappeared. Freedom for emancipated slaves cost slaveholders billions of dollars, while the value of real property declined by 30 percent in the South between 1860 and 1870.[2]

After the most destructive war in American history, almost immediately the question arose of how to rebuild the defeated South—not only physically but also constitutionally. What would rebuilding look like? How would southern secessionism be wrung out of the political system? What would happen to the old slaveholding class, and what would prevent their resurgence? Most importantly, what role would ex-slaves have? What did freedom mean for them, and what sort of position

[1] John Townsend Trowbridge, *The South: A Tour of Its Battlefields and Ruined Cities*, ed. John H. Segars (Macon, GA: Mercer University Press, 2006), 514. Originally published in 1866.
[2] Eric Foner, *Reconstruction. America's Unfinished Revolution, 1863–1877* (New York: Harper & Row, 1988), 124–125.

would they occupy in civil and political life? Reconstructing the South after the destruction of slavery was a highly contested process. Southern whites experienced a profound sense of defeat, coupled with a desire to justify their past and their sense of future. For black people, the aftermath of the war meant charting out freedom, even while a specter of slavery persisted.

Even before the war ended, northern invaders and occupiers began to debate how the South should be restored to the Union. In the occupied Confederacy, Union commanders sporadically governed, sometimes by military fiat, sometimes by appointing civilian governments in hopes that southern Unionists would emerge. Lincoln's wartime Reconstruction policies, which also depended on the existence of southern Unionists, encountered an unwilling southern white population and congressional critics who believed that the president did not go far enough to end slaveholder power. When John Wilkes Booth murdered Lincoln on April 14, 1865, the defeated South's future remained uncertain. Most important of these uncertainties was the status of freed slaves. How much freedom did black people possess in the post–Civil War South?

FREEDOM'S STRUGGLES

In July 1865, Louis Hughes and his wife, Mathilda, two enslaved African Americans from Panola County, Mississippi, traveled north on the Mississippi River to Memphis. After the Union army occupied Memphis in June 1862, the port city provided refuge for thousands of enslaved African Americans and served as a center for the recruitment of black troops. Seven regiments of black soldiers were stationed in the city; family members and other contrabands often accompanied them. By war's end, the black population of Memphis had tripled, with African Americans composing two-fifths of the city's population.

Arriving after a long trip, the Hugheses reported that it was crowded with ex-slaves "from all over the south, who cheered and gave us a welcome." Louis described how hundreds of black refugees "thronged the streets." "Everywhere you looked," he reported, "you could see soldiers. Such a day I don't believe Memphis will ever see again—when so large and so motley a crowd will come together." Cities such as Memphis, under the protection of Union military forces, provided sanctuary and protection, becoming hothouses of new experiences accompanying emancipation.[3]

The uncertainty that Louis and Mathilda Hughes experienced in postwar Memphis became a commonplace throughout the post–Civil War South. Whites were also uncertain about what defeat would mean. Some former Confederates, despairing about their ability to live in a conquered South, left the country. In June 1865, Gen. Joseph Shelby led a group of a thousand Confederates into Mexico. After making the 1,200-mile trip to Mexico City, the force disbanded. Emperor

---

[3] Hannah Rosen, *Terror in the Heart of Freedom: Citizenship, Sexual Violence, and the Meaning of Race in the Postemancipation South* (Chapel Hill: University of North Carolina Press, 2009), 24.

Maximilian, an Austrian-born monarch whom the French installed after invading and occupying Mexico in 1861, was an enthusiastic advocate of the immigration of ex-Confederates. Working with his emigration agent, Confederate naval commander Matthew F. Maury, Maximilian hoped to attract 50,000 exiles. Maury laid plans for a settlement, the New Virginia colony, in central Mexico, along with a 500,000-acre tract located in a new town, Carlota, between Vera Cruz and Mexico City. Eventually 2,500 moved to these settlements, including Confederate generals John B. Magruder, Edmund Kirby Smith, and Thomas C. Hindman. The withdrawal of French forces and the defeat and execution of Maximilian in July 1867 meant that the southerners were no longer welcome. Several thousand other southern whites moved to Brazil, owning slaves until 1888. Known as *Confederados*, many of them and their descendants remained in Brazil.

Soon after the end of the war, when Illinois newspaperman Sidney Andrews visited South Carolina, he noted a disjuncture between white and black attitudes regarding slavery's end. "I scarcely talk with any white man," Andrews wrote, "who fails to tell me how anxious many of the negroes are to return to their old homes." Andrews doubted that these observations were true, on two counts: first, it was rare that former slaveholders permitted ex-slaves to return, and, second, "I can't find any of those desirous of returning." He interrogated about one hundred freed people about whether they wanted to return to their masters. "I have yet to find," he reported, "the first one who hesitates an instant in answering 'No.'"[4] Slaveholders long deluded themselves with the fiction that they were serving a civilizing mission for slaves, who, in essence, preferred to be enslaved. Nothing could have been more untrue.

Possessing racial views leading them to view African Americans as inherently lazy, many southern whites were convinced that freed people would not work without the coercion of slavery's work regime. Whites had other fears associated with black freedom. They often objected to violations of racial etiquette, which they called "insolence." Whites also feared that the loosening of the bonds of slavery meant insurrection. "Serious apprehensions" about a general black revolt existed among whites during the months following the war, wrote a northern visitor in 1866, though he discounted these fears as "mere pretence and cant." There was not the "slightest danger from a rising from the blacks, nor will there be, unless they are driven to desperation by wrongs."[5]

The uncertainty of freedom became apparent in Kentucky, where a large portion of the state's slaves—70 percent of males—volunteered for the Union military in order to obtain their freedom. Despite large-scale emancipation, about 70,000 remained enslaved when the war ended. Their status was still uncertain in November 1865, when the Kentucky legislature refused to ratify the Thirteenth Amendment. During the months immediately after the end of the war, many planters and slaves did not immediately realize that slavery had ended. "The truth is," said one former

---

4 Sidney Andrews, *The South since the War, as Shown by Fourteen Weeks of Travel and Observation in Georgia and the Carolinas* (Boston: Ticknor and Fields, 1866), 22–23.
5 Trowbridge, *South*, 375.

slaveholder, "I had all my life, been accustomed to having someone call me master, and I can't get along without it now."[6]

Once the reality of emancipation sank in, further adjustment for other southern whites occurred. In Richmond, within months of the Confederate surrender, local authorities instituted pass and curfew restrictions to control black mobility and coerce labor. In June 1865 alone, eight hundred freed people were rounded up for violations and detained in makeshift jails in Richmond. In collaboration with occupying northern soldiers, freed people were intimidated verbally and physically. Black women, in addition, often suffered sexual abuse. According to one account of postwar Richmond, it became common to hear "women scream frightfully every night."[7]

In the Mississippi delta, white planters repeated the common misperception that ex-slaves worked only under white compulsion. Wherever slaves were freed, said one white, "they have for the most part ceased to work." Former slaves, observed another white commentator, possessed "false ideas" about freedom; city living lured them into degeneration and criminality.[8] Visiting the South in the summer of 1865, German émigré and former Missouri senator Carl Schurz described how southern whites remained convinced that a free-labor system could exist in the South only if ex-slaves were coerced. "You cannot make the negro work,

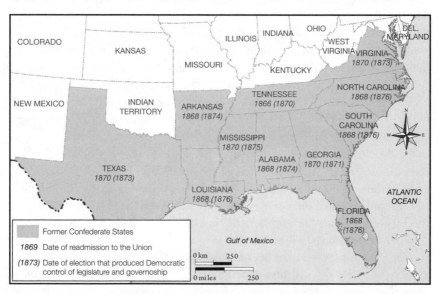

MAP 13.1 Readmission of Reconstructed States, with Dates of Redemption

[6] Anne E. Marshall, *Creating a Confederate Identity: The Lost Cause and Civil War Memory in a Border State* (Chapel Hill: University of North Carolina Press, 2011), 37.

[7] Elsa Barkley Brown, "Negotiating and Transforming the Public Sphere: African American Political Life in the Transition from Slavery to Freedom," in *Jumpin' Jim Crow: Southern Politics from Civil War to Civil Rights*, ed. Jane Dailey, Glenda Elizabeth Gilmore, and Bryant Simon (Princeton, NJ: Princeton University Press, 2000), 31.

[8] Rosen, *Terror in the Heart of Freedom*, 42.

without physical compulsion," former slaveholders informed Schurz. He heard this same sentiment "hundreds of times . . . wherever I went, . . . in nearly the same words from so many different persons."

Schurz, an exile from the German liberal revolutions of 1848 and an abolitionist, remained skeptical that the white South could easily abandon their past. Former slaveholders, he reported, wanted to return to the plantation regime, backed up by brutality and coercion. According to southern whites, Schurz wrote, former slaves were "too improvident" to take care of themselves and "must necessarily be consigned to the care of a master." Former masters were outraged when ex-slaves refused to submit to whipping—the slave regime's primary disciplinary tool—and their refusal seemed to demonstrate further that they were "unfit for freedom." Whites, according to Schurz, became so accustomed to violence against black people that their tendency to manage labor through brutality became "inveterate" and "almost irresistible." Former masters, seeking to "preserve slavery in its original form as much and as long as possible," harbored a "lingering hope" that slavery might survive.[9]

Ex-slaves' perceptions about the meaning of freedom were entirely different. Emancipation meant redemption from slavery's travails. Freedom, said one black preacher, "burned in the black heart long before freedom was born."[10] By the end of the Civil War, ex-slaves and free blacks lobbied for an expansion of rights that would accompany the northern conquest of the South. The Thirteenth Amendment solidified emancipation and the end of slavery, but northern abolitionists pushed for civil rights and even the suffrage for freed slaves. Others favored economic rights and a program of uplift targeting freed slaves. Some radicals advocated a punitive policy of confiscation of slaveholder lands and their redistribution to ex-slaves. The chairman of the House Committee on Public Lands, George W. Julian of Indiana, declared that only land reform would prevent ex-slaves from becoming imprisoned by "a system of wages slavery . . . more galling than slavery itself."[11]

Great confusion about African Americans' status characterized the immediate postwar years, punctuated by clashing white and black expectations. The experiences of Henry Adams, Louisiana ex-slave, are illustrative. Born in Newton County, Georgia, in 1843, at the age of seven Adams was taken by his master to De Soto Parish, in northwestern Louisiana. Sometime during the spring of 1865, a white man appeared, Adams recalled, "telling us that we were all free, and that we colored people could go where we pleased and manage our own affairs, and could work for who we pleased." During the war, Adams had accumulated property, including three horses and a "fine buggy," along with gold and silver. When the war ended, Adams's former master wanted him to remain, "because the poor white people did not like a rich negro no how." His former master urged him to "stay where we were living, and we could get protection from our old masters."

9 Carl Schurz, *Report on the Condition of the South*, 39th Congress, Senate Ex. Doc. 1st Session, No. 2 (1865).
10 Foner, *Short History of Reconstruction*, 35.
11 Foner, *Short History of Reconstruction*, 31.

Adams sought to assert his freedom, however, both in real and symbolic terms. "I fear God but not man," and "if I was free, I have to be free." "If I cannot do like a white man," he said, "I am not free." Whites wanted him to travel only with passes, and to work according to contracts that disadvantaged him. Seeing "how poor white people do," Adams declared that "I ought to do so too, or else I am a slave." Eventually, he left for the nearest town, Shreveport, where he joined scores of other former slaves seeking escape from the postwar plantation system.[12]

Henry Adams's experience suggests the conflicting emotions of ex-slaves' exhilaration and whites' anxiety about emancipation. Whites worried about the future, which required coerced, unpaid labor of enslaved African Americans and a social system resting on white supremacy. With slavery destroyed, black people expressed freedom by seeking things previously unavailable. Restricted by the pass system and slave patrols, freed people wanted to travel freely. Many sought to be reunited with families separated under slavery.

Once freed, many African Americans moved to southern towns and cities. Between 1865 and 1870 the black population in the South's ten biggest urban communities doubled. Prohibited by law under slavery from learning to read and write, freed slaves enthusiastically participated in makeshift schools. Once freed, ex-slaves—previously required to attend white churches—separated to form their own congregations. Clothed in plain homespun and inferior shoes, African Americans donned newer, fancier clothes, making a statement about their freedom. In many instances, they refused to give way to white people when they walked on sidewalks. Legally prohibited from owning dogs under slavery, freed people acquired them when freed. Ex-slaves also rode horses, a symbol of power and autonomy.

Above all, former slaves were acutely aware that slavery had deprived them of their livelihood and economic justice. When William Sherman asked Savannah black leaders in January 1865 what slavery meant, a black minister responded. "Receiving . . . the work of another man, and not by his consent" constituted slavery; freedom meant "placing us where we could reap the fruit of our own labor." Economic autonomy, escape from white authority, and control over their work and income became common objectives for freed people. For most nineteenth-century Americans, economic independence meant landholding; African Americans shared this faith in landownership. "Gib us our own land and we can take care ourselves," declared a Charleston emancipated slave. "Widout land, do ole massas can hire or starve us, as dey please."[13] Black people wanted to be elevated, former slave Bayley Wyat declared in a meeting in Tidewater Virginia in 1866. "We desires to do all we can to be educated, and we hope our friends will aid us all they can. I may state to all

[12] Henry Adams testimony, in *Proceedings of the Select Committee of the United States to Investigate the Causes of the Removal of the Negroes from the Southern States to the Northern States, March 9, 1880*, Reports of Committees of the Senate of the United States (Washington, DC: Government Printing Office, 1880), 190–192.

[13] Foner, "Rights and the Constitution in Black Life during the Civil War and Reconstruction," 870–871.

our friends and to all our enemies that we has a right to the land where we are lo-cated. Our wives, our children, our husbands, has been sold over and over again to purchase the lands we now locates on." Black people possessed "a divine right to the land," Wyat believed. "Didn't we clear the lands," he declared, "and raise the crops of corn and of cotton and of tobacco and of rice and of sugar and of everything?" Whites—southern and northern—had profited from slave labor. "They have grown rich, and my people are poor."

Whites regarded these symbols of freedom as evidence of a new spirit of rebel-lion, insubordination, and insolence. They searched for ways to reinvent the slave labor regime by coercive contracts binding ex-slaves to the land. Freed people re-sisted, preferring independent landownership outside the plantation system. Eman-cipated slaves, regarding cotton farming as working for the "slave crop," sought the self-sufficiency that they lacked under slavery. The "sole ambition of the freedman," said a northern visitor, was to "become the owner of a little piece of land, there to erect a humble home, and to dwell in peace and security at his own free will and pleasure." If ex-slaves grew cotton, they wanted to do so on their "own account, to be able to do so without anyone . . . [dictating] hours or system of labor." If they pre-ferred to grow food such as sweet potatoes or corn, their "desire and their hope" was to do so outside white control.[14]

Antebellum black evangelical Christianity served as a nerve center of slave cul-ture. Religion continued to define the freed people's postemancipation identity. A few independent black churches existed in the South before the war, despite white fears that black preaching might lead to insurrection. Existing black churches pro-vided an infrastructure for postwar growth. Baptists evangelized throughout the antebellum South; black Baptist congregations, after emancipation, grew exponen-tially. Originally northern denominations, the African Methodist Episcopal (AME) and AME Zion churches spread to some southern urban communities by the late antebellum era.

Emancipation brought great tumult to black Christianity. Frequently withdraw-ing from white churches, where they enjoyed an associate membership and were rel-egated to the galleries, blacks created their own denominations and churches. White and black missionaries encouraged African Americans seeking religious indepen-dence. Northern denominations, including Presbyterian, Congregational, and Epis-copalian, led the way in missionary activities. In many southern states, missionaries established black-controlled denominations affiliated with the northern denomina-tions that had split with southern churches before the Civil War. During the first year after the war, southern white Methodists lost half their black membership, with most of it migrating to the AME Church or to northern Methodist congregations. What remained of black Methodists in the white church organized a separate Col-ored Methodist Church, which became an independent denomination in 1870. In 1894, black Baptists founded the National Baptist Convention, the largest black de-nomination in the country.

[14] Foner, *Short History of Reconstruction*, 47–48.

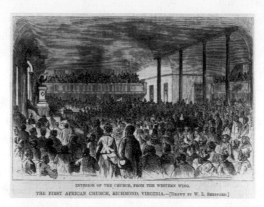

INTERIOR OF THE CHURCH, FROM THE WESTERN WING.
THE FIRST AFRICAN CHURCH, RICHMOND, VIRGINIA.—[Drawn by W. L. Sheppard.]

The First African Church, Richmond, Virginia—Interior of the Church, from the Western Wing, drawn by W. L. Sheppard. *Library of Congress.*

Henry McNeal Turner, perhaps the most successful religious organizer in the postwar South, became a key figure in the growth of the AME Church into a powerful national and international denomination. Born free in Newberry, South Carolina, Turner served as an AME minister in 1858, holding a pastorate when the Civil War began in Washington, DC. The first black chaplain in the Union army and seeing action in nine battles, Turner became a Republican and religious activist. Serving a Savannah pastorate for a decade, in 1880 he returned to Atlanta as the twelfth bishop of the AME Church. Turner also played a key role in expanding the AME Church to South Africa.[15]

Thousands of freed slaves looked to their churches as bastions of a new cultural independence. "The Ebony preacher . . . promises perfect independence from White control and direction carries the col[ore]d heart at once," wrote a northern white missionary. White preachers had admonished slaves to obey their masters; emancipation meant religious and cultural liberation. A southern white preacher picked up his Bible, remembered a former slave, and claimed "he gittin the text right out from the good Book." The white preacher told slaves: "The Lord say, don't you niggers steal chickens from your missus. Don't you steal your marster's hawgs." Social control and obedience was the primary message of white Christianity to black people. With freedom, slaves no longer needed to worship in secret, or under white scrutiny. "Bless God," said one freedman, "we don't have to keep watch at that door to tell us the patrollers are coming to take us to jail and fine us twenty-five dollars for prayin' and talkin' of the love of Jesus. O no, we's FREE!"[16]

In many churches, blacks either left the congregations or deposed their white ministers. In early 1865, at the Front Street Methodist Church in Wilmington, North Carolina, eight hundred members of the black congregation ignored the

[15] Stephen Ward Angell, *Bishop Henry McNeal Turner and African-American Religion in the South* (Knoxville: University of Tennessee Press, 1992), chapter 2.
[16] Reginald F. Hildebrand, *The Times Were Strange and Stirring: Methodist Preachers and the Crisis of Emancipation* (Durham, NC: Duke University Press, 1985), 36–37.

white minister, the Rev. L. S. Burkhead, as William H. Hunter, a black chaplain in one of the African regiments liberating the city and a former North Carolina slave, strode up the aisle and "took the seat usually vacated for the pastor." "The whole congregation was wild with excitement," Burkhead wrote, "and extravagant beyond all precedent with shouts, groans, amens, and unseeming demonstrations." Hunter, a recruiter for the AME Church, urged black congregants to seize on their new religious freedom. "One week ago you were all slaves; now you are free," he declared. He himself had left North Carolina a slave and returned a man. "The armies of the Lord and of Gideon," Hunter declared, had emerged victorious, with Rebels "scattered like chaff before the wind." Soon thereafter, most of the black members of Front Street left the white Methodist church to organize an AME church.[17]

THE NEW ORDER

In occupied Savannah in January 1865, Gen. William T. Sherman issued Special Field Order No. 15. It designated a large portion of Sea Island and Lowcountry plantations in the rice districts of Georgia and South Carolina for black settlement, in allotments of forty acres of land per family. Sherman also promised that the army would provide them each a mule—hence the phrase "forty acres and a mule" that came to characterize the most radical land redistribution programs. Eventually, 40,000 freed people took advantage of Sherman's order, in allotments totaling 400,000 acres. Yet Sherman's Field Order No. 15 became the exception rather than the rule, as no coordinated Union policy facilitated the transfer of plantation lands to freed slaves.

Created on March 3, 1865, the Bureau of Refugees, Freedmen, and Abandoned Lands—better known as the Freedmen's Bureau—existed under the War Department. Assuming control of the lands "abandoned" by fleeing southerners, the bureau assumed functions that Union occupiers had been performing for freed people. Remaining under military control and staffed by soldiers in uniform, the bureau directed the national effort to guide the transition from slavery to freedom. The bureau, engendering widespread hostility from southern whites, was no paragon of racial egalitarianism. Its officers frequently expressed racist or paternalistic attitudes; in many instances, they sympathized with former slaveholders and served their interests. Yet, for freed people, the bureau represented the only chance of federal protection.

Serving primarily as a relief agency, the bureau extended federal resources to help with the education, labor, and health of ex-slaves. It administered contraband camps and provided them with rations, reunited families, established schools for ex-slaves, supervised labor contracts, and ran hospitals. The bureau also helped coordinate and support extensive efforts by northern abolitionist groups, which had been engaged in the contraband camps during the war. Organizations such as the American Missionary Association (AMA) sent hundreds of northern teachers, many of them women, into the South to teach in new black schools.

---

[17] Litwack, *Been in the Storm*, 465–466.

Heading the Freedmen's Bureau, Maine native Oliver O. Howard fought with valor in the Army of the Potomac, losing an arm in June 1862. Promoted to major general, he was transferred to the western theater, where he commanded the Army of the Tennessee during Sherman's Atlanta Campaign. Serving as the Freedmen's Bureau's first and only commissioner, Howard strongly believed in free labor's transformative effects. "Until the system of free labor shall be practically understood in the south," he wrote in November 1866, "some agency like this bureau seems vital to the success of all those agricultural enterprises which depend upon the labor of the freedpeople." Ex-slaves were "willing and anxious" to work, but they needed federal protection from cruel ex-masters and an unjust legal system.[18]

Slavery's cruelest quality was the frequent separations of husbands from wives, and parents from children. With emancipation, former slaves rushed to reunite separated families, often with the aid of the bureau. A northern white missionary observed that freed slaves in a contraband camp near Richmond sought family reunification. "Mothers are having restored to them children whom they never expected to see again this side of eternity," he wrote. "Wives are brought upon their knees in praise to God at the appearance of husbands long ago torn from them and sold to the dreaded South and the meeting between these husbands and wives, parents and children no pen can describe." The missionary concluded that ex-slaves sometimes exhibited their pleasure in "loud salutation" but more often the "convulsive grasp of the hand and the tears of joy silently coursing down their cheeks tell of happiness too deep for utterance."[19]

Soon after emancipation, ex-slaves made extraordinary efforts to seek out lost relatives. Probably most failed, but many continued to try. Advertising in black newspapers, they described long-lost spouses and children separated by slave sales. In North Carolina, Marie Johnson, a freed slave, walked hundreds of miles in search of her husband, from whom she had been separated when her master moved from North Carolina to Mississippi. Arriving exhausted in Raleigh, she wrote how she had "now neither strength nor means to go further." In her case and many others, the Freedmen's Bureau provided passes to travel on the railroad while they searched for family members. Some agents were indifferent to the plight of freed people, but others were more energetic.[20]

As was true under slavery, black women were subjected to frequent sexual abuse. Many women migrated to urban areas in search of greater security. Ex-slave Lucy Williams moved to Memphis after the war. Her white plantation employer beat her because she participated in a meeting with the Freedmen's Bureau. According to her account, her white employer "commenced kicking and kicked so bad that I could not speak for several minutes. . . . He then told me to get off of his premises and never

[18] "Report of the Commissioner of the Bureau of Refugees, Freedmen, and Abandoned Lands, November 1, 1866," in *Annual Report of the Secretary of War*, 39th Cong., 2d Sess., House Executive Document No. 1, 705–707.

[19] Heather Andrea Williams, *Help Me to Find My People: The African American Search for Family Lost in Slavery* (Chapel Hill: University of North Carolina Press, 2012), 141.

[20] Williams, *Help Me*, 148–149.

Freedmen's Bureau agent officiating at the marriage of an African American soldier at Vicksburg, by Chaplain Warren of the Freedmen's Bureau, *Harper's Weekly. Library of Congress.*

return." Freed women assumed a leading role in urban life, in the growth of churches, in the development of mutual-aid societies, and, in a larger sense, in the construction of postwar families.[21] Women also pressured the Freedmen's Bureau to enforce wage contracts and to restrain planter violence, while they also used the bureau and its courts as weapons against sexual violence.

SELF-RECONSTRUCTION

In April 1865, President Andrew Johnson, succeeding the martyred Lincoln, extended his version of Lincoln's Reconstruction policies. Johnson, self-educated and a former tailor's apprentice, rose from obscure circumstances to become a wealthy landowner. Born in North Carolina but moving to eastern Tennessee, Johnson served in the state legislature and was elected to five terms as a US congressman, two terms as governor, and one as a US senator. Hostile to slaveholders, Johnson bitterly opposed secession, though he was no advocate of abolition or equal rights for freed people. Johnson served as military governor in occupied Tennessee and in 1865, though a Democrat, joined Lincoln in a bipartisan Union ticket.

Like Lincoln, Johnson favored a lenient peace and the quick reincorporation of the South back into the Union. Also like Lincoln, Johnson believed that secession was illegal and that the southern states had therefore never truly left the Union. Johnson used his power as president to issue pardons to former Confederates and to appoint provisional governors. On May 29, 1865, Johnson issued a presidential proclamation providing for amnesty and pardon to all Confederates except for fourteen classes of people, most of whom were high officeholders and owners of $20,000 or more in property. The latter were required to apply for pardons on a case-by-case basis.

Johnson showed little sympathy for emancipated slaves. Nor did he believe that they should possess civil and political rights. In the "progress of nations," he declared in his annual message to Congress in 1867, "Negroes have shown less capacity for

[21] Rosen, *Terror in the Heart of Freedom,* 52.

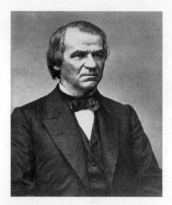

Andrew Johnson. *Library of Congress.*

government than any other race of people." No "independent government of any form has ever been successful in their hands," and they exhibited a "constant tendency to relapse into barbarism." Emancipated slaves were "not only regardless of the rights of property, but so utterly ignorant of public affairs that their voting can consist in nothing more than carrying a ballot to the place where they are directed to deposit it."[22]

Jefferson Davis was imprisoned for two years, freed on bail, and then successfully defended himself on treason charges in federal court, which eventually dismissed the charges. Aside from the execution of Henry Wirtz on November 10, 1865, for war crimes while commanding the Confederate prisoner-of-war camp near Andersonville, Georgia, no other Confederate military or political leader ever faced treason charges. President Johnson approved over seven thousand pardons of former Confederates exempted under his May 1865 proclamation. More than three years later, on December 25, 1868, he pardoned "all and . . . every person who, directly or indirectly, participated in the late insurrection or rebellion." Johnson also pursued a lenient policy toward the organization of new governments. In 1865–1866, appointing as provisional governors mostly former Whigs and reluctant secessionists, Johnson permitted southern states to organize themselves into new governments. These "self-reconstructed" governments oversaw the writing of new constitutions that invalidated secession, repudiated the Confederate debt, and ratified the Thirteenth Amendment. In elections for governors and legislatures, former Unionist Whigs were returned to governorships.

The southern governments assuming power in 1866 included many familiar faces, some of whom had participated in the Confederacy. At best, the new office-holders were Unionists who converted to secessionism after the attack on Fort Sumter. These new governments made no provision for black civil rights and enfranchisement. To the contrary, the legislatures enacted new laws defining a second-class status for ex-slaves. In late 1865, South Carolina and Mississippi became the first southern states to enact new "black codes," which most southern state legislatures eventually adopted. Reproducing the antebellum free-black codes, these laws provided that ex-slaves could own property, agree to contracts, marry, and testify against other black people.

More significantly, the black codes sought to control and regulate the black population. Under these codes, local governments were empowered to compel former slaves to work under white discipline; those resisting faced compulsion. Limiting former slaves to rural areas, the laws prohibited them from renting urban lands.

---

[22] Andrew Johnson, Third Annual Message, December 3, 1867; available at http://www.presidency.ucsb.edu/ws/index.php?pid=29508.

Freedmen's School, Edisto Island, SC, photograph by Samuel A. Cooley. *Library of Congress.*

Unemployed blacks could be declared vagrants and forced to work, while the state could also declare them "orphans" if they could not prove their parentage (in the aftermath of slavery, few former slaves could document their birth). These "orphans" could be apprenticed, with preference given to former masters. In South Carolina, black people pursuing other than farming or labor as a servant had to pay an annual tax. In addition, blacks' legal status was limited by prohibiting jury service and testimony against whites. The legislatures criminalized minor offenses, targeting ex-slaves and beginning a new system of mass imprisonment. At the same time, efforts were made to limit freed people's access to traditionally common lands for pasture, hunting, and fishing. Very often, former Confederate soldiers, filling the ranks of postwar police, militia, and sheriffs, enjoyed free rein in terrorizing black people.

The self-reconstructed governments made no provision for educating former slaves. To the contrary, the new governments remained hostile to black schooling. In North Carolina, Gov. Jonathan Worth, an antebellum Whig Unionist, successfully argued to the legislature that the state should abolish state-supported schools rather than educate black people. White schools, Worth said, meant that "we will be required to educate the negroes in like manner."[23]

Self-reconstruction ultimately failed for two reasons. First, freed people resisted attempts to reimpose slavery. Freedmen's conventions assembled while the self-reconstruction constitutional conventions met in 1865–1866, reminding the white leaders that they deserved a part in the political process. The Tennessee freedmen's convention, meeting in August 1865 in Nashville, sought "to impress upon the white men of Tennessee, of the United States, and of the world," said a black leader, "that we are part and parcel of the American Republic." The black codes were difficult to enforce, and conflicts frequently resulted. Race riots occurred in Memphis and New Orleans in late 1866 over whites' attempt to impose control. African Americans began to organize politically, advocating for increased federal protections. Black leaders also took early steps toward mobilizing black support for a new southern Republican Party. Second, the southern state governments' policies, especially the

[23] Foner, *Short History of Reconstruction*, 96.

Memphis Riot, 1866. *Library of Congress.*

black codes, provoked a backlash among the northern electorate, as did Johnson's obstinate opposition to congressional Reconstruction policies.

In December 1865, congressional radicals, favoring more punitive and far-reaching Reconstruction policies, organized a fifteen-member Joint Committee on Reconstruction. After Johnson vetoed key pieces of the radicals' program, including 1866 legislation extending the life of the Freedmen's Bureau as well as a new civil rights bill, public opinion turned against him. Johnson's truculence alienated much of the northern Republican Party; Congress overrode the presidential vetoes. In June 1866, in addition, Congress adopted the Fourteenth Amendment, which incorporated equality before the law and penalized southern states not fully enfranchising all males. Among the seceding states, however, only the Tennessee legislature ratified the amendment. Most significantly, in the congressional elections of November 1866, an overwhelming anti-Johnson majority was returned, able to overturn his presidential vetoes.

When the Thirty-Ninth Congress assembled in early 1867, radicals assumed full control. Marginalizing Johnson, Congress attempted to limit his power of appointment and dismissal with the Tenure of Office Act, enacted in 1867. A year later, Johnson was impeached and narrowly acquitted in a Senate trial, but his influence over Reconstruction remained greatly diminished. Meanwhile, in March 1867, Congress pushed Johnson aside, voting in the Reconstruction Acts over his veto. These laws swept away the self-reconstructed southern state governments, establishing five military districts in the ten states that had refused to ratify the Fourteenth Amendment. These military governments were charged with enfranchising black males, overseeing the holding of new constitutional conventions, and supervising a new round of elections.

REPUBLICAN GOVERNMENT

A majority of these new southern Republicans were newly enfranchised black males, loyal to the party of Lincoln and emancipation. After 1867, a massive mobilization of former slaves, occurring under the protective umbrella of military government,

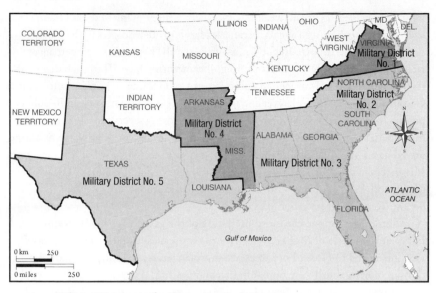

MAP 13.2 Military Districts under Reconstruction, 1867

brought a new era of African American political participation. Black voters mobilized through organizations such as the Union League, which became the most important vehicle of African American political mobilization in the postwar South. Beginning in 1867, Republican organizers relied on the Union League to recruit; black veterans played a key leadership role in a network that spread throughout the South and included AME churches with a message of religious and political liberation. "I commence as a preacher," declared a Mississippi AME preacher, "and end as a political speaker." Another AME organizer in Virginia announced he would speak "where they have cowed the black man," and, "by the help of God," he would provide "a dose of my radical Republican pills and neutralize the corrosive acidity of their negro hate."

Union League organizers established local councils in plantation districts. Their meetings were often held in secret, for fear of white retaliation or violence. They followed Masonic rituals, and the practices of black churches, which initiated new members into fellowship. The Union League spread during 1867–1868. In many districts, the organization claimed the allegiance of nearly all adult black males. Drawing on existing networks—plantation and kinship, as well as military veterans—the Union League schooled African Americans in political organization and leadership.

Union League organizers also mobilized white voters, but usually in districts with smaller black populations. The reality was that Republicans could not win elections with only black votes; only three southern states—South Carolina, Mississippi, and Louisiana—possessed majority black populations. As one contemporary put it, "a party sustained only by black votes will not grow old."[24] Biracial Republicanism— the uneasy coalition between whites and former slaves—constituted the party's most

[24] Foner, *Short History of Reconstruction*, 129.

significant achievement and weakness. Northern whites, many of them Union veterans or Freedmen's Bureau agents, became leaders and officeholders in the party.

These northern-born Republicans—pejoratively known as "carpetbaggers"—were not large enough to constitute a significant voting bloc. They included people such as Albion W. Tourgée, an Ohio veteran who came to Greensboro, North Carolina, after the war. A lawyer and judge, Tourgée involved himself in Republican politics in Reconstruction North Carolina, later writing several novels fictionalizing his experiences. Another carpetbagger, Adlebert Ames, originally from Maine, served as a Union general during the war and was elected to the US Senate from Mississippi in 1870. In South Carolina, Daniel Henry Chamberlain, a Massachusetts native and Yale graduate who commanded black troops during the Civil War, became Republican governor in 1874.

Tourgée was among the most interesting of the carpetbaggers. Suffering a back injury at the Battle of Manassas, he left military service in 1863 to teach school. In 1865, he moved to Greensboro to establish a plant nursery. Tourgée's main motivations in moving south were humanitarian and political. He soon became a Republican activist, serving in the North Carolina constitutional convention of 1868, where he helped reform the state's court system. For six years, Tourgée served as a superior court judge, where he did battle with the Ku Klux Klan's campaign of political terror. Departing North Carolina in 1878, in the next year he published *A Fool's Errand*, a fictionalized account of his time in Reconstruction.[25]

Carpetbaggers such as Tourgée joined with native-born southern whites to form another portion of this political coalition. These native-born whites—denounced as "scalawags" (a common nineteenth-century term for a low-grade, worthless person) by Reconstruction's enemies—were a diverse lot. Some had been antebellum Whigs who cast their lot with the new party. Wealthy Mississippi planter James L. Alcorn, who served as brigadier general in the Confederate army, was an antebellum Whig who, in 1867, became a Republican. He maintained that planter whites such as himself could attract the black electorate and cultivate the investment of northern capital. Similarly, Joseph E. Brown, who had been Confederate governor of Georgia, became a Republican, arguing that he could forestall more-radical changes pressed by northerners. Brown's position on Reconstruction represented both pragmatism and opportunism. Unenthusiastic about black suffrage and civil rights, he appeased northern interests in order to end Georgia's military occupation. His primary motivation, he wrote, was to see the state "restored to peace and prosperity upon the best terms that we could obtain."[26]

Scalawag voters often came from areas that were previously hotbeds of southern Unionism. In regions such as western North Carolina, Piedmont North Carolina,

[25] Mark Elliott, *Color Blind Justice: Albion Tourgée and the Quest for Racial Equality from the Civil War to Plessy v. Ferguson* (New York: Oxford University Press, 2006).

[26] Joseph E. Brown to William D. Kelly, March 18, 1868, box 3, folder 9, Joseph E. Brown Papers, MSS 40, Kenan Research Center, Atlanta History Center; Joseph H. Parks, *Joseph E. Brown of Georgia* (Baton Rouge: Louisiana State University Press, 1977). See also Joseph E. Brown to W. A. Bedell, June 17, 1868, box 3, folder 9, Brown Papers.

northwestern Arkansas, East Tennessee, southwestern Missouri, and northern Alabama, strongholds of wartime Unionism morphed into centers of southern white Republicanism. Because these regions lacked many African Americans, the race issue could be safely ignored—as long as it remained out of the political limelight. Nonetheless, the biracial Republican political coalition remained very fragile. For the most part, the party united around a platform of economic development through railroad improvement and public education, the end of corporal punishment (such as the whipping post), and equal rights for freedmen.

During 1867–1868, Republicans led efforts to rewrite southern state constitutions. With the antebellum southern political leadership either barred from participation or boycotting the elections, these new constitutional conventions contained Republican majorities. Whites were in the majority among the Republicans, but these conventions became the first significant meeting of elected representatives of any kind with an integrated membership. A Scottish visitor, David Macrae, observed Virginia's constitutional convention, which met from December 1867 to April 1868. Macrae noticed that the meeting was integrated, a "strange scene" in which "negro delegates from all parts of the State were occupying the seats vacated by the Confederate Congress, helping white men to frame a new Constitution for Virginia!" Blacks and whites, he noted, "sat side by side in the members' seats." A "mighty revolution" had occurred.[27]

Two hundred sixty-seven black delegates attended the Reconstruction-era constitutional conventions across the South during 1867–1868. However, African Americans were relatively underrepresented. Only in Louisiana and South Carolina did they make up a majority of delegates; in Florida, they numbered two-fifths. About forty of the black delegates to the constitutional conventions were Union veterans, while 129 black veterans eventually became officeholders. Black veterans continued to play a prominent role in Republican Party politics, and there were 138 northern free blacks who held office during Reconstruction. A number of black Republicans came from various backgrounds. Louisiana state senator Emile Detiège was the nephew of an officer in Napoleon's army who during the war had served as a lieutenant in the First Regiment, Corp d'Afrique. James H. Jones, who served as deputy sheriff in Wake County, North Carolina, worked as Jefferson Davis's personal servant and helped him to escape Richmond in April 1865.

Many of these officeholders were runaway slaves who returned from the North. Aaron A. Bradley escaped and moved to Boston in the 1830s, becoming an attorney. After the war, he became an advocate of black voting and the redistribution of Confederate lands and served in the Georgia constitutional convention and later the state senate.[28] The son of an enslaved woman and an Irish seaman, Abraham Galloway was an ex-slave brick mason from Wilmington, North Carolina, who escaped to Philadelphia in 1857. Serving as a Union spy during the war and working secretly during the Battle of New Bern in 1862, he organized a brigade of black troops.

---

[27] David Macrae, *The Americans at Home: Pen-and-Ink Sketches of American Men, Manners and Institutions* (Edinburgh: Edmonston and Douglas, 1870), I:145.
[28] Eric Foner, *Freedom's Lawmakers: A Directory of Black Officeholders during Reconstruction* (New York: Oxford University Press, 1993), xix.

Elected to North Carolina's constitutional convention in early 1868, Galloway served as state senator from Wilmington before his death in 1870. Always armed with a revolver, he insisted on equal treatment from whites.[29]

Other African Americans active in the war became postwar Republicans. Robert Smalls of Beaufort, South Carolina, who had piloted a Confederate transport into Union hands in May 1862, bought land and a store in Beaufort after the war, becoming a successful merchant. He also constructed a Lowcountry political power base. Elected to the South Carolina constitutional convention in 1868, Smalls served in the state legislature and five terms in the US Congress. A delegate to the Republican National Convention seven times, Smalls was collector of customs at Beaufort from 1889 to 1913.

The Reconstruction constitutional conventions needed to include at least several provisions if Congress would readmit the states into the Union. The constitutions were expected to include universal male suffrage, along with equal civil and political rights. Southern state governments were also required to ratify the Fourteenth Amendment, incorporating equality before the law, and the Fifteenth Amendment, recognizing the right of all citizens to vote. Finally, the Reconstruction constitutions made provision for state-supported public schools both for whites and blacks. Some constitutions went further. North Carolina's constitution of 1868, for example, abolished the oligarchic county court system of local government, replacing it with a popularly elected township system of commissioners. The North Carolina constitution created a statewide system of circuit courts, presided over by popularly elected judges. South Carolina's constitution permitted divorce, while in nine other southern states women gained the right to own separate property.

The most lasting accomplishment of the Reconstruction constitutions was the establishment of public schools. In the antebellum South, state schools existed with little public support and no guarantee of survival. At the same time, prewar southern states not only excluded blacks from public schools, they criminalized teaching slaves to read and write. The constitutional conventions of 1867–1868 could claim the establishment of the first system of public education to be one of their most-lasting legacies. During the late nineteenth century, these common schools—though erratically held and not generally extending beyond the elementary grade—spread throughout the South.

The new public schools did not, in general, provide integrated classrooms. Although South Carolina's constitution of 1868 mandated desegregated schools, schools officials refused to enforce the law. Black leaders in South Carolina also decided not to press the issue. Only in Louisiana did the new school systems establish racially integrated public education. In that state, the state constitution of 1867 banned racially separate schools and prohibited any school from denying admission on the basis of race. Especially in New Orleans, black and white pupils attended classes together. This extraordinary experiment lasted until 1877, when the New

---

[29] David S. Cecelski, *The Fire of Freedom: Abraham Galloway and the Slaves' Civil War* (Chapel Hill: University of North Carolina Press, 2012).

Orleans school board segregated the schools, and 1879, when a new state constitution prohibited school integration.

The legacy both of the Freedmen's Bureau and northern missionary educators figured prominently in the development of black education. The bureau built scores of black schools, often working in collaboration with AMA teachers. After Reconstruction constitutions incorporated black education as a state responsibility, most of these facilities became part of the public school system. Northern missionaries then refocused their objectives. After the writing of the late 1860s state constitutions, the AMA, for example, became primarily involved in black higher education. New AMA institutions such as Atlanta University, Fisk University, and Tougaloo College began a tradition of neo-abolitionist higher education for African Americans.

In states with the strongest traditions of upcountry political independence, such as North Carolina, yeomen resentment of long-standing planter domination of the state political structure solidified their loyalty to Republicanism. In 1868, North Carolinians, with strong white support, elected a Republican governor, William W. Holden, along with a Republican legislature. In other states, such as Georgia, Virginia, and Florida, native-born whites allied themselves with conservative whites. Georgia elected a new government in the spring of 1868, but when the legislature convened, it expelled all its black members. Congress refused to recognize the new government, however, forcing further changes.

Internal tensions prevailing in the Republican coalitions soon became apparent. The most basic of these tensions were racial. Southern-born white Republicans sometimes abandoned their alliance with black Republicans, attempting to attract conservative whites to the party. Republicans divided especially about how much former Confederates should be disfranchised; many blacks were reluctant to incorporate a principle of limited suffrage. In Virginia and Tennessee, opponents of Reconstruction allied themselves with white Republicans. Although the Virginia constitutional convention adopted sweeping changes in 1868, Republican governor Gilbert C. Walker and a majority of Republicans in the legislature thereafter formed an alliance with conservatives. A northern businessman and railroad entrepreneur, Walker joined forces with anti-Reconstruction forces to form a "New Departure." Excluding black Republicans, this alliance effectively ended Reconstruction in Virginia. Similarly, in February 1869 Tennessee Republican governor Dewitt Senter made overtures to the state's conservative Democrats by endorsing an end to anti-Confederate disenfranchisement provisions. Senter subsequently won reelection with significant Democratic support. An alliance of white Republicans and Democrats also ended Reconstruction in Missouri.

Republican regimes obtained power, if briefly, resulting in black officeholders. Relatively underrepresented, black Republicans, demanding more offices after 1870, criticized white Republicans who, as a Texas black politician declared, presented themselves as the "Big Gods of the negroes."[30] Especially during the 1870s, the number of black officeholders grew noticeably. During the Reconstruction years,

[30] Foner, *Freedom's Lawmakers*, xxvi.

1,465 African Americans achieved elective office. Three blacks were elected to Congress, including Hiram Revels of Mississippi, the first black senator in American history, and South Carolinian Joseph H. Rainey and Georgian Jefferson Long, both elected to Congress. Along with two US senators, thirteen other African Americans were eventually elected to Congress.

The numbers of black officeholders also increased at the state level. Nine served as secretaries of state, four as Speakers of the House of state legislatures, four as state superintendents of education, and six as lieutenant governors. All told, 782 African Americans served as state legislators during the Reconstruction era. At the local level, there were also numerous African American officeholders. About 111 served on county commissions, boards of police, and policy juries, while there were forty-one black sheriffs and twenty-five deputy sheriffs. While five African Americans served as mayors, 132 served on city councils or boards of aldermen, seventy-eight on school boards, 109 as police officers, and 228 as magistrates.[31]

Black officeholders were especially evident in some states. Possessing majorities in Mississippi and South Carolina, African Americans won eight statewide offices and three congressional seats in 1870. John Roy Lynch, son of an enslaved woman and Irish immigrant, was elected to the Mississippi state house in 1869, later becoming Speaker. In 1873, he was elected to Congress. Also in Mississippi, Blanche K. Bruce, son of a Virginia slaveholder and an enslaved woman, became a wealthy planter and established a political machine in Bolivar County in which he served as superintendent of schools, tax collector, and sheriff. In 1875, Bruce was elected to the US Senate.

Serious class tensions between blacks—separating those who had been free and those who were enslaved—divided the Republican coalition. In New Orleans, free black communities, dating before the Civil War, dominated Louisiana Republican politics after emancipation; the same was true in Charleston and South Carolina. In these two states, there were twenty-two black officeholders who had been slaveholders. Elsewhere, the antebellum free black population also exerted influence. Lighter-skinned blacks often resisted encroachments by newly arrived former slaves. Among

white Republicans, factional conflict divided upcountry yeomen and urbanites more interested in economic development. The Republican governments of the late 1860s were also affected by their inexperience; corruption became prominent, though it was exaggerated and sensationalized by anti-Reconstruction forces.

Republican-style Reconstruction never really took hold in the Upper South, where stiff resistance from the power structure frustrated Republican attempts to capture state governments. In other states, charges of high taxes and corruption undermined support among

The Ku Klux Klan, *Harper's Weekly*.
Library of Congress.

[31] Foner, *Freedom's Lawmakers*, xv.

upcountry whites. But most serious of all was the determined terror campaign targeting Republicans.

VIGILANTISM AND THE KLAN

In *A Fool's Errand*, Albion W. Tourgée's semiautobiographical novel, the hero, Comfort Servosse, a northern white, sought the advice of a northern friend, Enos Martin, about his disappointing experiences in the South. Though attempting to reunify the nation and to deal with freed people justly, Servosse announced that Reconstruction was a "magnificent failure." Northerners had assumed that the Emancipation Proclamation and the Thirteenth Amendment ended slavery. In reality, Tourgée wrote, the "power of the recent slave has been absolutely neutralized," while that of southern whites had grown. "Upon all questions touching the nation and its future," southern whites had become "practically a unit, and are daily growing more and more united as those who once stood with us succumb to age or the force of their surroundings." "The lords of the soil," he concluded, were "the lords of the labor still, and will so remain until the laborers have grown, through the lapse of generations, either intelligent or desperate."[32]

Probably the most important ingredient in Reconstruction's failure was the eruption of white violence to such an extent that it constituted a virtual insurrection. During the chaotic years after the end of the Civil War and the onset of emancipation, the return of thousands of Confederate veterans conditioned to combat violence shaped southern life. Often, ex-slaves became victims. In the late 1860s, the endemic lawlessness of the postwar South merged with an organized, full-throttled attempt to overthrow Republican rule. Most importantly, white supremacists employed a campaign of relentless terror designed to alienate white support for Reconstruction and pull apart the tenuous coalition supporting it.

Black veterans were accustomed to self-defense and to asserting their rights, and African Americans organized groups designed to protect themselves against white depredations. In coastal South Carolina, for example, United States Colored Troops (USCT) veterans organized a militia. When local Union occupiers ordered the group to disband, the group "positively refused." Black militias frequently appeared in public displays and commemorations, in a community assertion of their newfound power. Black militia paraded in Richmond on July 4, 1866, "with United States sabres and pistols." Southern whites—and sometimes even northern whites—often found militias' public displays obnoxious and even threatening. These fears eventually provided a pretext for white violence against freed slaves.[33]

Vigilante violence is most often identified with the Ku Klux Klan, a new organization first formally organized in eastern Tennessee in 1867. During the late 1860s and early 1870s, the Klan became a terrorist wing of the anti-Reconstruction forces.

---

[32] Tourgée, *A Fool's Errand, by One of the Fools: The Famous Romance of American History* (New York: Fords, Howard & Hulbert, 1879), 341–342.
[33] Emberton, *Beyond Redemption*, 88, 149.

Its explicit purpose was to break down the Republicans' ability to function as a political party. Much of Klan violence targeted black leaders. Peter Lemen, born a slave, became a literate landholder in Clarendon County, South Carolina. In 1868, he was elected county commissioner. There was a "great deal of grudge" against him because he was a Union army veteran; "they generally dislike" him, said one observer, because he was "a colored man who has been in the Federal Army." Lemen received a letter from someone requesting a meeting, but en route he was ambushed by a group of men, who killed him with shotguns.[34]

Black women also often experienced sexual violence, which became another method of enforcing white supremacy and intimidating ex-slaves. In July 1869, in Cherokee County, Alabama, forty masked white men visited freedman George Moore. Forcing Moore to kneel, the vigilantes whipped him with a peach tree branch and then raped a young girl visiting his family. Threatening to rape Moore's wife, they refrained only because she claimed that she had recently suffered a miscarriage. Bursting through the door of Moore's neighbor, Robert Roundtree, they pistol-whipped him and threatened to lynch him before he was able to escape. "The cause of this treatment," according to Moore, "was that we voted the radical ticket."[35]

African American officeholders also became victims of white violence, while Klan vigilantes also sought out white Republicans. In Sumter County, South Carolina, John J. Neason, a Savannah native and Confederate veteran, opened a merchandising store catering to the county's large black population. He offered credit to black cotton farmers, buying their unginned seed cotton. Sometime during October 1870, masked vigilantes visited Neason. They threatened him with a whipping if he continued to buy seed cotton from black farmers, a practice that allowed freedmen to bypass the planters owning cotton gins. In addition, Neason had permitted Republicans to hold meetings and barbecues at his store; the vigilantes insisted that these gatherings stop. Stores run by Democrats were left unharmed; only Republican-affiliated merchants were intimidated. The Klan operated in Sumter County, according to Neason, without fear of prosecution. The result was a chilling effect on Republicans, who wanted to "get away from there as quickly as they can; no man can feel safe there." "You cannot lie down there at night," he said of Sumter, "and feel safe."[36]

The Klan's campaign of violence became most intense in communities that were politically competitive. Vigilante violence reached a peak in the interior South—the Piedmont region of the Carolinas and Georgia—where Republicans most desperately tried to retain white voters. As the Republican governments faced reelection, they dealt with a growing anti-Reconstruction insurgency that proved difficult to

---

[34] Testimony of Leander Bigger, July 15, 1871, in *Testimony Taken by the Joint Select Committee to Inquire into the Condition of Affairs in the Late Insurrectionary States*, vol. III, South Carolina (Washington, DC: Government Printing Office, 1872), 286.

[35] Statement of George Moore, in *Testimony Taken by the Joint Select Committee*, vol. IX, Alabama, 1188.

[36] Testimony of John J. Neason, June 8, 1871, in *Testimony Taken by the Joint Select Committee*, vol. III, South Carolina, 41–46.

contain. In North Carolina, the Klan became active in the Piedmont, with vigilantes attacking black and white Republican officeholders. In May 1870, white Republican state senator John W. Stephens was attending a meeting of Democrats in the
Caswell County courthouse in Yanceyville; he was there to persuade a Democratic
leader to run as a Republican. Stephens had served as a Freedmen's Bureau agent, was
active in the Union League, and worked with African American leaders. Members
of the local Klan, many of whom were Democratic officeholders, participated in the
conspiracy. Always known for carrying arms, Stephens was lured into the basement
of the courthouse, where a group of masked men awaited him and murdered him by
cutting his throat.

On some occasions, anti-Republican violence took on a larger form, becoming
an open assault on Republicans en masse. In October 1870, in Laurensville, South
Carolina, white violence erupted into a "negro chase," as 2,500 armed whites murdered thirteen people and terrorized the black population. Laurensville (later renamed Laurens) was the county seat of Laurens County, in the heart of the
cotton-growing region of the Piedmont. The county, with a black majority, had just
returned a Republican slate in state elections, and the victims were prominent white
and black party leaders. Violence spread throughout the South Carolina upcountry
during the early 1870s.

Much of the Klan violence, explained a Florida Republican, sought "to kill out
the leading men of the republican party . . . men who have taken a prominent stand."
On the other hand, where African Americans took up arms to resist white violence,
they risked an even more violent white response. In Louisiana, state elections in 1872
led to a contested gubernatorial contest. In Grant Parish, black leaders, many of
them Civil War veterans, feared that white Democrats would attack. Black men
armed with rudimentary guns created entrenched defenses at Colfax, the county
seat. Holding out for three weeks, on Easter Sunday 1873 they were overcome by superior rifles and cannon that white attackers used against them. Fifty of the surrendering black defenders were executed. What became known as the Colfax Massacre
proved the bloodiest battle of the Reconstruction era.

The Klan held sway in portions of the Piedmont South, though determined enforcement succeeded in eradicating vigilantism. In Tennessee, Texas, and Arkansas,
governors responded strongly enough with arrests to limit the Klan's impact. In response to rising violence in Piedmont South Carolina, President U. S. Grant inaugurated federal enforcement efforts. Congress enacted new anti-Klan enforcement
laws in 1870–1871, empowering federal officials to intervene and to suspend habeas
corpus and conduct energetic prosecutions. Grant brought Amos T. Ackerman as
attorney general and Benjamin H. Bristow as solicitor general. Ackerman, a New
Hampshire native who served as a Confederate colonel and lived in Georgia, and
Bristow, a Kentucky Union veteran, had southern connections. Both energetically
pursued federal enforcement, and they expanded a federal apparatus that included
attorneys and marshals. The Ackerman-Bristow enforcement campaign yielded
hundreds of arrests, prosecutions, and convictions. In nine Piedmont South Carolina counties, the Grant administration declared a "condition of lawlessness,"

suspended habeas corpus, and arrested scores of Klansmen. Federal enforcement had effectively broken the Klan by 1872.

Despite the disappearance of the Klan, vigilante violence had proved an effective tool in neutralizing Republicanism. Federal enforcement was weak willed and inconsistent. Ackerman resigned in 1871; the Grant administration no longer intervened in southern affairs. Over time, Republicans suffered from the racial polarization that accompanied the Reconstruction years. Biracial Republicanism declined, while white supremacy became a rallying cry for the Democratic Party. After 1872, Republicans controlled only those state governments with a large African American presence and states such as South Carolina, Louisiana, and Florida, where federal troops remained. The experiment of biracialism was about to end.

14

INDUSTRIALIZATION

DURING THE GENERATION after the Civil War, the South experienced far-reaching social and economic changes. To be sure, some things remained the same. The plantation system—and the prevalence of single-crop agriculture, primarily cotton— persisted despite the end of slavery. New systems of labor and credit replaced those prevailing during the slave regime, yet most African Americans remained bound to the land. Other forces ushered in change. The expanding railroad network exposed long-isolated hinterlands to external markets as well as goods and services. New capitalist enterprises proliferated in the rise of mining, lumber, and other extractive industries. In addition, cotton mills provided a new landscape of industrialized manufacturing, which became an important feature of post–Civil War life. These economic changes spilled over into different areas of southern life, remaking old patterns of life.

THE NEW SOUTH

During the 1880s, the development of cotton mills became a panacea for southern boosters—newspapermen, promoters, and their business allies—seeking solutions to the South's poverty and underdevelopment. So-called New South advocates promoted economic development, promising expansion of the transportation infrastructure, industrialization, and the commercialization of agriculture. New South promoters predicted that the Old South of slavery and plantation agriculture would give way to railroad growth, industrialization, and scientific agriculture. Sectional peace, according to their vision, would also prevail. Much of what New South boosters had to say was salesmanship bordering on fantasy. Their primary purpose was to

Henry W. Grady. *Library of Congress.*

target northern audiences in an attempt to persuade capitalists that the South, a hospitable place for investment, was prepared to rejoin the nation.

Henry W. Grady, the best-known New South booster, was editor of the *Atlanta Constitution*. On December 22, 1886, he spoke before one of New York City's oldest and most distinguished organizations, the New England Society. Tickets to the event quickly sold out. To an enthusiastic crowd, he announced the end of sectional conflict. "When Lee surrendered, I say, and Johnston quit, the South became, and has since been, loyal to this Union." The South discovered a "jewel in the toad's head of defeat" in that the "shackles that had held her in narrow limitations fell forever when the shackles of the negro slave were broken." The Old South depended on slavery and agriculture, but this proved an inadequate basis for a healthy economy. The demise of slavery liberated southern whites, he announced, just as much as it had freed black people.

The Civil War proved a decisive event because it defined what the South was—and helped create what Grady called a "New South." Footsore Confederate soldiers, crushed by defeat and making their way back to their ruined homes and farms, found "their livestock and crops lost, their slaves freed, and their money worthless." Rebuilding southerners faced a daunting task, but the New South promised a refurbished, remade society. "As ruin was never before so overwhelming," Grady declared, "never was restoration swifter." The restored South, according to Grady, possessed a soul that had the "breath of a new life" and a "consciousness of growing power and prosperity." Defeat and sectional reconciliation meant prosperity, Grady promised. Southerners were being remade into thrifty people who had "fallen in love with work," permitting the economy to take root and "spread among us as rank as the crabgrass which sprung from Sherman's cavalry camps." The New South would contain a hundred farms for every plantation, "fifty homes for every palace," and a diversified industry that met the "complex needs of this complex age."[1]

Grady preached a mixture of sectional reconciliation and economic development. Southerners had returned to work after the Civil War, with "little bitterness in all this." The New South rejected slavery's legacy, realizing that the Confederacy's fight was against "the cause of human liberty, against which the arms of man cannot prevail." Those Confederate leaders determined to make slavery the "cornerstone of the Confederacy" were doomed, "committing us to a cause that reason could not defend or the sword maintain in the sight of advancing civilization."

While the Old South depended on slavery and agriculture, Grady continued in his speech, the New South embraced urbanization, industrialization, and commercial agriculture. As a resident of the booming city of Atlanta, Grady informed his

[1] "Honor to the Puritans," *Chicago Daily Tribune*, December 23, 1886.

northern audience that destruction at the hands of Gen. William T. Sherman had forced residents to create a "brave and beautiful city," just as the New South represented progress and capitalist growth. This new future, said Grady, meant a "fuller independence for the South than that which our fathers sought to win in the forum by their eloquence or compel on the field by their swords."[2]

Grady's New South address became an instant success among the largely northern audience. "Before half a dozen sentences had left his lips," commented *Frank Leslie's Weekly*, Grady swept his audience up "by storm."[3] Representing the South to northern whites, he "carried his audience with him from the first sentence to the last." Southerners present were also impressed with Grady's "manliness and frankness." Any description of the well-decorated hall was "utterly unimportant as compared with Grady's triumph." The audience rewarded Grady with sustained applause and a wild waving of hats and handkerchiefs, until he was forced to his feet in order to acknowledge the adulation.[4]

Grady's New South speech in 1886 succeeded not for its originality but for its timing. Before northern audiences, its wildly positive reception helped provide a new understanding of what the post–Civil War South might mean. "No postprandial oration of any recent occasion has aroused such enthusiasm in this city," declared the *New York Times*. It noted that Grady's delivery was "exceedingly forcible, and his clear, high, musical voice carried home every word with telling effect." He delivered a welcome message: "Thankfulness at the death of slavery, and at the better condition of the South now that the bondmen were free." Grady's promise of a new intersectional fraternalism evoked "boundless enthusiasm."[5]

Across the South, capitalists welcomed new opportunities in manufacturing, mining, lumbering, and extractive industries. Boosters publicized the advent of economic development with religious fervor and enthusiasm. They made their case especially to northern investors. Their vision of a New South was, in many respects, a fantasy. The southern economy remained underdeveloped, dependent on plantation agriculture, manufacturing, and extractive industries that relied on low-wage labor. The boosters also smoothed over racial injustice, ignoring the obvious inequities and barriers that African Americans faced on a daily basis. Boosters exaggerated the promise of wealth, saying little about the persisting problem of poverty.

The boosters' vision portended significant changes, above all the increasing advance of urbanization. Prior to the Civil War, the South remained the least urbanized place in the Union. In 1860, the only southern city ranking among the top-ten largest cities in the United States was New Orleans, while only six southern cities were among the nation's thirty largest. In the postwar era, the South remained more rural than the rest of the country. While the proportion of southerners living in

[2] Grady New South speech; available at http://www.anselm.edu/academic/history/hdubrulle/civwar/text/documents/doc54.htm.
[3] Quoted in the *Atlanta Weekly Constitution*, January 18, 1887.
[4] "Grady in New York," clipping, Henry W. Grady scrapbooks, Hargrett Rare Book and Manuscript Library, University of Georgia.
[5] "Boasting of Puritan Sires," *New York Times*, December 23, 1886.

urban areas grew from 7.2 percent in 1860 to 15.2 percent in 1900, the region remained the least urbanized in the country. Outside the South, in 1900 great metropolitan populations existed in New York (3.5 million), Chicago (1.7 million), and Philadelphia (1.3 million). The largest southern city in that year, in contrast, was New Orleans, with 287,000 inhabitants.

Still, the growth of urbanized places figured importantly in the post–Civil War South. Memphis, a prosperous antebellum Mississippi River port, grew after the Civil War as a result of the arrival of seven new railroad lines. During the 1880s, the population of Memphis increased from about 34,000 to nearly 65,000. The city also became a manufacturing center and a leading producer of milled lumber. In some respects, Memphis was exceptional: in general, the centers of southern urban growth, in contrast to the antebellum period, occurred outside port cities. Richmond, the most important industrial center in the antebellum South, saw its leading industries move elsewhere. With the rise of bright-leaf tobacco and cigarette manufacturing, tobacco factories shifted south to North Carolina towns such as Durham and Winston. Previously the center of the southern iron industry, Richmond saw its production shift to Birmingham, Alabama.

The rapid rise of smallish southern inland towns, especially those tied to the railroad network, became a late-nineteenth-century phenomenon. Inland cities such as Dallas, Birmingham, Houston, and San Antonio superseded older coastal cities. These cities grew from crossroads villages at a spectacularly rapid rate. Birmingham, Alabama, did not exist prior to 1871, when three towns merged to form a new community. Because of its strategic location on the junction of the Louisville and Nashville lines with several other railroads, Birmingham became home to coal and iron mining and, subsequently, the iron and steel industry. With a population of only 3,000 in 1880, the city claimed 133,000 inhabitants thirty years later.

The most-dynamic urbanizing centers were located in villages and small towns that popped up across the interior South. Between 1880 and 1910, the population of these smaller locales increased by five million people—by far the largest area of growth, and involving a subtler form of urbanization than was evident in cities. A community such as Big Lick, which housed only a few hundred people in southwest Virginia, was transformed after the arrival of the Norfolk & Western Railroad. Renaming itself Roanoke, the town boasted 25,000 inhabitants by 1892. Thousands of southern villages competed fiercely with each other to grow into towns. Small towns competed just as fiercely to grow into larger towns. These communities depended on their position as railroad depots, which enabled them to dominate agricultural products shipped on the transportation network. Merchants established outposts in the villages and towns to sell goods to farmers. The more successful towns and cities were those able to establish tributary communities, dependent on the urban market center for transportation and credit resources.

The growth of urban places in the South rested almost entirely on the migration of rural folks to towns and cities. Unlike northern cities, whose population increase resulted from European immigration, southern rural migrants, black and white, were mostly native born. Rural southerners came to regard urban communities as centers of opportunity. Towns attracted "those too poor to be able to live in the country," wrote one northern visitor, as well as "those too rich to be willing to live there."[6] African Americans were drawn to cities in order to escape the rural South's stultifying oppression. In cities such as Atlanta, a black middle class fashioned community institutions resting on black-owned business and black cultural institutions in lodges, mutual support organizations, and churches. In Atlanta, wrote W. E. B. Du Bois, an African American "may arise in the morning in a house which a black man built and which he himself owns," which black laborers had painted and papered, with furniture purchased at a white store but transported by black workers. The soap used for washing, along with other provisions, could be purchased at a black-owned grocery. Once a week, Atlanta blacks read a black newspaper, while their children attended schools taught by black teachers, and they belonged to churches with black ministers. Entertaining themselves in "amusements at places frequented and usually run by colored people," Atlanta blacks were "buried by a colored undertaker in a colored grave yard."[7]

The urban South offered markedly different physical spaces, compared to the rural communities still containing most of the region's population. Towns and cities led the way in installing modern conveniences. Although southern urban communities, in general, lagged behind their northern counterparts in these conveniences, they raced far ahead of the rural South. Urban areas became beacons of a new, modern world. Six southern cities by the turn of the twentieth century had introduced electricity, owned by municipal plants, while other communities began to install modern waterworks. In cities, new sewage systems came into existence for the first time. Southern towns and cities paved streets, while rural inhabitants traveled on dusty dirt roads. Telephones slowly made their entry into southern towns and cities by the 1890s, and, with 11 percent of the nation's population in 1902, the South possessed 22 percent of American phones. Streetcars came to typify urban life, too, especially in towns of fewer than 10,000 people, and increasingly many of these lines ran on electric power. The urban South counted 125 streetcar companies, which in 1902 ran on 2,252 miles of track. The advent of streetcars as a common form of transportation enabled further physical expansion into new suburbs. Cities began to fashion modernized public school systems, ahead of their rural neighbors, and in urban areas the first efforts were made to contain disease and ill health through public health measures.

All these conveniences provided markers of the urban South's progress, which town residents came to expect. In 1892, when Greenville, Alabama, opened its first streetcar, a local newspaper declared: "The next thing will be electric lights, then will come factories, etc. Let the good things come."[8] As electricity became more common in urban areas by the 1890s, cities lived in a new world startlingly different from

[6] Edward L. Ayers, *The Promise of the New South: Life after Reconstruction* (New York: Oxford University Press, 1992), 62.
[7] Dana F. White, "The Black Sides of Atlanta: A Geography of Expansion and Containment, 1870–1970," *Atlanta Historical Journal* 26 (Summer–Fall 1982): 213–214.
[8] Ayers, *Promise of the New South*, 72.

rural areas. "Our gas jets are lighted, our bells rung, our organs played, our sewing machines kept running," declared a Richmond enthusiast in 1895, "all by this wonderful power unknown to our grandparents." In 1902, electricity had become prevalent in the urban South—though limited to more-affluent areas—with six hundred power companies in existence. Indeed, on a per-capita basis, more electricity existed in the South than in the rest of the nation.

The urban ethos of the post–Civil War era found expression in the mania of expositions occurring in the 1880s and 1890s. In New Orleans, the World's Industrial and Cotton Centennial Exposition opened in December 1884 when President Chester A. Arthur flipped a switch, from the White House, turning on the fair's electricity—a new and fantastic form of technology. By the time it closed in May 1885, the New Orleans exposition had attracted over a million visitors. All the states and territories except Utah and Alaska sent delegations and maintained exhibits. The exposition featured not only the cotton textile industry but also other southern agricultural and industrial products, with more than three thousand exhibitors. The main exposition building, spanning thirty-three acres, stretching six miles long, and occupying 1.6 million square feet of space, was billed as the largest building in the United States. Electric lights illuminated the building, with fifteen thousand incandescent and eight hundred arc lights. The main building housed representatives from nearly thirty European, Latin American, and Asian countries. A music hall contained a large organ and held 13,000 people. The exposition's Horticultural Hall was the biggest greenhouse on the globe. Atlanta also participated in the mania, offering no fewer than three expositions in 1881, 1887, and 1895. Attendees of the 1895 exposition in Atlanta could travel across the spacious grounds by means of an electric railway constructed for the event.

THE RISE OF RAILROADS

The South's railroad network grew at a rapid pace during the two decades prior to the Civil War. During the antebellum era, state governments funded the earliest railroad lines, but in many instances overexpansion and financial collapse threatened public finance. During the 1850s, for example, Virginia incurred a huge debt resulting from a railroad-building boom, but repaying that debt in the late 1870s became so crushing that it brought on a major political revolt. Republican governments in many states promoted further expansion in the late 1860s, but these resulted in financial crises and accusations of corruption.

Explosive growth between 1870 and 1900, however, dwarfed the antebellum railroad system. By 1890, nine out of every ten counties in the South had tracks running across their borders. During the 1870s, much of the southern railroad system came under the control of northern capital. Thereafter northerners and the international bond market financed expansion. In 1868, the Virginia Central merged with the Covington and Ohio to form the Chesapeake and Ohio Railroad. Eventually coming under the control of northern capitalist Collis P. Huntington, in 1873 the combined

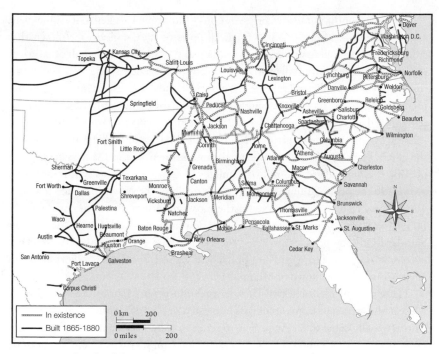

MAP 14.1 Railroads of the South, 1865–1880

system completed a 428-mile line from Richmond to Huntington, West Virginia, on the Ohio River. In 1871, the Pennsylvania Railroad, under the control of entrepreneur Tom Scott, scooped up the remains of twelve lines with two thousand miles of track in seven southern states. Scott sought to build a railroad network extending from Richmond to Atlanta. Even-bigger systems such as the Illinois Central and the Louisville and Nashville emerged through the acquisition of smaller, failing lines.

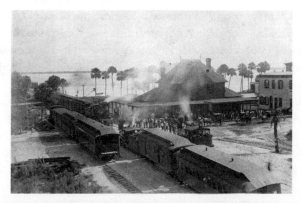

Trains at the South Florida Railroad Company Depot—Sanford, Florida. *State Archives of Florida.*

A turning point in railroad organization—and probably a key to its subsequent expansion—came after the severe financial crisis of 1873, a global meltdown that ruined many railroad financiers. Between 1873 and 1880, more than half of railroads in the South failed financially and were forced to reorganize. What was left of railroad companies, public and private, fell into the hands of northern investors. Entrepreneur Henry Bradley Plant purchased the Atlantic and Gulf Line, which he reorganized into the Savannah, Florida, and Western in 1879–1880. Acquiring other lines at bargain-basement prices, including the Charleston and Savannah, during the 1880s Plant began to build what became known as the Plant system. Plant became the most aggressive railroad builder in Florida, eventually linking citrus growers to the port of Tampa and capturing much of the steamship trade to Cuba. Tampa, as a result, grew into one of the most important port cities of the Gulf. Following Plant, Henry M. Flagler, who made a fortune with John D. Rockefeller's Standard Oil Company, constructed the Florida East Coast Railroad, which connected St. Augustine to West Palm Beach by 1894 and, a year later, to Fort Dallas in what became the new town of Miami.

Flagler's new railroad helped a new leisure industry in Miami and South Florida, while it also attracted scores of tourists interested in Florida's natural beauty. Flagler, who originally came to St. Augustine to retire in 1885, became the state's most important tourism promoter. He built a large hotel in St. Augustine, the Ponce de León, constructed between 1885 and 1887, as one of the first modernized buildings, and among the nation's finest hotels, with its own system of running water, indoor plumbing, and electricity. The hotel was also the first building constructed of poured concrete. John Carrère (1858–1911) and Thomas Hastings (1860–1929), leading American architects, designed the hotel in the Spanish Renaissance Revival style, with Louis C. Tiffany leading the interior design. Tiffany used mosaics, stained glass, and terra cotta relief on the walls and ceilings. He also commissioned murals by American artist George W. Maynard and Italian artist Virgilio Tojetti. As Flagler moved his railroad down Florida's east coast, he expanded his involvement in the state's tourism industry. At Lake Worth, in what would become Palm Beach, he constructed his first hotel in southeastern Florida, the Royal Poinciana, in 1894. Two years later, Flagler constructed another hotel on the Royal Poinciana's beachfront. Destroyed by fire twice, in 1903 and 1925, it was rebuilt in 1926, becoming one of the nation's premier hotels. The Breakers attracted elite visitors and made West Palm Beach into an exclusive beachfront community.

The railroads' arrival spurred on a nascent tourism industry. In the Sandhills region of south-central North Carolina, the state's commissioner of immigration sought to attract visitors by constructing the new town of Southern Pines in 1884, located on 675 acres through which a railroad passed. The town attracted the interest of James Walker Tufts, a Massachusetts industrialist who made a fortune producing silver plate flatware and soda fountain machines; Tufts purchased 5,800 acres of land that been pine forest but was logged over. Hiring landscape architect Frederick Law Olmsted to design the grounds, Tufts provided for the planting of 220,000 pine seedlings. He also hired Donald Ross, a Scottish golf course designer, to fashion four golf courses and to serve as golf pro. Tufts constructed a model village that he called Pinehurst, which opened in 1895 and consisted of a general store, dairy, and twenty cottages. In 1901, the Carolina Hotel opened for visitors, with its luxurious accommodations becoming a main attraction for northern tourists visiting the South.

As early as the 1880s, the mountains of western North Carolina attracted visitors, northern and southern, in search of cooler climes and impressive vistas. In 1880, the Western North Carolina Railroad linked Morganton and Asheville, opening that growing tourist town to travelers. Six years later, in 1886, the Asheville and Spartanburg Railroad was finished, creating a new path for visitors to western North Carolina. South Carolinians had traveled to the region since the antebellum era; towns such as Flat Rock were filled with Lowcountry planters. Hotels expanded, as did an entire service industry radiating in and around Asheville, which grew in population from 1,450 in 1870 to 50,193 in 1930. The city's Battery Park Hotel, constructed in 1886 as Asheville's first resort hotel, contained amenities such as running water and steam heat. It advertised itself as "the acknowledged center of fashionable life in the South during the summer."[9] By 1890, the city had twelve hotels and many more boardinghouses.

Hotels and resorts sprang up across the North Carolina mountains. Two entrepreneurs from Kansas, Samuel T. Kelsey and Clinton C. Hutchinson, constructed a community in Macon County that they called Highlands, attracting thousands of visitors and summer residents. Thirty-five miles north of Asheville, in Hot Springs, in 1890 northern investors constructed Mountain Park Hotel in Madison County, North Carolina. It provided luxurious accommodations that offered visitors stunning vistas and outdoor activities. During the hot East Coast summers, the mountains provided tourists an escape from heat and humidity, while the urban environment of Asheville became an escape from the mundane and ordinary. The construction of the 250-room Biltmore Estate by George Washington Vanderbilt in 1895 marked the region's coming of age. Biltmore, designed by architect Richard Morris Hunt and landscape architect Olmsted, indicated the depth of outsiders' interest in the mountains. It also immediately became a major tourist destination. The opening of Asheville's Grove Park Inn in 1913 established the hotel as one of the most luxurious in the South.

After the collapse of Tom Scott's Southern Railway system during the Panic of 1873, the Richmond and Danville system grew more powerful through various amalgamations, resulting in a conglomerate connecting the Southeast with the Mississippi valley. During the early 1890s, this conglomerate grew into the massive Richmond Terminal system, which extended nearly nine thousand miles into the Southeast. During the 1880s, further consolidation and expansion took place, and railroads penetrated farther into the hinterlands, regions heretofore off the transportation grid. The trend toward consolidation continued, culminating with the organization of the Southern Railway system, assembled after the Panic of 1893 left

---

[9] Richard D. Starnes, *Creating the Land of the Sky: Tourism and Society in Western North Carolina* (Tuscaloosa: University of Alabama Press, 2005), 29.

southern railroads in shambles. Organized by northern financier J. P. Morgan, the Southern became a dominant railroad system, possessing 7,500 miles of track. During the next decade, two other large systems, the Atlantic Coast Line and the Seaboard Air Line, were organized.

Railroad growth accelerated during the late nineteenth century, and the South laid more track than any other region except the West. Between 1880 and 1890, the total miles of track in the region doubled, from 16,605 to 39,108. Much of this growth occurred with the emergence of small, independent lines. In 1890, eighteen of the fifty-eight railroads operating more than one hundred miles of track had come into existence during the 1880s. Nonetheless, the bulk of southern growth came with the larger railroad operations.[10]

In November 1883, all the southern railroads agreed to standardized scheduling and a single, official time. Standard time soon became something that all southerners, and Americans, set their watches to. Meanwhile, southern railroads also converted to a standard rail gauge system. Gauge measured the distance between the inner rails, and it varied widely, nowhere more widely than in the South. In most parts of the country, railroads used standard gauge, at four feet eight and a half inches wide. In the South, in contrast, railroads commonly employed a much-broader gauge, but the system lacked a standard measure—fourteen different widths existed among southern railroads. That meant that traffic entering the South frequently had to stop to offload freight and passengers, transferring them to different trains. The standardization of gauge served as an important step in the integration of the southern transportation system. Between May 31 and June 1, 1886—two days!—nearly 13,000 miles of track were switched to standard gauge, and the remainder of the lines soon duplicated this effort.

In general, railroad expansion received an enthusiastic reception. When new lines opened, entire communities watched the arrival of the impressive steam engines. In the Ozarks in Arkansas, the town of Harrison greeted the arrival of the railroad during the 1880s. The scene was typical of how communities viewed the railroad's arrival with a combination of wonder and trepidation. Two thousand people showed up for the celebration, and the town celebrated the arrival of modernity. "Harrison is a Railroad Town at Last," read a local headline.[11] Railroad construction crews worked feverishly, but they brought with them a rough new tension to life. Workers were ruthlessly exploited; camps housing them were violent, and they lived beyond usual social bounds. The presence of railroad stations provided symbols of how the outside world had entered the locally oriented South. Railroads, and the communities they spawned, exhibited often-chaotic hustle and bustle of the modern world.

In many ways, railroads came to embody the forces of change sweeping through the post–Civil War South. A British traveler visiting the South in 1883 had heard

---

[10] John F. Stover, *Railroads of the South, 1865–1900: A Study in Finance and Control* (Chapel Hill: University of North Carolina Press, 1955), 196.
[11] Ayers, *Promise of the New South*, 11.

about how "jolting cars and rough roads" and rustic traveling characterized the erratic southern transportation system. She described "days gone by, when things generally were in a chaotic state, trembling in the balance between order and disorder." Surprised at what she experienced, the traveler reported about the expansion and improvement of the southern railroads. The South, she wrote, was redefining the sense of itself by way of railroads, as "new railways opening, great factories arising on every side, bear witness to the energy with which the south is throwing itself into the work of restoration." "North and south, east and west," she wrote, "all are animated by the same spirit of progress" and the "south of to-day is not the south of the yesterdays." Railroad builders "have laid down branch lines in all directions, running out like the arms of an octopus, grasping at distant towns and villages and halting in the most beautiful secluded spots in the inmost quarters of the land."[12]

A NEW INDUSTRIAL ECONOMY

During the generation after the Civil War, the Industrial Revolution transformed life for many southerners, white and black. In mining, lumbering, cotton textiles, and tobacco, capitalists opened up new ways to make money, exploit land and labor, and remake the physical environment. Southern forests, containing the nation's largest stands of hardwood forests, remained relatively untouched before the Civil War. Under the Southern Homestead Act (1866), Congress opened up forty-six million acres of lands, mostly forests, in Alabama, Arkansas, Florida, Louisiana, and Mississippi. Intended to assist freed people, the law, which awarded land in eighty-acre parcels, temporarily restricted logging and mineral speculators. Once the Homestead Act was repealed in 1876, a land rush followed, further encouraged by bargain prices that southern states charged for the sale of state-owned public lands. In addition, railroads disposed of their considerable land resources.

Log Dump, West Virginia. *West Virginia and Regional History Center, WVU Libraries.*

[12] Mary Anne Hardy, in R. Scott Huffard Jr., "Perilous Connections: Railroads, Capitalism, and Mythmaking in the New South" (PhD diss., University of Florida, 2013), 96.

After 1880, as a result, the most intensive period of logging in the South's history occurred. Speculators bought up large tracts of land, most of which ended up in the hands of northern companies. Of the lands acquired between 1881 and 1888, about two-thirds went to northern companies.[13] The most successful of these northern speculators, James D. Lacey of Grand Rapids, Michigan, assembled about five million acres of timberland, most of it in the South, between 1880 and 1900. Most of these lands were acquired from the federal government as part of the disposal of the public domain. Lacey resold his lands at a handsome profit.[14]

The timber industry expanded the use of naval stores, since shipbuilding depended on southern forests for supplies, such as tar and turpentine, to manufacture and maintain ships. Southern pine also provided ties for railroad expansion. The ties were usually covered with creosote to retard deterioration and rotting. Corporate control of southern forests also helped speed the transformation of the paper industry, which shifted to pulp paper produced from forest products.

The heart of the southern timber industry lay in the forested areas of the Atlantic coastal plain and the Gulf Coast, which contained rich stands of longleaf, slash, and loblolly pines. These regions accounted for a third of the lumber produced in the nation between 1900 and 1949. The lumber companies were highly capitalized enterprises employing mechanization to mill the felled timber. The industry depended on a largely African American workforce, often using convict laborers working under near-slave conditions. With little incentive to do otherwise, the timber companies ruthlessly exploited the timber resources with a "cut-and-get-out" approach that devastated the forests and then moved on to new ones.

In the process of southern industrialization, northerners and a new class of southern entrepreneurs led the way, though they usually possessed sufficient resources to do so. Washington Duke came from rural origins in Orange County, in central

Section Crew at William, WV, 1903. *West Virginia and Regional History Center, WVU Libraries.*

[13] Cowdrey, *This Land, This South*, 111–113.
[14] Paul Wallace Gates, "Federal Land Policy in the South, 1866–1888," *Journal of Southern History* 6, no. 3 (August 1940): 316.

North Carolina. Working as a tobacco peddler, he assembled enough resources to establish, in 1874, a business processing pipe and cigarette tobacco in the new railroad town of Durham. His son, James Buchanan Duke, took his father's business successes even further. Adopting the Bonsack Machine, which made possible the mass production of cigarettes, James B. Duke organized the American Tobacco Company, which, by the 1890s, dominated the cigarette-manufacturing industry. While American Tobacco's corporate offices were located in New York City, most of the production remained in North Carolina, in large tobacco factories near Durham. These factories employed African Americans, who were confined to the unskilled phases of the work. Tobacco manufacturing provided a new work opportunity for rural blacks migrating to Durham.

Another North Carolinian, R. J. Reynolds, also became a major player in the tobacco industry. His father was the largest slaveholder in Patrick County, in southern Virginia bordering North Carolina, growing primarily tobacco. Reynolds, inheriting his father's landholdings, moved to the nearest railroad town, Winston, and made it into a tobacco-manufacturing center. First working for Duke, Reynolds had by 1892 established two factories of his own in Winston, producing about a quarter of the chewing tobacco consumed in the United States. Reynolds then expanded into other products, introducing Prince Albert pipe tobacco in 1907. Developing the mammoth R. J. Reynolds Tobacco Company, which, with the development of packaged cigarettes—and the Camel brand—became one of the largest manufacturers in the world, Reynolds successfully used corporate organization and advertising to create a new market among Americans for cigarettes. By the 1920s, Reynolds Tobacco was producing two-thirds of the cigarettes manufactured in North Carolina.

The cotton textile industry became the most important manifestation of industrial manufacturing in the South. Textile mills first sprang up in New England in the early nineteenth century, and by the Civil War that region dominated the manufacturing in the United States. Beginning in the 1830s, cotton mills appeared in the Carolinas and Georgia. In North Carolina, entrepreneur Edward Michael Holt started mills in Alamance County, and during the 1850s his Alamance Plaids became nationally known. Other southern entrepreneurs established a foundation for postbellum industrial expansion. In South Carolina, William Gregg constructed a large textile complex at Graniteville, on the Savannah River. After the Civil War, the remnants of Gregg's operations provided the basis for mill expansion in southwestern South Carolina. Early textile mills were often located on rivers, using the waterpower resources of the region. Post–Civil War southern cotton mills were mechanized and relied on water or electrical power, with a regimented southern mill proletariat.

During the last three decades of the nineteenth century, the cotton textile industry in the South grew steadily. The overall capacity of southern mills increased during these years, in Georgia and the Carolinas, but also spread to Alabama and Mississippi to the west and, to the north, the southern part of central Virginia. By the early twentieth century, the cheap-labor advantage of southern mills proved a crucial competitive advantage. The unskilled end of the industry—unfinished and coarse cotton products—steadily moved south from New England mills.

Children working in textile mills, Cherryville, North Carolina. *Library of Congress.*

The heart of the cotton textile industry—where much of the region's capacity existed—could be found in the Carolina Piedmont. The Carolina mills were typically rural, located in mill establishments along rivers to take advantage of the rapidly flowing rivers of the area. Nearby towns embraced the arrival of mills. Small towns in the Carolina Piedmont became dotted with mills, though, over time, larger establishments came to dominate. The Carolina Piedmont attracted mills not only because of waterpower and enthusiastic boosters but also because the region possessed ample white labor drawn from the ranks of white yeoman farmers whom the pressures of the market economy had displaced. During their early years, mills did not have to go far to recruit workers, taking advantage of neighborhood and family networks. Over time, as the industry expanded and mills grew larger, mill recruiters fanned out, seeking people from the farther reaches of rural Piedmont and mountain areas.

W. J. Cash characterized the mill community as "a plantation, essentially indistinguishable in organization from the familiar plantation of the cotton field."[15] Between Reconstruction and World War I, mill paternalism prevailed. Workers, far from slaves, nonetheless became beholden to mill owners for housing, food, supplies, churches, and entertainment. Mill employees often worked as families, with wives and children—as they did on the farm—joining the workforce once they were older than nine or ten years old. This family-organized labor force meant that adult males formed a numerical minority in the mills, sometimes composing as few as a third of the total labor force. From the mill managers' point of view, the "family wage"—what the entire family earned—exceeded what families could earn on a farm.

Whatever their background, mill workers faced an abrupt transition from farm to factory. Textile mills imposed a work regime of regular shifts and hourly labor that contrasted with agricultural rhythms and lifestyles, which were geared to the seasonal cycles of the farm. Working hours were long, lasting from dawn until dusk six days a week. In 1904, textile workers in the Carolinas and Georgia worked about

[15] Quoted in Melton Alonza McLaurin, *Paternalism and Protest: Southern Cotton Mill Workers and Organized Protest, 1875–1905* (Westport, CT: Greenwood, 1971), 16.

sixty-six hours per week, as opposed to fifty-eight hours per week in Massachusetts.[16] The rigid work regime in textile mills contrasted with farm labor. According to a contemporary, like mill workers, farmers woke before daylight, "but there was something alarming in being ordered to rise by a factory whistle."[17] Workers, in another abrupt change, worked for a wage, remaining at the mercy of mill owners for their income. Typically, owners paid workers on a piece rate—according to how much they produced—and this resulted in great variation in wages. The net result was that wages were much lower than those paid to New England textile workers.

Another feature of industrial paternalism in the South was the mill village, company-owned housing located near the mill. Mill villages lay on the periphery of towns, usually on railroad lines in unincorporated areas beyond the purview of local government. Mill owners often constructed churches and schools under their control. The company store, also run by owners, sold supplies to workers. At the company stores, mill owners served as furnishing merchant to the workers, deducting the costs from their paycheck. During the late nineteenth century, mill village housing was typically rudimentary, erected as a way to provide housing for rural migrants. Very often these houses were two story, erected on pillars, but lacking running water and sewerage.

The cotton textile workforce, almost entirely white, forged a powerful identity. Most of the workers were of rural origins, and they retained cultural traditions of the farm in terms of language, music, and interactions. Moreover, owners, management, and town classes attached to the owners regarded mill workers as a separate, and often strange, cultural group. They were identifiable by language and dress, qualities that differed from the language and dress assumed by townfolk. Mill proletariats often came to be feared and despised, and they were derisively called "lintheads" or "cotton mill trash."

THE SURVIVAL OF COTTON CULTURE

Changes also came to southern agriculture after the Civil War. In the rice regions of Lowcountry South Carolina and Georgia, the gang labor system could not survive without coerced labor; wealthy plantations in the marshy coastlands collapsed for lack of workers. Tobacco planters in Virginia also had difficulty sustaining the antebellum system after emancipation. "How to get the estates formerly productive again brought into cultivation," wrote an observer in 1870, "occupies the minds of all classes with an intensity of interest to which no other public concern can be compared."[18]

In contrast, cotton plantations not only survived the end of slavery but to some extent even thrived. In 1881, *Atlanta Constitution* editor Henry W. Grady observed that cotton planters were "still lords of acres, though not of slaves."[19] Cotton planters

[16] McLaurin, *Paternalism and Protest*, table 3, p. 25.
[17] McLaurin, *Paternalism and Protest*, 26.
[18] Evan P. Bennett, *When Tobacco Was King: Families, Farm Labor, and Federal Policy in the Piedmont* (Gainesville: University Press of Florida, 2014), 9.
[19] Robert C. McMath Jr., *American Populism: A Social History, 1877–1898* (New York: Hill and Wang, 1993), 30.

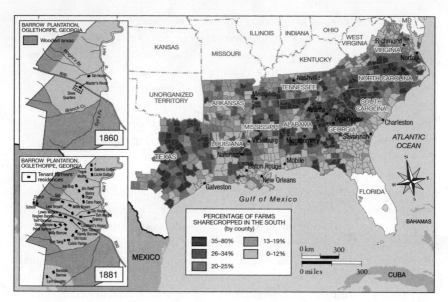

MAP 14.2 Sharecropping and Tenancy, 1880

quickly adapted to the postwar labor system. In the cotton-growing region extending from the Carolinas to eastern Texas, new forms of credit and labor emerged. Freed people, refusing to work under the old, coerced labor regime of slavery, wanted greater autonomy, a path toward landownership, and control over family labor. Subdividing their lands into rented portions, planters abandoned centralized control of the antebellum plantation. Farmers, many (though not all) of whom were ex-slaves, rented their land from the planters either for a share of the crop (as sharecroppers) or for a fixed cash rent (as tenant farmers). Sharecropping and tenancy offered a compromise between planters' desire to perpetuate the plantation system and freed people's desire for autonomy.

During the early days of the New South agricultural system, this system seemed mutually beneficial. High cotton prices helped sustain this impression. Eventually, however, this system of land and labor became onerous, serving to perpetuate racial oppression and poverty. Especially after the collapse in world cotton prices in 1873—and the prevalence of low prices during the next several decades—few of the proceeds trickled down to the tenants. Ex-slaves' loss of political power during and after Reconstruction gave considerable leeway to planters when they settled up with their sharecroppers at the end of the growing season. Possessing few resources, sharecroppers and tenants borrowed seeds, implements, and fertilizers from planters, but they remained at their mercy.

Planters' and merchants' high interest rates often reflected market forces: their tenants were bad credit risks, who, from the planters' point of view, justified higher charges. Planters and merchants possessed a monopolistic power over the share tenants, who had no alternative but to rent and borrow from the planters and to buy

Sharecropper near Jackson, Mississippi. *Library of Congress.*

provision at higher prices. Planters extended a line of credit to tenants, who found themselves subsumed in debt. The system further encouraged tenants to produce as much cotton as possible. Overall, the Cotton South in the post-Reconstruction era went from a food-exporting to a food-importing region. Tenants discovered that producing a cash crop trumped everything else: only by growing more cotton could they move out of debt, but the overproduction of the crop tended to depress prices.

In this way, the adaptation of the plantation system to post–Civil War conditions helped maintain the South's system of racial oppression. The new credit system provided levers for planter control. Landlords often adjusted their rates of credit, depending on the size of the crop. The share system, based on the extension of credit with the future crop as collateral, enabled merchants and planters to control the flow of wealth at the croppers' expense. In addition, after croppers harvested the cotton, it had to be ginned, and landlords and merchants controlled the ginning process. Typically, after tenants and sharecroppers paid their expenses for supplies and seed, little was left except a debt that was carried forward. Black sharecroppers possessed little recourse. "Colored men," said one black farmer, "soon learn that it is better to pay any account, however unjust, for he stands no possible chance of getting justice before the law."[20]

Prior to the Civil War, the upland South—the upper Piedmont region extending from North Carolina to Mississippi—remained insulated from market forces because it existed outside a modern transportation system. The agriculture in this region, largely subsistence, was dominated by so-called "yeoman" farmers, who owned few if any slaves. Raising enough crops to feed their families, yeoman farmers also pastured their livestock on the open range, while they hunted and fished on common lands. To the extent that they grew cotton, it was in small amounts and for local markets. With the extension of railroads after the Civil War, yeoman farmers became susceptible to price fluctuations, losing the self-sufficiency of the antebellum era.

[20] Nell Irvin Painter, *Exodusters: Black Migration to Kansas after Reconstruction* (New York: Alfred A. Knopf, 1977), 63.

As a result of the arrival of railroads, yeoman farmers became incorporated into the post–Civil War plantation system. Many Piedmont farmers grew cotton; others entered into a tenancy relationship with cotton planters. In the northern rim of the southern Piedmont, moreover, the advent of bright-leaf tobacco—which experienced a boom in prices and cultivation after 1870—drew still more yeoman farmers into the market economy. During the postwar era, the frontier of the Cotton South expanded to Texas, whose rich lands attracted migrants from all over the Southeast. Working as land development agents and even as landlords, railroads sponsored the westward extension of the cotton frontier.

Texas provided fertile breeding ground for a new form of agrarian radicalism that arose in response to the social and economic transformation of the last decades of the nineteenth century. Many Texas farmers were attracted to "producerism" as an ideology expressing their growing frustration with modern capitalism. Hostile to large economic enterprise, which it grouped together under the term "monopoly," producer ideology emphasized the traditional skills of agriculturalists and artisans. The core assumption of this ideology was that large economic enterprise, with the assistance of government, had undermined the economic and political rights of producers—laborers and farmers. In consequence, they sought to restore this apparent imbalance.

Across the South, railroads and large-acreage farmers objected to the open range, a prevailing tradition in which farmers let their livestock graze in common pastures. The open range served as a leveling influence: it permitted southern farmers to feed their livestock, especially hogs, without having to own much land. The open range also permitted smaller herdsman to sustain themselves and their livestock. Free-range cattle and hogs foraged, however, sometimes eating other farmers' crops and causing train crashes by wandering onto the rails. Railroads, large farmers, and Texas cattle ranchers spearheaded a modern enclosure movement that tried to end the open range by erecting barbwire fences and, where possible, legislating changes permitting them to exclude free-range livestock.

Widespread protest greeted these changes. Fencing laws became the subject of heated political debate, a long, protracted process involving special laws that proceeded by legislative enactment, community by community, over a period of years. The political controversy over fencing laws demonstrated the political power of large economic enterprise and how government had become unresponsive to the needs and desires of ordinary people. Much of this resentment focused on railroads, which dominated southern legislatures with money and lobbying. In some parts of the South, vigilantes protested railroad power, and the advent of train robbers—and the romanticization of anti-industrial bandits—became a part of the postwar South.

THE CONVICT LEASE SYSTEM

In 1893, the iconic black female leader Ida B. Wells denounced the convict lease system, along with lynch law, as the "twin infamies which flourish hand in hand in many of the United States." This heinous penal system operated predominantly in the

South, where nine-tenths of the convicts were black. Claiming poverty and inability to maintain prisons, southern states relinquished their responsibilities to maintain state convicts within prison walls by renting out convicts to railroads, mines, and farms. "These companies," she wrote, "assume charge of the convicts, work them as cheap labor and pay the states a handsome revenue for their labor."[21]

Convicts at work. *Library of Congress.*

Although the Thirteenth Amendment abolished slavery and involuntary servitude, it specifically exempted "punishment for crime whereof the party shall have been duly convicted." Exploiting that loophole, coerced labor in the postwar South survived in the convict lease, a system by which convicts were hired out by contract to employers. By 1876, all the state governments in the South had established some form of the convict lease. This system was particularly southern: in 1886, thirteen states leased their convicts; ten of them were in the South. Advertised as a system designed to reduce the costs of imprisonment, convict lease became a widespread system of labor that oppressed former slaves and their children.

The system was also racialized. Most southern convicts were African American under a criminal-justice system designed to keep whites out of the convict ranks. Courts imprisoned a high percentage of African Americans. In Florida, over 90 percent of the convicts were black in 1869. In 1878, Mississippi had 900 African American convicts and 112 whites. In 1889, an Alabama investigating committee found that 144 of the 147 convicts working in the state's coal mines were black. Into the twentieth century, the preponderance of black convicts persisted. In 1908, Georgia reported that 91 percent of its convicts were black.

The crimes for which African Americans were convicted were most often against property, in contested areas in which ex-slaves believed that they deserved access to economic resources. White fears of black criminality, a frequent postemancipation fantasy, drove a crackdown that targeted former slaves. Across the South, legislatures enacted laws providing for the criminalization of "black" crimes—typically small-time theft. In Mississippi, the legislature in 1876 adopted the notorious "Pig Law," which required a five-year sentence for stealing small animals worth a dollar or more. At the same time, vagrancy laws—enacted during Reconstruction and after—required proof of employment. Lacking such proof, vagrants could be imprisoned.

Petty larceny—the theft of crops or livestock—could often result in imprisonment, even harsh sentences. Out of the plantation regions, local whites dealt with the instability of the labor system and social order by treating alleged black

21 Ida B. Wells, "The Convict Lease System," in *The Reason Why the Colored American Is Not in the World's Columbian Exposition,* ed. Robert W. Rydell (Urbana: University of Illinois Press, 1999); available at http://digital.library.upenn.edu/women/wells/exposition/exposition.html#III.

criminality with an iron fist. There were significant incentives in this system. State governments severely reduced expenditures during the 1870s. Prisons and penitentiaries suffered harsh cuts, and a privatized system of incarcerating prisoners seemed attractive. In Florida, the Reconstruction government established a state prison at a former federal arsenal at Chattahoochee, in northern Florida, in 1869. But the Chattahoochee facilities were badly dilapidated; housing the prisoners cost $40,000 annually. In 1877, the Florida government—now composed of anti-Reconstruction Democrats—introduced a leasing system, and three years later the first prisoners were leased.

Between 1880 and 1920, many of these convicts were put to work in the lumber industry of northern Florida. Timber and naval stores became a major industry in the state, when twenty million acres of virgin longleaf pine and cypress were opened to exploitation for lumber, pine tar, and pitch. Convicts were also used in phosphate mines, a leading industry during the post-Reconstruction era. The turpentine camps of northern Florida housed many of the prisoners in harsh conditions. Convicts often walked without shoes for miles from their camp to the worksites. An investigation in 1907 found one camp in which none of the convicts had shoes. Palmettos lacerated the convicts' feet, with resulting inflammation, infection, blood poisoning, and even death. One convict reported that inmates were always in "intense pain." Beatings were a regular occurrence; inmates were described as having scars on their backs, some of them fresh.

Leasing convicts provided states with the most important source of state revenue in the post–Civil War era. In Georgia, North Carolina, Kentucky, Mississippi, and Arkansas, annual revenues from convict leasing reached $25,000 to $50,000. In Tennessee and Alabama, leases to coal mines were more profitable, yielding $100,000 per year to prison authorities and state governments. The criminal-justice system became geared toward producing revenue rather than rehabilitating convicts. States such as Mississippi adopted notorious laws imposing prison sentences for theft more than ten dollars in value. In Arkansas, the legislature in 1875 enacted a larceny law that made a felony a theft of anything valued more than two dollars. The state's prison population grew from one hundred in 1874 to six hundred in 1882.[22]

Local governments operated their own convict-leasing operations, also yielding them significant revenues. Convicts satisfied an intense demand for labor to construct the expanding transportation system, dig coal and mine iron ore, cut and process forests, drain swamps, and work sugar fields. Conglomerates gobbled up these laborers, secured in long-term contracts with penal authorities. Outright or implied corruption plagued the system; state officials benefited from the profits of the leases. Convicts were leased to favored clients; officials were part of a corrupt system. Joseph E. Brown, Georgia's governor during the Civil War and later a US senator, enriched himself through the lease system. In other states, convict lease profits greased political machines.

[22] Calvin R. Ledbetter Jr., "The Long Struggle to End Convict Leasing in Arkansas," *Arkansas Historical Quarterly* 52, no. 1 (Spring 1993): 6.

Sometimes, local government officials worked in collusion to generate a population of workers who could be sold off to contractors. In an investigative report published in 1907, a reporter described how a turpentine operator in Marion County, in central Florida, needed workers and agreed to pay the sheriff's fees plus five dollars per convict. Equipped with a list of eight local blacks whom they knew to be "good husky fellows, capable of a fair day's work," a deputy sheriff arrested the men over the next few weeks on petty crimes—assault, gambling, and disorderly conduct—conducted in roundups at local "shindies," or bars. The accused men appeared before a judge, who held the men over until the next court met six months later. Because the men could not afford bail, the turpentine operator stepped forward to pay their bond—and gained control over them and their labor.[23]

Enjoying leeway in managing convicts, employers often used brutal methods, including regular beatings, to compel the convicts to work. Reflecting white attitudes about the use of coerced black labor, officials and private companies leasing convicts saw little wrong with these practices. "The strap has to be used," said a Tennessee prison official, "and in almost every case when it is used on the class of indolent and worthless men, with a firm and relentless . . . hand, they came right up with their work." A prison guard reported that convicts expected brutality. "Treat him good and he will rear up and put his feet on your clean sheet," he declared. "When he misbehaves himself [he] has to be whipped."[24]

Little provision was made to ensure convicts' health and safety, with high mortality rates the result. In Arkansas, for example, in 1881 the death rate was reported to be 25 percent among convicts. In Louisiana, convicts' death rate, according to one account, "must exceed that of any pestilence that fell upon Europe in the Middle Ages."[25] Georgia counted more than 1,600 deaths between 1868 and 1908.[26] Women and men were housed together, and the system paid little regard to children, who were also convicted and leased. Overall, a significant majority of convicts were in their twenties or younger; many were juveniles. In 1893, Georgia reported that a third of their convicts were under the age of twenty, and fifteen of these convicts were under the age of twelve.[27] An Alabama prison official described the convict lease as "a disgrace to the state and the reproach of the civilization and Christian sentiment of the age."[28]

[23] Richard Barry, "Slavery in the South To-Day," *The Cosmopolitan* 42 (March 1907): 488–489.
[24] Mildred C. Fierce, *Slavery Revisited: Blacks and the Southern Convict Lease System, 1865–1933* (Brooklyn, NY: Africana Studies Research Center, Brooklyn College, 1994), 93.
[25] George Washington Cable, *The Silent South: Together with the Freedman's Case in Equity and the Convict Lease System* (New York: Charles Scribner's Sons, 1885), 171.
[26] Matthew J. Mancini, *One Dies, Get Another: Convict Leasing in the American South, 1866–1928* (Columbia: University of South Carolina Press, 1996), 85.
[27] Ayers, *Vengeance and Justice*, 199; Pamela Chase Hain, *Murder in the State Capitol: The Biography of Lieutenant Colonel Robert Augustus Alston (1832–1879)* (Macon, GA: Mercer University Press, 2013), 178.
[28] Quoted in Frederick Douglass, "The Convict Lease System," in *The Reason Why the Colored American Is Not in the World's Columbian Exposition*, ed. Rydell; available at http://digital.library.upenn.edu/women/wells/exposition/exposition.html#1.

Among the convict ranks were women and children, all convicted of various minor offenses. An investigating committee in Texas in 1909 uncovered that prison guards frequently abused black female prisoners. It was not uncommon for prisoners to bear children as a result of rape. A legislative inquiry in 1878 in Georgia found that there were twenty-five children born out of wedlock in the prison camps. Child convicts were housed together with adults and were expected to complete the same amount of work. In 1882, Alabama reported that one of its prison camps, at Walls, contained seven black women, with four of them under the age of eighteen. Two of them, Ella and Mary Edwards, were convicted of burglary at the ages of twelve and thirteen.

Convicts often worked relentlessly, with many of them starting work at dawn and finishing late at night. There was no prospect of labor unrest, no chance of unions. In 1872, the Tennessee Coal, Iron and Railroad Company, which used convicts, estimated that this form of labor provided a $70,000 advantage over its competitors. "Considering the depression in business throughout the country, the frightful upheavings of labor against capital of some of our sister States, its consequent injury and derangement of the general business of the country," wrote an Alabama warden in 1877, "we have cause to congratulate ourselves as to our financial success."[29]

The plantation districts of Georgia and Alabama provided a steady supply of laborers convicted of petty crimes. Planters used the criminal-justice system to intimidate workers and to rid themselves of troublemakers. Many black convicts in the mines stayed after their sentences expired. "After the convict has worked for several years," according to the US Immigration Commission in 1910, "he has learned a trade thoroughly.... Owing to the system of rigid discipline and enforced regularity of work, he becomes through habit a steady workman, accustomed to regular hours." Overall, however, the pool of cheap labor helped spur industrial development in centers such as Birmingham, Alabama. The Tennessee Coal, Iron and Railroad mines, producing three-fifths of the coal and iron in eastern Tennessee and northern Alabama by 1893, made heavy use of convicts. In its Tracy City, Tennessee, mines, for example, two-thirds of the workforce were convicts. The presence of convicts depressed wages for workers generally and discouraged unionization throughout the region.[30]

When writer George Washington Cable investigated the convict lease system in 1885, he found a great deal of variety in how it operated. He concluded, however, that the southern penal institutions were "the worst in the country by every evidence of their own setting forth." This system was cruel, "brutalizing, deadly." Too many convicts died by beating, shooting, drowning, or exhaustion. The convict lease system mocked "such intelligent sense of justice and mercy" as existed and among convicts made "his heart and conscience harder than the granite of his prison walls." This was a system, he concluded, that was "in every way a disgrace to civilization."[31]

[29] Ayers, *Vengeance and Justice*, 193.
[30] Alex Lichtenstein, "Good Roads and Chain Gangs in the Progressive South: 'The Negro Convict Is a Slave,'" *Journal of Southern History* 59, no. 1 (February 1993): 88.
[31] Cable, *The Silent South* , 154–155, 172.

The convict system prevailing in the post-Reconstruction South represented a new form of slavery and coerced labor, in which many whites had a stake. There were periodic calls for reform after the grossest examples of abuses became exposed. The power structure was closely tied to the system, however. In Georgia, figures such as former governor Joseph E. Brown and Senator Joseph Gordon reaped huge profits because they maintained the state's contract for convicts. In 1879, legislator Robert A. Alston presented a report critical of the management of the convict lease system, which he called a "disgrace," not only to Georgia, but "a disgrace to civilization." Alston, a Confederate veteran and Democratic legislator in charge of the state house's penitentiary committee, called for an end to the worst-offending camps, but his campaign enraged one of the sub-lessees (who leased from Gordon), Edward Cox. In March 1879, Cox shot and killed Alston in a sensational murder in the Georgia capitol building in Atlanta. Alston's killing was "not only a fresh illustration of the slight value which the violent men of the south place upon human life," commented the *New York Times*, it was also "a striking example of the terrible risks which are run by those who attempt to correct abuses in that section of the country." Alston, according to the *Times*, was a victim of his efforts to expose the maltreatment of black convicts, who were "dying by the score, dying like dogs, in the swamps and remote places to which they had been taken by the contractors."[32]

The post–Civil War South bred a particular kind of discontent; not everyone was satisfied with unsettling social and economic changes. The new industrial economy created greater wealth, but it also subjected people on the bottom of the social ranks, both white and black, to increased poverty and deprivation. African Americans suffered the exploitation inherent in the persisting plantation system, while they faced new oppressors as a result of the convict lease system. The growth of industrial manufacturing spawned the growth of towns and cities but seemed to diminish the status of traditional agriculture and farming. During the 1890s, especially, the New South order suffered a sharp political challenge in a mass uprising known as the Populist Revolt.

---

[32] Quoted in "The Latest Georgia Murder," *Atlanta Constitution*, March 16, 1879.

15

THE CRISIS OF THE 1890s

DURING THE 1890S, as the world plunged into a severe depression and distress gripped most sectors of society, a social and political crisis gripped the South and the nation. For rural southerners, the crisis proved especially significant. A severe depression affected agriculture and industry—and many more people—because of the wider reach of market capitalism. Aggrieved farmers could find little succor in the political system, which seemed unresponsive and to favor big business and industrialists over ordinary people. In the South, a racial crisis accompanied the social and economic crisis. Lynching and random antiblack violence spread. The rise of virulent racism gripped much of the South and the nation, leading to efforts to negate the Fifteenth Amendment by depriving black voters of their political rights. By the early 1900s, a new system of white supremacy became formalized through practice and legislature, defined in a new system of Jim Crow segregation.

THE AFTERMATH OF RECONSTRUCTION

During the winter of 1877, the presidential election of the previous November, pitting New York Democrat Samuel Tilden against Ohio Republican Rutherford B. Hayes, remained deadlocked in a disputed election. After Tilden polled about 253,000 more popular votes than Hayes, he fell short of attaining the presidency when he received 184 electoral votes—one shy of the necessary majority. With twenty disputed electoral votes in militarily occupied Louisiana, South Carolina, and Florida, an electoral commission attempted to settle the dispute and determine the new president. The crisis was averted only a few days before Inauguration Day, when Hayes was declared the winner.

The disputed election of 1876 was resolved, according to some historians, by what they called the Compromise of 1877. According to its terms, the white South acquiesced in Hayes's election in exchange for significant concessions. Republicans agreed to withdraw troops from these three southern states, the last to be occupied under Republican rule. More importantly, the Compromise marked a formal end to Reconstruction. After 1877, the North no longer mounted any further military intervention in southern affairs, and the South returned to the control of whites. Thereafter, in most of the South the Republicans lost power, where they still possessed it, to a resurgent Democratic Party.

In September 1877, President Hayes toured Virginia, Tennessee, Kentucky, and Georgia, the first time a president set foot on southern territory since April 1865, when Lincoln visited Richmond during the Civil War's last weeks. Hayes's trip indicated a new spirit of sectional reconciliation among whites. Visiting Louisville, Hayes was escorted by an honor guard of former Confederate soldiers. A local newspaper observed that blacks watching Hayes's visit were "less enthusiastic" about the sectional reconciliation "for which their old masters cheer so lustily." Subsequently speaking in Atlanta, Hayes struck a theme of reconciliation, making a return to white control. For African Americans, he said, their "rights and interests would be safer if this great mass of intelligent white men were let alone by the general Government" and permitted to solve their own problems. The white audience greeted this idea with "immense enthusiasm and cheering." Returning to Washington, Hayes announced that the nation was "again one and united!"[1]

Hayes's attempt at an alliance with business-oriented southern whites ultimately failed, yet his presidency marked a distinct change. For the next generation, the "redeemed" South—that is, governments captured by anti-Reconstruction forces—prevailed, as the governments employed extraordinary means to maintain power. Warning that Republicans would plunge the South into another era of Reconstruction, Redeemers conjured images of northern invasion that stuck in whites' psyche. Relentlessly exploiting the race issue, Redeemer politicians warned white voters that Republican power meant black officeholding and black police—in other words, African American men exercising power over white women. Using a rhetoric combining race and sex, Redeemers urged white voters to support them as a matter of social solidarity. Finally, in close elections Redeemers resorted to other methods to win elections, including violence designed to intimidate black voters into staying away from the polls, as well as redistricting, malapportionment, or ballot manipulation.

Redeemer political control solidified the grip of white supremacy. In the rural South, where most African Americans lived, there was little recourse to the revitalized plantation system, which assured the control of white planters over black labor. Black farmers found little sympathy from southern whites, who wanted a new system of labor and racial control. Black people, said the *New Orleans Times* in 1879,

[1] C. Vann Woodward, *Reunion and Reaction: The Compromise of 1877 and the End of Reconstruction* (Boston: Little, Brown, 1951), 229.

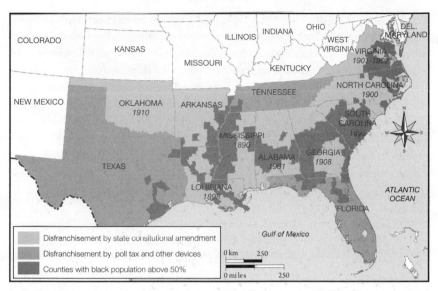

MAP 15.1 Disfranchisement, 1890–1908

had little reason to complain. "They themselves are more to blame for their condition," it claimed, "than anybody else. They are dissatisfied because, at the end of each
year they have accumulated nothing and are in debt. They do not seek to find out the
cause of this, but jump at the conclusion that they have been denied their rights,
robbed and misused generally." Rather, the *Times* claimed that "improvident"
African Americans were provided with credit but lived beyond their means "without any regard to their actual wants." In order to better themselves, advised the
newspaper, they needed to become more "thrifty and economical."[2]

The extent of Redeemer control varied from state to state. In Upper South states
such as North Carolina and Virginia, the political situation remained fluid. For the
most part, African American males continued to vote in North Carolina, especially
in the heavily black eastern third of the state. In Virginia, a large rebellion occurred
over the determination of the conservative Democratic government to honor a heavy
antebellum debt load incurred to finance internal improvements during the 1850s.
The "funders"—who favored full redemption of the debt—slashed public services,
most especially financial support for the new public schools. By the late 1870s, a coalition of aggrieved whites and African Americans created the Readjuster Party, which
proposed partially repudiating the debt by "readjusting" it. The Readjusters elected a
governor and two US senators, including former Confederate general William
H. Mahone.

In Deep South states, meanwhile, conditions worsened noticeably for African
Americans, especially in rural areas where white violence was common. In response,
in the Deep South, some black leaders advocated emigration from the South to

2 Painter, *Exodusters*, 64–65.

West Africa, or to the North. In 1878, Louisiana Redeemers resorted to ballot manipulation—switching polling places at the last minute, using violence and intimidation, illegally disqualifying Republican voters, and stuffing ballot boxes—to win elections. Henry Adams, an ex-slave and Republican activist, established a Colonization Council in response to these deteriorating conditions. Another ex-slave, Benjamin "Pap" Singleton, organized emigration efforts independent of Adams. Appealing to the US attorney general, Adams pleaded for the federal government to "give us some Territory to our selves—and let us leave these Slave holders to work their own land, for they are killing our race by the hundreds every day and night." Writing to President Hayes, another black leader described a "terror stricken and distressed people" who were driven from the polls, even murdered. Despite these pleas for federal intervention, none was forthcoming.[3]

On January 16, 1879, Minnesota senator William Windom offered a resolution authorizing an inquiry into the "expediency and practicability" of federal sponsorship of migration of African Americans from states where "they are not allowed to freely and peacefully exercise and enjoy their constitutional rights as American citizens, into such States as may desire to receive them and will protect them in said rights."[4] Windom's declaration encouraged emigrationist sentiment. During the spring of 1879, thousands of African Americans from Louisiana, Mississippi, and Texas —6,000 that year, followed by 15,000 a year later—traveled up the Mississippi River. Most of these "Exodusters" moved to Kansas, which became a Promised Land for black refugees. There were "no words which can fully express or explain the real condition of my people through the south," wrote one black leader, "nor how deeply and keenly they feel the necessity of fleeing from the wrath and long pent-up hatred of their old masters which they feel assured will ere long burst loose like the pent-up fires of a volcano and crush them if they remain here many years longer."[5]

Exoduster family in Nicodemus, Kansas. *Library of Congress.*

[3] Painter, *Exodusters*, 98.
[4] Heather Cox Richardson, *The Death of Reconstruction: Race, Labor, and Politics in the Post–Civil War North, 1865–1901* (Cambridge, MA: Harvard University Press, 2001), 157.
[5] Painter, *Exodusters*, 184.

Leonidas LaFayette Polk.
Library of Congress.

In terms of absolute numbers, the later, post–World War I departure of African Americans to northern states dwarfed the Exodusters' migration. However, the migration of the late 1870s was nonetheless significant. First, it charted out future routes of escape; the Mississippi River became a path for later generations. Second, the Exodusters made a decisive commentary about declining conditions for African Americans, how Reconstruction's promise of civil and political equality had failed. A new era in the South's postemancipation was inaugurated, but it contained dark auguries for the future.

ORIGINS OF DISCONTENT

Railroads, at the root of the rapid economic changes reshaping the post–Civil War South, brought mixed benefits. Between the late 1870s and early 1890s, the railroad network spread throughout the South—so much so, that few communities now lacked access to railroad transportation. Most communities greeted the railroads' arrival enthusiastically, seeing it as a measure of progress and as a promise of future prosperity. But railroads also brought subtle and not-so-subtle changes: the rush of store-bought goods whose prices usually were lower than locally produced goods, the incorporation of farm products into a commercial nexus, the new dependence on a cash economy, and the overall supremacy of an unrelenting and unforgiving market. In good times, these seemed like blessings, but in hard times, the crunch fell heavily.

The harshest consequences of the market economy were felt in the rural South. The postwar expansion of cotton culture reflected expanded access in the interior South to markets because of railroad connections. Increasingly, cotton farmers were indebted to merchants or large landholders. For farmers, railroads—seemingly possessing a stranglehold on their livelihood—became a frequent object of their ire. Increases in rates were greeted with complaints about monopoly power. Railroads symbolized the domination of the market and its controlling effect on their lives and livelihood.

As early as the 1870s, farmers organized to express grievances. During the 1870s, the Patrons of Husbandry, or the Grange, spread across the South. Appealing to the traditionalism of rural southern whites, the Grange was a voluntary organization uniting dispersed agricultural societies. The organization was a social group, but it also experimented with cooperative marketing and credit. Appealing to farmers with moderate amounts of cash, the Grange began a system of state agents that pooled purchases in order to obtain discounts from manufacturers. The group offered warehousing, in which cotton farmers could store their crop in order to seek a better price at the market. Some Grange leaders also wanted to establish their own manufacturing. "We have great facilities for manufacturing every implement needed on the farm," the master of the North Carolina Grange declared in 1875, "and I cannot but feel it a blemish on our good name that we, in a great measure, buy our plows, wagons, etc., in markets distant many hundreds of miles."[6]

There were limits to what the Grange could accomplish in the post–Civil War South. The organization was not especially radical. Large planters dominated the ranks; their concerns were not those shared by the rural masses. Where the Grange engaged in retailing, it insisted on cash purchases, effectively excluding cotton farmers who lived and died by credit. The Grange was also racially segregated, and indeed in some parts of the South, such as Georgia, it was reputed to be associated with the Klan. Although the Grange agitated for expanded agricultural education—including higher education—it generally avoided political involvement or any attempt to challenge the Redeemer power structure.

A very different version of agrarian radicalism emerged during the early 1880s. Founded in 1879 in eastern Texas, the Farmers Alliance included mostly small farmers opposing large cattle operations. Unlike the Grange, the Farmers Alliance attracted greater numbers of farmers lacking many resources. The order especially appealed to cotton farmers because of its deep suspicion of railroads and its willingness to criticize the credit system oppressing small farmers. By 1886, when the Alliance decided to expand beyond Texas, it had become a vehicle for mass protest.

The Alliance's popularity coincided with the rise of another protest organization, the Knights of Labor. Originating as a fraternal order, the Knights soon moved into protest politics. A surge in the Knights' growth occurred when it expanded its membership from 100,000 in 1885 to 700,000 a year later. Of this national membership, more than 21,000 organized into nearly 500 locals were southern workers. During the spring and summer of 1885, the Knights successfully challenged railroad speculator Jay Gould's railroad conglomerate. A year later, when Gould tried to break the union, he ignited the Great Southwest Strike, which began in East Texas and spread across the West. The Knights served as an appealing symbol of resistance to the corporate power of railroads, and especially so among railroad workers and factory laborers in the towns and cities of the South.

The Knights reached a diverse constituency in the South. Active in cotton mills and coal mines, they organized strikes in the cotton mills of Augusta, Georgia (1886), and Cottondale, Alabama (1888). The Knights also led strikes by lumber workers and sugar workers. Unusual for its time, the union was biracial. Typically organized into separate black and white locals, in some cases they also functioned in integrated locals—this in contrast to most trade unions, which completely excluded black members. The Knights tapped into the late-nineteenth-century culture of "producerist" radicalism that tapped into traditions of independent artisan workers as well as farmers. With numerous rural members, the group organized cooperatives that would provide an alternative to merchants. In Raleigh, North Carolina, the Knights established the National Cooperative Tobacco Company in 1884. Other

[6] Theodore Saloutos, "The Grange in the South, 1870–1877," *Journal of Southern History* 19, no. 4 (November 1953): 482.

members of the union created a cooperative coal mine in Mercer Station, Kentucky, while an African American local established a cooperative cotton gin in Stewart's Station, Alabama.[7]

The Knights' struggle against organized capital solidified their appeal among Texas alliancemen. During the railroad strikes of 1885–1886, armed conflict raged, while workers asserted themselves against state police power. The Texas Alliance adopted much of the Knights' utopianism and radical political ideology. Some alliancemen urged a sympathetic boycott against the railroads, while more-conservative leaders in the order opposed any political involvement. Alliance rank and file became what one newspaper called "the spinal column of this great railroad war."[8] After the failure of the strike, the radical wing of the Texas Alliance adopted a vigorously politicized language. The "combined capital" had imposed an "unjust oppression of labor," declared one Alliance resolution, which was "casting a gloom over our country." Capital was "thoroughly organized," said another Texan, "but when the laboring class begins to organize, they call it communism and other hard names, which is unjust. I am proud the morning sunlight of labor's freedom is shining in the political horizon of the east."[9]

In August 1886, the Texas Alliance met outside Dallas, in Cleburne, and, after much infighting, committed to a program of political action. The meeting adopted a manifesto of seventeen "demands" urging action to secure "to our people freedom from the onerous and shameful abuses that the industrial classes are now suffering at the hands of arrogant capitalists and powerful corporations." The Cleburne Demands authorized the establishment of Alliance cooperative stores and a national bureau of labor statistics, while they also called for an end to the convict lease system. Bitterly antirailroad, the Texas Alliance endorsed the national regulation of railroad rates and practices. Criticizing the inadequacies of the national finance and currency system, the Alliance also called for a federal national bank to manage the currency.

With 200,000 members in the state, the Alliance was poised for significant expansion.[10] In early 1887, the group decided to recruit new members beyond Texas. Under President Charles W. Macune, the Texas Alliance dispatched lecturer-organizers across the cotton South. Organizers promised to overcome the credit and debt problems of the southern farmer by establishing centralized buying and selling in cooperatives, and by extending credit in advance of the cotton crop. Alliance cooperative exchanges were established at the county, district, and state level—with a powerful grassroots appeal. The lecturer-organizers were Texans, but they were often sent to their home states. Thus J. B. Barry, a native North Carolinian who had migrated to Texas, wrote about the reception he received in Wake County, North Carolina. "I met the farmers in public meetings twenty-seven times, and twenty-seven times they

[7] Frederic Meyers, "The Knights of Labor in the South," *Southern Economic Journal* 6, no. 4 (April 1940): 486.
[8] Lawrence Goodwyn, *The Populist Moment: A Short History of the Agrarian Revolt in America* (New York: Oxford University Press, 1978), 41.
[9] Goodwyn, *Populist Moment*, 42.
[10] Goodwyn, *Populist Moment*, 47–50.

organized," he wrote. The farmers seemed "like unto ripe fruit—you can gather them by a gentle shake of the bush."[11]

Nominally nonpolitical, the Alliance aggressively represented the besieged rural culture. It specified that its membership was only open to farmers, laborers, mechanics, teachers, physicians, ministers, and editors of agricultural journals. Specifically excluded were those associated with the market economy and corporate bullying—lawyers, bankers, railroad men, cotton merchants, warehousers, and storekeepers. The Alliance also formed coalitions with existing protest groups across the South. In early 1887, it merged with the Louisiana Farmers' Union, adopting the name of National Farmers' Alliance and Co-operative Union of America. In Arkansas, the Agricultural Wheel, which claimed a region-wide membership of 500,000, also joined forces in December 1888.

By 1889, the Alliance claimed a peak membership of several million. With headquarters established in Washington, DC, the organization maintained a network of stores, exchanges, and warehouses that attracted new members. Adopting a revival-style approach to organizing, the Alliance maintained 35,000 lecturers whose main purpose was to beat the bushes for new members and to promote an "education" program preaching "cooperation" to the rank and file. The cooperative exchanges became wildly popular across the South, and they drove much of the order's rapid growth.

Part of the Alliance's rapid expansion into the rural South lay in its militancy, its willingness to slay the dragon of "monopoly" that seemingly oppressed rural southerners. In one of the organization's more spectacular successes, in 1888 it took on the so-called jute-bagging trust. The manufacturers of jute, a fabric used for cotton bagging, conspired to raise unilaterally the price of jute from seven to eleven cents per yard. The Alliance, organizing themselves in Birmingham, mounted a boycott in the spring of 1889 against the trust. They instructed alliancemen to use cotton fabric for bagging instead. The state Alliances agreed to make arrangements with cotton mills cooperatively; the membership avidly embraced this cause. "The Standard of Revolt is up," declared Georgia editor Tom Watson, "Let us keep it up and speed it on." By 1890, the jute trust had collapsed.[12]

Despite these successes, the Alliance confronted many obstacles. Some farmers remained discouraged and dispirited. Organizing in Alabama, Alliance lecturer J. M. Perdue complained that farmers were often "so crushed under the crop mortgage system that they have lost almost all hope of bettering their condition." Many depended for their livelihood on local merchants, who intimidated the farmers into apathy.[13] Henry W. Grady, the boosterish editor of the *Atlanta Constitution*, called the Alliance "deluded brothers" with socialist tendencies whose principles, "if carried out, would revolutionize our entire system of government, shutting out

[11] Goodwyn, *Populist Moment*, 58.
[12] Goodwyn, *Populist Moment*, 88.
[13] Goodwyn, *Populist Moment*, 59.

all competition, placing the commerce, the producer and manufacturer in the hands of one man, closing up all stores save their own."[14]

In truth, the Alliance was an unwieldy organization with divisions of geography, class, and politics. Its sudden expansion, which brought in members from the Plains and Upper Midwest grain belt, made these differences even more obvious. In some sense the cooperative movement papered over internal tensions. Macune realized this, but from the beginning the market pressures to succeed worked against the exchange system. In late 1889, Macune used the pages of the national Alliance journal, the *National Economist*, to outline a new effort to seek to overcome the credit problems of cotton farmers. Macune proposed a nationally established system of subtreasuries, or warehouses, where farmers could store their crops and receive currency in advance of the sale of their crops. Subtreasury certificates of deposit would serve, the Alliance's 1889 platform stated, as "full legal tender for all debts, public and private." The certificates would provide the basis of legal notes up to 80 percent of the crop's value. The subtreasuries would also try to stem the endemic price deflation that characterized the American economy during the last third of the nineteenth century.[15]

The subtreasury plan led the Alliance into politics. Adopting the subtreasury required an act of Congress, and during the congressional elections of 1890 the organization lobbied hard. At Democratic nominating conventions, candidates were presented with the "Alliance yardstick" requiring them to support or oppose the subtreasury. Across the South especially, the Alliance yardstick yielded results, as candidates endorsing it were elected and those opposing it were defeated. During the same year, alliancemen elected "Alliance legislatures," which bore the mark of the mobilization of agrarian protest. In Tennessee, fourteen of thirty-three state senators, forty of ninety members of the state house, and the governor all were Alliance-backed candidates. In North Carolina, during elections the entire congressional delegation pledged support for the subtreasury, as did legislative and statewide officers. In Georgia, the governor and a large majority of the legislature were Alliance candidates. Other southern states reported the success of the Alliance yardstick. The Alliance, officially nonpolitical, was becoming increasingly politicized. At a meeting in Ocala, Florida, in December 1890, the Alliance again endorsed the subtreasury plan but also included in its platform the abolition of national banks, the expansion of the money supply through the monetization of silver, greater control over railroads, a graduated income tax, and a constitutional amendment providing for the direct election of US senators.

Ultimately, the Alliance found their experiences in politics disheartening. The subtreasury plan quickly stalled in Congress, and its sponsor, North Carolina senator Zebulon Vance—who had endorsed the Alliance yardstick—voted against it,

---

[14] C. Vann Woodward, *Origins of the New South, 1877–1913* (Baton Rouge: Louisiana State University Press, 1951), 198.

[15] Goodwyn, *Populist Moment*, 92.

saying that he could not support this "great and radical departure."[16] Regular Democrats consistently outmaneuvered Alliance Democrats, and in numerous states the agrarian legislatures accomplished little. In states such as Georgia, where the "Farmers' Legislature" elected conservative Democrat John B. Gordon to the US Senate, the "silk-hat bosses" remained in charge.[17] Despite majorities elsewhere, important Alliance proposals were frustrated. In Texas and South Carolina, respectively, Democrats such as James Hogg and Ben Tillman used the Alliance to build up their machine organizations to elect themselves governor and to seize control of the state Democratic parties.

The question remained how much the Alliance could expect from the Democratic Party. "Being Democrats and in the majority," reasoned one member about the Alliance's prospects, "we took possession of the Democratic party." As the *National Economist* commented, the order believed that it had "by one effort revolutionized the politics of the nation."[18] But the events of 1891–1892 indicated otherwise. Democrats seemed intent on neutralizing the economic radicalism in the order, and on subduing its membership.

POPULISM

For a generation after Reconstruction, race and the imperatives of white supremacy imposed stability over the political system. All white men were told that maintaining racial solidarity, preventing "negro rule," and defeating the Republican Party served as cardinal principles of politics. Democratic leaders exploited race to maintain political power. Increasingly, they became committed to policies favoring railroads, corporations, and the wealthy classes of the New South in a way that seemed contrary to interests of the mass of white southerners. The failure of the Alliance led to political crisis in the South. Their grievances targeted the political system itself, and especially the Democratic Party.

The Alliance, however, remained profoundly divided over its mission, purposes, and future. A large portion of the order was politically conservative, unwilling to desert racial orthodoxy. Democratic leaders attacked the subtreasury and other Alliance proposals that would bring greater governmental intervention in the economy as dangerous, even socialist. Vance declared the subtreasury and other Alliance proposals as "demagoguism and communism."[19] In contrast, a vocal radical wing, suspicious of the intentions of Democratic leaders, promoted direct involvement in politics.

During 1891–1892, the subtreasury plan continued to serve as a litmus test. It remained what the *Progressive Farmer* called "the one real living issue" among

---

[16] Stuart Noblin, *Leonidas LaFayette Polk: Agrarian Crusader* (Chapel Hill: University of North Carolina Press, 1949), 242.

[17] Woodward, *Origins of the New South*, 237.

[18] Woodward, *Origins of the New South*, 204.

[19] Woodward, *Origins of the New South*, 240.

Ho for Kansas!

Brethren, Friends, & Fellow Citizens:
I feel thankful to inform you that the
REAL ESTATE
AND
Homestead   Association,
Will Leave Here the

15th of April, 1878,

In pursuit of Homes in the Southwestern
Lands of America, at Transportation
Rates, cheaper than ever
was known before.
For full information inquire of
Benj. Singleton, better known as old Pap,
NO. 5 NORTH FRONT STREET
Beware of Speculators and Adventurers, as it is a dangerous thing
to fall in their hands.
Nashville, Tenn., March 18, 1878.

One of the many posters calling on southern blacks to leave for Kansas.

Poster advertising Exoduster
migration. *Library of Congress.*

rank-and-file alliancemen. "The people are learning," commented an Alabama agrarian, "that the sub-treasury means final freedom from serfdom."[20] Radicals in the Alliance used the issue to point out their divergence from Democrats. Two states with large Alliance membership and charismatic leadership, Georgia and North Carolina, illustrate how this process unfolded. In Georgia, Alliance leadership was divided between conservative Democrat and Alliance president Lon Livingston and newspaper editor Tom Watson. Livingston supported loyalty to the Democratic Party; Watson favored radicalization. Elected to Congress as an Alliance Democrat in 1890, Watson became alienated from the Democratic leadership, emerging as an articulate advocate of the farmers' plight. "Here is a tenant—I do not know, or care, whether he is white or black, I know his story," Watson declared. "Railroad kings" were enriched by the New South's economic system, which ground down ordinary farmers.[21] Advocating that agrarian radicals bolt to an independent third party, in October 1891 Watson founded the *People's Party Paper* as a platform for his cause.

In North Carolina, Leonidas L. Polk similarly promoted third-party political involvement. Polk had been active in the North Carolina Grange and was state agriculture commissioner and the well-respected editor of the North Carolina *Progressive Farmer*. Polk had much to do with building one of the strongest Alliance organizations in the South. But, like Watson, he faced a bitter fight with establishment Democrats. One newspaper contended that Polk had appealed to prejudice and was a "disturber of the peace." The newspaper denounced Polk as a "failure as a soldier, . . . a failure as a farmer, . . . a failure as Commissioner of Agriculture."[22] Polk became convinced that the Democrats had betrayed the Alliance cause and no longer represented the mass of North Carolina farmers. At the National Alliance convention in Indianapolis he told members "to be deceived no longer" by "arrogant party dictation."[23]

Although hardly a radical by disposition, Polk felt that Democratic leaders had abandoned the subtreasury plan, "so near to the heart" of the mass of rural North Carolinians.[24] Like other Alliance leaders, Polk favored the organization of a third party. Elected president of the National Alliance in 1889, Polk announced his

[20] Goodwyn, *Populist Moment,* 161.
[21] Goodwyn, *Populist Moment,* 160–161.
[22] Noblin, *Leonidas LaFayette Polk,* 233.
[23] Goodwyn, *Populist Moment,* 163–164.
[24] Noblin, *Leonidas LaFayette Polk,* 246.

Benjamin Ryan Tillman.
Library of Congress.

position at a meeting of the Confederation of Industrial Organizations in February 1892. The time had come, he declared, for the "great West, the great South and the great Northwest, to link their hands and hearts together and march to the ballot box and take possession of the government, restore it to the principles of our fathers, and run it in the interest of the people." This new mass movement intended to rectify the political system, "if we have to wipe the two old parties from the face of the earth!"[25] The St. Louis meeting essentially verified the exodus of large numbers of Alliance members into a new third party, the People's Party, or Populists.

At the same time, other members of the Alliance could not stomach deserting white supremacy, sentiments that Democrats worked hard to encourage. Elias Carr, president of the North Carolina Alliance, was elected governor as a Democrat. In other states, Democrats also tried to retain the agrarian vote. On the other hand, a large portion of the order supported the Populists, though deserting the Democrats was not easy. When a Virginian cast a Populist ballot, he said it was "like cutting off the right hand or putting out the right eye."[26]

In June 1892, southern Populists suffered a grievous blow when Polk died suddenly at age fifty-five, only a month before the new third party was scheduled to meet in Omaha, Nebraska. The Omaha convention endorsed Alliance principles but also attempted to appeal to an urban-industrial workforce. The convention's nomination of James B. Weaver, an Iowan and former Union general, for the presidency had little appeal in the South. Weaver did not carry any southern states. Populists, however, assembled state tickets, which, in some states, challenged Democratic hegemony. In Alabama, Reuben Kolb ran for governor under a Jeffersonian Democratic banner, but he was defeated by the regular Democratic candidate after massive fraud and what one Democratic newspaper admitted was "trickery and corruption." In Georgia, Tom Watson lost his reelection campaign for Congress after ballot chicanery and political violence tilted the election to his Democratic opponent.[27] In other states, Populists composed a significant minority, though they still faced the determined opposition of the political establishment. South Carolina's Ben Tillman maintained a stronghold over the farmers' movement, but he was determined to undermine its influence. With Tillman in charge, the Alliance collapsed. In other states such as Tennessee, Mississippi, Florida, and Virginia, the Alliance for various reasons did not convert to Populism.

Perhaps the most effective Populist insurgency appeared in North Carolina. As elsewhere, the Alliance was split over support for a third party, but after their defeat

25 Noblin, *Leonidas LaFayette Polk*, 273–274.
26 Woodward, *Origins of the New South,* 244.
27 Goodwyn, *Populist Moment*, 188.

Thomas E. Watson, ca. 1920.
Library of Congress.

in the presidential election of 1892, Populist leaders, led by newspaper editor and future senator Marion Butler, decided to form a coalition, known as "fusion," with the state Republican Party. In the legislative elections of 1894, the Populist/Republican fusion alliance captured control of the legislature. Two years later, it elected Republican Daniel L. Russell governor. Fusion rule in North Carolina lasted only four years, but the government swept away vestiges of Democratic oligarchy. Ending partisan control of the electoral machinery, the Fusion regime restored democratically elected local government and opened up voter registration to include greater numbers of poorer white and black voters.

In most of the South, Populists challenged the political orthodoxy and threatened the established order. Proclaiming the solidarity of the "producer" class, Populists were sharply critical of the power of corporations and of railroads as symbols of concentrated economic power. By 1896, however, Populism was in decline. The political establishment struck back with whatever means were required to maintain power. Most commonly, the race issue divided Populists. In North Carolina, the Fusion coalition fell victim to a furious race-based campaign and political violence in legislative elections during 1898.

The mouthpiece of the organization Democrats, the *Raleigh News and Observer*, launched a viciously racist campaign assailing "black rule" during Fusion, with sexual innuendo about the implications of black political power. In a "White Supremacy" campaign, organized vigilantes on horseback, Red Shirts, prevented black voters from reaching the polls in closely contested precincts. And in Wilmington, the center of black political power, a full-scale racial massacre arose from the political contest.

RACIAL CRISIS

Following emancipation, racial violence became a common, nearly everyday part of life in the rural South. Whites in the antebellum South, already accustomed to brutalizing black people under slavery, continued to use organized violence after emancipation in order to maintain the caste system. With the assertion of black civil and political rights during Reconstruction, vigilantism of the Klan and other groups exhibited sometimes unofficial, sometimes state-sponsored violence that became endemic during the late 1860s and early 1870s. Federal intervention only partially limited its scope, duration, and presence.

In the antebellum South, lynching of black people remained rare, perhaps because slaves were considered valuable as property and because state-conducted executions brought compensation to masters. Mob violence grew out of the disorder of the Civil War, when resistant slaves were dealt with summarily and brutally.

Following the end of the Klan's extralegal vigilante violence, white violence against black people increased during the 1880s in an epidemic of lynching. Extralegal forms of punishment, committed by informal groups, had been common in American culture throughout the colonial era and nineteenth century. Sometimes this involved a form of shaming, such as a tarring and feathering. Lynching extended this tradition of extralegal punishment, involving a group of individuals sometimes working in small groups, sometimes in a larger mob. Most important, lynching involved murders of people, by hanging or other means.

Although lynchings occurred in the western states, over time it became a predominantly southern phenomenon. In the 1880s, 82 percent of lynchings occurred in the South; by the 1920s, this proportion had reached 95 percent. Lynching also became more racial. Of the 3,943 people lynched in the South between 1880 and 1930, 3,220, or 82 percent, were black. In contrast, outside the South, 83 percent of the victims were white.[28] "It is obvious," concluded a sociological study of lynching in 1933, "that lynching is becoming more and more a Southern phenomenon, and a racial one."[29]

In general, lynching occurred in rural communities and small towns, and less frequently in cities. Vigilante justice most frequently occurred in counties that were whiter, less frequently in counties that were blacker. Sparse settlement also seemed to be a factor. According to one estimate, a resident of the 250 more sparsely settled counties in the South had sixty times the probability of being lynched than people living in the region's largest cities. The lynching rate was statistically the highest in Florida and was greatest in terms of absolute numbers in Mississippi. Both states were frontier societies, with more-fragile legal and social systems. Next to Florida, the next highest rates of lynching appeared in Arkansas, Oklahoma, and Texas.[30]

Large Crowd Looking at the Burned Body of Jesse Washington, 18-Year-Old African American, Lynched in Waco, Texas, May 15, 1916. *Library of Congress.*

[28] W. Fitzhugh Brundage, *Lynching in the New South: Georgia and Virginia, 1880–1930* (Urbana: University of Illinois Press, 1993), 8.
[29] Arthur F. Raper, *The Tragedy of Lynching* (Chapel Hill: University of North Carolina Press, 1933), 25.
[30] Raper, *Tragedy of Lynching*, 28–29.

According to the lynchers, the rise of organized racial violence reflected a break-down of law and order. "With sophomoric judges, Demosthenian lawyers, and juries well sprinkled with cranks," complained the *Savannah Morning News*, "the criminal has a good chance of escaping even conviction."[31] Improved transportation led to more mobility and migrants who rode the rails as "hoboes." Migrants, especially African Americans, were regarded suspiciously. Among black people, moreover, there was a profound mistrust of the system of justice, which imprisoned and op-pressed them. Ironically, southern lynchers described themselves as defending their civilization and society, but they did so in the most horrific and grotesque ways.

Defenders of lynching contended that racial violence was directed at sexual vio-lence by black men against white women. According to the novelist Thomas Mann Page, lynching resulted from whites' resolve "to put an end to the ravishing of their women by an inferior race."[32] Whites, fearing black bestiality, fantasized about black male hypersexuality. It was "with this crime that lynching begins," said North Carolinian Clarence H. Poe, "here and here only could the furious mob spirit break through the resisting wall of law and order." It was only because "lynching for rape is excused that lynching for any other crime is ever attempted."[33] That did not mean, however, that most lynchings occurred because of rape. "Generation after generation of Southern whites," concluded NAACP president Walter White after a lengthy in-vestigation in 1929, shared common assumptions: "That Negroes are given to sex crimes, that only lynching can protect white women, that unmentionably horrible deeds can be prevented only through the use of extreme brutality."[34] More often, lynching resulted from nonsex crimes such as theft, assault, or acts of defiance against white authority.

Ida B. Wells. *Public domain.*

Although most lynchings did not result from sexual assault, the rhetoric about vigilante violence often referred to it. Ida B. Wells suggested that at least some of the rape charges against black males arose from consensual sexual relationships with white women. Lynch mobs killed their victims, in some instances, with the "full knowledge" that the relationship was "voluntary and clandestine." In her investigation, Wells concluded that rape charges de-clined over time. "To the unprejudiced, fair-minded person it is only necessary to read and study . . . [these data] in order to show that the charge the Negro is a moral outlaw is a false one, made for the

[31] Ayers, *Vengeance and Justice*, 227–228.
[32] Brundage, *Lynching in the New South*, 58.
[33] Ayers, *Vengeance and Justice*, 240.
[34] Walter White, *Rope & Faggot: A Biography of Judge Lynch*, with a new introduction by Kenneth Robert Janken (Notre Dame, IN: University of Notre Dame Press, 2001), 6. Originally published in 1929.

purpose of injuring the Negro's good name and to create public sentiment against him."[35]

Local law enforcement—which was all-white—generally either looked the other way or possessed insufficient power to combat mob violence. During the nineteenth and early twentieth centuries, there existed little tradition of state or federal intervention in law enforcement. Federal officials lacked constitutional authority; governors only rarely dispatched troops or militia into local communities. As a result, lynchers operated in a power vacuum in which county sheriffs and their deputies were either indifferent to or supported racial violence. "Do you think I'm going to risk my life protecting a nigger?" a southern sheriff exclaimed in the late 1920s. Others agreed with the mob's version of justice. "Except for my oath and bond," said another sheriff, "I'd have killed him myself as soon as they brought him within shooting distance." In many cases, local police were in cahoots with the mob.[36] With feeble law enforcement systems, the legal system depended on extralegal support. Community law enforcement provided manpower when the alarm sounded. Lynch mobs fit into the traditions of the *posse comitatus*, a common-law concept in which the adult male population could assist police in event of a crime. But informal law enforcement developed a life of its own. Enraged mobs focusing on alleged black criminals spent no time with legal niceties. Instead, they administered their own version of summary justice, especially during instances of sensational crime.

In the 1890s and after, lynching sometimes became public spectacles that attracted huge crowds and were administered in ritualistic ways. Two lynchings that occurred during the 1890s illustrate how mob violence became events of public violence seeking to restore community honor. In February 1893, Henry Smith, a black man in Paris, Texas, was accused of brutally murdering three-year-old Myrtle Vance. A mob captured Smith in Arkansas. After he confessed, vigilantes transported him by train back to Paris, where a large crowd of 10,000 people awaited him. Smith was placed on a carnival float mocking him; a large crowd escorted him through town. Encircling Smith on his scaffold in a diameter extending outward six hundred yards, the crowd ripped off his clothes piece by piece. Myrtle Vance's relatives burned him with hot irons. Smith was tortured repeatedly on his stomach, back, and arms, and then the hot irons were thrust down his throat. At last, the scaffold was covered in oil and set ablaze while Smith was still alive. In its sadistic violence, Smith's ritualistic torture and murder went well beyond a public execution. It became a public sport that attracted gawking crowds intent on inflicting vengeance. The law "had no punishment to fit such a deed," commented a local resident. Law "never contemplated such a deed. The people who make the law sat in judgment on the case, and rendered a verdict; the people who uphold and respect the law executed the criminal."[37]

---

[35] Ida B. Wells-Barnett, *On Lynchings*, with an introduction by Patricia Hill Collins (Amherst, NY: Humanity Books, 2002), 108, 202.

[36] Raper, *Tragedy of Lynching*, 13.

[37] Amy Louise Wood, *Lynching and Spectacle: Witnessing Racial Violence in America, 1890–1940* (Chapel Hill: University of North Carolina Press, 2009), 43.

Six years later, in Coweta County, Georgia, southwest of Atlanta, twenty-one-year-old Sam Hose, an African American, was accused of murdering his employer, Alfred Cranford. After the two men argued, Cranford threatened Hose with a gun. Hose responded by throwing an axe, which hit Cranford and killed him instantly. It was reported, inaccurately, that Hose had sexually assaulted Cranford's wife and daughter. A subsequent investigation by antilynching activist Ida B. Wells acknowledged the murder but declared the rape accusation "absolutely false."[38] As an outsider to Coweta County, Hose could easily be depicted as a black "brute." He was a "monster in human form," according to one account, who had "crept into that happy little home . . . with an ax knocked out the brains of that father, snatched the child from its mother, . . . and then by force accomplished his foul purpose." The newspaper press in the area, and in Atlanta, whipped up public sentiment, predicting "determined men" would seek justice by lynching. The press further warned authorities not to obstruct "the people's will." The "black brute, whose carnival of blood and lust has brought death and desolation to the home of one of our best and most worthy citizens," said the *Newnan Herald and Advertiser*, should be "run down and made to suffer the torments of the damned in expiation of his hellish crime."[39]

The mob caught Hose while in flight, on a train at Newnan, Georgia. Railroad officials provided a special train—actually, a locomotive pulling one car—to return to the scene of the crime at the Cranford home. Word of Hose's capture prompted trainloads of people to head toward Newnan, but the mob took more-immediate action. In a ritualized, almost ceremonial way, the mob took Hose to Mattie Cranford, Alfred Cranford's widow and the supposed rape victim, to identify him. She refused to appear, but her mother identified Hose. Denying raping Mattie, he claimed that he killed Cranford in self-defense. The mob wanted to lynch Hose on the spot, but Mattie requested that they move on. Not far down the road, they tied him to a pine tree. A rush of people from the surrounding area arrived, transported by six special cars operated by the railroad; a second special train of ten cars arrived a little later. Four thousand visitors arrived from Atlanta to view the lynching; they expected a spectacle. The mob tortured Hose, cutting off his ears, fingers, and genitals. They then dumped a can of kerosene on him, and he was set ablaze. When it was over, the onlookers left with body parts as souvenirs of the event.[40]

DISFRANCHISEMENT

A cornerstone of Reconstruction had been freed male slaves' voting rights. The franchise served as a bulwark of freedom, considered instrumental to the remaking of the South. For most southern whites, black voting symbolized what they most despised in northern intervention during Reconstruction. Black voting fundamentally

---

[38] Wells-Barnett, *On Lynchings*, 200.
[39] Philip Dray, *At the Hands of Persons Unknown: The Lynching of Black America* (New York: Random House, 2002), 4–5.
[40] Dray, *At the Hands of Persons Unknown*, 9–15.

threatened the racial order, and they remained opposed to it. During the 1870s and 1880s, African American voting survived in voting places across the South, but rarely did its existence go unchallenged.

The Fifteenth Amendment, adopted and ratified in 1870, stipulated that the franchise should not "be denied or abridged" by state or federal governments on the basis of "race, color, or previous condition of servitude." Before readmission to the Union, former Confederate states during Reconstruction adopted new constitutions that provided for black voting. Much of the Klan-inspired violence of the late 1860s and early 1870s was intended to intimidate and suppress black voting and to limit African American officeholding. But if vigilante violence proved especially necessary during Republican rule, it was less so thereafter. Once Reconstruction was reversed during the 1870s, however, the southern states began to impose restrictions on black voting.

Throughout the South, Democratic-controlled legislatures maintained power by partisan control over the machinery of voting, awarding local boards of elections greater discretion to disqualify voters. This partisan stranglehold over the electoral system was based on fraud, sometimes massive fraud, requiring the ruling order's constant vigilance. As a consequence, the post-Reconstruction southern political system became markedly less democratic. For example, in North Carolina, the constitution of 1868 provided for the popular election of local government. When anti-Reconstruction Redeemers revised the state constitution in 1875, they abolished democratic county government, empowering the state legislature to appoint local officials.

Later, in the early 1890s, southern state governments expanded suffrage restriction. The secret ballot, which was widely adopted in the United States between 1889 and 1891, became a way of limiting or even eliminating the black vote. The secret ballot, announced one of its advocates, provided the South "with the only method by which they can get rid of the great bulk of the colored vote in a legal, peaceable, and unobjectionable manner."[41] Secret-ballot laws of the early 1890s supplemented earlier efforts to suppress the vote. In Virginia, for example, in 1893 the Democratic legislature passed the Walton Law. It provided for a secret ballot, stipulating that voters had to draw a line through all the candidates whom they did *not* support. The candidates whom they favored could have no markings whatsoever. Election judges exerted wide latitude in disqualifying ballots that were incorrectly marked, and they used these powers to target black voters. Between 1893 and 1897, as a direct result of the Walton Law, voting among African Americans declined precipitously. In other states, such as Texas, North Carolina, and Tennessee, secret-ballot laws were applied only in areas where blacks were in a majority.

For much of the post-Reconstruction era, southern Democrats, using these methods, held black voters and their white allies at bay. However, during the 1890s two factors changed matters. First, northerners who had been key supporters of

[41] Michael Perman, *Struggle for Mastery: Disfranchisement in the South, 1888–1908* (Chapel Hill: University of North Carolina Press, 2001), 20.

black enfranchisement permitted southern whites to impose their own solution. Second, the chaotic political conditions of the 1890s—with the Populist challenge and some biracial political alliances—unnerved southern Democrats. Many feared that popular discontent might bring in—as it had with North Carolina Fusionists—new regimes possessing different assumptions about how government should function. White southerners intent on excluding black males searched for more-permanent solutions.

The movement for permanent disfranchisement—as opposed to ballot manipulation—led to a more complete elimination of African American voters. Some states pioneered new methods of political exclusion. In Florida, a state convention adopted a new constitution in 1885 that authorized a poll tax, which was used to eliminate black voting. Four years later, in Tennessee, the legislature enacted four laws in 1889 that initiated a secret ballot, required advance registration, and created a poll tax designed to eliminate the black electorate by requiring a cash payment that many of them could not afford and were unwilling to pay. These combinations of laws had the "most noticeable effect," said one contemporary, of causing the "absence of the colored voter."[42] Disfranchisement in these states set off a chain reaction. In 1891, Arkansas centralized the state electoral machinery, giving the state Democratic Party absolute control over elections. A year later, the restricted electorate ratified a constitutional amendment that included a poll tax. Along with the subsequent adoption of a "white primary"—which limited voting in the Democratic primary to whites—Arkansas Democrats effectively eliminated the black vote.

Other southern states moved to adopt constitutional amendments institutionalizing suffrage restriction. In 1890, Mississippi called a constitutional convention that focused on the revision of voting laws. The convention, described by the *Memphis Appeal* as the "most important deliberative assemblage that ever gathered in the South," proposed constitutional amendments requiring advance voter registration, instituting a restrictive secret ballot, and imposing stiff voting requirements (which permitted the disqualification of voters on a variety of grounds). Since these restrictions targeted illiterate voters, they potentially eliminated many white voters. In a measure designed to prevent the disfranchisement of whites, the convention provided local registrars with the power to test voters' ability to read or understand portions of the state constitution. At registrars' discretion, illiterates might vote despite the disfranchising measures.

What became known as the "Mississippi Plan" supplied a model for other states. In South Carolina, using its notorious "eight-box" ballot law, the legislature had already imposed significant restrictions over the electoral process in order to ensure white supremacy. The eight-box law required voters to cast ballots in a different box for each office; ballots misplaced could be disqualified. In addition, the law required registration and awarded local election officials considerable discretion in disqualifying voters. The South Carolina convention also added a poll tax (paid six months in advance of the election) and, as a new item in the disfranchising menu, a literacy

[42] Perman, *Struggle for Mastery*, 58.

test. Banning interracial marriages and requiring segregated schools, the new constitution endorsed white supremacy.

Leading the South Carolina campaign for disfranchisement was Benjamin "Pitchfork Ben" Tillman, former governor and longtime senator. Tillman described the "black serpent" that the convention should confront. The existing electoral system, he claimed, resulted in widespread fraud with a "sword of Damocles suspended over our heads by a single hair."[43] In perpetrating "fraud and intimidation," white South Carolinians had fallen into a "bog and mire that we have been wallowing in for the past twenty-five years.[44] "We have done our level best," Tillman later announced on the floor of the US Senate. "We have scratched our heads to find out how we could eliminate every last one of them. We stuffed ballot boxes. We shot them. We are not ashamed of it."[45]

Disfranchisement did not go unprotested. Black delegates to these constitutional conventions, though badly outnumbered, offered prophetic dissents about the process of electoral "reform." At the South Carolina convention, only six black delegates were present, as compared to 154 whites. "Men upon this floor are clamoring for white supremacy," said black delegate William J. Whipper, while they "call us niggers with the flippancy of barroom attendants." The "brawny arm of the negro," he said, had "cared for you in your cradle" and "protected you in your homes, and yet this is the man you propose to rob of his right to vote." According to white delegates, the trouble with the political system lay with "negro rule." Did such a thing ever exist? he asked. There were more blacks "on your farms," yet "don't your wife rule?" Though nothing he said would change any votes, "sooner or later, God being always right, right will eventually prevail."[46]

Tillman favored disfranchisement as a way to stabilize the existing system of voter suppression. Borrowing from suffrage restrictions adopted in Mississippi, the new constitution adopted restrictions that were designed to evade the Fifteenth Amendment. In measures targeting blacks unable to document their residency, voters had to live in South Carolina for at least a year, and in the voting precinct for four months. Voters could be disfranchised for theft, adultery, arson, wife beating, burglary, and rape (all considered "black crimes"), while murder and assault (considered "white crimes") were omitted. The constitution also required that voters pay taxes on at least $300 of property. In an escape clause for white voters, the new constitution specified that, prior to January 1, 1898, anyone able to read the state constitution or to "understand and explain it" would be declared a lifetime voter. If voters missed these voting requirements, they could be permanently disfranchised.[47]

---

[43] Perman, *Struggle for Mastery*, 111.
[44] Francis Butler Simkins, *Pitchfork Ben Tillman, South Carolinian* (Baton Rouge: Louisiana State University Press, 1944), 295.
[45] Chandler Davidson and Bernard Grofman, eds., *Quiet Revolution in the South: The Impact of the Voting Rights Act, 1965–1990* (Princeton, NJ: Princeton University Press, 1994), 194.
[46] Paul D. Escott and David R. Goldfield, eds., *Major Problems in the History of the American South*, vol. 2, *The New South* (Lexington, MA: D. C. Heath, 1990), 180–182; Simkins, *Pitchfork Ben Tillman*, 300.
[47] Simkins, *Pitchfork Ben Tillman*, 297.

In 1889, Henry Cabot Lodge, a Massachusetts congressman, proposed legislation requiring federal supervision of elections. The House of Representatives approved the measure, but it failed passage in the Senate. With support among northern Republicans, the Lodge "force" bill aroused a firestorm of southern opposition. While white people had "an inborn capacity for free institutions," claimed Mississippi senator James Z. George, black voters were "an unsafe depository of political power."[48] However, after the failure of the Lodge bill, northern Republicans abandoned black voting in the South. The trend instead moved in the opposite direction, as federal intervention in southern elections became a still more remote possibility. Once Democrats regained control of the presidency and Congress in 1892, they undid any further federal intervention in southern voting. The ability of these southern state conventions to institutionalize the political disempowerment of black males—and the abrogation of the Fifteenth Amendment—clearly reflected northern acquiescence.

The success of disfranchisement depended also on the posture of the US Supreme Court. During the 1870s, the court refused to endorse direct federal intervention in elections. In response to the disfranchising conventions, the court expanded on this ruling. In *Williams v. Mississippi* (1898), it unanimously rejected a challenge to Mississippi disfranchisement. The decision rested on the specious logic that the impact of the constitutional changes was distinct from their intent, which was not discriminatory. The law, the justices said, applied equally to "weak and vicious white men as well as weak and vicious black men, and whatever is sinister in their intention . . . could be prevented by both races by the exertion of that duty which voluntarily pays taxes and refrains from crime." Mississippi's election laws, said the court, "do not on their face discriminate between the races, and it has not been shown that their actual administration was evil; only that evil was possible under them."[49] Five years later, in *Giles v. Harris* (1903), a case involving disfranchisement in Alabama, the court similarly refused to intervene.[50]

Between 1890 and 1908, following the examples of Mississippi and South Carolina, most of the South adopted suffrage restriction. The preferred methods became constitutional convention or amendment. In 1898, Louisiana imposed a literacy test and a property requirement of $300 per voter, combined with a "grandfather clause" exempting from suffrage restriction anyone and their descendants who had voted prior to January 1, 1867. In North Carolina, voters by referendum adopted constitutional amendments providing for a literacy test to limit the electorate. Subsequently, Alabama (1901), Texas (1901), Virginia (1902), and Georgia (1908) all adopted radical restrictions over the electorate, seeking the elimination of black voters.

The results of these measures became immediately apparent. Across the South, African American voters could not vote, with only a few exceptions. The instance of

---

[48] Perman, *Struggle for Mastery*, 42.
[49] *Williams v. Mississippi*, 170 U.S. 213 (1898).
[50] *Giles v. Harris*, 189 U.S. 475 (1903).

Louisiana is illustrative. In 1896, prior to disfranchisement, over 130,000 black voters were registered to vote. By 1900, this number had been reduced to slightly over 5,300. Ten years later, only 730 African American voters remained on the state's registration rolls. In South Carolina, with a black majority, there were only 5,500 black voters in the entire state by 1896. Alabama's black electorate declined from over 181,000 to about 3,000 between 1900 and 1902.

The arrival of state-required segregation followed on the heels of the exclusion of African Americans. Much of such segregation involved public spaces, especially public accommodations, restaurants, and railroad and streetcar transportation. The Supreme Court's decision in *Plessy v. Ferguson* (1896), which involved testing whether a Louisiana segregation law violated the Fourteenth Amendment's equal-protection clause, ruled that governments could require segregation in transportation if the dictum of "separate but equal" could be maintained. "Separate but equal" provided a formula for evading the Fourteenth Amendment's requirement of equal protection under the law. Around the turn of the twentieth century, legislatures and municipal governments began requiring the segregation of railroad cars. Louisiana enacted a law in 1890 requiring the segregation of all railway cars; the law mandated that black and white passengers ride in separate cars.

A more complex set of issues arose around electric streetcars, which were becoming a popular form of local conveyance in the 1880s and 1890s. In 1891, the Georgia legislature enacted the first law segregating transportation, providing a vague standard of requiring it "as much as practicable," with enforcement by the transportation companies. Transportation companies opposed these laws because of the difficulty of enforcing them, but that did little to stop the momentum toward segregation. Local ordinances were passed in 1900 in Atlanta, Rome, and Augusta, Georgia, along with Montgomery, Alabama. Between 1901 and 1903, Jacksonville, Mobile, Columbia, and Houston all enacted laws requiring segregated streetcars. These laws became progressively more stringent, as a number of states enacted measures requiring streetcar segregation.

This form of Jim Crow was especially humiliating to African Americans, who were often subjected to rough treatment by drivers and conductors, who enforced the segregation. Separate seating was "so humiliating that the better class of our folk seem to share in a feeling of mingled disgust and bewilderment," commented an observer in Tennessee in the early 1900s. Nearly four decades after emancipation, Tennessee had "imposed obloquy and shame upon those of her citizens whom she should encourage and lift up." Many African Americans refused to ride streetcars, "being rather ashamed of the disgrace."[51]

Across the South, spontaneous and sometimes well-organized boycotts emerged in protest of the segregation of transportation. Between 1900 and 1906, boycotts occurred in some twenty-eight southern cities. Calling the Virginia law "a gratuitous insult . . . to every one with a drop of Negro blood," a group of Lynchburg blacks

---

[51] August Meier and Elliott Rudwick, "Negro Boycotts of Jim Crow Streetcars in Tennessee," *American Quarterly* 21, no. 4 (1969): 757.

urged a boycott, saying "Let us touch to the quick the white man's pocket." Although these boycotts failed, they foreshadowed subsequent organized movements to overthrow the segregation of public spaces a half century later.

In 1904, when Clifton Johnson traveled throughout the South, publishing his account *Highways and Byways of the South,* he concluded with a chapter titled "The Niggers." Traveling across the Mason-Dixon line, he noticed the ever-present segregation of railroad cars, something that was "characteristic of the whole social structure of the entire South." Black people occupied a "position of servility and inferiority" in which they were "constantly reminded" of their inferiority. The term "nigger" was a common phrase that was "opprobrious" but a necessary term reminding blacks of their inferiority. To most southern whites, a "negro must constantly in word and action acknowledge the whites' superiority." Black people must always show deference, while it was "optional" whether whites "shall be respectful in return."[52]

Rapid changes came to the South during the closing decade of the nineteenth century. The economic transformation unhinged social moorings, resulting in a crisis atmosphere, compounded by the severe depression, during the 1890s. The Populists challenged the status quo, proposing a reassertion of the traditional primacy of agriculture and resisting how market forces had altered life. Populism suffered defeat and collapse, virtually disappearing as a political force by 1900. By the end of the 1890s, many of the lingering questions after emancipation were answered, for the most part at the expense of African Americans. Political exclusion of most black voters, along with the imposition of state-sanctioned white supremacy, marked a low point in the status of black people. Disfranchisement paved the way for the formal adoption of additional measures of Jim Crow segregation throughout the South.

The elimination of most black voting rendered the Republican Party uncompetitive in southern politics, ensuring a Democratic monopoly on officeholding. The one-party, Democratic state, based on disfranchisement and white supremacy, ushered in what was known as the Progressive Era in a program of sectional harmony, modernized basic services, and economic development through industrialization and modern agriculture.

[52] Clifton Johnson, *Highways and Byways of the South* (New York: MacMillan Company, 1904), 330–333.

16

THE PROGRESSIVE SOUTH

IN THE SOUTH, the Progressive Era featured modernizing leadership emanating from the growing urban areas. That leadership depended on disfranchisement and one-party rule, and early-twentieth-century reformers favored exclusion of African Americans from politics and the new system of segregated public spaces. United by a common belief in a new political order, these reformers sought a fuller reunification and an end to sectional animosity that would bring the South into the national mainstream. The Progressive Era also marked a coming of age for middle-class women, who played a large role in shaping and directing reform, especially social reform. During the early years of the twentieth century, women exerted unprecedented public involvement in leadership by claiming their positions as mothers and protectors of the family.

FOLLOWING THE COLOR LINE

On the day after the fiftieth anniversary of the end of the Battle of Gettysburg, on July 4, 1913, President Woodrow Wilson spoke to a gathering of veterans. "Look around you upon the field of Gettysburg," he declared, calling on the audience to visualize the "fierce heats and agony of battle, column hurled against column, battery bellowing to battery!" Both sides, North and South, exhibited valor "greater no man shall see in war; and self-sacrifice, and loss to the uttermost; the high recklessness of exalted devotion which does not count the cost." Creating a nation, the bloody Civil War required the "blood and sacrifice of multitudes of unknown men lifted to a great stature in the view of all generations by knowing no limit to their manly willingness to serve."

Fiftieth anniversary of the Battle of Gettysburg, July 1913. *Library of Congress.*

Wilson suggested more about the meaning of the Civil War for early-twentieth-century Americans. Rather than "ghostly hosts," Wilson foresaw commanding another army that "might work out in days of peace and settled order the life of a great Nation." This new army would comprise "the people themselves, the great and the small, without class or difference of kind or race or origin; and undivided in interest, if we have but the vision to guide and direct them and order their lives aright in what we do." The army's enlistment lay in constitutions and political order; the recruits were "the little children crowding in"; and the army's provisions lay in the nation's factories, shops, mines, forests, and fields. The army's objective was "their freedom, their right to lift themselves from day to day and behold the things they have hoped for, and so make way for still better days for those whom they love who are to come after them." Every day the army pushed its campaign forward, "by plan and with an eye to some great destiny."[1]

Wilson's Gettysburg speech addressed the national process of reconciliation and the continuing, disputed nature of what the Civil War meant. In particular, almost as soon as the guns were silenced, various groups contested the meaning of the war—and how they remembered it. While African Americans stressed emancipation and the destruction of slavery, many white southerners saw the war as a matter of states' rights and a dispute between fundamentally similar societies. By the time Wilson delivered his Gettysburg speech, the southern white view had largely prevailed, and reconciliation meant a smoothing over of the past of slavery and a war fought to end it.

Many white southerners, with the American victory over Spain in the war of 1898, urged a new nationalism that would seek reconciliation and reintegration. Observers noted that the American military armada that invaded Cuba was staged from the Gulf Coast ports of Tampa and New Orleans. The American military that smashed Spanish resistance in 1898 and destroyed the Spanish fleet in the Philippines included many southerners, including even some Confederate

---

[1] Address at Gettysburg (July 4, 1913), Woodrow Wilson; available at http://millercenter.org/president/speeches/detail/3787.

veterans. Southerners joined the volunteer force eagerly, in the first war fought since Appomattox. "Northerner and Southerner," said one observer, "stood, in blue again, side by side in a common cause." Former Confederate cavalry officer Joseph Wheeler, at the sprightly age of fifty-two, volunteered and, commissioned as a major general, commanded a cavalry division and led his men into battle. The war, according to this account, had caused the memory of disunion and secession to "grow dim and opened a vista to all America."[2]

This new attachment to the American nation reflected the racial settlement of the 1890s that brought disfranchisement and Jim Crow segregation; the new era meant one-party rule, white supremacy, and modernization mixed together. Charles Brantley Aycock was elected governor of North Carolina in 1900 after an organized white supremacy campaign that featured racially charged editorials, cartoons, and language designed to inflame fears of "negro rule." Aycock's election came on the heels of the violent overthrow of the Republican local government in Wilmington in 1898 and, in 1900, the passage of a constitutional amendment providing for suffrage restriction by a literacy test. At his inauguration on January 15, 1901, Aycock explained his version of post-Reconstruction southern history—a version that prevailed among white southerners seizing power during the 1890s. During the decades after the Civil War and emancipation, "we struggled in every way against the evils of a suffrage based on manhood only." North Carolina black voters supported the Republican Party and helped them gain power. The result, Aycock claimed, was "new evils and wrongs," while "lawlessness stalked the State like a pestilence." Political power, he contended, emboldened black males' sexual aggression and the "screams of women fleeing from pursuing brutes." In Aycock's telling, the white supremacy campaign of 1898 became a "victory for good government" in which whites secured "life, liberty and property." Aycock also equated disfranchisement, an obvious injustice, with progress. The literacy test and suffrage restriction, he argued, meant improved public education. Henceforth, he announced, "in every home there will be the knowledge that no child can attain the true dignity of citizenship without learning at least to read and write." Political citizenship meant literacy, which required a new effort in support of public schools. Industrial development required intelligence, not of the few but of the many, and education brought concrete economic benefits. It was of the "utmost importance from a material point of view that our whole people should be educated."[3]

Most of what Aycock claimed—that disfranchisement meant progress—was a sham, but it became a common mantra among early-twentieth-century reformers. Others made the connections among sectional reconciliation, southern allegiance to an American nationality, and the political exclusion of African Americans. Many were southerners who left their native region but remained actively interested in the

[2] Peter J. Hamilton, "The South in National Politics, 1865–1909," in *The South in the Building of the Nation*, vol. 4, *Political History*, ed. Franklin L. Riley (Richmond, VA: Southern Historical Publication Society, 1909), 551, 555.

[3] R. D. W. Connor and Clarence Poe, *The Life and Speeches of Charles Brantley Aycock* (Garden City, NY: Doubleday, Page, 1912), 228–238.

South. North Carolina native Walter Hines Page was ten years old when the Civil War ended. In 1883, after a stint in newspapers in Kentucky, Missouri, and New York, Page found a newspaper in Raleigh, North Carolina, the *State Chronicle*. Page used the *Chronicle* to advocate modernization of the state through education and industry, but his program fell on deaf ears. Leaving Raleigh in 1885, Page wrote four letters bitterly denouncing North Carolina's leadership as "mummies" who lived in the past and kept the state backward. The rest of Page's career was outside the South, as editor of the *Forum* and the *Atlantic* and then as the founding publisher of Doubleday & Page. Though an expatriate, he remained a cosmopolitan interpreter of the South in speeches and publications, and an enthusiastic advocate of reform.

Another southern expatriate, William Garrott Brown, expressed similar views. Entering Harvard in 1889, he earned a master's degree and then became the university's archivist. A prolific historian, Brown was also an interpreter of the late-nineteenth- and early-twentieth-century emerging South. Disfranchisement had lamentably occurred, because the "responsible public men of the North" were "disinclined to interfere." Yet, the political exclusion of black people, Brown wrote, had helped reintegrate the South back into the nation. White southerners were "restive under the restraints which keep them from entering actively and fearlessly into the larger life of the Republic." There had been an increase in "Americanism," a new "pride in the flag, pride in the prosperity and prestige of the United States." The South was now "too much alive to outer things, too cognizant of a civilization ampler than its own, not to feel keenly the limitations upon its participation in national political contests."[4]

Another southern-born expatriate, Woodrow Wilson, was elected president in 1912—the first southerner to occupy the White House since the Civil War. Inaugurated March 4, 1913, Wilson brought with him an administration filled with white southerners and a Congress dominated by southern Democrats. William G. McAdoo, a native Georgian, became his secretary of the treasury; Texan Albert Burleson, his postmaster general; Josephus Daniels, his secretary of the navy; and David F. Houston of Texas, his secretary of agriculture. "All the way from styles in head-gear to opinions on the tariff," said one observer, "the flavor and color of things in Washington are Southern." It was the "spirit and disposition, the purpose and inspiration, the tendency and direction which we note in the guiding forces of affairs. All these point unerringly to the South. In Washington you feel it in the air, you note it in the changed and changing ways of business."[5]

Congress, controlled by a Democratic majority after the 1912 elections, also had a distinctively southern flavor. Because disfranchisement had established undisputed Democratic control in their home states, southern congressmen enjoyed seniority—the key to power. In the Sixty-Fifth Congress, nine of the fifteen ranking Democrats in the Senate were southern, and they held key committee chairmanships. Southern

[4] William Garrott Brown, *The Lower South in American History* (New York: Macmillan, 1902), 259–260.
[5] Woodward, *Origins of the New South*, 480.

Democrats also controlled twenty-eight of the fifty-nine standing committees in the House of Representatives. In the Senate, Confederate veteran and Virginia senator Thomas S. Martin was majority leader, while North Carolinian Claude Kitchin held a similar post in the House.

Wilson's inauguration exhibited themes of sectional reconciliation. The South, which was "beaten, bleeding, prostrate" only a half century earlier, said one observer, had now "come back to rule the Union." Chief Justice Edward Douglass White, a Louisianian and Confederate veteran, administered the oath of office at Wilson's inauguration. With a warm March day, the inaugural parade was greeted by a vocal group, a number of whom were southerners. The four-hour procession from the Capitol to the White House involved three thousand marchers, and a Rebel Yell or a rendition of Dixie by the band broke out whenever a southerner passed.[6]

Seven years before Wilson's inauguration, between September 22 and 24, 1906, a major race riot in Atlanta became one of the more important examples of racial violence in the Progressive Era urban South. State militia finally intervened, but only after Atlanta's black community responded by arming and defending themselves; the militia did little to arrest white perpetrators, instead apprehending three hundred black residents. The violence cost an unknown number of deaths of black people, with estimates ranging from twenty-five to more than a hundred. Officially, there were only two white deaths, although black leaders claimed many more had actually died. To some extent, the Atlanta Riot exposed the contradictions in that city, supposedly the paragon of what the New South meant. For advocates of reconciliation, the New South meant racial harmony, and at the end of the nineteenth century white southerners asked for a settlement that would assure white supremacy in exchange for racial stability.

This combination of hope and oppression became an emblem of the Progressive Era. What occurred in Atlanta seemed to typify an unraveling of the social order across the South, the inability of public and private institutions to manage social and political stresses and strains. Early-twentieth-century reformers were cosmopolitans, generally from the new urban areas of the South, well educated, often female, and middle class in orientation. They were acutely aware of the growing distance between the industrializing North and Midwest and the rural, economically underdeveloped South. They thus sought to modernize their region by revamping institutions.

THE GALVESTON HURRICANE

On September 8, 1900, the worst natural disaster in American history, a terrible hurricane, struck Galveston, Texas. Four days earlier, after passing over Cuba as a tropical storm, the storm turned west and, over warm Caribbean waters, gathered

---

[6]   George Brown Tindall, *The Emergence of the New South, 1913–1945* (Baton Rouge: Louisiana State University Press, 1967), 1–2.

significant strength. In the absence of accurate weather forecasting or ship-to-shore communications, the hurricane struck the Texas coast with little warning. The category 4 storm reached peak destructive force during the early evening. A massive, fifteen-foot-high storm surge struck the island where Galveston was located, inundating the city of 38,000 people, in what residents called a "giant swell" flooding the island.

The great hurricane utterly destroyed Galveston. Six thousand people perished, most of them drowning victims. Another six thousand fled within a month of the disaster. The worst areas of devastation were located in the south and east sides of the city, facing the Gulf, with entire neighborhoods and four thousand structures washed away. "We looked out of the window," wrote one survivor the morning after the hurricane, "and of all the beautiful homes that were between our house and the beach not one was left. It is a just a clean sweep; nothing but desolation."[7] Most of Galveston's infrastructure similarly disappeared, including the bridges connecting the island to the mainland, as well as electrical, telegraph, and telephone lines. Everywhere in the destroyed city were corpses, debris, and the remains of the city.[8]

Galveston's reconstruction required a massive effort. An immediate challenge was the disposal of thousands of corpses decomposing in the September heat. Deputies commandeered fifty black men to load seven hundred bodies on a barge to dump eighteen miles out in the Gulf. But the bodies soon returned and washed ashore. "The sea as though it could never be satisfied with its gruesome work washed these bodies back upon the shore," one commentator wrote, "the waves being the hearses that carried them in to be buried under the sand." Bodies were thrown into temporary graves or stored in ad hoc morgues. Drastic measures were required, including the cremation of the corpses, work that took into November to complete.[9]

Aftermath of the great Galveston hurricane of September 1900.
Library of Congress.

The longer-term needs of Galveston's reconstruction were to restore basic services. The police force was small, about seventy men, unequipped to deal with the aftermath of looting and crime. The state militia restored order, but local government was simply unable to perform its most important functions. In response, the mayor established a Central Relief Committee (CRC) to take charge of basic public services and relief. The CRC organized early efforts at reconstruction by distributing relief among Galveston's twelve wards, each

[7] Elizabeth Hayes Turner, *Women, Culture, and Community: Religion and Reform in Galveston, 1880–1920* (New York: Oxford University Press, 1997), 33.
[8] Patricia Bellis Bixel and Elizabeth Hayes Turner, *Galveston and the 1900 Storm: Catastrophe and Catalyst* (Austin: University of Texas Press, 2000), 17–43.
[9] Bixel and Turner, *Galveston,* 48.

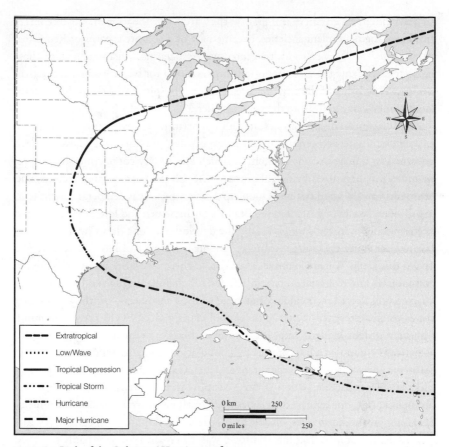

MAP 16.1 Path of the Galveston Hurricane of 1900

with a commissary directing activities and food and relief distribution. The ward chairmen in charge of the commissaries directed cleanup and debris removal, drafting the able-bodied into the effort. A building committee began the massive job of rebuilding the destroyed city. Subsequently, the rebuilding of Galveston included an immense program to prevent future disasters, including a massive seawall.

The Galveston disaster attracted national attention, with contributions arriving from all over the world. Along with the army, organizations such as the Salvation Army, the Children's Aid Society, and the American National Red Cross became involved. Ten days after the hurricane, famed nurse and Red Cross president Clara Barton rode a special train to Galveston loaded with relief supplies. Working with the CRC, the primarily female workforce and leadership of the Red Cross employed its experience and expertise in administering relief activities. As a result of its national appeal, supplies poured in, along with financial support.

The Red Cross's involvement offered an opportunity for the emergence of Galveston's white middle-class female activists. The organization provided a relief structure that supplied each of the city's twelve wards with provisions but stipulated that female chairmen run the program at the ward level. The women, mostly coming from existing benevolent societies, became part of a volunteer corps of Red Cross auxiliaries. The Women's Health Protective Association, organized out of these auxiliaries, became the most important organization for white women activists in the city. "The ladies of the city," declared Barton, "in spite of the shock, grief, mutilated homes, came grandly to the work of relief."[10]

The Galveston disaster also created an opportunity to restructure government. Like most nineteenth-century urban communities, pre-hurricane Galveston was governed by a mayor/council system in which twelve city council members represented wards organized by neighborhood. Though inefficient, cantankerous, and often corrupt, the ward system of municipal government was democratic, representing diverse class and racial interests. Leading businessmen and families who wanted better public improvements, especially the development of a deep-water port, long favored changing this system to make it more efficient and less democratic. The Galveston Deep Water Committee, an elite eighteen-member group of banking, commercial, and real-estate interests, lobbied for changes. In 1890 and 1895, the city charter was altered to provide for at-large council members—on the theory that these would represent a "better" class of politicians with citywide interests in mind. The new system made it impossible to elect black aldermen, although African Americans composed a fifth of the city's population, and also eliminated working-class representation. In 1900, the extent to which Galveston's system of local government failed is debatable, yet its inability to cope with the hurricane disaster provided the opportunity for reformers to experiment with new forms of local government. "I cannot say the storm is responsible for all the bad conditions now existing," wrote one resident, "for it is a fact that our town was, to say the least, very badly governed for some time past."[11]

In November 1900, the Deep Water Committee drew up a new city charter with emergency powers. According to this new charter, presented to the legislature in January 1901, an appointed board of commissioners would govern Galveston on a businesslike, efficient basis, maintaining basic services and administering them effectively. Two commissioners were elected at-large; the other three were appointed by the governor. All five served two-year terms. While one commissioner served as mayor, the other four ran public safety, streets and public works, water and sewerage, and finance. Requesting that the Texas legislature enact the new charter, a group of reformers declared that it was "a question with us of civic life or death." In April 1901, the legislature enacted the measure.[12]

What became known as the "Galveston Plan"—the so-called commission form of government—became a model for urban government across the United States. It

[10] Turner, *Women, Culture, and Community*, 190.
[11] Bradley Robert Rice, *Progressive Cities: The Commission Government Movement in America, 1901–1920* (Austin: University of Texas Press, 1977), 6; Turner, *Women, Culture, and Community*, 195–196.
[12] Bixel and Turner, *Galveston*, 92; Rice, *Progressive Cities*, 13.

became especially popular in the early-twentieth-century South. In Texas, the use of the commission plan spread to six other cities, including Houston, Dallas, and Fort Worth. Like Galveston, an appointive municipal government seemed to make possible more-rapid modernization of public services. The Galveston Plan became the "Texas Idea," and other municipalities sought to adopt the model. "In every city we visited," reported a visiting committee from the Illinois legislature, "we found the almost unanimous sentiment of the citizens favoring the commission form of government." Seeking out the opinion of "all classes of citizens," they concluded that popular enthusiasm was "hardly describable." There was a "marked improvement in the conduct of affairs of these cities under this plan of municipal government."[13] The commission plan was refined with a significant adaptation that occurred in the small city of Staunton, Virginia. Rather than adopt the commission system, Staunton hired a city manager to oversee the running of municipal government.

Reformers' attempts to modernize the functioning of government formed an essential part of Progressivism all over the United States. The impetus for change came out of towns and cities, and from the urban middle classes populating them. Reformers looked to corporate models of organization; the business standard of "efficiency" served as a buzzword. The attempt to reform government also shaped the operation of state government, as coalitions elected reform governors and legislatures in various states, dedicated to making government more modernized. Both at the local and state levels, efforts to reform government were in many respects antidemocratic. It seemed to many reformers that excessive democracy caused corruption and inefficiency; the "best people," they contended, should manage public affairs. Progressive reform in the South emerged in the post-disfranchisement environment, and the restricted electorate provided the political basis for reform.

WOMEN AND REFORM

During the generation after the Civil War, the status of women slowly changed in the South. Although Victorian taboos restricted women's ability to work outside the home, women became involved in activism in the public sphere. New opportunities for work opened up, as a handful of women were able to become physicians and lawyers. Scores of other women joined the workforce in the burgeoning textile mills springing up across the Piedmont South. Women became a powerful force behind early-twentieth-century reform, and their involvement coincided with their expanded public presence.

In the post–Civil War era, women became more active in missionary societies, women's clubs, and reform-minded organizations designed to protect the home. Home and foreign missions attracted southern Protestant women as churches organized women's boards of missions. Mission activities often involved charity work with the poor. Laura Askew Haygood, graduating from the all-women's

[13] Rice, *Progressive Cities*, 31.

Wesleyan College in Macon, Georgia, became active in southern Methodist home missions. She helped create the Trinity Home Mission in Atlanta in 1882, the goals of which included the "physical, mental and moral elevation of the poor of the city."[14]

The Woman's Christian Temperance Union (WCTU), founded in 1874, first appeared in the South five years later. Although segregated, the organization existed in separate chapters that communicated occasionally across racial lines. By the 1880s and 1890s, the WCTU had become the largest female reform organization in the South. Its appeal lay in expressing women's moral power and its assertion over the primarily male world of saloons and drinking. In addition to pressing for temperance and prohibition, some WCTU activists became involved in causes such as education, child labor, prison reform, and antilynching campaigns. The group became an organizational training ground for female leadership. The women's organization served as "the golden key that unlocked the prison door of pent-up possibilities" and the "generous liberator, the joyous iconoclast, the discoverer, the developer of Southern women," said Mississippi reformer Belle Kearney. After she attended a national WCTU convention, she remarked that she had acquired a "new vision of woman's life."[15]

Many other women became active in the women's club movement, which grew in popularity after the mid-1880s. Early clubs were historical and literary, often reading groups by women in a single-sex setting. Soon clubwomen became involved in social concerns related to traditional female spheres of influence—children, education, and the home. The "improvement of health, the betterment of morals, the modernizing of education and humanizing of penology are perhaps the most vital matters in which North Carolina women have interested themselves," declared a North Carolina clubwoman.[16] The women's club movement spread across the South, with every state in the region represented by 1907 and all participating in the General Federation of Women's Clubs by 1910. Women's clubs provided yet another setting for activism.

Black women also used women's clubs as an outlet for public activism. Much of the ugly racism of the Progressive Era—lynching, disfranchisement, and segregation—was focused on black men and the alleged threat that they presented. Black women found a niche under Jim Crow that had not previously existed. Ida Wells Barnett, a vocal critic of lynching, was a leading organizer of black women's clubs, and these in many ways mirrored the same activities of white women's clubs—activism in children's issues, neighborhood improvement, education, and health. Black women's clubs focused especially on racial uplift in the age of Jim Crow. In 1896, the National Association of Colored Women's Clubs (NACW) was organized, with Mary Church Terrell serving as its first president. Born in Memphis in 1863, Terrell graduated from

[14] Anne Firor Scott, *The Southern Lady: From Pedestal to Politics, 1830–1930* (Chicago: University of Chicago Press, 1970), 142–143.
[15] Belle Kearney, *A Slaveholder's Daughter* (New York: Abbey, 1900), 118.
[16] Scott, *The Southern Lady*, 159.

Oberlin College in Ohio and moved to Washington, DC. A suffragist, Terrell participated in the National American Woman Suffrage Association.

Local black women's clubs were actively involved in reform efforts. In Atlanta, Lugenia Burns Hope helped organize the Neighborhood Union in 1908. The Neighborhood Union proved one of the most effective of the black women's clubs in its emphasis on racial uplift, education improvement, sanitation and health, arts and recreation facilities, and antiprostitution efforts. The wife of Morehouse College president John Hope, Lugenia enjoyed the relative autonomy of a larger southern city and the security of marriage to a prominent black leader. But she became one of the most important black women leaders in the early-twentieth-century South. Most of black and white women's activities occurred in isolation from each other. Not until after World War I were there efforts to cross the racial divide.

Middle-class white women's missionary and club activities often led them toward projects in public health, education, city beautification, parks and playgrounds development, poor relief, and antiprostitution efforts. Clubwomen became especially involved in improving the physical environment of cities. Many of them became involved in efforts at conservation, for example by organizing local Audubon societies to prevent the wholesale slaughter of birds by plume hunters (who used the popular feathers for women's hats) and sportsmen, often to the verge of extinction. Clubwomen were also especially interested in urban schools, creating orphanages and establishing kindergartens.

As in the urban North and Midwest, settlement houses became centers of social improvement, with women running their operation. Founded in 1896 by Episcopalian rector Beverley Warner, the Kingsley House in New Orleans became one of the South's better-known settlement houses. A Princeton graduate and New Jersey native, Warner was deeply influenced by the Social Gospel, the movement of liberal evangelicals to use Christianity to solve social problems. In 1885, Warner published a novel, *Troubled Waters*, which examined the problems of the urban working poor. Warner described a "trinity of problems"—labor, poverty, and wealth—that were leading to "the proportions and hideousness of a trinity of trouble for present and future generations of this republic to deal with." Everything touched "everybody in this world," he wrote. "Everything comes back upon us. . . . We may suffer Poverty to go on increasing, with no new effort to stay or prevent it but that maudlin and mistaken one of doing everything for the poor, without providing them the means at far less expense to do for themselves. . . . Poverty works upward as well as downward."[17]

Although Warner helped found Kingsley House, its success depended on a group of women who soon came to run its affairs. Jean Gordon, active in anti-child-labor campaigns in New Orleans, started a day nursery. Eleanor Laura McMain, a native Louisianian, moved to New Orleans in the 1890s to work in the Free Kindergarten Association. In 1900, McMain became head of Kingsley House. She studied leading

[17] Beverley Ellison Warner, *Troubled Waters. A Problem of To-Day* (Philadelphia: J. B. Lippincott, 1885), 323.

settlement houses elsewhere, such as Hull House in Chicago, in search of useful models. Kingsley House, which soon became nonsectarian, focused its activities on health, education, and social betterment of the New Orleans poor. Operating a health clinic, the settlement house also ran a kindergarten, adult education, a library, athletics programs, and playgrounds. McMain became a key figure in the creation of the Woman's League in New Orleans, the leading social reform organization in the city.

The expansion of education in the South, public and private, opened up new opportunities for women. As elsewhere in the United States, women dominated the ranks of schoolteachers. All-female teacher-training institutions came into existence in new "normal" schools—named for the French *écoles normales*. Normal schools produced teachers, providing new educational opportunities. In 1884, the Virginia legislature established the State Female Normal School in Farmville, in southern Virginia, while Mississippi established the State Industrial Institute and College. By the 1890s, most southern states had normal schools to produce teachers for the public schools. In most instances, normal schools were little more than high schools, with limited educational opportunities. Still, teacher training provided an opening wedge for some expansion of the public presence of women.

Perhaps the most ambitious teacher-training institution was the North Carolina State Normal and Industrial School for Women, established in 1891. President Charles Duncan McIver ran the school, remaining its dominant figure until his death in 1906. Graduating from the University of North Carolina (UNC) in 1881, McIver taught in public schools in Durham and Winston, North Carolina, before running popular and successful teachers' institutes across the state in 1889. McIver, with a strong force of personality, possessed a passion to expand women's role in education. "He was from the beginning a presence and a force," remembered Walter Hines Page, a UNC classmate and fellow educational reformer.[18] In 1891, McIver created the State Normal with a distinctive philosophy in mind.

McIver came to believe that women's education held the key to transforming southern society, constituting a "strategic point in the education of the race." Wives and mothers were "priestess[es] in humanity's temple," presiding at the "fountain head of civilization," while the centers of modern civilization were homes and schools, which were "made by women rather than by men." The "cheapest, easiest, and surest road to universal education," he once said, was to "educate those who are to be the mothers and teachers of future generations." An educated man might father illiterate children, but the "children of educated women are never illiterate." Men held political power, McIver said, but the political structure bore "both the marks of masculinity and neglect . . . [which were] plainly visible." "Educate a man and you have educated one person," he often told audiences. "Educate a mother and you have educated a whole family."[19]

[18] Walter H. Page, "McIver, a Leader of the People," *World's Work* XIII (December 1906): 8265.
[19] Charles L. Coon, "Charles Duncan McIver and His Educational Services, 1886–1906," in *Report of the Commissioner of Education for 1907*, 329–339 (Washington, DC: Government Printing Office, 1908); available at http://archive.org/stream/charlesduncanmci151coon/ charlesduncanmci151coon_djvu.txt.

McIver pushed North Carolina young women toward public involvement, but the lines separating such involvement from politics often proved thin. Southern women's activism during the Progressive Era, though nominally operating within established gender norms, almost inevitably veered toward political questions. How could women establish what they called "municipal housekeeping" if they were deprived of the vote? The more women became involved in social reform, the more many of them recognized a connection between social problems and the absence of female political power.

Woman suffrage thus seemed a natural consequence of activism. Suffragists had existed in the South since the Civil War, as part of a larger national movement to achieve voting rights for women. Yet, the energizing impact of club, missionary, and temperance campaigning, along with Progressive Era reforms, created momentum as a new generation saw the suffrage as the culmination of social reform. Nellie Nugent Somerville was a Methodist woman who became active in church missions, women's clubs, and the WCTU. In 1894, she became the corresponding secretary of the latter organization. In 1897, Somerville joined the suffrage movement, helping found the Mississippi Woman Suffrage Association. In 1915, she became vice president of the National American Woman Suffrage Association.

Inhabitants of southern towns and cities, most of these "new suffragists" were generally affluent white women. Madeline McDowell Breckinridge came from distinguished Kentucky lineage and lived in Lexington. Lila Meade Valentine, a suffragist possessing First Family of Virginia lineage, lived in Richmond. In Texas, Minnie Fisher Cunningham of Houston led a statewide movement that enjoyed substantial support from Dallas. Pattie Ruffner Jacobs was the energetic president of suffrage

Madeline McDowell Breckinridge. *Library of Congress.*

leagues in Birmingham and Alabama. The "greatest grip" of the suffrage movement in Birmingham, according to one account, was among the homes of the "most exclusive women." Suffrage activism appealed to "old and aristocratic families" with "culture, high social position and wide personal influence."[20] "The women of the leisure class," observed Jacobs, "can afford to go around stirring up enthusiasm for the movement which the women of other classes cannot do."[21]

Many elite women made a transition from women's clubs and social activism to suffrage. How could Christian women love their neighbors as themselves "without feeling compelled to take part in the betterment of the conditions of her neighbors, namely of the community?" declared Virginian Adele Clark. But

[20] William A. Link, *The Paradox of Southern Progressivism, 1880–1930* (Chapel Hill: University of North Carolina Press, 1992), 185.

[21] Marjorie Spruill Wheeler, *New Women of the New South: The Leaders of the Woman Suffrage Movement in the Southern States* (New York: Oxford University Press, 1993), 46.

how could this occur unless women participated in choosing "the officers who shall govern and serve the community?"[22] Conscious of their disfranchisement, reforming women came to see their political disempowerment as an obstacle to reforms in prohibition, education, health, and child labor.

All-male legislatures elected by all-male electorates were responsible for moral ills such as the age of consent for sexual intercourse, which was kept typically very low in the South by modern standards. In many southern states, children as young as twelve years old could legally marry. Reformers favored raising the legal age to protect children and provide a higher moral standard. Children needed protection against "Cruel and Heartless Parents who are more desirous of having them earn a little money rather than receive an education," said one reformer. Children were not responsible for their existence, but they were often "robbed" of their childhood, "deprived of an education and denied the God given days of youth for money."[23] "Just give to women this right of representation," said a southern suffragist in 1915, and an eight-hour law for women, widows' and mothers' pensions, child labor regulation, and "cleanliness and purity" would prevail. "We will see to it that the men who are elected to the municipal offices are as clean in their manipulation of city affairs as they are supposed to be in their private homes."[24]

Nowhere did the connection between social reform and the suffrage exist more strongly than in Kentucky, where, in 1907, the legislature reformed school organization by centralizing local schools into county units. This legislation also disfranchised women in school board elections, though women had possessed some form of that right since 1838. For the next five years, Kentucky female reformers made the restoration of school suffrage for women a top objective. The most important education, said Breckinridge in 1908, was "of ourselves." It was no longer "dignified to work for the schools without a voice in their government." In recent years, what defined "womanly" had changed. Some might think it "unwomanly" to vote for sheriff, but fewer thought it so for school trustees.[25] Kentucky women had emerged into public prominence in order "to shelter and protect the great brood of Kentucky children growing up in ignorance, almost forgotten." Men were "too largely absorbed" in business to care about education.[26]

22 Adele Clark to the *Roanoke Times*, ca. January 1913, Virginia Woman Suffrage Papers, 1910–1925, Archives Branch, Library of Virginia.
23 Andy B. Ludwig to Madeline McDowell Breckinridge, June 25, 1903, Papers of Madeline McDowell Breckinridge, Breckinridge Family Papers, Manuscripts Division, Library of Congress.
24 "Unrepresented" to the editor, *Richmond Virginian*, ca. 1915, Virginia Woman Suffrage Papers, 1910–1925, Archives Branch, Library of Virginia.
25 Desha Breckinridge, "The Educational Work of the Kentucky Federation of Women's Clubs," from General Federation of Women's Clubs, *Ninth Biennial Convention Proceedings*, June 1908, Papers of Madeline McDowell Breckinridge, Breckinridge Family Papers, Manuscripts Division, Library of Congress.
26 Madeline McDowell Breckinridge to J. A. Sullivan, circular letter, November 26, 1909, Papers of Madeline McDowell Breckinridge, Breckinridge Family Papers, Manuscripts Division, Library of Congress.

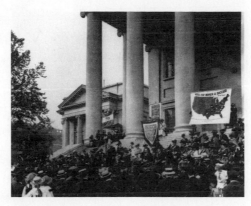

Suffrage rally, Richmond. *Courtesy of the Virginia Historical Society.*

Across the South, Progressive Era women organized equal-suffrage leagues to press for the vote by state enactment, and, after 1916, by national constitutional amendment. Organizing the movement acquired momentum between 1910 and 1917, when suffrage groups in Alabama increased from two to eighty-one and in North Carolina by ten times.[27] In Virginia, suffragists in 1918 claimed 175 leagues in all of the state's one hundred counties, with 30,000 men and women having signed prosuffrage petitions. Of this total, 12,000 came from Richmond alone.[28]

Southern suffragists faced strong opposition, and some of it came from women. Most voters in his district, complained one Virginia legislator in 1913, were opposed to equal suffrage, and among them were a "majority of women."[29] "There is such a strong sentiment" against suffrage, said another activist in 1917, "that the more timid have not the courage to come out & declare themselves in favor of this glorious work."[30] Most people probably opposed the suffrage, said an activist, but that was true of most needed social change. "Was there ever any reform desired by all whom it was designed to benefit? "[31] The suffragists encountered fears about race from opponents, who suggested that enfranchising women meant votes for African American women. Although they regarded these charges as nonsense, suffragists often combated them by asserting that woman suffrage reinforced, rather than challenged, white supremacy.

In the end, the Nineteenth Amendment, submitted to the states in early 1919, became the main focus of reforming women. Of states in the South and Border

[27] Scott, *The Southern Lady*, 179.

[28] "Brief for Federal Suffrage Amendment," 1918, Virginia Woman Suffrage Papers, 1910–1925, Archives Branch, Library of Virginia.

[29] John W. Chalkley to Lila Meade Valentine, November 11, 1913, Virginia Woman Suffrage Papers, 1910–1925, Archives Branch, Library of Virginia.

[30] Mrs. Preston B. Moses to Edith Cowles, January 29, 1917, Virginia Woman Suffrage Papers, 1910–1925, Archives Branch, Library of Virginia.

[31] Jessie Townshend to Woodard [local representative to GA], December 28, 1913, Virginia Woman Suffrage Papers, 1910–1925, Archives Branch, Library of Virginia.

Equal Suffrage League of Virginia, rally at Capitol Square. *Courtesy of the Virginia Historical Society.*

South, seven out of seventeen ratified the amendment—Oklahoma, Kentucky, Missouri, West Virginia, Texas, Tennessee, and Arkansas—an indication of the depth of antisuffragist sentiment in the region and the attachment to traditional gender roles. Tennessee was the final state to ratify, despite attempts by opposing legislators to delay by fleeing the state and preventing a quorum. In the end, the Tennessee legislature ratified the amendment when eastern Tennessee Republican Harry T. Burn changed his vote after his mother insisted that he do so. Tennessee's vote provided the thirty-sixth state necessary for final ratification of the amendment. When antisuffragists mounted an unsuccessful attempt to recall the vote, suffragists made "an uproarious demonstration" in Nashville, where women "screamed frantically" and threw their arms around each other and danced in joy. "Hundreds of suffrage banners were waved wildly," said one account, "and many removed the yellow flowers they had been wearing and threw them upward to meet a similar shower from the galleries."[32]

THE REFORM CRUSADES

Identifying with the urban-industrial world that had overtaken much of the United States, motives of class and race motivated most reformers. More-affluent middle-class people who lived in the urban South dominated their ranks; they expressed an urban-industrial worldview. If not all of them were avid white supremacists, many of them were. What they saw in the South, on the basis of these attitudes, was an underdeveloped region whose population was undereducated and often traditional in their attitudes, resistant to modernization of institutions and practices. Progressive Era southern reformers were also profoundly influenced by religious motives and imagery.

---

[32] "Tennessee Completes Suffrage Victory," *New York Times*, August 19, 1920.

Reformers also exhibited a softer, more humanitarian side: they strongly believed that human action could assist the Christian perfection of society. Most were Protestants. Most subscribed to the Christian notion of a Kingdom of God—a perfected society that Jesus's Second Coming would inaugurate. Reformers articulated this Christian humanitarianism through their strong interest in children and what became known as "child-saving." Protecting children from adulthood—by limiting their work and by requiring them to attend school—became a central goal. The "fusing power" behind social reform, a reformer explained, was the notion that "the great social duty of our age is the saving of society." But this salvation depended on saving the child. All progress began "with the little child."[33]

Reformers confronted the problem of persuading a resistant southern population of the need for these changes. They turned to a familiar form of popular mobilization—the evangelical crusade—to shape and mold public opinion. Reformers used the crusade model in two campaigns, all occurring roughly between the 1890s and World War I: prohibition and moral reform; and education, health, and social-efficiency reform.

The crusade for moral reform, focusing on prohibition and anti-vice campaigns, sought to reform the South's social environment. Prohibition, by far the most popular social reform of the Progressive Era—and the most important moral reform—had long roots extending to early-nineteenth-century efforts at temperance. Only during the 1890s did a national campaign emerge that targeted the manufacture, sale, and distribution of alcohol. Using effective public relations and mass mobilization, the Anti-Saloon League (ASL), which was founded in Westerville, Ohio, in 1895, led campaigns to institute statewide prohibition in the South. After 1900, southern prohibitionists recorded a number of successes, making the region the driest in the country. The South, wrote one observer in 1910, experienced a prohibition movement that swept "onward with relentless and irresistible force, gaining new converts and increasing in power every year."[34]

The prohibition crusade especially focused on the saloon, the source of the alcoholic culture and, according to one reformer, "the mother and the breeder of all anarchy in this and every other country." Drunkenness, prohibitionists claimed, destroyed moral capabilities, leaving the victim a "wretched wreck." Alcoholism wrecked family stability, encouraging crime and disorder. Prohibitionists assigned more blame on systemic conditions than to individual depravity. Alcoholics, they believed, were "as much a victim of disease as the consumptive." Saloons wielded considered political power, corrupting and dominating city government. Organized liquor had become the "mightiest combine on the face of the earth," colluding with government to "defeat law and to rule over the ruins of law, religion, public decency and all good." Nothing short of complete prohibition could work, they

[33] Link, *Paradox of Southern Progressivism*, 129.
[34] Link, *Paradox of Southern Progressivism*, 96.

reasoned, because of the "portentous and continuous menace" to social and political institutions.

Employing a crusade model of popular campaigning, one very familiar to most Victorian Americans, the ASL tried to alter public opinion through a staged manipulation of public opinion, communication of a message through pamphlet literature and public meetings, and nearly constant pressure on legislators. Operated on an evangelical-style model of mobilization—which stressed public meetings and individual conversion to the cause of reform—the ASL focused on the single issue of saloons in nonpartisan fashion. Its goal was what a Virginia prohibitionist called "the elimi[na]tion of the saloon as an institution in American life." Prohibition meetings exhibited the characteristics of a revival. One reform meeting employed, according to one account, "rather terrifying and rather coarsely emotional oratory from pulpit and platform," which was "interspersed with singing and praying" and women's and children's participation, "drilled for the purpose." The passage of statewide prohibition legislation in several states was frequently accompanied by the singing of the doxology, often on the floor of state capitols.

Expanding to the South after 1900, the ASL became the primary organizing focus to mobilize public opinion, and the results were very successful. After 1900, prohibitionists pressed for local-option laws empowering counties to declare themselves dry. After about 1908, the campaign shifted toward the enactment of statewide prohibition, and for the next six years what a contemporary described as a "prohibition wave" swept through the South, with only South Carolina, Kentucky, Texas, and Florida remaining outside the statewide prohibition camp.

Public education, both for blacks and whites, became universally available during Reconstruction. As the price of ending federal intervention, Congress required that southern states include educational provisions in their state constitutions. During the Reconstruction era, southern state governments established public school systems by constitutional enactment. But the establishment of state-run black schools tainted public education in the eyes of many southern whites, who resisted the support of schools with tax revenues. For the most part, southern state government supported public education only anemically.

School modernization became a major objective early on among southern reformers. The formation of the Southern Education Board (SEB) in 1901 sealed an emerging intersectional alliance of southern reformers and northern philanthropists. The SEB, combining southern white school reformers with northern philanthropists such as the Rockefellers into a new coalition, operated as a regional coordinating organization, helping to run a new educational crusade. Northern philanthropies such as what eventually became the Rockefeller Foundation served as what one northerner called "silent partners" of white educational uplift. Although northern philanthropists were interested in black education, they agreed with southern whites' request that they focus on white schools, on the reasoning that reformers depended on altering white attitudes. Northern philanthropists were motivated not only by the desire to stabilize the South, but also by humanitarianism. The "betterment of humanity" was "demanded by Divine authority," wrote New York philanthropist and department store magnate Robert Curtis Ogden, "through the living purpose clearly revealed in Holy Writ, providential guidance and human consciousness."[35]

THE EXPANSION OF THE STATE

Using reform crusades, reformers in a variety of causes galvanized public opinion in support of a new approach to state policy. For example, child-labor reformers, interested in eliminating the work of children in textiles mills and coal mines, sought to publicize the extent of working children. Ultimately, they sought state laws restricting the practice. But in this instance and others, translating the rhetoric of the campaign into specific policy changes, reformers sought a stronger state with greater power over local affairs. The reform crusades' successes provided a public mandate justifying interference. Southern underdevelopment, reformers believed, comprised the root problem, which they sought to change through a campaign of modernization.

The state, as such, functioned as a very weak entity in nineteenth-century America. The federal government, aside from running the post office, had little influence in the dispersed communities of the rural and small-town South. For Progressive Era reformers, the "state" meant state government, heretofore an even-weaker entity than the federal government. Knowing that nineteenth-century state and local government was generally ineffective, reformers placed great faith in greatly empowered state-based interventions in social policy. They sought to construct a new bureaucratic and administrative system in place of locally controlled, decentralized government.

This revitalized state depended especially on changes in southern public education and health. Because of excessive local control, both health and education were neglected, they believed. Public schools were, in their analysis, underfunded, ill-housed, and limited in their ability to shape children. Southern children were the least educated in the United States; adults were the most illiterate. Attending school only three or four months a year, most schoolchildren were not educated beyond elementary grades. Facilities mirrored the rural landscape, more resembling barns and outbuildings than modern public schools. Reformers similarly discovered—and publicized—prevalent health problems among southerners that were seemingly the product of excessive local control. Nutritional deficiencies were common, as were disease and parasites—many of them preventable by modern health and hygiene, and modern public health.

Northern philanthropy, especially Rockefeller philanthropy, played a key role in creating the social-efficiency state. The Rockefeller-financed General Education Board (GEB), established in 1902, initiated an ambitious intervention in southern public education. Building up bureaucratic resources, the GEB used its considerable

[35] Link, *Paradox of Southern Progressivism*, 129.

largesse to promote state control over local schools. In 1905, the GEB established high-school agents in each southern state to promote secondary education among southern whites. These agents were paid by the GEB but became part of the southern educational hierarchy. They lobbied communities to finance schools, urged legislatures to make greater expenditures, and cajoled state education officials to intervene more aggressively. The GEB officials encouraged structural changes in educational government by encouraging the consolidation of the smaller, one-room schools into larger schools, which were increasingly under state-level control. They also promoted high schools, the lengthening of the school year, and the renovation of school facilities. The GEB infused funds but insisted on the creation and strengthening of new school bureaucracies to manage change.

The Rockefellers' intervention in southern public education was supplemented by their involvement in public health. Operating between 1909 and 1914, the Rockefeller Sanitary Commission (RSC) employed tactics of the evangelical crusade, using demonstrations and meetings to publicize parasitic infection and to demonstrate methods—such as sanitary privies—of prevention. The most successful event in the commission's antihookworm crusade became the county dispensary. Beginning in 1910 in Mississippi, these free demonstration clinics combined health education and evangelical camp meeting. In the county dispensaries, Rockefeller workers delivered old-style political stump speeches at courthouses. They avidly employed new media, borrowing from early-twentieth-century educational crusaders, by using displays and even stereopticon and slide shows.

Hookworm infection served as an ideal disease around which to organize public opinion. The parasite, known as *Necator americanus*, was present in soil infected with human feces and was transmitted by skin contact, usually on bare feet. It was by no means the South's only public-health problem. Malaria was prevalent and, in certain areas, endemic; yellow fever appeared periodically in devastating and terrifying epidemics. People, especially in rural areas, suffered from various nutritional ailments. For example, in the early 1900s the US Public Health Service uncovered

Hookworm dispensary. *Rockefeller Foundation.*

the prevalence of pellagra, a nutritional deficiency related to the lack of niacin—a result of the dependence of farmers on store-bought, bleached cornmeal in the Cotton South.

Reformers focused on hookworm because organizing a public-health campaign to eradicate it could provide a model. Hookworm had an easily identifiable cause: parasites that were transferred by contact of barefooted southerners with fecal matter. Constructing sanitary outhouses provided an easy fix. Seemingly, hookworm could be cured almost immediately, indeed almost magically—something like the religious conversion experience that the county dispensaries sought to imitate. In those states where the dispensary was most successful—Alabama, Kentucky, and North Carolina—RSC campaigns, relying on able state directors, enjoyed political support and a powerful base in the state health bureaucracy. "I have never seen the people at any place," Kentucky director Arthur T. McCormack wrote, who were "so wrought up and so full of interest and enthusiasm." The dispensary was like a "big, old-time camp meeting," and the local population talked "of nothing but hookworm and hookworm disease."[36]

There were, however, limits to what the hookworm crusade could accomplish. Reformers had done little more than conduct "raids into the enemy's country," according to a contemporary. Once reformers departed, the favorable impression gradually evaporated and rural folk soon became indifferent.[37] Reformers invested in a long-term campaign spearheaded by northern philanthropy and relying on state intervention. Two semipermanent entities, the International Health Commission (IHC) and its successor, the International Health Board (IHB), immediately followed the RSC. Both adhered to the general pattern that the GEB had already established. The primary objective of Rockefeller philanthropic involvement, either in schools or in health, was the stimulation of state bureaucratic development. The Rockefeller Foundation's attack on ill health became an "entering wedge," according to a Rockefeller official, by which the South "could be induced to build up permanent machinery to take care of the whole problem of public health."

Health and school modernizers during the 1910s and 1920s often worked hand in hand. A goal of public-health reform was to ensure that every schoolhouse in the South had a sanitary privy, which became a symbol of rural school modernization. Health reformers advocated the construction of sanitary privies and the education of rural southerners about their proper use and maintenance. At the urging of reformers, communities often sought outside help in privy building. In Cherokee County, in southwestern North Carolina, the county board of education in December 1914 petitioned state health officials for their help in installing privies to correct the "unwholesome conditions" that existed near schools. "In our opinion," the board declared, "every School should have proper means for caring for and

[36] Link, *Paradox of Southern Progressivism*, 152.
[37] Link, *Paradox of Southern Progressivism*, 154.

disposing of the bowel movements and other body excrements in a way that will prevent disease."[38]

It was only natural that a loose association emerged between educational and health reformers in the early-twentieth-century South. Their alliance shared similar problems associated with anyone seeking to impose state bureaucratic power on backwoods rural communities. Health and school reformers tried to persuade traditional rural populations to exchange local control for the promise of improved facilities, along with better schools and improved health. Unlike other social reformers of their generation, educational and health reformers needed to organize larger numbers of southerners and to determine their exact compliance with state policy. Both soon turned to bureaucratic methods, about which they learned more through the growing influence of northern philanthropy. Northern philanthropists played a determinative role in shaping the new social-efficiency state. They had figured prominently both in the school crusade and the antihookworm crusade. Now, through the judicious use of their funds, they continued to shape educational and health policy.

By attempting to integrate the South into the nation by reforming its social and political institutions, the Progressive Era brought significant changes. Arising mostly in towns and cities and appealing to the middle classes, various reform efforts featured a new and unprecedented public role for women. Though there were limits to what reformers could accomplish, they did succeed in changing the operation of local and state government. Government acquired a stronger presence, becoming part of a new administrative state, portions of which appeared in the South before World War I. The new administrative state began to peek into the corners of the hinterlands of the South, though further, more significant changes awaited the course of the twentieth century.

[38] Link, *Paradox of Southern Progressivism*, 205.

PART FIVE

WORLD WAR AND DEPRESSION

17

THE GREAT WAR

⟨⟩ _____

THE SPREAD OF market capitalism after the Civil War linked the region to a world-wide economic system. The transportation revolution shortened distances between countries and opened markets; the construction of a world communication network made the transmission of news and information nearly instantaneous. What Europeans called the Great War enhanced these tendencies, forcing southerners to consider their place in the world. With the onset of European war and the subsequent American intervention, southerners became exposed to a transformative military experience abroad. White and black southerners, serving in the American military, found their views about themselves and their communities had changed. In the end, more than any other event since 1865, World War I solidified their patriotism and heightened their nationalism. In addition, the war's economic effects were long lasting, setting in motion powerful forces. Although lasting less than two years, American participation in the war brought on a new set of social, economic, and cultural changes.

THE COMING OF WAR

After the outbreak of war on August 3, 1914, cotton markets remained closed for three months. The disruption of international trade and a British naval blockade of German ports, along with German submarine warfare against Allied shipping, sent cotton markets into chaos. Prices effectively collapsed. Only after federal intervention and government-run merchant ships were outfitted to transport the cotton did the crisis pass. Anti-British sentiment, prevalent in the South, emerged among southern Democrats in Congress. The British embargo, said Mississippi senator James K. Vardaman, was destroying the southern economy. To Vardaman, "the conduct of Germany is not half so reprehensive and offensive to the American people as that of Great Britain."[1] The British eventually realized the political significance of the cotton crisis and defused southern hostility. As a result, beginning in August 1915 they agreed to purchase southern cotton that would have been exported to Germany and Austria in order to assuage southern public opinion.

Nonetheless, there was no groundswell of sentiment for war between 1914 and 1917, when the United States remained officially neutral. Southern congressmen, in general, remained antiwar and anti-interventionist. In 1915, when President Wilson sought congressional support for a military buildup in his preparedness plan, many southern Democrats opposed the president. Antimonopoly sentiment and hostility to military establishments made them suspicious of the motives of munitions manufacturers and so-called war profiteers, who they suspected were fomenting war fever. Adoption of preparedness, warned North Carolina's Claude Kitchin, meant "a nation given over to navalism and militarism."[2] In Congress, the strongest opponents of the military buildup were southern Democrats Cole Blease of South Carolina, James K. Vardaman of Mississippi, Oscar Callaway of Texas, Henry De La Warr Flood of Virginia, and William C. Adamson of Georgia.

With Wilson's election and the Democrats' capture of both houses of Congress in 1912, southern antimilitarists possessed a great deal of power. Southern Democrats shaped Wilson's domestic policies, pushing him further to the left on important measures such as the Federal Reserve Act (1913) and the Clayton Anti-Trust Act (1914). They also successfully obtained legislation establishing federal programs in rural finance, agricultural extension, and highway construction. House Majority Leader Claude Kitchin of North Carolina initially opposed preparedness, bolstered by a strong antimilitary sentiment among his constituents, but then supported the legislation and reshaped it to his liking. Kitchin insisted that preparedness be financed through progressive taxation. Rejecting the Wilson administration's proposal of excise taxes to pay for mobilization, Kitchin and his supporters imposed new taxes on the very wealthy. In the Revenue Act of 1916, Congress raised the income tax from 1 to 2 percent and increased taxes on incomes above $2 million to 13 percent. In addition, the act provided for a graduated inheritance tax, a tax on profits in the munitions industry, and additional taxes on corporate profits. Even with these concessions, many southern congressmen opposed the preparedness plan to the bitter end. Although the House adopted it in early 1916, 123 southern congressmen voted against enlarging the army and 129 voted against the expansion of the navy. Even after the Germans announced unrestricted submarine warfare against all shipping in January 1917, provoking a diplomatic crisis with the United States, southerners remained hesitant. A substantial portion

---

[1] Anthony Gaughan, "Woodrow Wilson and the Rise of Military Interventionism in the South," *Journal of Southern History* 65, no. 4 (November 1999): 775.

[2] Gaughan, "Rise of Military Interventionism," 777.

Claude Kitchin. *Library of Congress.*

of public opinion opposed intervention even after Woodrow Wilson's call, on April 2, 1917, for a declaration of war on Germany.

Claude Kitchin remained antiwar, even during congressional debate about a war resolution in April 1917. A native of Halifax County, North Carolina, Kitchin was first elected to Congress in 1900. Prior to North Carolina's suffrage restriction amendment, his Second Congressional District had regularly sent African Americans to Congress. After North Carolina adopted the literacy test in 1900, Kitchin became so secure in his congressional seat that he eventually served twelve terms. Although a product of the one-party system, Kitchin was known for his fiery, anti-big-business political message and his championing of the interests of white farmers. His long tenure in Congress provided him the seniority to become a dominant figure in the US House of Representatives.

A little after midnight, on April 6, 1917, Kitchin spoke on the floor of the House. According to the *New York World*, he cut "an impressive figure," adorned in a "blue business suit, a high white vest, and a black string tie." Kitchin's speech was the most important delivered by any opponent of American intervention. It took little courage "to declare a war for others to fight," he told the audience. Support for war demonstrated "neither loyalty nor patriotism for one to urge others to get into a war." There was no invasion of American soil; that was the ultimate test, and "not a foot of our territory is demanded or coveted." Proceeding "barefooted and alone," Kitchin realized that the war resolution would pass, but he made up his mind to walk a lonely road with the "undoubting conclusion" that he would vote against the measure. Half the world had become a "slaughter-house for human beings," and the United States was the "last hope for peace on earth." With American entry into the war, the "demons of inhumanity will be let loose for a rampage throughout the world."[3]

In the end, a declaration of war overwhelmingly passed the House, with fifty dissenting votes, only six of which came from southern congressmen. Within months, public opinion swung in favor of the war effort. Probably most agreed with Alabama congressman Tom Heflin, who maintained that Kitchin did not "speak for the people of the South." "No man born South of the Mason-Dixon line," he said, "is ready to surrender his country's self-respect and honor and lie down and crawl."[4] Kitchin became the subject of criticism even within his own state. If those North Carolinians who disagreed with Kitchin's antiwar stance "were to write or wire

[3] Alex Mathews Arnett, *Claude Kitchin and the Wilson War Policies* (Boston: Little, Brown, 1937), 226–237.

[4] Jeanette Keith, *Rich Man's War, Poor Man's Fight: Race, Class, and Power in the Rural South during the First World War* (Chapel Hill: University of North Carolina Press, 2004), 34.

him," said one newspaper, "he would be swamped beyond recall. It would take a snow plow to unearth him."[5]

Once the crisis occurred, southerners rallied around the flag and supported war. Hal Flood, a Virginia congressman, announced that America was defending "our fundamental rights" and fighting for the "preservation of the rights of humanity." This war was "as sacred and noble as the war of 1776." In the Senate, Mississippi senator John Sharp Williams argued that the United States was fighting "on the side of liberty and democracy and free speech and free institutions against militarism and autocracy."[6]

THE DRAFT AND THE EXPANSION OF FEDERAL POWER

World War I resulted in a major expansion of the power of the federal government. Not since the Civil War and Reconstruction had the national government so systematically intruded in local matters, doing so in the name of the war effort. Across the country, in the name of military necessity, federal authorities commandeered transportation, agricultural, mining, industrial, and financial resources. Even more importantly, a new conscription act met wartime manpower needs by inaugurating a massive—and unprecedented—mobilization of human resources.

The Selective Service Act of May 18, 1917, nationalized the recruitment of military manpower, which heretofore had been filtered through the states. About a month after the passage of the draft, on June 15, 1917, Congress enacted the Espionage Act, which empowered federal authorities to imprison those who deliberately obstructed the war effort or persuaded others to do so. About a year later, on May 16, 1918, the Sedition Act strengthened legal restrictions against antiwar speech and publications that involved "disloyal, profane, scurrilous, or abusive language" about the American government. Postmasters could suspend the mailing privileges of any publication involved in the "willful obstruction" of the war effort. The latter stipulation provided an effective way to suppress antiwar publications.

These measures attracted some support among southern congressmen. The draft was based on "Jeffersonian principles of equal rights for all and special privileges for none," said Congressman Thomas Harrison of Virginia.[7] Rep. Edwin Y. Webb of North Carolina, who guided these measures through the House, supported the provisions for press censorship, which, he said, "protects the innocent and catches the guilty." A free press became expendable during wartime, according to most congressmen. "Of course, we must have a censorship," argued William W. Venable of Mississippi, "for you cannot conduct wars except through dictators." Southerners embraced the wartime nationalism and fear of foreigners with exaggerated enthusiasm. Southerners faced a "hydraheaded monster of treason," said Rep. Joe H. Eagle of Texas. "For me," he

[5] Gaughan, "Rise of Military Interventionism," 800.
[6] I. A. Newby, "States' Rights and Southern Congressmen during World War I," *Phylon* 24, no. 1 (1963): 39.
[7] Newby, "States' Rights," 41.

declared, "there is no longer any tolerance for foreign sentiment in our midst. Either a man is for America or he is a base traitor to America and a hired or craven slave to foreign monarchy."[8]

The more unpopular of these measures was undoubtedly the draft. Conscription represents coercive government at its most extreme; throughout history, wherever it was attempted, conscription met popular opposition. Southern antimilitarists, once war was declared, worried how the new, massive American Expeditionary Force (AEF) would be organized. Drawing on antimonopoly ideology, they warned that the draft disproportionately benefited the wealthy and fell most heavily on poor people—especially white people. Adopting conscription told the "same old story," complained Georgia congressman James Wise. "We need not fool ourselves about who will do the fighting and dying in this war. . . . The helpless will be compelled to go."[9] The same people behind the war, antimilitarist southerners claimed, also supported the draft—the munitions manufacturers, war financiers, and eastern elites. These "selfish interests," said Texas congressman Jeff McLemore, made "money out of war." Commercial interests favored war and the draft, he argued, while agrarian interests opposed the draft and reluctantly participated in warfare. Others criticized the draft's class bias. Conscription was "state slavery," said Rep. George Huddleston of Birmingham, Alabama, "in which the rewards are to place and not capacity, in which servile obedience is the highest virtue and independence and individuality the most serious vice."[10]

Others portrayed the draft as a violation of individual rights. An expanded military could be "easily mobilized and used by powerful interests with a friendly administration to crush or oppress the people," warned Georgia congressman Rufus Hardy. The draft, added Oklahoma senator Tom Gore, risked "substituting military despotism for democracy in America."[11] "I am not going to consent to the humiliation of the white men of this republic," Vardaman announced, "by providing for compulsory military service until the citizen has had an opportunity to show his patriotism." Tennessee senator Kenneth McKellar favored the bill but wanted to include more voluntary incentives for enlistment. The draft abandoned the "traditions and the history of the Anglo-Saxon race for the first time since William the Conqueror," he argued, "and we are asked to pattern after the military despotism of Germany and of Russia and Austria."[12]

Some southern congressmen maintained that the most insidious part of the Selective Service Act was its nationalization of military enlistment. James F. Byrnes, a South Carolina congressman and future senator and Supreme Court justice, opposed the draft because it eliminated state-based military units. Byrnes favored retaining the system in existence since the Civil War, which preserved state

[8] Newby, "States' Rights," 42.
[9] Keith, *Rich Man's War*, 49.
[10] Keith, *Rich Man's War*, 49–50.
[11] Gaughan, "Rise of Military Interventionism," 783.
[12] Newby, "States' Rights," 40.

identities. The federal government would become empowered, he warned, to "have a man from South Carolina assigned to a company with men from Massachusetts or Oklahoma." The national government could even order a South Carolina boy "by the side of a negro from Indiana." In that event, Byrnes declared, "they would not have to go to Europe for war."[13]

Others also expressed skepticism. Tom Watson, former Populist, became vocally antiwar. Conscription, he wrote in *Watson's Magazine*, forced "millions of our best young men into foreign servitude and death in foreign lands." The foreign threat, thousands of miles away, was not "actual and imminent." Real militarists were not in Berlin but Washington, and those who "campaign for world democracy . . . by subverting our Constitution, must consider us stupid." These were "revolutionary new laws" that had been "sprung upon a betrayed people." Had "you and I predicted that such a state of affairs would have resulted from the re-election of President Wilson," Watson wrote, "we would have been derisively hooted all over the land."[14] "The world must be made safe for democracy," Watson said on another occasion, "even though none is left in these United States."[15] Watson's inflated rhetoric brought a swift response. Using the powers of the Espionage Act, *Watson's Magazine* was denied access to the federal mails and effectively silenced.

The least enthusiastic participants in conscription were African Americans, though they were conscripted in greater numbers than whites. A black Mississippian, in an anonymous pamphlet, urged black men to avoid military service. "Well educated Negroes," he charged, had "urged young black men to be killed for nothing." The *Washington Bee*, a leading African American newspaper, complained that the "self styled spokesmen of the black people had no right to offer the services of blacks to the government." The newspaper urged "bootlickers who accepted disenfranchisement and segregation" to "volunteer their own services for the fighting."[16]

During June 1917, in the first registration of eligible young men for the draft, black inductees were underrepresented. According to one estimate, in several southern states more than half of African American males did not register, perhaps 200,000 men. Some were confused about the law (which they thought applied only to whites), while others were discouraged by white employers to participate in the draft. Federal enforcement efforts yielded disproportionately more arrests of black suspects for draft evasion. In one case in Beaumont, Texas, a Bureau of Investigation (the predecessor to the FBI) agent arrested Ollie Eaglin four days after the June 1917 registration date. Eaglin produced witnesses testifying that he was underage; he claimed that he did not know his birthday and was unaware that the Selective Service Act required him to register. Eaglin spent a month in jail before he was released and drafted.

[13] Newby, "States' Rights," 42.
[14] "Editorial Notes and Clippings," *Watson's Magazine* XXV, no. 4 (August 1917), 237–240.
[15] Gaughan, "Rise of Military Interventionism," 796.
[16] Calvin White Jr., *The Rise to Respectability: Race, Religion, and the Church of God in Christ* (Fayetteville: University of Arkansas Press, 2012), 57.

Applied unequally, the draft often reinforced the existing caste system. Planters in many cases deliberately misinformed African American sharecroppers and laborers, sometimes to keep them in the workforce, sometimes later to turn them in to conscription authorities in order to collect a reward for apprehending "slackers." In March 1918, Congress provided furloughs for drafted men needed to help with harvests, and camp commanders were often only too willing to provide planters with a source of conscripted labor. Meanwhile, in another amendment to the Selective Service Act, local draft boards were empowered to draft any men not working in essential war-related employment. This "work or fight" provision became another way to draft labor for planters, since sharecroppers had to demonstrate employment in order to obtain the exemption. Supplemented by state legislation, "work or fight" became a sort of new vagrancy law awarding planters even-greater leverage over their workers. The "work or fight" laws—which were applied to women as well as men—became so unpopular that they invigorated the NAACP in the rural South, which campaigned against them.

Frequently, delinquency and draft evasion reflected the racial hierarchies of the plantation system. A federal official found that, in the cotton districts of Georgia, cases of delinquent draft registration were "attributable to the ignorance, isolation and conditions prevailing in out of the way locations." Sharecroppers depended on planters for registration information, and, in many instances, having them read the instructions to them. A southern Georgia sharecropper, Thomas Johnson, was arrested for evading delinquency. He contended that he was told about the registration only after it had occurred. Johnson immediately went to the white sheriff in Valdosta, and he was taken in handcuffs to the induction center at Camp Wheeler.

Although the Selective Service Act made provision for religious objections to military service, the status of conscientious objectors remained ill-defined. All-white draft boards in the South had little sympathy for them, least of all black conscientious objectors. The Church of God in Christ (COGIC), a black Pentecostal denomination, required its members to refuse to serve in any war. The church, founded in California, attracted members in the rural South. Although the church's leader, Bishop Charles H. Mason, supported the war effort, he urged members to avoid the draft. Suspicious whites detected signs of subversion or even pro-German sentiment, though little real evidence substantiated these charges. Federal investigators conducted surveillance against church leaders, while local whites harassed them. In April 1918, a COGIC preacher was tarred and feathered in Blytheville, Arkansas, after telling his church that the war was a "white man's war" and that "the Kaiser [was] . . . as good a man as the president."

Soon conflict emerged between religious conviction and federal enforcement of the draft. In August 1917, a black church member in Lexington, Mississippi, Jack Wright, refused induction. Apprehended in Jackson, he told federal interrogators that Mason and the church instructed members not to serve. Soon agencies such as the Bureau of Investigation and Military Intelligence Division of the War Department began surveillance of Mason and church leaders. In June 1918, Mason was arrested in Lexington, Mississippi, on draft obstruction charges, while a number of congregants were rounded up and sent to induction centers. In July, military intelligence arrested Henry Kirvin, a COGIC pastor in Paris, Texas, for draft resistance. They also arrested Mason, and the two men, along with church leader William B. Holt, but a federal grand jury in Paris refused to indict them.

War policies aroused intense nationalism among southerners, as they did among other Americans. Wilsonian repression quieted opponents of the war, but the crackdown disguised grassroots opposition. When the Selective Service System was first implemented, southern draft boards reported that four-fifths of the men requested exemptions. By 1918, there were 95,000 southerners listed as deserters, about 16 percent of those who were inducted. According to one estimate, as many as half a million people from the South evaded the draft by refusing to register.[17]

Antiwar sentiment focused on legally debatable issues that the Espionage Act did not prohibit, such as war finance and mobilization. On the heels of the Revenue Act of 1916, legislation in 1917 and 1918 shifted the burden of paying for the war to the affluent. This legislation expanded the income tax to include more people, but it also increased levies on larger incomes: incomes above $1 million were taxed at a 77 percent rate, while "excess profits" were taxed at 65 percent and 25 percent on inheritance. Others resisted the expansion of governmental controls. Early in the war, Wilson nationalized the railroads, an extreme measure by peacetime standards but considered appropriate during wartime. The Lever Act, in addition, empowered federal control of food production and consumption. Many southerners worried about national, centralized control of the economy. McLemore denounced the Lever Act as "the most extraordinary and the most un-American piece of legislation ever presented to Congress," while Vardaman said it resulted in the creation of a "benevolent altruistic food despot." But, in general, public opinion favored these controls in order to maximize production and ensure that distribution occurred fairly and efficiently.[18]

The draft mobilized a huge American army, but it also became an opportunity for social engineering. The military administered intelligence (IQ) testing, an attempt to measure innate ability among supposedly average Americans. The testers, who used methods of testing that were skewed by race and class, found differences between North and South in that southerners scored significantly lower. They also found differences between white and black. Scholars such as George O. Ferguson of the University of Virginia and Carl C. Brigham of Princeton University asserted that the gaps in intelligence between southern and northern soldiers resulted from the presence of black soldiers, who, they claimed, were innately inferior. Other testers pointed out that the difference was regional; northern whites tested better than southern whites, and northern blacks tested better than southern blacks. Nonetheless, these dubious racial theories emerging out of wartime intelligence testing reinforced conclusions about differences between whites and blacks.

[17] Keith, *Rich Man's War*, 1.
[18] Newby, "States' Rights," 43.

The mobilization also provided an opportunity to extend early goals of Progressive Era social reformers. Raymond B. Fosdick ran the Commission on Training Camp Activities, in charge of fostering a healthful environment for the training of troops in camps across the United States. He described the commission's "permanent contribution" to towns in the South in furthering a sense of community responsibility in social work. Many of them, he wrote, "never had any experience whatever in community work, and they never had any cohesiveness so far as a community program was concerned." Now these towns were developing a "social consciousness." The commission was "making a permanent addition to the life of the towns that will last long after our war camps have been forgotten."[19] The commission's most important effort involved its campaign to eradicate prostitution and red-light districts located near training camps. In addition, the commission launched a public-health crusade focusing on the reduction of venereal disease (VD)—the most ambitious federal public-health campaign in American history. The federal government subsidized anti-VD campaigns by state health services, bolstering the public-health and social-welfare bureaucracies in the South.

About a million southerners served in the military forces during World War I, with 600,000 of them drafted. Their military experiences thrust them into the wider world. The South hosted many of the training camps, exposing the region to non-southerners and making some communities into boomtowns. The war transformed the Norfolk, Virginia, area into a center of shipbuilding and dry dock for expanding American naval forces in the Atlantic. As a result of the military buildup, Norfolk's population nearly tripled during the war years, while nearby Newport News grew from 24,000 to 60,000 in only a few months in 1917. Other naval bases in New Orleans, Charleston, and Pensacola experienced similar war-induced booms.

The 1917–1918 military expansion spilled over to most sectors of industry and agriculture. The lumber industry became so overheated that yellow pine was no

Training at Fort Meyer, Virginia. *Library of Congress.*

[19] Raymond B. Fosdick, "The Commission on Training Camp Activities," *Proceedings of the Academy of Political Science in the City of New York* 7, no. 4 (February 1918): 163–170.

Oil fields, Bull Bayou, Louisiana, ca. 1919. *Library of Congress.*

longer sold on the private market. The need for explosives, especially nitrate, spurred hydroelectric power and petrochemicals. During the war, federal authorities constructed Wilson Dam, at Muscle Shoals, Alabama, as the centerpiece of the wartime hydroelectric projects in the South. The war spurred demand to clothe the military; southern cotton textile mills experienced prosperity and profits. The tobacco industry produced many more cigarettes, successfully marketing them to military men. The need for coal to fuel factories and navies opened up new coalfields in regions such as eastern Kentucky. Similarly, as a result of the wartime boom, new oil fields opened up in Oklahoma and Texas. In agriculture, cotton prices increased to historically high levels of twenty-seven cents per pound, and income soared across the Cotton South.

In the end, the Great War, despite antiwar sentiment prior to intervention in 1917, marked a further step in national reconciliation. "The fact is," declared a Mississippi newspaper in 1918, that prior to the war "there was very little national spirit" in the South. By war's end, however, southerners stood "shoulder to shoulder" with other Americans.[20] After World War I, the South became the region most loyal in its support of an internationalist foreign policy and the most stalwart backer of a strong military. Wilson's appeals to national unity during wartime and his Protestant-infused rhetoric resonated with southerners. America's mission in the world, as explained by Wilsonian internationalist rhetoric, became a struggle of Christian democracy against German secularism—an appealing message. There was "little hope for the cause of Christ in this world until the world is first made safe for democracy," declared a Mississippi newspaper in March 1918.[21]

AFRICAN AMERICANS AND THE WAR

Prior to the war, most African Americans in the regular military served in the army. The prewar regular army maintained four all-black units—the Ninth and Tenth Cavalries, and the Twenty-Fourth and Twenty-Fifth Infantries The navy, in addition, severely restricted the number of black volunteers, and those serving were consigned to mess duty. Both the marine corps and coast guard barred blacks from their ranks. Military service put thousands of black men in uniform, many of whom served overseas. Within weeks of the declaration of war, the four regular army units

[20] Gaughan, "Rise of Military Interventionism," 803.
[21] Gaughan, "Rise of Military Interventionism," 790.

were full to capacity, and none participated in the AEF. The bulk of black service-men were draftees.

All-black units from the Ninety-Second and Ninety-Third Divisions were among the first American units to join the fight in late 1917, and they suffered 1,647 and 3,534 casualties, respectively. In the Ninety-Third Division, the 370th, 371st, and 372nd all fought with distinction under French command. The 371st spent three months on the front lines in the Champagne offensive, earning the Croix de Guerre for the entire unit. The so-called Harlem Hellfighters, the 369th Infantry, participated in the September–October Allied counteroffensive that eventually turned the tide of the war. In total, the 369th fought on the front lines of the war for 191 days, longer than any other American unit in the war, earning 171 Croix de Guerre.

Black troops who served in combat, however, composed a small minority. Most were instead relegated to support positions. Both in the United States and in Europe, 180,000 and 120,000 African American men, respectively, worked in the Services of Supply (SOS), where, according to a contemporaneous account, they served as "nothing more than laborers in uniform."[22] SOS troops performed mainly manual labor in loading and unloading, construction, and gravedigging, along with work in depots, hospitals, factories, and repair shops. Black draftees composed a seventh of all conscripts; they made up half of the SOS ranks. White officers, often southerners, commanded black troops in the SOS; white commanders subjected these troops to severe restrictions. Fearing contact between black males and French women, the military often issued orders banning contact with locals.

The wartime mobilization established training camps around the country, each provided with racially segregated facilities. Army leaders also dispersed black units to maintain what they called a "safe ratio" of white and black inductees. Although in general white officers led black units, early in the war about six hundred black offi-cers were trained and commissioned at Fort Des Moines, in Iowa. Black officers suf-fered prevalent discrimination of segregated quarters and mess; white officers and enlisted men often refused to salute them. Black troops were the last to receive sup-plies and provisions, and they sometimes found themselves without uniforms or even blankets.

In training camps located in the South, black troops experienced white hostility while away from the base. Tensions brewed between armed black troops and local whites, sometimes erupting into violence. White military officials made it clear that black troops should respect local Jim Crow customs. Gen. Charles J. Ballou, com-manding the all-black Ninety-Second Infantry Division, ordered Camp Funston, Kansas, soldiers to stay on base because in town "their presence will be resented." "White men made the Division," Ballou wrote, "and they can break it just as easily it becomes a troublemaker."

[22] Adriane Lentz-Smith, *Freedom Struggles: African Americans and World War I* (Cambridge, MA: Harvard University Press, 2009), 95.

The worst outbreak of wartime racial violence occurred in Houston, where black soldiers stationed at Camp Logan took up arms against local police and the white community after ample provocation. Local authorities, in anticipation of the arrival of black troops, tightened up segregation. African American troops defied the laws by refusing to sit in segregated sections of streetcars and theaters and by tearing down Jim Crow signs. On August 23, 1917, a black soldier intervened after a white policeman beat a black woman; he was beaten and arrested. Although the soldier was soon released, rumors spread of his death. An angry group of armed black soldiers marched into the city, and a shootout occurred, resulting in the deaths of seventeen whites and two blacks. Army officials arrested 156 black soldiers for mutiny, and following military trials during December 1917, thirteen were convicted and hanged. Sixteen more were condemned to die. Although President Wilson commuted the sentences of ten of these, the remaining six were hanged. The hasty disposition of military justice aroused an uproar. "We would rather see you shot by the highest tribunal of the United States Army because you dared protect a Negro woman from the insult of a southern brute in the form of a policeman," commented a black newspaper in San Antonio, "than to have you forced to go to Europe to fight for a liberty you cannot enjoy."[23]

The experience of World War I proved disappointing for many black conscripts. Desertion rates ran three times higher among black troops as compared to white troops. Unquestionably, discrimination and day-to-day humiliation were hard on morale. White army officers had little confidence in them, often complaining that black inductees were "shiftless" or unreliable. A contemporaneous song expressed black soldiers' sense of isolation about a Jim Crow war:

> *"I been digging in Mississippi, diggin' in Kentucky,*
> *Diggin' in Georgia, diggin' all over God's heaven.*
> *Lawd, lawd, guess I can dig in France.*
> *Ruther be in corn-field workin' hard,*
> *Than be back private in national guard.*
> *But I'm on my way, can't turn back."*[24]

Despite the discrimination that they suffered, the training and arming of this many black soldiers was significant. The use of firearms, and in some instance, combat experience, made black soldiers less willing to return to everyday indignities. World War I was fought, in Woodrow Wilson's famous phrase, "To Make the World Safe for Democracy," yet Jim Crow practices were ever present. If black men were told that they "must come forward in the performance of a common duty," wrote the *Greensboro Daily News*, would it be possible to tell them "in the future that whereas

---

[23] H. C. Peterson and Gilbert C. Fite, *Opponents of War, 1917–1918* (Madison: University of Wisconsin Press, 1957), 90.

[24] Theodore Kornweibel Jr., *"Investigate Everything": Federal Efforts to Compel Black Loyalty during World War I* (Bloomington: Indiana University Press, 2002), 83.

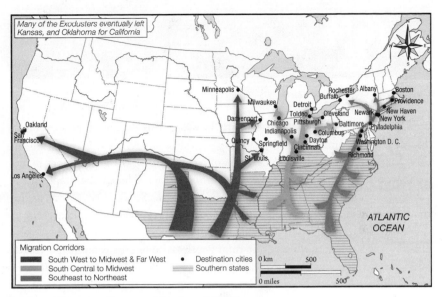

MAP 17.1 Migration Patterns of the Great Migration

... [they] must register for a possible casualty list, ... [they] cannot register for the voting list?"[25]

The war marked the beginning of the Great Migration, one of the most important social changes in modern America. Between early 1915 and mid-1916, 300,000 African Americans left the South; for the war years as a whole, the figure was perhaps a million. Wartime migrants tended to be predominantly male rather than female, first moving to southern cities and from there migrating to urban communities in the North, Midwest, and West. Only after the farm-to-city pattern was established within the South did African American migrants begin to look toward opportunities in the North.

The wartime African American exodus resulted from a cutoff in European immigration. The numbers of Europeans moving to the United States declined from 1,218,480 in 1914 to 110,618 in 1918. African Americans filled the need for workers, with most originating in the Deep South, a region that had previously seen little out-migration. Northern mills and factories dispatched labor agents who scoured the South looking for black workers. A contemporary described how labor agents recruited by arranging for transportation for workers. Black immigrants often traveled by railroad in large numbers, according to this observer, who told of witnessing "the sending north from a Southern city in one day a crowd estimated at twenty-five hundred." This group was shipped on a three-sectioned train, crammed into coaches with their

Downtown Norfolk, Virginia, ca. 1915.   *Library of Congress.*

belongings. "For the Negroes of the South," he wrote, "this was the happy blending of desire with opportunity."[26]

African Americans migrated because of factors pulling them away from home, along with those pushing them away. The "pull" factors included new employment and higher income. Wages in industrial jobs outside the South were as much as five times what could be earned in agricultural employment. In northern cities, African Americans enjoyed more political and civil rights, along with better schools. "Push" factors—the harsh oppression of the rural South—also figured prominently. Black migrants often simply wanted to escape grinding oppression. "To die from the bite of frost," said the *Chicago Defender*, was "far more glorious than at the hands of the mob."[27] "Confidence in the sense of justice, humanity and fair play of the white South is gone," wrote a black newspaper. "I should have been here twenty years ago," a black migrant wrote home. "I just begin to feel like a man.... My children are going to the same school with the whites and I don't have to humble to no one. I have registered. Will vote in the next election and there isn't any yes Sir or no Sir."[28]

Many southern planters reacted with alarm to the black exodus. Where would white employers "get labor to take their places?" the *Montgomery Advertiser* asked.[29]

Group of Florida Migrants on Their Way to Cranberry, New Jersey, to Pick Potatoes: Near Shawboro, North Carolina, photograph by Jack Delano. *Library of Congress.*

[26] James Weldon Johnson, *Black Manhattan* (New York: Alfred A. Knopf, 1930), 151.
[27] Roger Biles, *The South and the New Deal* (Lexington: University Press of Kentucky, 1994), 9.
[28] Joe William Trotter Jr., "The Great Migration," *OAH Magazine of History* 17, no. 1 (October 2002), 31–32.
[29] Isabel Wilkerson, *The Warmth of Other Suns: The Epic Story of America's Great Migration* (New York: Random House, 2010), 162.

Southern state and local governments obstructed migration by antienticement legislation and by imposing steep fees on labor agents. These efforts did little to stem the rising flood. With the end of the Great War, black migration continued; 615,000 African Americans went north during the 1920s. Like other immigrants throughout history, southern blacks in the Great Migration left in patterns of familiarity, only after networks of communication and community provided well-known destination points. Black newspapers such as the *Chicago Defender* or the *Pittsburgh Courier* served as sources of information about work, housing, and methods of migration.

Prior to the 1940s, most black migrants moved to northeastern and midwestern cities. During World War I, the black urban population grew rapidly, increasing by 66 percent in New York City, 148 percent in Chicago, 500 percent in Philadelphia, and 611 percent in Detroit. Migrants to midwestern cities came from the Mississippi delta. From South Atlantic states—Florida, Georgia, the Carolinas, and Virginia— African Americans migrated up the Eastern Seaboard to northeastern urban areas. Later black immigrants moving to the West Coast during the late 1930s and 1940s came from the trans-Mississippi South states of Arkansas, Louisiana, and Texas. These black migrants gained a foothold in manufacturing. Between 1910 and 1920, the proportion of black males in industrial employment increased by about six times in cities such as Cleveland, Pittsburgh, Detroit, and Milwaukee. Black women made gains in factory work also, though at a much-slower rate.

In his autobiography, *American Hunger*, novelist Richard Wright recalled his experiences in moving north. Born in rural Mississippi, he migrated to Memphis and then, in 1927, to Chicago. He found the city unwelcoming. "My first glimpse of the flat black stretches of Chicago," he wrote, "depressed and dismayed me, mocked all my fantasies." Chicago seemed unreal, with "mythical houses . . . built of slabs of black coal wreathed in palls of gray smoke, houses whose foundations were sinking slowly into the dank prairie." Wright remembered that he was "seized by doubt" about his move to a strange new place, but he realized that "going back was impossible." He had "fled a known terror, and perhaps I could cope with this unknown terror that lay ahead." "Wherever my eyes turned," he wrote, "they saw stricken, frightened black faces trying vainly to cope with a civilization that they did not understand. . . . I had fled one insecurity and had embraced another."[30]

Black migrants such as Wright encountered a hostile white reaction, to be sure. Segregated into all-black neighborhoods, African Americans often found that work was confined to the lowest rungs of the labor ladder, with mobility into better occupations limited. Although possessing the right to vote, black migrants faced widespread contempt and hostility. Wartime migration spawned outbreaks of violence. In New York City in May 1917, a small race riot occurred, with one African American killed and another seven injured. In East St. Louis, which experienced heavy wartime immigration, racial tensions erupted over competition for housing and jobs. On July 2, 1917, carloads of whites drove into black neighborhoods,

[30] Richard Wright, *American Hunger* (New York: Harper & Row, 1977).

shooting randomly into houses. Black residents responded with gunfire, but they shot into a police car, killing several whites, including a policeman. An explosion of violence followed in a full-fledged massacre, with scores dead, one of the worst outbreaks of racial violence in American history. Also during the summer of 1917, antiblack violence erupted in Chester, Pennsylvania; Memphis; and Waco, Texas.

THE WORLD WAR AND RACE CONFLICT

When the Armistice ended World War I in November 1918, racial violence continued. In the immediate aftermath of the war, a terrible racial conflagration occurred in Chicago. The city witnessed heavy black immigration during the war, and the return of veterans after the Armistice created acute competition for jobs and housing. In July 1919, whites attacked and killed a black swimmer in Lake Michigan when he violated the unofficial racial segregation of the city's beaches. Violence raged between rival white and black mobs for about a week, with fifteen whites and twenty-three blacks killed. More than a thousand black homes were destroyed. Other riots occurred during the summer of 1919 in Washington, DC; Omaha; Longview, Texas; and Knoxville. This violence involved massacres in which white mobs indiscriminately attacked black homes and businesses. Two years later, in June 1921 white mobs attacked black residential and business districts in Tulsa, Oklahoma. In the aftermath of the violence, 10,000 blacks were homeless, thirty-five city blocks were destroyed, and 1,256 homes were leveled.

In still another example of postwar violence, a white mob attacked and destroyed the small all-black town of Rosewood, Florida, in June 1923, after false accusations were circulated that a black man had raped a white woman. Rosewood was destroyed, its inhabitants fleeing. The white press mostly ignored the massacre until 1982, when *St. Petersburg Times* reporter Gary Moore uncovered the event. In 1993, the state of Florida compensated victims for having failed to protect Rosewood against white violence. The story of the Florida massacre was later fictionalized in John Singleton's film *Rosewood*, which appeared in 1997.

In the face of white hostility and violence, northern blacks looked inward, creating cultural and political enclaves. The best-known of these emerged in New York and Chicago. African Americans were among the earliest residents of colonial New York, though prior to 1860 black settlement was mostly confined to lower Manhattan. After 1890, a steady flow of southern migrants moved to the city. By the 1920s, this flow had become a flood, with much of the black population moving into northern Manhattan in Harlem. Founded in the 1870s as a northern suburb, Harlem remained on the outskirts of Manhattan until a real-estate boom followed the construction of a subway line in the late 1890s. The bustling district was dominated by brownstones constructed along boulevards and was inhabited by Russians, Germans, Irish, and Jews, with Italians settling in working-class East Harlem. After 1910, Harlem began to acquire a black character. In 1914, 50,000 African Americans lived in the neighborhood. By 1920, the portion of Manhattan between 130th and 144th Streets, and between 5th and 8th Avenues, counted 73,000 black inhabitants, the largest urban black community in the world. By 1930, there were nearly 330,000 black inhabitants of Manhattan—a figure that exceeded the African American populations of St. Louis, Memphis, and Birmingham combined.[31]

More than any other place in the United States, in Harlem African Americans enjoyed unrestricted cultural and political freedom. Originally from Jacksonville, Florida, African American activist, poet, and academic James Weldon Johnson lived in New York for more than two decades. Working with the NAACP, he recognized the cultural and political power that accompanied this large black community. In his *Black Manhattan* (1930), Johnson called Harlem the "greatest single community anywhere of people descended from age-old Africa." He noted New York's position as "incongruous." Over the years, the city housed Dutch, Irish, and Jewish newcomers. Now it was home to a "Negro metropolis and as such is everywhere known." Throughout black America, Harlem had quickly become the "recognized Negro capital," what he earlier called "the greatest Negro city in the world." It was a "Mecca for the sightseer, the pleasure-seeker, the curious, the adventurous, the enterprising, the ambitious, and the talented of the entire Negro world." Containing more black people than any other place in the world, it was a "phenomenon, a miracle straight out of the skies."[32]

Harlem's inhabitants were largely migrants escaping the poverty of the rural South. Especially during the 1920s, cheap housing became more available, but its quality deteriorated significantly. Landlords found that they could make handsome profits in the cheap rental market. "In the golden days," wrote a *New York Times* reporter, "when vacant apartments and rents were cheap, a Harlem landlord who let

down the bars of his tenement to admit a colored family brought down wrath upon his head. For instantly that house, and presently the entire block, became doomed for white occupancy; and flat after flat was given over to colored tenants. . . . The unwritten law of Manhattan of those days was that white and black could not dwell side by side as neighbors."[33]

During and after World War I, one of the manifestations of the hopes and aspirations of southern blacks was the attractiveness of the social movement associated with black nationalist Marcus Garvey and his Universal Negro Improvement Association (UNIA). Born in Jamaica, Garvey

James Weldon Johnson. *State Archives of Florida.*

[31] Gilbert Osofsky, *Harlem: The Making of a Ghetto; Negro New York, 1890–1930* (New York: Harper & Row, 1966), 128–129.
[32] Johnson, *Black Manhattan*, 3–4; Johnson, "Harlem: The Culture Capital," in Alain Locke, *The New Negro: An Interpretation* (New York: Albert and Charles Boni, 1925), 301.
[33] "Negro Colony Growing; 150,000 in Harlem Section," *New York Times*, July 29, 1923.

lived in London, where he was influenced by Pan-African ideas. In 1916, he visited the United States, where he promoted UNIA as an organization espousing a world-wide back-to-Africa campaign. UNIA expanded thereafter, claiming over two million members by 1919 and four million members a year later. Garvey founded the Black Star Line, which outfitted passenger liners to transport colonists to Africa. Garvey, perceived as a profound threat, was subjected to a federal prosecutorial campaign that culminated in his conviction for mail fraud. Serving two years in federal prison, he was deported in 1927.

Garveyism retained a powerful appeal during the 1920s, especially in rural areas. Of UNIA membership in the United States, about half its local chapters were composed of black farmers. Rural membership tended to come from property holders, lawyers, and ministers—in other words, the elite among rural African Americans. UNIA offered a fraternal order where black autonomy, self-defense, and leadership became emphasized. "A man who thinks that he is fitted for something better and is willing to work and suffer to get it," said one Missouri Garveyite, "will eventually reach a higher plane. . . . We are masters of our destinies, and if we fail, we can blame nobody but ourselves."[34]

UNIA provided a vehicle for protest, just as migration also made a statement against white supremacy. The organization drew members from urban areas where rural blacks had migrated. In Hampton, Virginia, which experienced heavy black migration during the war, longshoremen were attracted to the racial solidarity and nationalism that Garveyism represented. In 1919, Garvey toured the area and organized a UNIA division in Newport News. The area attracted seven thousand members, making this group the second-largest division in the country. In Florida, UNIA found receptive audiences among Bahamian and Jamaican immigrants of Miami and Key West. The Florida UNIA divisions were radicalized by the West Indians' disillusionment with the segregation and exclusion that they suffered in Jim Crow Florida. Garveyites organized paramilitary units and displayed a spirit of defiance, which attracted the attention of state and federal authorities.

Marcus Garvey, 1924. *Library of Congress.*

The Garvey movement continued to grow during the 1920s. The ports of New Orleans, Charleston, and Mobile became fertile organizing grounds among black longshoreman. By 1921, New Orleans alone had three divisions, with more organizations near the city. UNIA also spread to rural Louisiana, especially in the sugar plantation areas of the Mississippi valley. By 1926, Louisiana claimed eight divisions in the state. Similarly,

[34] Jarod Roll, *Spirit of Rebellion: Labor and Religion in the New Cotton South* (Urbana: University of Illinois Press, 2010), 65.

Mobile hosted a significant UNIA presence, which expanded to the rest of Alabama during the 1920s. Birmingham's iron and coal districts saw significant UNIA expansion.

The most-dynamic areas of growth for Garveyism existed in the rural South, with a strong appeal to workers and farmers. In Georgia, a center of strength existed in the cotton plantation district in the southwest portion of the state. Into the delta regions of Mississippi and Arkansas, UNIA continued to expand, with an appeal to plantation workers. According to one estimate, 75 percent of the Garveyites in southwestern Georgia were agricultural workers, most married, literate, and parents. Elsewhere in the cotton South, black farmers were drawn to the organization. Bolivar County, Mississippi, in the delta, possessing a population over 80 percent black, boasted seventeen UNIA divisions.[35]

Everywhere, the message that black people found most appealing was empowerment. UNIA did not preach disloyalty, said a Georgia organizer, but instead the "Redemption of Africa, our Motherland." African Americans did not want "social equality, but social rights." Black people, the organizer declared, would "never be anything until they possess strong power; not until then will we be respected."[36] Members included longshoremen, railroad workers, and shipbuilders, as well as timber cutters, sawmill workers, and construction workers. In addition, the agricultural proletariat was naturally drawn to a message of independence and empowerment.

UNIA's back-to-Africa program had a mostly ideological appeal. Garvey and UNIA represented racial pride, autonomy, and self-defense—all qualities appealing to African Americans during the Jim Crow era. "This is a white man's country," said an organizer in North Carolina, but the time was ripe to establish a black man's country in Africa. In that state, the organization attracted followers in Piedmont towns, with membership reaching black professional and middle classes. Winston-Salem became a center of Garveyism, and it attracted black workers at R. J. Reynolds Tobacco plants.

The entrance of UNIA into black communities often had a divisive impact. The organization's rapid growth unnerved established black leaders. Northern civil rights groups criticized UNIA methods and goals, while local ministers in the South were frequent opponents. At the same time, some of the most successful organizers were local ministers who embraced the cause. Adam D. Newson, a black minister with three churches in Bolivar County, Mississippi, became a highly effective organizer. Very often local divisions met at churches, retaining a religious affiliation. Each local organization was required to have a chaplain, reinforcing the presence of black ministers in the organization. UNIA meetings often involved prayers and hymns; in communities where the order grew, it often reflected a strong religious character. The order's musical director, Arnold J. Ford, wrote a Universal Ethiopian Anthem. Its chorus declared: "Advance, advance to victory! / Let Africa be free! / Advance to meet the foe with the might of the red, the black, and the green."[37]

[35] Mary G. Rolinson, *Grassroots Garveyism: The Universal Negro Improvement Association in the Rural South, 1920–1927* (Chapel Hill: University of North Carolina Press, 2007), 107–112.
[36] Rolinson, *Grassroots Garveyism*, 96.
[37] Rolinson, *Grassroots Garveyism*, 119.

The UNIA survived in the South through most of the 1920s, peaking in membership by about 1927. After Garvey was deported, the organization became beset by division and infighting. UNIA became increasingly superseded by the NAACP, which moved into the South and organized communities aggressively. Other protest organizations, such as the interracial Southern Tenant Farmers Union, also siphoned off membership as a more attractive vehicle for protest. Nonetheless, UNIA laid a basis for future black protest, while promoting an ideology of armed self-defense and self-reliance, along with a message of black separatism.

In the World War I era, an ugly racism dominated various levels of southern—and American—society. In an Atlanta pencil factory where Leo Frank worked as a manager, a young worker, Mary Phagan, was murdered in April 1913. Frank was Jewish, and the case immediately attracted the attention of the press, with lurid accusations against Frank. A large crowd waited outside the courthouse during the twenty-five-day trial. Tom Watson, who had been viciously anti-Semitic and anti-Catholic in his *Watson's Jeffersonian Magazine*, took up the cause. After Frank was convicted of murder in September 1913, his lawyer exhausted appeals, including an appeal to the US Supreme Court. The governor of Georgia, John M. Slaton, commuted the sentence because of his doubts about the case. Local residents became outraged. In August 1915, a mob stormed into the state prison at Milledgeville, Georgia, drove Frank to Marietta, Phagan's hometown, and lynched him.

The atmosphere of officially sanctioned racism received the backing of the academic and cultural leadership of the South. Virginia's leading eugenicist was John Powell, a composer and music professor at the University of Virginia who organized the Anglo-Saxon Clubs, a movement promoting racial purity. Powell believed that segregation needed to go further in "achieving a final solution" to the "negro problem" and a decline toward a "Negroid Nation." It was insufficient, Powell wrote, "to segregate the Negro on railway trains and street cars, in schools and theaters." Disfranchisement meant little "so long as the possibility remains of the absorption of Negro blood into our white population." Powell rejected the usual standard—that people having one-sixteenth or more African heritage were "black"—and argued instead that any African heritage at all equated with blackness.[38]

Powell adhered to eugenics—the pseudoscience of genetic management—which encouraged racial "purity" as well as efforts to "purify" the racial development of southern whites. These included supposedly genetically "defective" people such as the poor and mentally ill; remedies sought to institutionalize them, and even to sterilize them by force. In 1924, the Virginia legislature enacted the Racial Integrity Act. It required all Virginians to register their racial status, while the law also provided measures against race mixing. The law imposed a much more restrictive notion of whiteness. Whereas previous legislation mandated that "colored" included anyone

---

[38] J. Douglas Smith, "The Campaign for Racial Purity and the Erosion of Paternalism in Virginia, 1922–1930: 'Nominally White, Biologically Mixed, and Legally Negro,'" *Journal of Southern History* 68, no. 1 (February 2002): 71.

with one-sixteenth African American lineage, the Racial Integrity Act declared that "white persons" were only those with "no trace whatsoever of any blood other than Caucasian." Marriage between any nonwhite and white people became illegal.[39]

Also in 1924, the Virginia legislature enacted the Virginia Sterilization Statute, which enabled the sterilization of persons at four state institutions who were deemed to be "feebleminded," including the "insane, idiotic, imbecilic, or epileptic." Virginia was not alone in these policies; by 1956, twenty-four states had laws providing for involuntary sterilization on their books. By the late 1970s, when the practice stopped in Virginia, nearly seven thousand people underwent forced sterilizations. In 1927, the Supreme Court, in *Buck v. Bell*, allowed the practice. The case involved Carrie Buck, who was born in Charlottesville, Virginia, and, at age seventeen, was committed to the Virginia Colony for Epileptics and Feebleminded after she was raped and impregnated by the nephew of her foster parents. In 1924, after the birth of her child, the colony's superintendent, Albert Sidney Priddy, sought and obtained approval to sterilize Carrie. Claiming that she had the intelligence of a nine-year-old, Priddy argued that she posed a larger threat to the genetic health of society.

Deciding *Buck v. Bell* on May 2, 1927, the Supreme Court endorsed the eugenicist argument for involuntary sterilization. Buck, wrote Justice Oliver Wendell Holmes Jr., was the parent of "socially inadequate offspring," and her sterilization benefited her and served a social good. Mental "defectives" such as Buck "already sap the strength of the State"; sterilization prevented "our being swamped with incompetence." It was "better for all the world, if instead of waiting to execute degenerate offspring for crime, or to let them starve for their imbecility, society can prevent those who are manifestly unfit from continuing their kind." Just as vaccination had become compulsory, so too the state was justified in instituting forced sterilization. "Three generations of imbeciles," wrote Justice Oliver Wendell Holmes Jr., "are enough." Nationally, nearly 60,000 sterilizations occurred by the 1970s.[40]

The Great War left a deep imprint on the South. Exposing the South to the wider world, it marked the beginning of the end of the long-standing social and cultural isolation of the region from the rest of the country. Mass migration of people from the South began an ongoing depopulation of the countryside, a process that would continue in earnest over the next half century. As the South began to experience powerful external forces, exposure to new ideas and influences was not always enthusiastically welcomed. Undergoing sweeping changes after World War I, during the 1920s the South expressed a new mood of unease, evident elsewhere in the United States. The war spurred nationalism and heightened patriotism, but these forces translated into powerful forces demanding a defense of white supremacy and the reassertion of old patterns of racial hierarchy. Similarly, southerners expressed their unease by attempting to return to a past of cultural homogeneity.

[39] Pippa Holloway, *Sexuality, Politics, and Social Control in Virginia, 1920–1945* (Chapel Hill: University of North Carolina Press, 2006), 21–22.

[40] *Buck v. Bell*, 274 U.S. 200 (1927); Susan K. Cahn, *Sexual Reckonings: Southern Girls in a Troubling Age* (Cambridge, MA: Harvard University Press, 2007), 158–159.

18

CHANGE AND CONFLICT IN THE 1920s

RAPID CHANGES CAME during the 1920s, and managing and understanding that change occupied southerners. The new postwar society spawned other responses across a diverse spectrum of life. Cultural elites criticized traditionalism as a Southern Renaissance in literature, the arts, and academics emerged. The expanded industrial economy heightened corporate control but also spurred labor conflict, as incipient unions attempted to establish a foothold in a region with fewer unions than any other in the country. Labor conflict became so acute that the social harmony of the modern South appeared seriously frayed.

Ordinary people's responses to these changes often reflected an attempt to reimpose order by returning to old ways of life. The popularity of the Klan during the 1920s expressed disquiet about change and, especially, threats to white Protestant cultural and racial dominance and traditional roles for men and women. Revitalized Christianity also sought to impose order by reasserting past traditions. Coalescing during World War I, fundamentalism appeared on the public stage during the 1920s. Fundamentalist Christianity—insisting on biblical inerrancy and opposing Darwinian evolution—was unrelated to the Klan, though it expressed many of the same anxieties. White conservative evangelicals denounced vigilantism, but the Klan and fundamentalists shared a common determination to restore the cultural hierarchy.

Despite traditionalists' attempts to manage change by controlling it, the genie was out of the bottle. Conflict and change during the 1920s exposed a social fragility. Indeed, the region was on the verge of a transformation that was foreshadowed during this period, and the 1920s experienced serious crises. The speculative fever that gripped the American economy also occurred in the South, most apparently in the real-estate mania that gripped Florida in the middle of the decade. A major environmental disaster, the great Mississippi flood of 1927, also revealed the uncertainty with which political elites dealt with crisis.

THE URBAN ETHOS

In the 1920s, cities became magnets of a new southern culture—more obviously "modern," connected to the urban North and Europe, more secular, more commercialized, but also more stratified by race and class. The urban South of the 1920s embraced consumerism, the new economy and culture that accompanied the advent of electricity, and popular attractions such as commercial sports, radio, and movies.

No place better exemplified the urban ethos of the 1920s than the city of Atlanta, Georgia. Reminding outsiders that they were the New South city of Henry Grady, boosters advertised the city as an attractive location for northern capital. They promoted an "Atlanta spirit" of openness to outsiders, emphasizing economic development and growth and harmonious social and racial progress. During the first three decades of the twentieth century, Atlanta underwent intense growth and expansion. The advent of streetcars in the 1880s enabled the city to expand into a ring of suburban neighborhoods. The popularity and prevalence of automobiles further spurred growth. New skyscrapers appeared in the downtown, creating an urban landscape that advertised the urban identity. Between 1900 and 1930, Atlanta's population tripled. Meanwhile, the city's economy shifted from manufacturing to finance and transportation.

Boosters in the Atlanta Chamber of Commerce launched a national promotion campaign, Forward Atlanta, selling the city to the world. The city spent $722,000, raised privately, in a national promotional campaign. In 1924, the chamber established an Industrial Bureau to lead promotional efforts. The campaign yielded results during the 1920s, as large companies such as Sears, Roebuck & Company, and General Motors located distribution centers in the city. Leaders of the promotional campaign claimed that the Forward Atlanta movement succeeded in luring 679 firms and 17,400 workers to Atlanta. Other southern cities followed suit, using chambers of commerce and auxiliary organizations to lure new businesses.

Another prominent southern metropolitan center of the first half of the twentieth century was Birmingham, Alabama. Prior to the 1870s, the city did not exist. Its location on key railroad locations and near rich deposits of coal, limestone, and iron made it into an important industrial center. Birmingham's steel industry became especially important, and the city's population growth proved spectacular. In 1900, Birmingham had about 38,000 residents. Twenty years later, about 179,000 people lived there—one of the fastest-growing urban areas in the United States. During the 1920s, Birmingham's growth continued, with the city's population reaching about 260,000 by the end of the decade.

Many of Birmingham's new residents were migrants. The coal mines and steel mills near the city employed eastern Europeans and African Americans, while many of the mill and mine managers were northerners. Although the total immigrant population was not large, about two-fifths of the city residents were black. Black residents lived in neglected areas—along the railroad lines, in back alleys, and along creek beds. Their housing was inferior, often shacks; African Americans lacked streetlights, sewage and running water, and paved streets. Housing for black people was further limited by a pattern of residential segregation, which kept the city racially segregated. Although many of its residents lived in squalor, city boosters emphasized the future rather than the past. Birmingham, said one, was "predominantly a child of the twentieth century, and it has no old traditions that cause men to regret the passing of old landmarks." The city was known for its prominent skyline, and city boosters proclaimed the city center as "the South's most developed downtown corner."[1]

Cities after World War I increasingly depended on electricity, which created a distinctive urban lifestyle of consumer products and household goods such as lighting fixtures, washing machines, refrigerators, radios, and vacuum cleaners. Because of hydroelectric power, the production of electricity expanded by 156 percent between 1921 and 1930. There was considerable consolidation in the electric-utilities industry; at the end of the 1920s, seven main conglomerates controlled most of the electrical industry in the South. Of these seven, three—Duke Power, Commonwealth and South, and Electric Bond and Share—controlled more than 70 percent of the market. Because of the South's heavy usage of hydroelectric power, energy costs were cheaper than anywhere else in the United States, a factor that provided southern textile mills a competitive advantage.

The 1920s saw the continued departure of cotton mills from New England to the South. More than two-thirds of people employed in the textile industry worked in the South by 1933. Large textile conglomerates dominated. Burlington Mills, which industrialist J. Spencer Love established in North Carolina in 1923, became the largest textile manufacturer in the world. Southern mills, along with the textile industry worldwide, expanded into the production of rayons and other synthetics. Meanwhile, larger textile manufacturers eroded the traditional paternalism of southern mill villages. These enterprises, organized along corporate lines and often multinational in organization, responded to intense pressure to compete and to report profits to shareholders.

Other industries expanded during the 1920s. Tobacco manufacturing grew with increased consumption of cigarettes at home and abroad. On the heels of R. J. Reynolds's development of the popular Camel brand of cigarettes, other producers developed brands that depended on heavy advertising and marketing. Cigarette manufacturing concentrated among the Big Three producers—R. J. Reynolds, Liggett & Meyers, and American Tobacco—and accounted for nearly nine-tenths of production. Most manufacturing was located in North Carolina, in the center of the bright-leaf tobacco growing region. Petrochemicals, established as a war industry, also became a major industry in the

---

[1] Blaine A. Brownell, "Birmingham, Alabama: New South City in the 1920s," *Journal of Southern History* 38, no. 1 (February 1972): 23.

post–World War I South. An oil boom accompanied the expansion of the automobile industry, with Oklahoma, Texas, and Louisiana composing the heart of the southern oil patch. The Gulf Coast became a center of oil refineries, with a network of pipelines transporting gasoline to markets around the nation.

The ascendancy of the urban South found expression in cultural turmoil. The Southern Renaissance, which historian Richard King defines as an attempt by writers and intellectuals to "come to terms not only with the inherited values of the Southern tradition but also with a certain way of perceiving and dealing with the past," became an important phenomenon. Participants in the Southern Renaissance sought to re-create and reimagine the past, attempting to discern how it had shaped the present. This inquiry involved attention to "past and present" and coming to terms with the particularities of the American South.[2] A broad cultural, literary, and academic movement, the Southern Renaissance encompassed a variety of areas of life. World War I—which exposed southerners, and Americans generally, to the wider world—had an effect, providing the chance, as Allen Tate wrote, for southerners to "rejoin the world."

Most prominently, the Southern Renaissance was a literary movement. Journals such as *Virginia Quarterly Review*, the *South Atlantic Quarterly*, and the *Sewanee Review* became leading venues for southern writers. The most important of these writers were novelists. Thomas Wolfe described life in his hometown of Asheville, North Carolina, in his *Look Homeward, Angel* (1929). Georgian Erskine Caldwell depicted the life in the rural South in *Tobacco Road*, which became one of the most important American novels of the twentieth century. And William Faulkner portrayed the tangled web of race, class, and gender in his portrayal of human relationships in fictitious Yoknapatawpha County, Mississippi.

Like the Lost Generation of American writers, southerners' experiences in Europe during World War I had a significant impact. The war, and the exposure to global conditions, undermined southern parochialism. People coming of age during the war questioned previous bedrock values. The greatest of the southern writers of this era, William Faulkner, served in the war, and his experiences encouraged an inquisitorial spirit about southern traditions. William Alexander Percy, a young Mississippian, traveled to Europe in 1916, before the United States joined the war, to work on the Commission for Relief in Belgium. Later, he enlisted in the infantry and served in the American offensive in 1918 in the Argonne Forest. Like Faulkner, a Mississippian, Percy wrote his autobiographical *Lanterns on the Levee* in 1940. In it, he described how young southerners returned from the war altered in their perspectives about their home. Once the war ended, Percy remembered telling himself, "the only great thing you were ever a part of" was over. He found it difficult to return "to the old petty things without purpose, direction, or unity.... You can't go on with that kind of thing till you die."[3]

[2] Richard H. King, *A Southern Renaissance: The Cultural Awakening of the American South, 1930–1955* (New York: Oxford University Press, 1980), 7, 13.
[3] William Alexander Percy, *Lanterns on the Levee: Recollections of a Planter's Son* (New York: Alfred A. Knopf, 1941), 223.

In November 1917, Baltimore journalist Henry Louis Mencken published a short piece in the *New York Evening Mail* describing the South as a "Sahara of the Bozarts." Mencken, a native of Baltimore, wrote for the *Evening Sun* in that city, and after 1914 he edited national journals the *Smart Set* and the *American Mercury*. Since the Civil War, the state of civilization south of the Potomac had declined, he claimed. There were "single acres in Europe that house more first-rate men than all the states south of the Potomac." If the entire South were engulfed by a tidal wave, "the effect upon the civilized minority of men in the world would be but little. . . . It would be impossible in all history to match so complete a drying-up of a civilization." In this "gargantuan paradise of the fourth-rate," there was not a "single picture gallery worth going into, or a single orchestra capable of playing the nine symphonies of Beethoven, or a single opera-house, or a single theater devoted to decent plays, or a single public monument that is worth looking at, or a single workshop devoted to the making of beautiful things." No historians, philosophers, or theologians of any distinction worked in the region; it was an "awe-inspiring blank—a brother to Portugal, Serbia and Albania." The literary scene in the South was equally dismal; there was not a single southern writer who could "actually write." Assessing composers, painters, sculptors, and architects, Mencken concluded that there was "not even a bad one between the Potomac mudflats and the Gulf."[4]

Seeking a reaction, Mencken was deliberately provocative. The Nashville Agrarians organized themselves as a response to Mencken's criticisms. Based at Vanderbilt University in Nashville, Tennessee, they were led by writers such as John Crowe Ransom, Allen Tate, and Donald Davidson. In *I'll Take My Stand: The South and the Agrarian Tradition* (1930), the Agrarians criticized the cultural status quo, though from a romantic-conservative perspective. Including essays by twelve southerners, the book was a manifesto from intellectuals Ransom, Tate, and Davidson; poet John Gould Fletcher; novelist Andrew Nelson Lytle; and Vanderbilt historians Herman C. Nixon and Frank Owsley.

I'll Take My Stand reasserted southern cultural traditions as against the triumphant industrial values that seemed to be overcoming America. The volume was backward looking and anti-industrial. The Nashville group supported a "Southern way of life against what may be called the American or prevailing way," they wrote in the manifesto that opened the book, "and all as much as agree that the best terms in which to represent the distinction are contained in the phrase, Agrarian *versus* Industrial." The Nashville Agrarians criticized not only the collectivism of industrial values but also its heartless and soulless qualities. The "theory of agrarianism," the manifesto posited, was that a "culture of the soil" could provide an alternative path to progress, and that the South was the best example of this agrarian culture.[5]

Despite changes found most obviously in urban areas, the South was a region of contrasts. Even with new industry, new forms of cultural transmission, and the

---

[4] H. L. Mencken, "The Sahara of the Bozarts," in *The American Scene: A Reader*, ed. Huntington Cairns (New York: Alfred A. Knopf, 1977), 158–159.
[5] Introduction, in Twelve Southerners, *I'll Take My Stand: The South and Agrarian Tradition* (New York: Harper, 1930).

physical presence of cities, a powerful traditionalism remained. For many rural southerners, life had not changed that much compared to what it was for their parents and grandparents. The rural South remained largely isolated from the swirl and tumult of modernization. Heavily populated, the countryside included a dense concentration of poor people who composed a pool of cheap, available labor for plantation agriculture that was practiced in essentially the same way that it had been for the previous century. Nationally, the South was, by far, the poorest, worst nourished, and least educated region in the United States. The more that pockets of modernity appeared and grew, the more this disparity became obvious.

LABOR CONFLICT

In the post–World War I South, the prosperity of the 1920s disguised serious structural inequalities. The rural South remained a center of poverty, which was tied to a system of oppression, racial and economic, that accompanied cotton culture and the plantation system. This system depended on the existence of cheap labor, and management was determined to avoid any union inroads. As industry, mining, transportation, and extractive industries faced pressures to compete and generate profits, added pressure fell on southern workers. The result was a period of labor turbulence and revolt evident by the late 1920s.

Southern industrial workers were underpaid, compared to counterparts elsewhere in the country, earning on average between three-fifths and two-thirds of the wages of workers outside the region. Southern workers were overworked, laboring between eleven and twelve hours daily, as compared to substantially shorter days for nonsouthern workers. To a greater extent than elsewhere in the United States, though the incidence of child workers was declining during the 1920s, child labor persisted in the South. Federal legislation outlawed child labor in 1916 and 1919, but in both instances the Supreme Court invalidated these laws.

Most southern mill workers lived in company-owned mill villages. Larger mills modernized these facilities, installing running water, plumbing, electricity, and modern sanitation. According to one study of North Carolina mill villages, most had modernized facilities, with about 93 percent of workers living in new housing. Some of the mill villages also created a system of welfare capitalism by providing churches and schools, as well as social workers and organized leisure and sports activities. Baseball became popular in the southern textile community because of mill-sponsored leagues. The flip side of mill paternalism was the total control that owners and managers exerted over workers. "We govern like the Czar of Russia," said a South Carolina manager. "We are monarchs of all we survey." Police and the legal system remained under the control of mill owners.[6] The mill village became a bastion of class

---

[6] Lois MacDonald, *Southern Mill Hills: A Study of Social and Economic Forces in Certain Textile Mill Villages* (New York: Alex L. Hillman, 1928), 44.

identity, as the clothes, language, schools, and churches segregated mill workers from townspeople and bred a mutual dislike.

Labor organizers in the South made few inroads, despite frequent attempts. The United Textile Workers (UTW), affiliated with the American Federation of Labor, increased southern membership during World War I, but management reversed these gains during the postwar economic slump. Other union organizers encountered resistance. Oil workers successfully organized the Texas fields during World War I, only to see the union extinguished thereafter. Tobacco workers organized in Winston-Salem but encountered opposition in Reidsville and Durham and eventually folded. In the coalfields, the United Mine Workers (UMW) won a strike in 1917 and achieved further gains, but the union was dealt a mortal blow in 1920, when management responded with strikebreakers. After black lumber workers went on strike in Bogalusa, Louisiana, in 1919, vigilantes attacked and broke up the strike.

Larger corporations introduced popular synthetics such as rayon, providing the fabric for women's hose, which become popular during the 1920s. Over 70 percent of rayon production occurred in the South by the 1940s, with most factories located in Virginia and Tennessee. The 1920s were challenging times for textile manufacturers. Facing intense competition from abroad, management looked for ways to reduce costs. With unions reeling during the 1920s, southern industrialists instituted their own labor policies. Textile manufacturers, in this new economic environment, turned to efficiency experts to find ways to boost production and cut labor costs. Commonly known as the "stretch out" by workers, these cost-cutting measures brought added work responsibilities and production quotas without any commensurate increases in pay. Across the textile belt, workers deeply resented these practices. The result was a spate of labor conflict across the Piedmont South.

Labor organizers, seizing on the opportunity to organize mills, found a receptive audience. In 1929, strikes erupted across the Piedmont and mountain mill towns. Elizabethton, in eastern Tennessee, housed two huge rayon plants employing several thousand workers. Two German corporate giants, J. P. Bemberg Company and Vereinigte Glanzstoff-Fabriken, operated plants located along the rim of the Appalachian Mountains. On March 12, 1929, 523 female workers spontaneously struck at the Glanzstoff-Fabriken plant after a worker was demoted for asking for a pay increase and after complaints about bad pay and management harassment. Two days later, the plant closed after other workers joined the strike. During the next week, workers at the Bemberg plant also went on strike.

The leaders and participants in the Elizabethton strike were women, who made up 30 percent of the workforce at the Bemberg plant, which employed 886 men and 384 women. At the Glanzstoff-Fabriken mill, 44 percent of the workers were women. Most were single females, who received lower wages than male workers. Women workers were subject to petty rules forbidding them from wearing makeup and, in some instances, requiring uniforms. Female workers were required to have a pass to use the washroom, where they were watched and scrutinized, while male workers used the facilities whenever they wanted. These women, resenting new labor controls that German managers introduced, spearheaded the strike. Women workers saw the labor system as something imposed by outsiders, in collusion with the town classes. The local townspeople advised the German corporation that "women wasn't used to working," recalled one female striker, "and they'd work for almost nothing, and the men would work for low wages."[7]

Strikers were united not only by a common sense of grievance, but also by their rural roots and traditions. The strikers affiliated with the UTW but lacked local allies. Labor unions also faced the united opposition of the company and the Elizabethton local government. A local court issued an injunction preventing strikers from picketing and to stop the plants' operation. After a temporary truce, the workers struck again on April 15, 1929, after two union organizers were kidnapped and transported out of the county and after union members were dismissed from jobs. Management responded by hiring strikebreakers. Violence erupted in arson and dynamiting, presumably committed by strikers. The governor of Tennessee responded to the violence by dispatching eight hundred National Guard troops to protect the plants. The troops created an armed camp, and 1,250 strikers were arrested. The strike ended in May 1929, when management agreed to concessions, though refusing to recognize the union.

Across the mountains, to the east, in the small town of Marion, North Carolina, another protest strike among textile mill workers erupted against low wages, bad working conditions, and long hours. Like other strikes during 1929, in Marion the owners were intransigent, refusing to recognize the unions or make concessions. In violence occurring on October 2, 1929, police fired tear gas into a crowd, and deputies fired live ammunition, killing six workers. The sheriff and his deputies were later acquitted on murder charges, and the strike fizzled.

In the latter half of 1929, strike fever spread to the southern Piedmont, especially in the Carolinas, with similar strikes based on similar grievances. By far, the most serious explosion of labor conflict took place in Gastonia, North Carolina. There, the Manville-Jencks Corporation of Pawtucket, Rhode Island, ran the massive Loray plant, which employed 3,500 workers. With absentee ownership, the mill maintained a mill village and ran forms of welfare capitalism but, like other mills during the 1920s, instituted cost-cutting measures that greatly increased workloads. Management also reduced wages and downsized the workforce by about a third.

In 1928, the National Textile Workers Union (NTWU) organized in Massachusetts, with affiliation with the Communist Party of America. The union began an aggressive effort to organize the Loray Mill. Organizers' arrival in Gastonia formed part of a strategy to politicize the South by politicizing white workers and mobilizing African Americans. The head of the Communist unionizing effort, Fred Beal, arrived in early January 1929 and began a two-month campaign. After the Loray Mill dismissed five union members, a thousand workers voted to go out on strike. The union demanded

[7] Jacquelyn D. Hall, "Disorderly Women: Gender and Labor Militancy in the Appalachian South," *Journal of American History* 73, no. 2 (September 1986): 369.

Ella May Wiggins. *Library of Congress.*

better wages and working conditions, but management was unwilling to negotiate or recognize the union. Communists outside Gastonia were eager to radicalize things as a part of their larger effort. North Carolina, declared one Communist official, was "the key to the South, Gaston County is the key to North Carolina, and the Loray Mill is the key to Gaston County."[8]

The strike achieved little progress and ended in mid-April 1929. However, with a contingent of about 250 strikers remaining, management evicted the strikers from company-owned housing. The strikers erected a tent colony in a nearby field, but, on June 7, 1929, when local police raided the settlement, shots were fired, killing Chief of Police Orville F. Aderholt. Authorities responded with mass arrests, imprisoning seventy-one people. A reign of terror ensued in Gaston County, while a group of strikers, including Beal, were tried in Charlotte under spectacular national scrutiny. On September 14, 1929, shots were fired into a truck occupied by five workers, and Ella May Wiggins, a strike leader and balladeer, was killed.

Wiggins was a twenty-nine-year-old mother of five, and a legendary female striker. She was drawn to the strike as a protest against oppression. "I never made no more than nine dollars a week," she said in a speech, "and you can't do for a family on such money." "That's why I come out for the union, and why we all got to stand for the union, so's we can do better for our children, and they won't have lives like we got." During a brief period of about six months during the spring and summer, Wiggins composed twenty-one ballads. Using the melodies of popular "hillbilly" and mountain musical traditions, she crafted lyrics that spoke to the workers' conditions and urged radical action. In her best-known ballad, "The Mill Mother's Lament," she explained how "We leave our homes in the morning, / We kiss our children good-bye, / While we slave for the bosses, / Our children scream and cry." The bosses could be defeated only by union strength: "But understand, all workers, / Our union they do fear. / Let's stand together, workers, / And have a union here."[9]

Beal and six other strikers were convicted in November 1929 and given long prison sentences. Released on bail, Beal toured the Northeast, giving a series of speeches about management's oppression of labor in the South. After the North Carolina Supreme Court rejected their appeal in September 1930, the union leaders fled the country and moved to the Soviet Union. Disillusioned with the Soviets and communism, Beal later returned to the United States and served part of his prison sentence.

[8] Gregory Taylor, *The History of the North Carolina Communist Party* (Columbia: University of South Carolina Press, 2009), 22.
[9] Lyrics can be found at http://www.traditionalmusic.co.uk/folk-song-lyrics/Mill_Mothers_Lament.htm.

FUNDAMENTALISM

During the late nineteenth and early twentieth centuries, the intellectual and cultural force of modernism reshaped mainstream Protestantism. Modernism, as applied to Christianity, involved adapting belief to modern standards of science and secularism. In some denominations, modernist scholarship in literature and history questioned the absolute veracity and literal truth of the Bible. Trained in Germany, these biblical scholars turned their attention to the historical Jesus and the Gospels, which they interpreted as products of the culture and social conditions of their time. Alongside modernism was the Social Gospel, a doctrine that emphasized the social-justice re-sponsibilities of the church. Social Gospelers favored human interventions in social problems, believing that Christians could hasten the arrival of the Kingdom of God and a perfected society. Social Gospel advocates also urged churches to adapt to modern culture—a notion that fundamentalists came to reject thoroughly.

The most explosive issue in American Protestantism concerned the Protestant response to Charles Darwin's theory of evolution. First published in 1859, Darwin's *Origin of Species* soon stirred controversy. James Woodrow, a professor at the Columbia Theological Seminary in South Carolina (and an uncle of Woodrow Wilson), was tried for heresy for expressing the view that evolution and religious faith were compatible. In December 1884, Woodrow was stripped of his seminary professorship and was banned from teaching. Southern Presbyterians took a strong antievolution stance after the Woodrow controversy. In an important turning point, denominational leaders, well into the twentieth century, strongly opposed the teaching of Darwin in schools.

Fundamentalists insisted on orthodox "fundamentals"—a belief in the inerrancy of the Bible, the Virgin Birth and Atonement, Christ's death and resurrection, and his ascension to heaven. In 1910, two Southern Californians published *The Fundamentals*, pamphlets asserting conservative Presbyterianism. In 1916, the World's Christian Fun-damentals Association, espousing the same antimodern agenda, met at Montrose, Pennsylvania. In May 1918, a Prophetic Convention attracted five thousand partici-pants to Philadelphia, and the attendees agreed to combat modernism.

Fundamentalists expressed anxiety about how the remaking of the economy affected the social structure. "My friends, we are in a terrible hour," fundamental-ist J. Frank Norris told the Texas legislature in 1923. He warned of a "reign of lawlessness" prevailing in the land. "Our penitentiaries are crowded, our jails are crowded and our juvenile courts are working overtime." This social breakdown was attributable to the rise of secularism and "liberalism"—the tendency to exalt humans over God. "There is a wave of liberalism sweeping over this country," he continued, in which marriage vows were invalid; Americans were in the "age of free-loveism."[10]

---

[10] Michael Lienesch, *In the Beginning: Fundamentalism, the Scopes Trial, and the Making of the Antievolution Movement* (Chapel Hill: University of North Carolina Press, 2007), 88–89.

A small but vocal group of theological moderates opposed these views. William L. Poteat, born in Caswell County, North Carolina, in 1856, joined the faculty of Baptist Wake Forest College in 1880 as a natural-science instructor. Between 1905 and 1927, Poteat served as Wake Forest president. During the early 1900s, he popularized the view that it was possible to reconcile modern science and religious faith. In lectures at Louisville Seminary in 1901, later published as *Laboratory and Pulpit*, Poteat presented himself as an enthusiastic evolutionist. Darwin's ideas, he declared, were "the most potent instrument for the extension of natural knowledge which has come into men's hands since the publication of 'Newton's Principia.'" Poteat argued that religious faith and belief should guide science in a "re-statement of the Christian conception from the view-point of evolution." God, Poteat said, was the source of a "proper environment of the growing ethical nature." With a directive hand on the organic process, God could "put into it more and more of moral and spiritual significance until it reaches a point where it is altogether meaningless apart from the nobler nature which he has grafted upon it."[11]

Within Protestant denominations, a fight erupted as fundamentalists tried to purge modernists from pulpits and seminaries. For the most part, fundamentalists prevailed. They encountered a stiffer fight outside the denomination regarding the teaching of evolution in public schools and the state's role in prohibiting Darwinian biology. Much of the fundamentalist campaign concerned public high schools and colleges. Mississippi evangelist T. T. Martin published a pamphlet, *Hell and the High Schools*, which claimed that modern education was subverting the moral and religious order. Evolution, Martin claimed, was being "drilled into our boys and girls." Martin was especially concerned about high schools and the threat that they posed to young minds and the "most susceptible, more dangerous age of their lives."[12]

Starting in 1921, former Democratic presidential candidate William Jennings Bryan led a national campaign to ban evolution in the public schools. "Under the pretense of teaching science," Bryan warned, "instructors who draw their salaries from the public treasury are undermining the religious faith of students by substituting belief in Darwinism for belief in the Bible." "Quietly and unnoticed," he said, "the enemies of the Bible have been substituting irreligion for religion."[13] In state legislatures, fundamentalists attempted to enact legislation preventing Darwinian biology from being taught in high schools and universities. Nationally, forty-five antievolution bills were introduced in twenty-one state legislatures. The most-intense antievolution efforts occurred in the South. In 1926, proposed bills in Virginia, West Virginia, Georgia, and South Carolina were beaten back. In Texas, fundamentalists attacked evolution, and the University of Texas's faculty senate responded by adopting a

[11] William Louis Poteat, *Laboratory and Pulpit: The Relation of Biology to the Preacher and His Message* (Philadelphia: Griffith & Rowland, 1901), 31, 39–40.
[12] Lienesch, *In the Beginning*, 74.
[13] Bryan, "The Menace of Evolution"; available at http://law2.umkc.edu/faculty/projects/ftrials/scopes/bryanonevol.html.

resolution prohibiting employment of anyone who was "infidel, atheist, or agnostic."[14] On the other hand, five southern legislatures—in Mississippi, Arkansas, Florida, Oklahoma, and Tennessee—enacted laws prohibiting the teaching of Darwinian biology in state-supported schools.

Perhaps the most-heated struggles occurred in the North Carolina and Tennessee legislatures. Fundamentalists introduced a bill in the North Carolina legislature seeking to ban Darwin from public schools and universities. This proposal enjoyed strong support from the state's Presbyterians, doggedly antievolutionist, and from organizations such as the North Carolina Anti-Evolution League and the North Carolina Bible League. After a determined campaign by University of North Carolina president Harry Woodburn Chase, Poteat, and the state's Protestant mainline leadership, the bill was defeated.

In 1925, Tennessee became the first state to enact an antievolution law. In 1923, the University of Tennessee fired psychology professor Jesse W. Sprowls and five others when Sprowls assigned James Harvey Robinson's *The Mind in the Making: The Relation of Intelligence to Social Reform*. The university remained silent after Tennessee representative John Washington Butler introduced his bill and it was enacted into law. The act made it illegal "for any teacher in any of the Universities, Normals and all other public schools of the State which are supported in whole or in part by the public school funds of the State, to teach any theory that denies the story of the Divine Creation of man as taught in the Bible, and to teach instead that man has descended from a lower order of animals."[15]

The Tennessee "Monkey Law" attracted worldwide attention when a high-school biology teacher, John T. Scopes, agreed to test the law's constitutionality by intentionally teaching evolution in his classroom. The American Civil Liberties Union (ACLU),

which had been organized in 1920 to oppose government suppression of free speech during World War I, defended Scopes. The trial, held in Dayton, in southeastern Tennessee, became a national spectacle. The ACLU lawyer, Clarence Darrow, was a controversial defense attorney and an atheist. The prosecutor brought in William Jennings Bryan to help with the case.

The area surrounding Dayton had diversified from the coal and iron mines, developing a profitable strawberry-growing business. The town was also a commercial center, boasting an energetic group of local capitalists. Boosters saw the publicity from the Scopes trial as helping put their community on the map. To visiting contemporaries, however, the town

John T. Scopes. *Library of Congress.*

[14] Norman F. Furniss, *The Fundamentalist Controversy, 1918–1931* (New Haven, CT: Yale University Press, 1954), 87.
[15] Tennessee Evolution Statutes, 1925; available at http://law2.umkc.edu/faculty/projects/ftrials/scopes/tennstat.htm.

embodied a cultural divide in the South—and America. The town remained caught between change and tradition, between what one newspaper called "fundamentalist fervor and . . . the love of the limelight,"[16] which was something that the trial exposed. "Under the stress of the evolution trial," wrote a visitor from Atlanta, "Dayton is struggling to take on such big city ways as are necessary to give comfort to the visitors." Despite their efforts, there remained a "genuine hospitality that springs from kindly hearts rather than from polished manners."[17]

Dayton attracted media from around the country, and much of the attention paid to the town was unflattering. Generally, national correspondents portrayed Tennesseans as narrow minded and provincial. H. L. Mencken, reporting for the *Baltimore Evening Sun*, described fundamentalism in mocking terms. At the root of the Scopes trial, Mencken saw southern buffoonery and mass ignorance. The assumption that the average person was more enlightened than previously was erroneous, he claimed. The "great masses of men, even in this inspired republic," Mencken wrote, were "precisely where the mob was at the dawn of history. They are ignorant, they are dishonest, they are cowardly, they are ignoble. They know little if anything that is worth knowing, and there is not the slightest sign of a natural desire among them to increase their knowledge." Antievolutionists were nothing more than "conspiracies of the inferior man against his betters" who expressed a "congenital hatred of knowledge, . . . [a] bitter enmity to the man who knows more than he does, and so gets more out of life." Fundamentalists hated knowledge and science "because it puts an unbearable burden upon . . . [their] meager capacity for taking in ideas."[18]

The trial, taking place in July 1925, pitted Darrow against Bryan. In a crucial moment, on the seventh day of the trial, Darrow called Bryan to the stand, and the two men—and two worldviews—stood opposite each other in two hours of testimony. Bryan explained that he was testifying because he wanted the "world to know that this man, who does not believe in God," was trying to use the trial to spread his views. Darrow relentlessly questioned Bryan about the inconsistencies in the Bible, asking the Great Commoner to explain himself. Although Bryan originally maintained under questioning that "everything in the Bible should be accepted as it is given there," he eventually admitted that a literal interpretation of scripture made little sense. Most observers viewed Darrow's questioning as humiliating Bryan, and six days after the trial he collapsed and died.

The outcome of the Scopes trial was inconclusive. After only nine minutes of deliberation, the jury found Scopes guilty, and the judge fined him $100. A year later, the Tennessee Supreme Court affirmed the constitutionality of the Butler Act but dismissed the charges against Scopes in what the decision called a "bizarre" case. The law remained on the books until 1967, when the Tennessee legislature repealed it. A year later, the US Supreme Court issued a decision declaring a similar law in

---

[16] "Dayton Drops 'Strawberryville' and Basks as 'Monkeyville,'" *Baltimore Sun*, July 5, 1925.
[17] "Listening In on Dayton," *Atlanta Constitution*, July 8, 1925.
[18] *Baltimore Evening Sun*, June 29, 1925.

Arkansas to be in violation of the First Amendment. Darrow "appealed directly to the country and to the world," Mencken commented in the pages of the *Baltimore Evening Sun*, by exposing "these recreant Tennesseans by exhibiting their shame to all men, near and far." Darrow succeeded in turning the state "inside out" by demonstrating "what civilization can come to under Fundamentalism." Would Tennesseans "cling to Fundamentalism or will they restore civilization?"[19]

During the 1920s, college and university campuses experienced a period of significant growth, but higher education—which projected secular values and modernism—attracted fundamentalist ire. The University of North Carolina (UNC) at Chapel Hill after World War I became a leading location of the academic investigation of the social conditions and problems of the South. UNC gained the support of legislative leaders for the expansion of the university into a major academic center and an engine of modernization. Sociologist Howard W. Odum established UNC as a leading center of the study of social problems. Under visionary presidents—Edward Kidder Graham, Harry Woodburn Chase, and Frank Porter Graham—UNC recruited new faculty, expanded its facilities, and revamped the university's role in public life. By 1931, the student newspaper, the *Daily Tar Heel*, proclaimed that UNC's growth had been "astounding."[20]

Howard W. Odum came to embody UNC's particular public role. Born in Georgia, in what he later described as the "ruralest of the rural South,"[21] Odum earned two doctorates: at Clark University, in psychology, and at Columbia, in sociology. After stints at the University of Georgia and Emory College, Odum was recruited to UNC in 1920 as the founding director of a new School of Public Welfare. Within a few years, Odum was running an academic empire. He began the Institute for Research in Social Sciences (IRSS), whose mission was to apply new methods in economics, political science, sociology, and history to understand southern social problems. In 1922, Odum founded a new journal, the *Journal of Social Forces* (shortened to *Social Forces* in September 1925), a forum of engagement between the university and the wider world. The IRSS attracted foundation support that funded graduate students and additional faculty.

Odum became a fundamentalist target when the *Journal of Social Forces* published two articles in January 1925 that appeared to undermine traditional Christian faith. One article, written by L. L. Bernard of Cornell University, described religious faiths as the "products of the folk imagination," while another, by sociologist Harry Elmer Barnes, questioned the role of religion in morality. Barnes suggested that the Bible, the "alleged sacred book," had not provided a "reliable and definitive body of rules for conduct, either personal or social." *Social Forces* and Odum came under immediate attack. A social-scientific, clinical approach to religious faith meant "godless science as the only guide for mankind," said one minister. Not only did the publication of these

---

[19] *Baltimore Evening Sun*, September 14, 1925.
[20] Charles J. Holden, *The New Southern University: Academic Freedom and Liberalism at UNC* (Lexington: University Press of Kentucky, 2012), 16.
[21] Willard B. Gatewood Jr., "Embattled Scholar: Howard W. Odum and the Fundamentalists, 1925–1927," *Journal of Southern History* 31, no. 4 (November 1965): 375.

articles suggest "an insidious attack upon the whole supernatural revelation," said a Charlotte Presbyterian minister, but UNC seemed to be fostering an environment of "carnality, sensuality, communism, and the Red Flag."[22]

The loudest opponent of Odum's social science was William P. McCorkle, a Presbyterian minister of Burlington, North Carolina. Publishing numerous articles attacking Odum, McCorkle also wrote a pamphlet, *Anti-Christian Sociology as Taught in the Journal of Social Forces: Presenting a Question for North Carolina Christians.* Appearing in 1925, the pamphlet criticized UNC's "infidel propaganda campaign," which, he claimed, was "not only anti-Christian but anti-religious." McCorkle reviewed past issues of the *Journal of Social Forces*, locating additional evidence of heresy. He objected to a book reviewer's assertion of an "intellectual awakening and growing emancipation from the traditional repressions and controls" of religious belief. McCorkle attacked especially "Darwinian sociology" and objected to UNC's acceptance of the theory of evolution, which slandered Christianity and undermined the "fundamental verities of the Christian faith." The secularist army, camped at UNC, wanted to make Christianity as "extinct as the dodo."[23]

For McCorkle and other fundamentalists, the key issue was that the state had subsidized an "anti-Christian" publication and encouraged the erosion of traditional values. The people of North Carolina should have the right to suppress the publication of "bald infidelity" in a journal edited and produced by UNC faculty. The university was "our school," depending on "our funds, devoted to specific educational uses." The faculty, employed by the state, were obliged to oversee the welfare of students "to be educated for usefulness in life." Should the university really be devoted to the promotion of "agnosticism and materialism?"[24]

In the end, Odum headed off the criticisms of McCorkle and other fundamentalists. Odum, along with UNC President Frank Porter Graham, challenged taboos about race and class, though both were also politically adept. When push came to shove, they tried to accommodate hostile political forces. But their larger success lay in their ability to protect UNC from political pressure. After the 1920s, in many respects, the university enjoyed a flowering that formed a key part of the larger Southern Renaissance.

THE KLAN

On Thanksgiving Eve 1915, at Stone Mountain, Georgia, outside Atlanta, a group of men assembled, adorned in white robes. The group included two veterans of the first, Reconstruction-era Klan. The Speaker of the Georgia house numbered among the participants. The group gathered around an altar with a flag and a Bible and burned

[22] Gatewood, "Embattled Scholar," 380–381.
[23] Gatewood, "Embattled Scholar," 384; William P. McCorkle, *Anti-Christian Sociology as Taught in the Journal of Social Forces: Presenting a Question for North Carolina Christians* (Burlington, NC: A. D. Pate, 1925).
[24] McCorkle, *Anti-Christian Sociology*, 27.

a cross. At midnight, the group resolved to "call up from its slumber" the long-dormant Ku Klux Klan, and they lit a cross to conclude the ceremony. In this way the Invisible Empire, Knights of the Ku Klux Klan—a fraternal order whose name was registered into a charter a few days after the meeting—came into existence.

The leader of the meeting, William Joseph Simmons, was a former Methodist circuit rider, Spanish-American War veteran, southern historian, salesman, and Atlanta-based fraternal organizer for the Woodmen of the World. A white supremacist whose father was an officer in the first, Reconstruction-era Klan, Simmons promoted this second Klan as representing a rebirth of the modern South with a new vision of racial nationalism. He organized the Klan along the lines of a fraternal order, adopting curious naming practices and a modern business plan in its organization. On paper, the Klan comprised regional, state, district, and local chapters, with officials such as "Imperial Wizard" (heading the entire organization), "Grand Dragon" (state leader), "Great Titan" (district leader), and "Exalted Cyclops" (chapter leader).

Simmons deliberately scheduled the first meeting of the Klan to coincide, a week later, with the opening of the feature-length movie blockbuster *Birth of a Nation*. The film, directed by D. W. Griffith, inaugurated a new era of big-budget movies seeking a mass audience. *Birth of a Nation* was mainly the creation of the minister, politician, writer, and actor Thomas Dixon. Based on Dixon's novel *The Clansman* (which, in 1905, he produced into a popular touring play), the movie told the story of the Civil War and Reconstruction in a way that glorified the white South, ridiculed the political capabilities of African Americans, and depicted the Klan as a heroic organization defending white womanhood.

Birth of a Nation evoked widespread protest; the NAACP launched a national campaign in a number of cities to prevent its screening. Despite these protests, the film was wildly successful, implanting in popular discourse a version of history—targeted at a national audience—that was severely distorted. In New York City alone, during the first year of its appearance, there were nearly 6,300 screenings of the film. Dixon succeeded in gaining a White House screening from his old friend Woodrow Wilson, adding luster to the production and seemingly validating the film's truth. "Every man who comes out of one of our theatres," Dixon wrote, "is a Southern partisan for life."[25]

Birth of a Nation thus inspired William J. Simmons's new Klan. Its purpose, Simmons would later write, was "to inculcate the sacred principles and noble ideals of chivalry, the development of character, the protection of the home and the chastity of womanhood, the exemplification of a pure and practical patriotism toward our glorious country, the preservation of American ideals and institutions and the maintenance of white supremacy." Simmons claimed to oppose lynchings and vigilante violence and to take "no part as an organization in any political or religious

[25] John Hope Franklin, "'Birth of a Nation': Propaganda as History," *Massachusetts Review* 20, no. 3 (Autumn 1979): 430.

Ku Klux Klan parade, Washington, DC,
September 13, 1926. *Library of Congress.*

controversy." He also espoused a good-government approach that would "purify" government and regulate moral behavior. But the organization was based on white racial nationalism. Membership was limited to "white American citizens." More ominously, Simmons announced that the organization opposed "strikes by foreign agitators" while favoring "sensible and patriotic immigration laws."[26]

Simmons's revived Klan at first attracted little attention. Atlanta newspapers ignored him; the group had a minimal impact. In 1920, the Klan claimed members concentrated mostly in Georgia and Alabama cities. But the war and especially its aftermath saw a significant growth spurt. The war effort excited a spirit of "Americanism," an exaggerated patriotism and nationalism that questioned national, religious, and ethnic minorities. The Klan adopted the slogan of "One Hundred Percent Americanism," attaching the organization to wartime nationalism and anti-immigrant and anti-Catholic sentiment. By exalting this jingoism, the Klan appealed to war sentiment. Its appeal was predominantly urban, in cities such as Atlanta, Birmingham, and Richmond, where a more diverse population became targets.

The new, twentieth-century Klan became a romanticized version of the earlier, Reconstruction-era Klan, mimicking an idealized version of white supremacist heroes. But there were important differences. The new Klan was not simply white supremacist, it was also anti-Catholic. Much of its appeal lay in towns and cities, and, as the organization spread, much of its growth occurred outside the South. The new Klan was also thoroughly modern, adapted to concerns about the changing social order, the apparent decline of moral values, and the emergence of non-Protestants across America. Klansmen appealed to the erosion of white male control over the modernizing environment. With a message crafted to appeal to anxieties about social and cultural changes, the new Klan adopted modern measures and methods, even communicating themes about a romanticized past.

The Klan adopted an aggressive strategy to market this message, which William Alexander Percy called its "mumbo-jumbo ritual" and "its half-wit principles."[27] In 1920, Simmons allied himself with two public-relations specialists of dubious background, Edward Young Clarke and Mary Elizabeth Tyler. Their Southern Publicity Association had successfully worked in public relations with organizations such as the

[26] Guy B. Johnson, "A Sociological Interpretation of the New Ku Klux Movement," *Journal of Social Forces* 1, no. 4 (May 1923): 441.

[27] Percy, *Lanterns on the Levee,* 235.

Anti-Saloon League, the YMCA, and the Red Cross. In June 1920, Simmons contracted with the two to expand the Klan. During the next three years the group expanded rapidly. The Clarke-Tyler management team also refined the order's message, extending its appeal to a broad audience fearful of racial, ethnic, religious, political, and moral changes. The Klan became more explicitly anti-Catholic and anti-Semitic, playing on the nationalism that had emerged from the war years. The order promoted traditional moral values, appealing to a society that was undergoing significant changes in the roles of women and the family. It also defended Prohibition, which was instituted nationwide in 1920 as a result of the Eighteenth Amendment. Clarke and Tyler remade the Klan into a secret society, which appealed to the conspiratorial tendencies of many Americans. They also instituted a new system of recruitment in which Kleagles, recruitment agents, beat the bushes for new members and chapters. At the peak of the Klan's expansion, 1,100 Kleagles conducted a massive campaign to attract new members. The Kleagles, as well as Clarke, Tyler, and Simmons, all received a percentage of membership dues. Klan recruitment became, in effect, a giant pyramid scheme.

In 1923, a UNC sociologist, Guy Johnson, concluded that the advent of modern life—so apparent during the 1920s, really for the first time—had unnerved many Americans. The "complexity of modern life," he wrote, decreased religious authority, and the appearance of new amusements and recreation such as automobiles, movies, and dancing "has lessened the inclination toward religious conformity." Parents seemed to have less control over their children; the "Puritanic home of yesterday, with its unspared rod, its altar, and its taboos, is now a mere joke." For those who feared cultural innovation and change, according to Johnson, the Klan had "drawn a goodly number of recruits."

The real basis of the Klan's racial nationalism lay in its attitude toward ethnic, racial, and political minorities—Roman Catholics, Jews, and Communists, as well as black people. Clarke instructed organizers to target minorities in their region in order to create appropriate scapegoats. In the South, the Klansman looked "with misgivings as he watches the color line gradually grow dimmer to the negro"; the Klan appealed to white southerners' fears that "the race problem of today is nothing compared to the race problem that will come." "Anyone reared in the South," Johnson wrote, "can testify to the intricate maze of thought which greets the southerner when he tries to contemplate the future of the Southland with the negro possessing a degree of social and political equality which would give him a voice in the control of his own legal status." The white masses were "blindly afraid of 'social equality'"—the fear of sexual equality—and the Klan became "merely a more frank way of expressing what they have begun to feel so strongly in the past two decades."[28]

Women—including Elizabeth Tyler—exerted a key role in the Klan's expansion. In 1921, a congressional investigation claimed about Tyler that "in this woman beats the

---

[28] Johnson, "Sociological Interpretation of the New Ku Klux Movement," 442, 444.

real heart of the Ku Klux Klan today."[29] She organized a women's auxiliary, appointing five hundred women from around the country. Women involved in the Klan pushed for full membership, and there were competing organizations, such as the Grand League of Protestant Women, that paraded in such places as Atlanta demanding "white supremacy, protection of womanhood, defense of the flag." Other organizations, such as the White American Protestants, pledged not to hire any governess, teacher, or caretaker of children who was foreign born, nonwhite, or non-Protestant. Facing increasing competition from outside groups, the Klan in 1923 organized the Women of the Ku Klux Klan. By late 1923, this group included 250,000 members in thirty-six states.

Appealing to popular disquiet about cultural changes that crystallized during the war, the Klan expanded rapidly after 1920. It grew by as many as 100,000 members during 1920–1921, mostly in the South and Southwest. In the next year, that figure doubled. An expose by the *New York World* in 1921, which documented more than 150 cases of violence, seemed only to spur further growth. In 1924, membership stood at about four million, and it may have reached five million a year later, with about five thousand chapters. An internal power struggle toppled Simmons in 1922, and Hiram Evans, a Dallas dentist, took control of the organization, eventually purging Clarke and Tyler. There had been persistent charges about financial malfeasance and immorality (Clarke and Tyler were involved in a long-standing liaison).

Nonetheless, the Klan continued to expand. Much of the growth in membership occurred outside the South—in the Midwest and on the Pacific Coast, into states such as Indiana, California, and Oregon. The organization pitched itself to a mainstream America as a fraternal order preserving traditional America, but increasingly it also practiced terror tactics. The most violent Klan existed in Texas. Texas Klansmen, according to the *Houston Chronicle* in 1921, had "beaten and blackened more people in the last six months than all the other states combined."[30] Terror and vigilantism, even with a veneer of respectability, remained a major part of Klan operations. In January 1922, hooded Klansmen in Texarkana, on the Texas-Arkansas border, abducted a twenty-year-old black man, Clarence Weatherford, and whipped him for "fooling about a white woman." Klan terror in Arkansas extended beyond antiblack violence. In Little Rock, in early 1922, three hooded men whipped a pool hall operator, ordering him to close his business.[31]

In Arkansas, much of the Klan violence focused on an apparent breakdown of the social and moral order. In the oil-producing part of the state, in El Dorado, Klansmen fought against prostitution and vice. The organization enforced a stricter moral code elsewhere as well. In April 1922, a group of hooded vigilantes abducted a Clarksville white man, J. E. Brock, and ordered him to leave the county because of

[29] Kathleen M. Blee, *Women of the Klan: Racism and Gender in the 1920s* (Berkeley: University of California Press, 1991), 22.

[30] Charles C. Alexander, "White-Robed Reformers: The Ku Klux Klan Comes to Arkansas, 1921–1922," *Arkansas Historical Quarterly* 22, no. 1 (Spring 1963): 14.

[31] Alexander, "White-Robed Reformers," 20.

accusations that he was having an adulterous relationship with a young woman. Brock promptly left town. In November 1922, disguised members of the Klan led a "Clean-up Committee" in Ouachita and Union Counties, burning brothels, saloons, and gambling dens. After an ensuing shootout, the Klan whipped and tarred and feathered perpetrators. It claimed to have run off two thousand vice operators from the scene.

Elsewhere, Arkansas Klansmen enforced Prohibition by terrorizing bootleggers. Vigilantes conducted their own raids on stills, publicly demonstrating their belief in Prohibition. Klansmen ran for political office at the state and local levels on a record as defenders of the social and moral order. A Klansman running for governor of Arkansas in 1924, Lee Cazort, claimed that the organization had been responsible for rooting out bootleggers in Johnson County. There had been "a mighty crew of bootleggers and innumerable liquor dispensaries," Cazort claimed, "which were debauching the youth of Lamar and of the county. I joined the Klan and with others sat on juries and backed up the prosecuting attorney and circuit judge until we cleaned up Lamar and Johnson County."[32]

The Klan reached a peak of popularity and political power about 1924. In Georgia, the order helped elect a governor; in Texas, a US senator. During the presidential election of 1924, the Klan pushed hard, though unsuccessfully, to nominate a presidential candidate with its support. Despite its attempt to reach middle-class respectability, the Klan in the South became involved in vigilante violence. Striking out at blacks across the South, the Klan also worked as an organization regulating public morals by disciplining adulterers, wayward women, and bootleggers. Much of its appeal in the South lay in the new, growing urban centers of Tulsa, Dallas, Birmingham, Atlanta, and Houston. In states such as Oklahoma, Louisiana, Alabama, and Georgia, the Klan determined state elections. Undoubtedly, the organization was stronger in the Deep South and Southwest, with a particular appeal in urban areas.

Overseas Highway to Key West, Looking Southwest from Lower Matecumbe. *State Archives of Florida.*

[32] Alexander, "White-Robed Reformers," 22.

After the mid-1920s, the Klan went into decline. Partly, that decline reflected heightened scrutiny over its violence, and the more its terror campaigns came to light, the more the Klan alienated its middle-class, urban supporters. Questionable financial practices by the national organization, along with state orders, also undermined its respectability. The widespread popularity of the Klan, however brief, offered evidence of a mass reaction to the unsettling changes that accompanied the modern world—a world that seemed to come into focus during the 1920s.

TWO CRISES

During the 1920s, no southern state saw greater change than Florida. During the late nineteenth century, industrialist Henry Plant expanded rail connections to Tampa and the Gulf Coast. The advent of the Atlantic Coast Line (which absorbed Plant's lines) and the Seaboard Air Line opened up other avenues into Florida's interior. After the completion of the Florida East Coast Railway from St. Augustine to Miami, South Florida underwent rapid development, especially during and after World War I. The railroad, which was eventually extended to reach Key West, made the subtropical and tropical climate of Florida available to tourists, and the building of new roads such as the Dixie Highway and US Highway 1 further spurred automobile visitors.

Transportation access encouraged real-estate development, and in 1924 the state of Florida adopted constitutional amendments banning an income and inheritance tax. After 1910, developers began draining the Everglades and the mangroves and swamplands of South Florida. During World War I, Florida's appeal expanded further. Carl Fisher, a native of Indianapolis who had made his fortune in auto racing, developed a new resort on an island south of Miami, Miami Beach, where mangrove swamps were drained. Meanwhile, Biscayne Bay was dredged to produce solid land. Fisher planted trees and shrubs and laid out lots for auction. Fisher, said Will Rogers, was the "first man to discover that there was sand under the water . . . that could hold up a real estate sign. He made the dredge the national emblem of Florida."[33]

Growing in population from 5,000 people in 1915 to 47,000 in 1923 to 70,000 in 1925, Miami became a boomtown. "Thousands of persons are leaving," wrote the *Indianapolis Times*, "in search of something for nothing in the land of oranges and speculators."[34] By 1924, a real-estate frenzy was gripping South Florida, with speculators from all over the nation participating in an escalating market, fifty to seventy-five Pullman cars arriving daily, and agents waiting for them in the depot. Thousands of people visited Miami in search of a quick buck, and the city's streets were jammed and often impassable because of the press of humanity. Speculators purchased real

---

[33] William Frazer and John J. Guthrie Jr., *The Florida Land Boom: Speculation, Money, and the Banks* (Westport, CT: Quorum, 1995), 33.

[34] Jack E. Davis, *An Everglades Providence: Marjory Stoneman Douglas and the American Environmental Century* (Athens: University of Georgia Press, 2009), 265.

Florida real-estate boosters. *Public domain.*

estate on credit and then resold it at fantastic profits. The Miami Kiwanis Club even complained to city commissioners about real-estate agents who "accosted strangers" on Flagler Street and elsewhere "for the purpose of selling real estate." Flagler Street had no other "businesses but real estate offices," according to a contemporary, who complained that "you couldn't walk down the sidewalks, it was so crowded. You had to walk out on the street if you wanted to get anywhere." "Ten minutes to half an hour in any spot in the State," said a reporter for the *New York Times*, "would convince the most skeptical eyes and ears that something is taking place in Florida to which the history of developments, booms, inrushes, speculation, investment yields no parallel."[35]

West of Miami, Coral Gables became another center of the speculative fever. Developed by George Merrick in a Mediterranean Revival architectural style, the town opened in 1921 on a 10,000-acre tract of land, attracting considerable interest from investors. William Jennings Bryan became a full-time resident; other luminaries joined him. Merrick developed a successful promotional operation relying on aggressive advertising and national marketing. He also used Bryan to hawk Coral Gables; the Great Commoner often addressed crowds from the town's Venetian Casino. Bryan was an indefatigable booster of all things Florida. "We have what the people must have," Bryan explained: "God's sunshine." Miami was "the only city in the world where you can tell a lie at breakfast that will come true by evening."[36]

By 1925, however, the real-estate boom had spiraled out of control. In downtown Miami, the prices of some lots increased from $1,000 in the early 1900s to $400,000 to $1,000,000 in 1925. Lots in Miami Beach increased from $7,000 to $35,000 during the first six months of 1925. New buildings sprang up almost instantaneously. The great Florida land boom came to a crashing end in late 1925.

[35] Paul S. George, "Brokers, Binders, and Builders: Greater Miami's Boom of the Mid-1920s," *Florida Historical Quarterly* 65, no. 1 (July 1986): 33.
[36] George, "Brokers, Binders, and Builders," 39.

The Internal Revenue Service (IRS) more carefully scrutinized the activities of speculators, dampening the expansionist spirit. The Florida legislature, suspicious of the boom, also imposed restrictions. Other states published dire warnings of an impending collapse. Those tempted by "stories of fabulous fortunes being made in Florida real estate," wrote a Minnesota official, should "think twice and investigate closely before offering themselves as possible victims of the most monumental real estate boom that has ever been artificially produced in the United States, if not on the globe." "When the boom bursts," he warned, "it will result in a crash the likes of which has never been experienced in this country."[37] While the boom lasted, the rush of goods became so intense that the Florida East Coast Railroad imposed an embargo on all freight entering South Florida, and this was not lifted until the spring of 1926. Similarly, the port of Miami could not handle the cargo coming into the community. The end of the boom became complete when a powerful hurricane slammed into Miami in September 1926, causing the death of more than one hundred residents and the widespread destruction of physical property.

Another great catastrophe of the 1920s was environmental: the Mississippi River flood of 1927. The flood, remembered William Alexander Percy, was "a torrent ten feet deep the size of Rhode Island; it was thirty-six hours coming and four months going; it was deep enough to drown a man, swift enough to upset a boat, and lasting enough to cancel a crop year." The delta, he wrote, became a "mill-race" of 7,500 square miles "in which one hundred twenty thousand human beings and one hundred thousand animals squirmed and bobbed."[38] One of the greatest natural disasters in American history, the flood had a host of consequences for the South of the 1920s.

Beginning in August 1926, the upper Mississippi valley, including several hundred thousand acres in the Upper Midwest, experienced drenching rain. By September, much of the region was underwater, but still more rain arrived. The water emptied into the Missouri, the Ohio, and, ultimately, the Mississippi Rivers. During the fall, observers noted that river levels had reached the highest marks ever recorded. In October 1926, the river gauge in Vicksburg, Mississippi, reached more than forty feet. Previously, the highest record had been thirty-one feet. After a lull during the autumn months, precipitation returned in December, with flooding by Christmas. Storms and heavy rains continued in February and March 1927, with tornadoes and severe weather in the lower Mississippi between March 17 and 20.

The rising waters challenged the system of dams and levees that held the river back. When large numbers of white people first came to the lower Mississippi during the 1830s and established booming cotton plantations, individuals constructed private levees. But private levees created pressure elsewhere, as the river sought outlets when it was high. For the most part, individuals' efforts to control the river failed—and were even counterproductive. Human activity in the

---

[37] George, "Brokers, Binders, and Builders," 48.
[38] Percy, *Lanterns on the Levee*, 249.

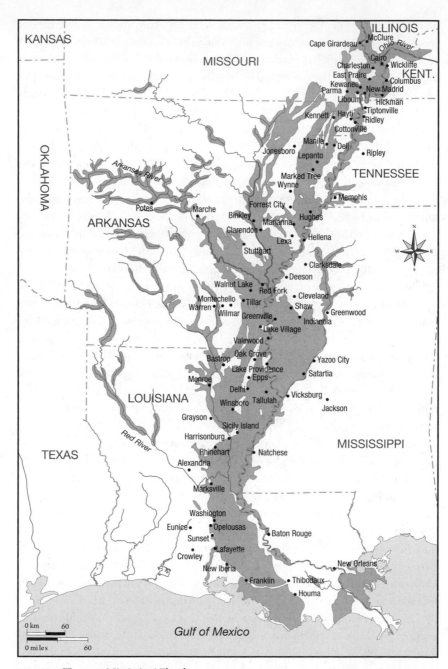

MAP 18.1 The 1927 Mississippi Flood

valley—especially the expansion of commercial agriculture—silted up the tributaries and the river, worsening the natural process of flooding. The clearing of the
forests, which had, before the advent of whites, lined the river, eliminated a buffer
that could absorb the rains.

The nineteenth-century private levee system was overwhelmed by its ineffectiveness. The Swamp Acts of 1849 and 1850 provided federal support, in public
lands, to state-run flood control. In 1879, following a flood five years earlier, Congress established the Mississippi River Commission to coordinate efforts. State and
federal governments, involving local levee boards, expanded the system. By 1927, a
mile of levee on average held 421,000 cubic feet of earth. Huge fortifications and
earthworks, the levees were intended to fend off a raging river. Massive structures
planted in durable Bermuda grass to help hold the structure together, with large
banquettes buttressing them on the land side, the levees rose as high as thirty feet
tall and nearly two hundred feet wide. A marvel of modern technology's effort to
control nature, the levees provided a "safe and adequate channel for navigation,"
said an Army Corps publication in 1926, and it was "now in condition to prevent
the destructive effects of floods."[39]

The river challenged the ability of modern civilization to control nature, and
technology appeared to have triumphed. But others were dubious. Working as a
steamboat pilot during the late 1850s, Mark Twain published a memoir about his
experiences in 1883, *Life on the Mississippi*. Returning to the river after the Army
Corps' levee system was in place, he remained skeptical. The federal government
had remade the Mississippi "into a sort of two-thousand-mile torch-light procession" that illuminated the levee system with clear-burning lamps. "You are never
entirely in the dark, now," he wrote, for there was always "a beacon in sight, either
before you, or behind you, or abreast." Ultimately, Twain saw this massive effort
as futile, despite the Army Corps' brash confidence. West Point engineers, he
wrote, "have not their superiors anywhere; they know all that can be known of
their abstruse science; and so, since they conceive that they can fetter and hand-
cuff that river and boss him, it is but wisdom for the unscientific man to keep still,
lie low, and wait till they do it."

The Mississippi River Commission's military engineers tried to make "the
Mississippi over again,—a job transcended in size by only the original job of creating it." They constructed "wing-dams here and there," Twain wrote, "to deflect the
current; and dikes to confine it in narrower bounds; and other dikes to make it stay
there; and for unnumbered miles along the Mississippi, they are felling the timber-
front for fifty yards back, with the purpose of shaving the bank down to low-water
mark with the slant of a house-roof, and ballasting it with stones; and in many
places they have protected the wasting shores with rows of piles." But anyone who
knew the Mississippi recognized that "ten thousand River Commissions, with the
mines of the world at their back, cannot tame that lawless stream, cannot curb it or
confine it, cannot say to it, Go here, or Go there, and make it obey; cannot save a

[39]   Pete Daniel, *Deep'n as It Come: The 1927 Mississippi River Flood* (Fayetteville: University of
     Arkansas Press, 1996), 3; Christopher Morris, *The Big Muddy: An Environmental History of
     the Mississippi and Its Peoples, from Hernando de Soto to Hurricane Katrina* (New York:
     Oxford University Press, 2012), chapter 8.

shore which it has sentenced; cannot bar its path with an obstruction which it will not tear down, dance over, and laugh at."[40]

During the spring of 1927, the sheer quantity of water on the Mississippi created an astounding volume, with nowhere to flow but southward. As flooded tributaries poured into the river, a logjam appeared. The Ohio River actually reversed course for a few days because of the congested flow of water. Between southern Illinois and New Orleans, the rising river tested the levee system, and 1,500 workers manned the levees, attempting to forestall breaches by moving earth and piling on sandbags. Many of the workers were convicts, mostly African Americans, working in desperate and brutal conditions. If matters worsened, the managers had the authority to impress black plantation workers into service. Despite cracks in the system, the levees held until the latter part of March 1927.

The arrival of yet another storm system broke the back of the levee system. More than fifteen inches of rain pelted New Orleans on April 15, 1927, with standing water everywhere in the city. Similarly, heavy pain deluged the rest of the river valley. On April 16, a levee at Dorena, Missouri, was breached, inundating 175,000 acres. Five days later, on April 21, major breaches occurred in Mound Landing, Mississippi, and Pendleton, Arkansas, and the river flooded a seven-state region, with Arkansas and Louisiana experiencing the worst damage. The breach at Mound Landing created the most significant crevasse in the lower Mississippi—the largest ever to occur anywhere in the Mississippi River valley. Breaking through the levee with a force twice as powerful as Niagara Falls, a wall of water stretching three-quarters of a mile wide and one hundred feet high poured into the delta farmlands.

This immense quantity of water flooded the lower Mississippi for months, eventually covering 2.3 million acres and displacing over 172,000 people. By April 22, 1927, downtown Greenville, Mississippi, was submerged under ten feet of water, while thousands of refugees fled. As far as Yazoo City, Mississippi, seventy-five miles from Mound Landing, the river rose above rooftops. Eventually the flood waters flowed back into the river at Vicksburg and then breached the levee at Cabin Teele, Louisiana, flooding 6.2 million acres and displacing nearly 278,000 people. In Arkansas, where 5.1 million acres were flooded, other breaks appeared in levees in the Mississippi, as well as in the Arkansas, White, and Red Rivers. The Arkansas floodwaters gushed south into Louisiana. All told, in three states the great flood created forty-two crevasses. The wreckage was unprecedented.

The great Mississippi River flood of 1927 wreaked widespread havoc. Once the floodwaters receded, 27,000 square miles remained flooded, a huge swath of territory in the heart of the Cotton South. The destruction was devastating, with 246 reported deaths, more than 130,000 homes destroyed, and 700,000 people homeless. Property damage was also extensive, estimated to be about $5 billion in today's dollars. Relief efforts at first were unable to deal with the disaster. The main relief agency was the Red Cross, which housed more than 307,000 refugees in temporary

[40] Mark Twain, *Life on the Mississippi* (Boston: James R. Osgood, 1883), 299–302.

camps in three states while also feeding about 289,000 people outside the camps. There were 129 refugee camps in Arkansas, Mississippi, and Louisiana, including a facility housing 15,000 refugees on Vicksburg battlefield. In Greenville, Will Percy headed up local relief efforts, but the large number of rural black refugees alarmed white residents, who feared a mass exodus from the plantations. Secretary of Commerce Herbert Hoover, with a reputation for his successes in Belgian relief during World War I, organized federal relief efforts.

The refugee camps, housing mostly black occupants, offered scenes of great distress. Hoover created a Colored Advisory Commission, composed of black leaders such as the Tuskegee Institute's Robert Russa Moton, to investigate. When the commission discovered desperate conditions, Hoover suppressed the report. Eventually, the flood and its aftermath spurred continued African American emigration from the Mississippi delta, with half of the region's black population leaving, according to one estimate. The disaster spotlighted structural deficiencies affecting the Deep South, the inequities of the social system, and the need for greater federal involvement in solving them. The mass conscription during the emergency fell especially hard on African Americans, and there were outbreaks of official violence, including the death of a black man in Mississippi, at the height of the crisis, when he refused to join a levee gang.

The 1920s concluded with a mixed legacy. The decade brought rapid economic growth in the South, with changes in industry, transportation, and agriculture. Change also brought adversity and conflict. The advent of "modern" attitudes evident in the Southern Renaissance represented a literary and intellectual effort to bring the South into line with the rest of the country. Modernism proved profoundly disturbing to many southerners, especially Protestant fundamentalists, who feared that technology and science were undermining the traditional social system. The expansion of industry brought growth, but the globalization of industry put added pressure on management to reduce costs at the expense of workers. The South was not far from disaster, whether financial or natural, as evident in the Florida real-estate bust of 1925 and the Great Flood of 1927.

19

THE GREAT DEPRESSION

THE GREAT DEPRESSION, AFFECTING the South as severely as any region in the nation, constituted the most serious economic crisis in American history. The financial system's collapse set off a cascading series of adverse economic consequences, including the collapse of the agricultural and industrial sectors. The extent of southern poverty worsened, highlighting the injustices of caste and class already accompanying the plantation system. The Depression spurred national efforts to revive the southern economy, placing a spotlight on the gap between the South and the rest of the country. The New Deal became the first major effort to develop and modernize the southern economy through federal intervention—a milestone change in governmental power. During the 1930s, southerners began to consider a different future.

ECONOMIC COLLAPSE

After the great stock market crash of October 1929, the American economy went into a tailspin. Southern farmers suffered from low prices and high debt during the 1920s, but these problems became greatly aggravated after 1929. Cotton prices declined from 20.19 cents per pound in 1927 to 9.46 cents in 1930, and to 5.66 cents in 1931. Tobacco prices fell from 18.3 cents per pound in 1929 to 10.5 cents by the early 1930s. With such a severe price decline, farm income collapsed. Cotton farmers saw their income drop between 1929 and 1932 from $1.5 billion to $45 million. The income of tobacco farmers dropped by two-thirds, while income earned by peanut farmers decreased by a similar amount (68 percent). A historic drought affecting the Southwest and the lower Mississippi valley compounded the economic misery.

The effects of the agricultural collapse spilled over into the entire economy. The cotton trade was so reduced that port cities depending on it were badly hurt. New Orleans saw the value of the cargo passing through its port decline by about half between 1928 and 1933. Hard times at ports brought higher unemployment for dockworkers and stevedores. Department stores were unable to sell merchandise; automobile lots remained full of unsold vehicles. The financial shock undermined the stability of the banking system, which was, by 1931, further worsened by the inability of farmers to meet their debt obligations. Real estate was also in shambles, along with the infant tourism industry that had sprung up after World War I and had spurred the Florida land boom of the 1920s. The real-estate crash fed into the general financial crisis, as property owners could not make their mortgage payments and faced foreclosure. The rising rate of foreclosure placed additional strain on the financial system. After the Florida collapse, real-estate values also fell rapidly in tourist destinations such as Asheville, North Carolina.

Other sectors of the southern economy were devastated. Railroads experienced a severe decline in business, and by July 1933, of the twenty-one largest lines, seven were in receivership. The Depression adversely affected manufacturing in key industries such as cotton textiles. Profits fell off sharply as a result of declining prices. Meanwhile, the tobacco-manufacturing industry was dubbed "depression proof" because consumers continued to smoke cigarettes, and factories worked at full capacity. While prices for cigarettes held steady, prices for the tobacco crop dropped, adding to the manufacturers' profits. The oil industry, which grew rapidly during the 1920s, suffered from excess capacity. Oklahoma and East Texas discovered major finds in oil, but a glut resulted in a price collapse. In August 1931, the situation was so desperate that the governor of Texas declared martial law in East Texas in order to prevent runaway oil production.

The evidence of hard times came in rising unemployment throughout the American economy. Unemployment rose to as high as a third of the workforce in many southern cities. Mines and manufacturing were especially hard hit. Many of the most desperate joined the ranks of homeless transients, who rode the rails in search of work. These transients flocked to cities, which attempted to limit their presence. In 1934, Florida became so concerned about transients that it banned them from the state.

The financial system sustained a severe shock about a year after the stock market crash. The collapse of leading banks set off a general financial panic. In 1930, the Nashville financial conglomerate Caldwell & Company went into bankruptcy, as did many of its affiliate banks, setting off a panic that resulted in the failure of 120 banks in seven states. The state of Tennessee lost $6.5 million in the collapse and had to be propped up financially by emergency loans from other banks. A string of bank failures continued through early 1933.

The economic crisis also resulted in plunging tax revenues, paralyzing state governments. During the 1920s, the states engaged in a spending spree, paid for by borrowing, to finance school modernization and road building. Some states faced delinquency or even default; in 1932, Arkansas could not meet its financial obligations. The South possessed more delinquent governmental units than any other region during the 1930s. State governments responded to the fiscal crisis by slashing spending and scaling back support for public services. Georgia in 1932 imposed a 21 percent budget cut in order to avert financial disaster. North Carolina, reorganizing state government, took over control of roads and schools while the state's three senior public colleges and universities were consolidated. A number of states instituted sales taxes as a new source of revenue, even while they took over revenue and governmental functions previously exerted at the local level.

The collapse of the manufacturing, mining, agricultural, and financial sectors created widespread distress. Poverty became so widespread in coal-mining Harlan County, Kentucky, that 231 children died of malnutrition between 1929 and 1931. Between 1930 and 1932, 41 percent of the banks in Mississippi failed, while during a single day in April 1932, 25 percent of all of Mississippi's farmland was sold at bankruptcy auctions. Writing from South Carolina in 1930, a teacher recounted "deserted negro cabins by scores, ruined mansions, denuded fields, poor whites in huts, hound dogs, dust, cotton mills."[1]

Because local and state governments had experienced precipitous declines in revenue, their capacity to deal with the economic crisis was limited. High unemployment, the absence of social security or unemployment insurance, and social attitudes that equated unemployment with personal failings of the worker made the crisis much worse. In the immediate aftermath of crash and depression, pressure mounted for federal intervention to alleviate the distress. Representative George Huddleston of Birmingham, Alabama, urged the establishment of a $50 million fund for the unemployed. Other congressmen and senators from the South called for "direct" federal relief—despite a taboo against this practice. Under President Herbert Hoover, federal intervention began with the Reconstruction Finance Corporation (RFC), which began to administer loans in the fall of 1932 and also provided states with the resources for unemployment relief.

The entire country suffered from the Depression, yet the poverty and economic deprivation made the crisis even more severe in the South. Increasingly, policymakers seeking to restore the economy saw a connection between southern poverty and the national economic crisis. Any attempted solution to the crisis, in other words, had to consider the peculiar problems existing south of the Mason-Dixon Line.

FEDERAL INTERVENTION

In accepting the Democratic nomination for president, on July 2, 1932, New York governor Franklin D. Roosevelt promised a "New Deal" for the American people, a "call to arms" in a "crusade to restore America to its own people."[2] Winning the

[1] Dewey W. Grantham, *The South in Modern America: A Region at Odds* (New York: Harper-Collins, 1994), 117.
[2] The New Deal: A Speech Delivered by President Franklin D. Roosevelt; quoted at http://www.danaroc.com/guests_fdr_021609.html.

election with a decisive mandate and inaugurated on March 4, 1933, Roosevelt pushed through an ambitious legislative program. These New Deal programs were designed to halt the decline in farm income, stabilize the financial system, reinvigorate manufacturing, and alleviate the sufferings of the unemployed.

An immediate challenge was to extend support for the large number of unemployed. In May 1933, the Federal Emergency Relief Administration (FERA) began to funnel money to the states; in September, the agency supplied relief to a fifth of all families in Oklahoma, Florida, and Virginia. By October, one in every eight southerners received relief. The New Deal expanded public-works programs, which attempted to build infrastructure while providing work to the unemployed. Much of this relief went to impoverished African Americans; in 1935, a quarter of all black families were on relief.

Many southern whites worried that relief would encourage their tenants to leave the land. As one South Carolina farmer complained, relief funds were "buzzing in our Niggers' heads."[3] Frequently, however, relief administrators worked in concert with landlords. According to Howard Kester, leader of the Southern Tenant Farmers Union (SFTU), "the relief machinery of the federal government is all too frequently used as a club to force the unfortunate day-laborer and sharecropper into accepting arduous and difficult labor in the cotton fields at less than starvation wages." Kester claimed that the federal government often "sided against the disinherited in making them slave in the fields for those who were in a position to exploit them."[4]

The Civilian Conservation Corps (CCC) hired hundreds of thousands of young, unemployed urban southerners organized in work camps to drain swamps, plant trees, rehabilitate forests, and build parks and recreational areas. The CCC also worked in projects in soil conservation. FERA funds were used in another agency, created by presidential order, named the Civil Works Administration (CWA), which financed public-works projects until its demise in the spring of 1934. The Public Works Administration (PWA) provided hundreds of millions of dollars to construct roads, bridges, hospitals, schools, public housing, and post offices. PWA funds paid for the Skyline Drive and the Blue Ridge Parkway in Virginia, among the 740 projects completed in the state. In Kentucky, the PWA built the federal vault at Fort Knox. In Tennessee, its funds constructed the state supreme court

Civilian Conservation Corps worker on scaffold. *Library of Congress.*

[3] Kari Frederickson, *The Dixiecrat Revolt and the End of the Solid South, 1932–1968* (Chapel Hill: University of North Carolina Press, 2001), 19.
[4] Howard Kester, *Revolt among the Sharecroppers* (New York: Covici-Friede, 1936), 35.

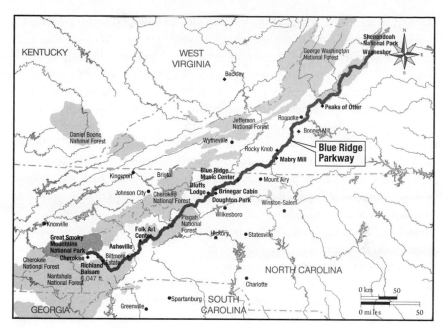

MAP 19.1 The Blue Ridge Parkway

building and renovated the state capitol. After its establishment in 1935, the Works Progress Administration (WPA), the largest public-works agency in American history, poured funds into the South.

The New Deal programs attempted to revive the economy and also to change labor practices. The National Industrial Recovery Act established the National Recovery Administration (NRA), which attempted to revive the economy by sponsoring self-regulation and consolidation among businesses. The cotton textile industry, under NRA supervision, developed and adopted codes that set production levels as well as working hours and wages. During the NRA's first year of existence, this system was popular among cotton manufacturers. Soon, however, they feared that the NRA would raise wages and costs even while cotton prices were increasing. The Supreme Court struck down the NRA in May 1935, but federal intervention spurred rationalization of the textile industry, sponsored labor unions, and added pressure for higher wages and improved working conditions.

During the two years of its existence, the NRA made similar efforts in other sectors of the economy. Oil producers were organized into an Oil Compact Association and were encouraged to draft codes regulating production, business practices, and marketing. This code-making authority also instituted new labor standards. Coal mine operators formed a code-making authority, though it foundered on disagreements about labor standards and wages. Lumber mills organized themselves under an NRA umbrella to standardize lumber operations, production, grading, and terms of sale. In each instance of NRA intervention, despite early enthusiasm, businessmen objected to the ineffectiveness of the program and the impact that it was having in raising labor costs.

The New Deal pursued ambitious agricultural policies. The Agricultural Adjustment Act (AAA) of May 1933 inaugurated a program of voluntary crop reduction. This program restricted production through governmental subsidies—in the hope that lowered production would lead to higher prices and income. In the South, the AAA during the summer of 1933 reduced the cotton crop, after it had already been planted; in that year, the crop dropped by nearly a third. The AAA used the existing infrastructure of 22,000 county extension agents to conduct a "plow under" of much of the already planted cotton crop. All told, 10.5 million acres of cotton were destroyed at a cost of $162 million in government subsidies; production was 4.5 million bales less than expected. Although this immediate fix proved ineffective in raising prices, a permanent program followed that included government loans and subsidies to cotton farmers, under the Commodity Credit Corporation, established in October 1933.

Other federal projects were designed to benefit farms, such as the Soil Conservation Service, which sought to modernize farm practices and to prevent soil erosion. The Tennessee Valley Authority (TVA) built hydroelectric plants in order to distribute cheap energy and stimulate economic development in the Deep South. Constructing sixteen dams on the Tennessee River, the TVA established a system of flood control and hydroelectric power. Federal authorities subsidized the introduction of

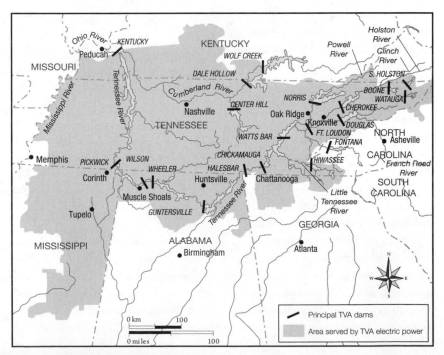

MAP 19.2 The Tennessee Valley Authority

electrical appliances into a region where only 3 percent of the population in 1933 possessed electricity. Producing fertilizer for farmers, as well as educational programs about modern agricultural methods, the TVA attempted to become an engine of rural planning and economic growth. Despite bitter opposition from private power companies, the TVA used local electric cooperatives to extend energy to the southern heartland. Private utilities, meanwhile, were forced to compete by lowering their rates and extending service.

Since the 1820s, the South had dominated world cotton production, but this position was eroding after 1920. Foreign competition contributed, as cotton cultivation sprang up around the developing world. American cotton producers cultivated about three-fifths the world's cotton in 1911, but, by 1921, this proportion had declined to about half, and by 1937 to about a quarter. The adoption of New Deal policies raised prices but also made American cotton less competitive abroad. Ultimately, this helped reduce the economic power of King Cotton and marked the beginning of the end of cotton monoculture.

THE PROBLEM OF RURAL POVERTY

The Cotton South historically relied on cheap labor. Until the 1930s, much of the southern countryside remained densely populated, filled with an impoverished population. During the 1930s, federal intervention shone a national spotlight on southern poverty. "I have seen mothers go from the curing barns late in the night," an observer commented, "worn out and exhausted, their small children sleepy and pitiful, and crying like hungry pigs following the sow. I have seen men, strong men, bow down between the tobacco rows, like an inverted V, cropping in the August sun, with not a dry thread on them." Many of the southern destitute became migrants out of desperation. Thousands of displaced sharecroppers were evident in the South, according to one reporter, "lonely figures without money, without homes, and without hope."[5]

Rural poverty gained added exposure with work by sociologists, novelists, and journalists exposing these conditions. Erskine Caldwell wrote semi-lurid accounts of rural deprivation in novels such as *Tobacco Road* and *God's Little Acre*. John Steinbeck's *Grapes of Wrath* dealt with rural poverty and migrants nationally. James Agee's *Let Us Now Praise Famous Men* dramatized the condition of sharecroppers and tenants, but it did so sympathetically. Sociologists such as Charles S. Johnson, in *The Shadow of the Plantation* and *The Collapse of Cotton Tenancy*, dealt with the consequences of southern rural poverty.

Southern rural poverty was also displayed through visual media and documentary photography. In 1937, photographer Margaret Bourke-White, working as a photojournalist for *Life* magazine, toured the South and then published her photographs in a book titled *You Have Seen Their Faces*. Novelist Erskine Caldwell provided commentary for this volume. "Whatever the cause of the South's despair," he wrote, "it

[5] Biles, *The South and the New Deal*, 37–38.

becomes more evident as each day passes that it is now a worn-out agricultural empire." Whereas cotton had always been the predominant crop, now "the day of the plantation is over, . . . and cotton is not king any longer." The rural poor, Caldwell wrote, were "trying to hold onto a spinning world" until they became "enabled to get a grip on a better way of life."[6]

The Roosevelt administration included advocates both of modernization and relief, and this created a tension in New Deal policies. AAA director George Peek favored a business-oriented program of agricultural modernization; Jerome Frank and the AAA's legal division were more concerned about the impact of New Deal policies on the rural poor. In general, however, the landlords and planters prevailed in AAA policies. They ran the local committees administering the AAA programs; federal agricultural officials looked to the bigger planters for leadership. The land-lords usually received federal subsidies, little of which trickled down to the poor. Planters reduced acreage by cutting the workforce and, in many cases, evicting the rural poor from the land.

The AAA's programs could not hide persisting southern rural poverty. In 1937, a presidential commission on farm tenancy estimated that a quarter of all American farmers—and a large share of them in the South—lived in poverty, ill health, and ignorance. The AAA did little to alleviate these problems. By the mid-1930s, there were numerous charges that the AAA had spurred mass evictions of tenants. Social-ist Norman Thomas, visiting Arkansas in 1934, reported that "under the operation of the AAA hundreds of thousands . . . are either being driven out on the roads without hope of absorption into industry or exist without land to cultivate by the grace of the landlord in shacks scarcely fit for pigs."[7] To blame all distress on the AAA is perhaps unfair, but federal policies certainly accentuated significant changes in southern agriculture.

The AAA's subsidies—known as benefit payments—were supposed to be dis-tributed to sharecroppers and tenants, but this rarely happened. About this issue, the AAA contained divergent and often-conflicting views. When Jerome Frank issued an order requiring protection of sharecroppers and tenants, Secretary of Agriculture Henry Wallace dismissed Frank in a purge of the department. Subsequently, pres-sure from below only increased, keeping the issue of rural poverty in the spotlight. The Communist Party made an effort to recruit the rural poor when they organized the Alabama Sharecroppers Union in 1932.

Some New Deal programs addressed these issues. In January 1934, FERA began a program of rural rehabilitation with fourteen experimental communities, which took farm families off the relief rolls and placed them in cooperative farms. The cre-ation of the Resettlement Administration (RA) in April 1935 directed federal efforts toward displaced poor farm families through the organization of cooperative farms

[6] Erskine Caldwell and Margaret Bourke-White, *You Have Seen Their Faces* (Athens: University of Georgia Press, 1995), 2. Originally published in 1937.
[7] Tindall, *Emergence of the New South*, 414.

Farm Security Administration, Transylvania, Louisiana, June 1940. *Library of Congress.*

and the use of federal loans to assist debt-plagued farmers. In July 1937, the Bank-head-Jones Farm Tenant Act established the Farm Security Administration (FSA); it superseded the RA. Southerner Will W. Alexander, who headed the RA, became the FSA's first director. Alexander, a Methodist minister and longtime executive director of the Commission on Interracial Cooperation (CIC), was one of the South's leading liberals on racial matters.

The FSA focused on rural poverty, emphasizing rural rehabilitation and enabling tenants to become landowners. Much of what the FSA attempted was free-

Boll Weevil Monument in Downtown Enterprise, Alabama. The monument was erected in 1919 to express appreciation for the insect, which forced farmers to diversify their crops. Photo taken in 2010. *Library of Congress.*

style and experimental: for example, the agency funded an ambitious photographic project that hired photographers to document the everyday life of the rural poor. The FSA expended much of its effort in the South, with half the rehabilitation loans and more than two-thirds of the purchase loans going to southern farmers. The FSA experienced the hostility of landlords and the agricultural establishment, most of whom saw these programs as undermining the rural South's power structure. During World War II, the FSA fell victim to a conservative backlash, and Congress gradually reduced its jurisdiction.

Larger economic forces also overshadowed federal antipoverty policies. Cotton culture experienced the infestation of the boll weevil (*Anthonomus grandis*), a beetle that consumed cotton buds and flowers. Arriving from Mexico, the insect first appeared in Texas in the 1890s and spread throughout the region by the 1920s. Boll weevils attracted widespread attention and forced southern farmers to consider alternative crops, such as peanuts and soybeans. During the 1930s, the cotton culture underwent further decline. Falling victim to foreign competition and the rise of synthetic fibers, the labor-intensive cotton culture, which depended on the massive exploitation of human labor, disintegrated under its own weight. In addition, southern farmers replaced cheap labor with the use of machinery.[8]

New Deal agricultural policies to some extent aggravated rather than solved rural poverty. Federal authorities tried to raise income by modernizing agriculture, but their policies also made the low-wage, large agricultural proletariat unnecessary. As landlords began to capitalize—between 1933 and 1940 replacing mules with 100,000 tractors—there was less need for cheap labor. This was a trend that continued over many decades: the numbers of tractors grew by four times during the 1920s, then doubled again in the 1930s, then doubled once more in the World War II years. With tractors came cultivators, which greatly reduced the need for manual labor. In cotton agriculture, the mechanical cotton picker, introduced during the 1930s and 1940s, also had an impact.

Over time, southern agriculture was depopulated of its large, marginalized poor population, and the rural poor migrated to cities in the South and the North. In one Georgia farm during the early 1930s, for example, a landlord oversaw twelve tenant families and owned ten mules. By the end of the decade, ten of the tenant families were turned out, while eight of the mules were sold. In Greenville, in the Mississippi delta, another planter replaced 130 out of 160 tenant families with twenty-two tractors and thirteen row cultivators. Between 1935 and 1940, the number of tenants decreased by a quarter, while wage laborers increased by 14 percent. Overall, the number of black tenants declined by 192,000 and white tenants decreased by 150,000 during the 1930s.[9]

Collectively, the New Deal's expansion of federal power shaped the 1930s South. Relief and other programs to address unemployment were popular among ordinary southerners, yet these programs, and federal intervention, injected new ideas about how society should be organized. The labor system, predicated on the availability of low-cost labor, was undermined by federal protection for union organizers and by new mandates raising wages and establishing maximum hours. For black southerners, although the New Deal was often administered in a way that privileged whites, the 1930s offered new hope of change.

LABOR AND THE NEW DEAL

The New Deal offered an unprecedented opportunity for labor unions in the South. Section 7(a) of the National Industrial Recovery Act stipulated the right to collective bargaining and, for the first time, provided federal protection for unions. In a

---

[8] James C. Giesen, *Boll Weevil Blues: Cotton, Myth, and Power in the American South* (Chicago: University of Chicago Press, 2011).

[9] Robert J. Norrell, *Dixie's War: The South and World War II* (Tuscaloosa: Center for Southern History and Culture, University of Alabama, 1992), 13; Frederickson, *Dixiecrat Revolt*, 17; and Bruce J. Schulman, *From Cotton Belt to Sunbelt: Federal Policy, Economic Development, and the Transformation of the South, 1938–1980* (New York: Oxford University Press, 1991), 20.

historically low-wage region, the New Deal attempted to raise wages and improve working conditions. Expanded unionization reflected these objectives, but it was a thoroughly alarming development for managers and owners. Workers' expectations, mixed with managers' resolve to hold the line, made for volatile, often-violent labor relations.

During the 1930s, union organizers achieved some inroads. The Tobacco Workers International Union organized successfully, though generally most of industry remained nonunion. Workers' heightened expectations increased activity by unions, and determination by management to remain nonunion led to conflict. Between 1933 and 1936, nearly a million southern workers went on strike. Among the more important centers of union organizing were the southern coalfields. In northern Alabama, the Communist Party made substantial inroads. In June 1930, Communists founded a newspaper, *Southern Worker*, published in Birmingham, which appealed to black workers and sharecroppers east of the city.

Communists organized a sharecroppers union, but their meetings faced violent intimidation from local law enforcement. An assessment in 1939 concluded that black Communists encountered "almost ruthless resistance" by police, vigilantes, and white trade unions. "The police have raided Negro homes by the score, sometimes brutally beating occupants of the houses, and searching at will for literature which could be in any way labeled revolutionary."[10] In 1932, two black Communists were murdered. Their bodies were brought to Birmingham, where their supporters proclaimed that they had been "fighting for the rights of the poor people, and against race oppression." Communists also drew black members in Birmingham's iron and steel industry. According to one estimate, the Communist Party had perhaps 1,000 followers in Birmingham.

The most important, and biggest, strike of the early New Deal was the general strike in the cotton textile industry, involving perhaps 200,000 southern workers. The Depression hit the industry hard. With cotton mills operating at 72 percent capacity by June 1934, owners retrenched by instituting pay cuts, stretch outs, and layoffs. Owners also tried to uproot the United Textile Workers (UTW), a union affiliated with the American Federation of Labor (AFL). In September 1934, the UTW organized a general strike, seeking a reduction in the work week, improved conditions, elimination of the stretch out, and union recognition. The strike included much of the southern Piedmont textile belt. Strikers promoted the effort by using "flying squadrons," car caravans of union workers who tried to close mills by stirring strike enthusiasm. Some three hundred mills were closed in this fashion. Throughout the region, owners used guards and armed deputies to keep the plants open; the authorities sided with management. In the Carolinas and Georgia, the governors used state militia to enforce sanctions against union attempts to picket. In Augusta, Georgia, a picketing worker was killed when a policeman fired shots. Police

[10] Horace R. Cayton and George S. Mitchell, *Black Workers and the New Unions* (Chapel Hill: University of North Carolina Press, 1939), 338–339.

in Greenville, South Carolina, beat five strikers, while police and strikers exchanged gunfire in Trion, Georgia. At Honea Path, South Carolina, six workers were killed and fifteen were wounded in a similar outbreak of violence.[11]

Workers responded with violence, including arson and bombings. In Georgia, Gov. Eugene Talmadge, though friendly to unions during the 1920s, sent four thousand National Guard troops into textile communities, where he imposed martial law. The state militia in Atlanta attacked the strikers and jailed them in an internment camp at Fort McPherson. By the end of September 1934, despite Roosevelt's intervention and his appointment of an investigative board, the general strike had collapsed against unwavering opposition from management, abetted by the full support of state governments.

Some of the most violent conflict occurred in the efforts of the United Mine Workers (UMW) to organize West Virginia and Kentucky coalfields. The NRA's code-making authority governing mines sponsored unionization; by 1935, 95 percent of miners belonged to the union. Along with the UMW, the International Union of Mine, Mill, and Smelter Workers—known as Mine Mill—organized black miners in northern Alabama. That organization included white miners, and the union reserved the presidency for a white and the vice presidency for an African American. Mine Mill was known for its radicalism; it was also suspect because of its racial egalitarianism. The UMW also organized white and black miners and, like Mine Mill, stipulated that the presidency and vice presidency in their locals would be separated by race.

The epicenter of the conflict in the mines was located in Harlan County, Kentucky. The entire county depended on mining, but it was completely under the economic and political control of the mine operators. The county contained thirty company towns, with stores, homes, streets, and everything else under company ownership. These towns provided living arrangements under management control for 45,000 workers. The owner-controlled Harlan County Coal Operators' Association hired a private army to maintain control. Law enforcement remained in the pocket of the association, which represented the owners. "Bloody Harlan" became a center of labor violence when the UMW encountered an all-out war by the local authorities. Under the umbrella of the NRA code-making authority, unions had expanded into Harlan, but union membership declined from 5,000 to 1,200 between 1933 and 1935. When the UMW renewed its organization campaign, violence erupted. However, after a US Senate investigation headed by Sen. Robert M. La Follette Jr. in March–May 1937, the extent of officially sanctioned terrorism became nationally known. That investigation culminated in the indictment of forty-seven men. A year later, in 1938, the UMW obtained a contract from mine operators. When the operators attempted to break the union in 1939, a strike resulted in the miners' favor, solidifying the UMW's position in Harlan.

---

[11] F. Ray Marshall, *Labor in the South* (Cambridge, MA: Harvard University Press, 1967), 167.

Union organizing gained a new spirit of militancy with the rise of the Congress of Industrial Organizations (CIO), established in 1937. Organized by AFL dissidents John Lewis of the UMW, Sidney Hillman of the Amalgamated Clothing Workers, and David Dubinsky of the International Ladies' Garment Workers Union, the CIO tried to organize entire industries. Once again, federal intervention in the New Deal spurred union development with the passage of the National Labor Relations Act of 1935, which provided federal enforcement authority in protecting attempts to unionize. In the North, the CIO led major organizing drives in steel and automobiles. There were southern workers in these industries; the first sit-down strike by the United Automobile Workers occurred in Atlanta in 1936. The CIO organized the mammoth steel industry in Birmingham, and in 1937 the industry became unionized.

The CIO also attempted to organize oil drilling and refining, rubber manufacturing, and tobacco, but with mixed success. The CIO-affiliated Textile Workers' Organizing Committee (TWOC), which was established in 1936, encountered continued and determined hostility from management during its organizing campaign a year later. Using 160 southern organizers, the TWOC conducted a well-planned, well-coordinated campaign. Despite some initial inroads, little progress was achieved until World War II. The AFL-affiliated union, the United Textile Workers, also continued efforts at organizing southern mill workers, but they claimed only about six thousand members by 1942.

The unionization drive encountered determined opposition during the 1930s. The CIO's challenge to racial orthodoxy provided a weapon used by its opponents; another weapon was the union's Popular Front approach, in which the CIO sometimes allied itself with Communists. Localism and white southerners' long-standing suspicion of outsiders also worked against organizing. In general, the unions faced the united opposition of the established classes, who viewed them as threatening the South's cheap labor advantage and, beyond this, as subverting the foundations of white supremacy. Owners frequently used their access to brute force, sometimes state enforced, in order to combat unionism.

The culmination of efforts for federal protection of organized labor came in Congress's enactment of the Fair Labor Standards Act of 1938. Providing for national standards of wages and hours, the law created the first national minimum wage, outlawed child labor, and imposed maximum hours of the work week. The law had an important effect. Some economists argue convincingly that federal intervention, especially the minimum wage, resulted in increased unemployment. But minimum-wage legislation confirmed an important trend occurring in southern labor during the 1930s: the decline of a low-wage economy and the nationalization of work standards. Increasingly, the disparity of wages that had long existed between southern and nonsouthern workers was diminishing. Whereas in 1937 southern workers earned 63.2 percent of the national average, by 1947 that figure had increased to 74.1 percent.

Despite the growth of unions during the 1930s, the South remained strongly antiunion. The CIO was generally successful only in those industries with a national presence, such as steel, automobiles, and mining. Encountering determined opposition and often-lukewarm responses from southern workers, southern union organizers were frequently frustrated. By 1940, about a tenth of the southern workforce was unionized, as compared to about a fifth nationally. Yet, the labor-organizing campaigns of the 1930s undermined the seeming invincibility of the power structure in the South, with a spillover effect on the solidity and stability of the Jim Crow system.

THE SOUTHERN LEFT

A sharp polarization of political attitudes and ideology accompanied the New Deal. Roosevelt and his policies were popular among the southern masses, black and white. He also enjoyed the support of a young group of southern New Dealers. In 1935, the Southern Policy Committee (SPC) attracted young southerners in Washington who had been entranced by the New Deal's possibilities for changing the region. Clark Foreman, a white Georgian involved in efforts to bring African Americans into positions of responsibility in the Roosevelt administration, was a leader. So were Alabamians Hugo Black, Clifford Durr, and J. Lister Hill. In 1938, Roosevelt appointed Hill to the Senate to represent Alabama. Foreman, representing a new sort of southern white liberal, became one of the most effective New Deal southerners. Born to privilege in Atlanta, as a young student at the University of Georgia he witnessed the sadistic lynching of accused black rapist John Lee Eberhardt, an experience that, he wrote, brought him "face to face with the barbarism" of racism and left an "indelible impression."[12] After graduation, Foreman studied at Harvard and traveled to Europe. In 1924, he became secretary of the Georgia chapter of the CIC.

Also influential was Virginia Foster Durr, Clifford Durr's wife. Born into privilege in Birmingham, Alabama, Virginia Durr was educated at Wellesley College, where she encountered black female students—the first time she experienced African Americans on an equal basis. Moving with her husband to Washington, DC, in 1933, Durr became a keen New Dealer. The Durr household in northern Virginia provided a social and intellectual center for many like-minded southern New Dealers. In addition, Durr participated with the Woman's National Democratic Club, the Democratic National Committee, and later in the anti-poll-tax campaign. She was also a founding member of the Southern Conference for Human Welfare, becoming vice president of its civil rights subcommittee.

Much of the attention of southern New Dealers was on the problem of rural poverty. H. L. Mitchell, son of a tenant farmer, preacher, and small-town cleaning business owner, founded the STFU (Southern Tenant Farmers Union) in northeastern Arkansas in 1934. Mitchell had become involved in Socialist Party politics, and in February 1934, he met party leader Norman Thomas during his visit to Memphis.

---

[12] Patricia Sullivan, *Days of Hope: Race and Democracy in the New Deal Era* (Chapel Hill: University of North Carolina Press, 1996), 27.

H. L. Mitchell, June 1938. *Library of Congress.*

Describing himself as a "small-town rebel who had read too many books," Mitchell sought out tenants in the Arkansas delta. He took Thomas to rural areas, where they met a family of six who had been evicted. Asked why they had been thrown off the land, the father of the family responded: "The landlord said we were no longer needed after plowing up the cotton last spring." The STFU was then formally organized in July 1934 as an interracial organization.[13]

Along with Mitchell, another key figure in STFU was Howard Kester. Born in Virginia, Kester was a Social Gospel minister who studied with theologian and re-former Reinhold Niebuhr, worked with Walter White at the NAACP, and became a Socialist. Kester traveled deep into eastern Arkansas to organize farmers. He was also an avid publicist about the plight of the rural poor. In his *Revolt among the Sharecroppers* (1936), Kester described how visitors to cotton country might be ini-tially deceived about the delights of rural living. In reality, the rural masses faced "unremitted and unrequited toil in the cotton fields." They usually lived in shacks, "miserable abodes of cotton workers" that were "unfit for humans." The roofs and walls leaked, and there were no screens to keep the mosquitoes out. Sanitation was crude, without even outhouses. "All a sharecropper needs," said one planter, "is a cotton patch and a corn cob." Sharecroppers and their families, Kester continued, consumed paltry meals of biscuits, molasses, and fatback. "Hundreds of thousands of sharecroppers and tenant farmers have never known any other kind of breakfast and today they consider themselves fortunate to have even this." Children went to work at the age of six, entering into the "service of King Cotton." Working all day in the fields, the entire family trudged sadly back home at dusk in a "weary walk to the place they call home." Southern sharecroppers, Kester said, were "weighed down by

[13] H. L. Mitchell, *Mean Things Happening in This Land: The Life and Times of H. L. Mitchell, Co-founder of the Southern Tenant Farmers Union* (Montclair, NJ: Allanheld, Osmun, 1979), 40.

indescribable misery and suffering, exploitation and greed." Though they were "honest, courageous, and long-suffering," sharecroppers struggled "against the combined forces" that had kept them "enslaved so long."[14]

The SFTU crafted an appeal that was based on agrarian radicalism and religious enthusiasm. Claude F. Williams, a Presbyterian minister from Tennessee, preached a message of empowerment to landless farmers. Williams urged his listeners to "build to the Kingdom of God on earth." The Kingdom, Williams said, was "not of this world, but it is in this world." Like early Christians, SFTU members were infused with the Holy Spirit. The Pentecost, Williams said, represented unity, organization, and power by the disempowered. With recruiters such as Williams exciting mass appeal, the SFTU grew into a truly grassroots organizations that drew on traditions of protest and evangelical belief.[15]

By 1937, the STFU had expanded to six states and claimed 30,000 members—a third of them African American. Planters responded to union organizers with evictions. Surviving the counterattack, the union spread into Oklahoma. The organization went into decline after 1937, but the group publicized the dire poverty of the mass of rural southerners, white and black, and the conditions of peonage and near-peonage under which many of them lived. The STFU organized farmers against evictions of tenants and sharecroppers in the western cotton belt. Although white Socialists such as Mitchell, Clay Easter,

Evicted Sharecroppers along Highway 60, New Madrid County, Missouri, January 1939, photograph by Arthur Rothstein. *Library of Congress.*

and Howard Kester founded the organization, these leaders encouraged local participation and control. Union organizers operated by using religious ritual and imagery. "When they first started talking about the union," said one white sharecropper, "I thought it was a new church."[16] To a large extent, black sharecroppers were drawn to the organization. In late 1935, the union mounted a successful cotton-picking strike in northeastern Arkansas, and because of this membership spread to Tennessee, Texas, Mississippi, and Oklahoma.

The STFU also publicized inequities in New Deal farm subsidies, which benefited planters over sharecroppers. In 1936, it became public that the Lee Wilson & Company plantation, one of the largest in the Arkansas delta, had received almost $200,000 in payments during 1934–1935. The Wilson plantation was huge, encompassing 65,000 acres of rich cotton and timber lands that had been cleared and drained over the previous

[14] Kester, *Revolt among the Sharecroppers*, chapter 3.
[15] Roll, *Spirit of Rebellion*, 100.
[16] Roll, *Spirit of Rebellion*, 96–97.

decades. The STFU claimed that the Wilson plantation shifted its labor force from sharecropping to day labor in order to avoid sharing the federal subsidies. Many of the sharecroppers, it contended, were evicted and forced onto federal relief. The Lee family disputed the STFU's charges, but the controversy added pressure to congressional debate about the inequities of the AAA system. The result was that federal payments were suspended for six years to the Wilsons.

The views of this group of younger white southerners found expression in the famous *Report on the Economic Conditions of the South*, which was submitted to Roosevelt through the National Emergency Council in July 1938. Clark Foreman spearheaded the report; Clifford Durr, who worked as a lawyer for the RFC, Oklahoman John Fisher, and Arthur "Tex" Goldschmidt of Texas also contributed. This group produced a draft, which a larger, twenty-two-member committee, headed by University of North Carolina president Frank Porter Graham, considered and approved. The *Report*, after it was made public, provided the basis for Roosevelt's declaration that the South was the "nation's number one economic problem."

Describing an "economic unbalance" between the South and the rest of the nation, the *Report* concerned itself "primarily not with what the South has, but with what the South needs."[17] Examining fifteen different dimensions of southern life, it argued that basic problems of inequality and poverty dominated the region. The report entirely (and deliberately) avoided the subject of race, focusing instead on social inequality. Ever since the Civil War, the South had remained the poorest region in the nation; the "richest State in the South ranks lower in per capita income than the poorest State outside the region." Farmers earned less than half of what farmers outside the region earned, and only a fraction of their income was left for them to purchase food, clothing, and the basics. More than half of southern farmers did not own their farms; their condition was "comparable to that of the poorest peasants in Europe." Consumer goods lay outside the reach of country folk. Industrial workers, according to the report, were little better off. A substantial wage gap divided southern workers from the rest of the nation, with the South's industrial workers earning about 71 percent of the national average.[18]

The consequence of the South's economic backwardness was the underdevelopment of key institutions and practices in public health and public education. The South remained the most illiterate part of the country. Higher education was stunted, as the combined endowments of all southern colleges and universities were less than those of Yale and Harvard. Poverty also affected health, and the region was a "belt of sickness, misery, and unnecessary death." Southerners suffered disproportionately from venereal disease, malaria, pneumonia, and tuberculosis because of inadequate public health. People lacked modern sanitation; poverty and substandard living

[17] National Emergency Council, *Report on the Economic Conditions of the South* (Washington, DC: National Emergency Council, 1938), 1, 3.
[18] National Emergency Council, *Report on the Economic Conditions of the South*, 21–22.

Eugene Talmadge, on the right in a cream-colored suit, visiting the White House, June 1935.
On the left is Clark Howell, publisher of the *Atlanta Constitution*. *Library of Congress.*

conditions lowered the quality of life. The report estimated that half the southern population lived in inadequate housing.[19]

While the southern Left became more prominent, so also did a new conservatism. Indeed, as elsewhere in the country, the New Deal sharply polarized ideological positions, and, just as a southern Left emerged, a new, southern Right also began to coalesce. The implications of federal intervention—especially for white supremacy—alarmed such senators as Carter Glass and Harry Byrd of Virginia, Joseph Robinson of Arkansas, and Josiah W. Bailey of North Carolina. Glass warned that the NRA's Blue Eagle emblem was a "bird of prey" that created a "reign of terror among thousands of struggling, small industries."[20] Other southern conservatives feared that relief and massive federal financing would undermine the southern social system. Georgia governor Eugene Talmadge said that urban recipients of relief were "bums" and "chiselers." The best way to deal with the urban poor, he said, was to "line them up against a wall and give them a dose of castor oil." Government programs such as NRA and TVA were, Talmadge declared, "all in the Russian primer and the President has made the statement that he has read it twelve times." The Georgia governor organized an anti-Roosevelt convention, which met in Macon, Georgia, in January 1936.[21]

Conflict between New Dealers and conservatives erupted over Roosevelt's so-called "court-packing" plan in 1937, in which he sought legislation that would enable him to expand the court's membership and nominate a pro–New Deal court. Congress revolted over the court-packing plan; an anti–New Deal coalition began to emerge. Not all the members of this coalition were southern, though many were. In December 1937, Senator Bailey, and other supporters, issued a "Conservative Manifesto," which called

[19] National Emergency Council, *Report on the Economic Conditions of the South*, 29–34.
[20] Frederickson, *Dixiecrat Revolt*, 23.
[21] Biles, *The South and the New Deal*, 64.

for reduced taxes and spending, a reduction of competition by the government with private enterprise, and the restoration of states' rights.[22]

Flush from his landslide reelection in 1936, Roosevelt felt confident that he had strong public support. And in many respects he did. "Every house I visited," wrote a journalist about the South, "had a picture of the President. . . . He is at once God and their intimate friend; he knows them all by name, knows their little town and mill, their little lives and problems."[23] According to the Gallup poll, a majority of southerners favored his court plan. Beyond this, throughout the 1930s, Roosevelt's approval rating among southerners was consistently higher than in the rest of the country. Some southern governors, such as James V. Allred of Texas, Bibb Graves of Alabama, and Eurith D. Rivers of Georgia, were New Deal supporters and even endorsed "little New Deals" enacted by their state legislatures. A group of younger Democratic congressmen, such as Lyndon B. Johnson, who had served as head of the National Youth Administration (NYA) in Texas and was elected to Congress in 1937, or Claude Pepper, elected to the Senate from Florida in 1936, were strong New Dealers.

Believing that he possessed a strong base in the South, Roosevelt struck back at his conservative opponents. In an attempted "purge" during the elections of 1938, the president campaigned for Lawrence Camp over Georgia incumbent senator Walter George; Gov. Olin Johnston of South Carolina over incumbent conservative "Cotton Ed" Smith; and William Dodd Jr. in his challenge to unseat conservative Virginia congressman Howard W. Smith. In March 1938, speaking before a group on a stage in Georgia he shared with banker and philanthropist (and distant cousin) Walter George, Roosevelt described the low-wage economy that had kept southerners oppressed, amounting to a "feudal economic system." The region needed better education, healthcare, and highways, but it would accomplish these goals only with congressmen whose minds were "cast in the 1938 mold and not in the 1898 mold."[24]

Roosevelt's 1938 purge of southern conservatives backfired. The conservatives, remaining committed to white supremacy, portrayed Roosevelt's policies and campaigning as a potentially dangerous intervention that undermined the racial order. George denounced the president's intervention as "a second march through Georgia," and he reminded voters that "we answered this question before when federal bayonets stood guard over the ballot box."[25] Roosevelt's 1938 purge was a failure: in no instance did his candidates oust established conservatives.

These developments emboldened anti–New Deal conservatives, who made common cause with northern Republicans in Congress. The anti–New Deal coalition possessed enough power in 1939 to launch attacks on relief, labor, and housing

[22] Grantham, *The South in Modern America*, 127.
[23] Patrick J. Maney, *The Roosevelt Presence: The Life and Legacy of FDR* (Berkeley: University of California Press, 1998), 71.
[24] Sullivan, *Days of Hope*, 62.
[25] Sullivan, *Days of Hope*, 65.

programs. Their opposition embraced an ideology of anticommunism. After 1939, the Special Committee on Un-American Activities, chaired by Rep. Martin Dies of Texas, held regular hearings seeking to expose Communists in the New Deal. Moreover, by the early 1940s Roosevelt began a retreat from the liberal coalition that he had constructed, in large part because his attention turned increasingly to international issues and the looming prospect of world war.

Nonetheless, the events of 1938—the attention on the South focusing on the *Report on the Economic Conditions in the South*, along with Roosevelt's tilt to the left politically—emboldened a liberal coalition in the region. This coalition included racial liberals, black activists in the NAACP and other organizations, Communists, Socialists, and others. Many of these activists underwent a flirtation with Marxism. F. Palmer Weber, a white Virginian, became involved in Communist Party and labor politics at the University of Virginia during the 1930s. He was one of the leaders of a campus student movement and was affiliated with the Communist-influenced National Student League. Weber, realizing a connection between labor and class and racial oppression, became an advocate of equal civil rights.

Others saw a convergence between labor organizing and Jim Crow oppression. The Young Women's Christian Association (YWCA) and Young Men's Christian Association (YMCA) organized students with campus-based meetings that stressed social and racial equality, within acceptable bounds. Many of the campus Ys became involved in labor and racial issues, and many of the people associated with these organizations were women. The CIO also became a leading force for racial change in the South. It hired black organizers, who were dispatched to organize black industrial workers, such as those in tobacco factories. The CIO also attempted to organize industries such as mining, steel, and tobacco that had both white and black workers.

From the outset the union pursued a biracial approach. In Alabama, slightly more than half of coal miners were African American. UMW locals were organized to accommodate the two races in separate locals. Typically, the local president was white, and seating was separate without being "Jim Crow." At a national level, the CIO included black members. The union also sponsored the Highlander Folk School, located in Monteagle, Tennessee, which was founded in 1931 as a training center for activists seeking to institute worker democracy and racial justice. "Everything at Highlander is high," wrote a participant, "its ideals, its standards, and its purpose. The school is an experience in real democracy."[26]

Women such as Lucy Randolph Mason, along with others associated with the Southern Summer School for Women Workers in western North Carolina, formed a core group of activists among CIO organizers. Born into a prominent Virginia family in 1882, Mason became a suffragist and then worked as industrial secretary for the YWCA. In September 1932, Mason served as general secretary of the National Consumers League, a position that exposed her to New Deal policies. Mason was

[26] Lucy Randolph Mason, *To Win These Rights: A Personal Story of the CIO in the South* (New York: Harper & Brothers, 1952), 161.

especially drawn to the CIO because of its position on race. Southern whites, she recalled, had constructed "road blocks to democracy and justice and equal opportunity," and "evil weeds" spreading from poverty and ignorance had "spread in many directions." White supremacy had "darkened and impoverished" the South; the white man had "narrowed his own soul." Drawn to the CIO because the organization grasped the connection between race and labor, she saw it as offering "more to southern progress" than any other group.[27]

On the heels of the publication of the *Report on the Economic Conditions of the South*, Mason helped organize a meeting in Birmingham, Alabama, in September 1938. The meeting, which included 1,200 delegates, about a fifth of whom were black, fashioned itself as a promoter of the new, progressive policies on labor and race in the South. With leaders such as Mason, SPC leader H. C. Nixon, and First Lady Eleanor Roosevelt, the new Southern Conference on Human Welfare (SCHW) came into existence.

The SCHW took a strong stance in opposing white supremacy. Although not overtly integrationist, the group was biracial. On the third day of the Birmingham meeting, when police chief Eugene "Bull" Connor threatened to break up the meeting because it violated segregation ordinances, the SCHW arranged seating so that the main auditorium placed whites on one side, blacks on the other. Eleanor Roosevelt made a point of sitting with the African American delegates. During the meeting, the delegates agreed on a resolution promising never to hold a segregated meeting in any future gathering.

After 1939, the SCHW campaigned to repeal the poll tax. The organization pointed out that the poll tax, which was in operation in much of the South by 1908, disfranchised lower-class white voters as well as African Americans. In 1939, one newspaper concluded that nearly two-thirds of southern voters were disfranchised by the poll tax, with white voters more affected than African Americans.[28] Although three southern states—North Carolina, Louisiana, and Florida—repealed the poll tax during the 1920s and 1930s, eight states kept it. The SCHW helped organize a Committee on Civil Rights and the National Committee to Abolish the Poll Tax (NCAPT). The anti-poll-tax efforts met strong opposition from southern conservatives, who saw it as an opening wedge of federal regulation of voting in the South—and the end to suffrage restriction. The campaign became the most important issue in the SCHW's agenda. Eventually, with the adoption of the Twenty-Fourth Amendment in 1964, the poll tax was repealed everywhere.

The SCHW also established a civil rights infrastructure, which, growing slowly during its first several years, later expanded. Southern liberals such as Frank Porter Graham participated, as did veteran organizers Clark Foreman and James Dombrowski. An Emory graduate and a Methodist minister, Dombrowski helped organize the Highlander Folk School, serving as its staff director. One account described

---

[27] Mason, *To Win These Rights*, 164.
[28] Sullivan, *Days of Hope*, 106.

Foreman as "assertive, decisive, and perhaps a little rash," while Dombrowski was "self-effacing, cautious, at times inefficient." Foreman was "impatient for a better world"; Dombrowski was "more inclined to stoicism and quiet, diligent labor."[29]

ROOTS OF THE CIVIL RIGHTS MOVEMENT

The Great Migration altered the demographic and political balance of power; by 1930, a fifth of all black Americans lived in the North. A decade later, that proportion had increased to a quarter, following the outmigration of another 425,000 African Americans during the 1930s. A growing African American political bloc in the North had important consequences. Politically, after the midterm elections of 1934, a shift took place in political allegiances of black voters from Republican to Democratic. During the presidential election two years later, about three-quarters of the black electorate voted for Roosevelt. In the South, voter registration of African Americans expanded, as over 300,000 were registered during the 1930s, mostly in North Carolina, Kentucky, Oklahoma, Tennessee, and Texas. This trend was aided by long-standing Republican "lily-white" policies, which excluded black leaders from party councils. Under Herbert Hoover, there were fewer black appointees than ever; federal offices remained segregated, and lily-white political practices were expanded.

Soon after Roosevelt was inaugurated, Will W. Alexander and Edwin Embree, two southern whites, who headed, respectively, the CIC and the Julius Rosenwald Fund, lobbied for the establishment of a position to monitor race relations in the New Deal. Organized in 1919, the CIC included white liberals and black leaders, in an effort to achieve racial "cooperation." Short of integration, racial "cooperation" meant an expansion of opportunities under the limitations of racial segregation. With Alexander serving as its director, the CIC was headquartered in Atlanta and organized state chapters that brought together cooperating groups of whites and blacks. A Methodist minister and racial liberal, Alexander probed the limits of Jim Crow racial etiquette.

Embree offered to use Rosenwald resources to pay for a new "special adviser" on race matters in the Interior Department. NAACP leaders objected after Clark Foreman, a white male, was appointed to this position. Yet, he succeeded in bringing black leaders into the Roosevelt administration. In 1933, Foreman hired Robert Weaver, an economist and Harvard graduate from the faculty of the North Carolina A&T State College. He was followed by William Hastie, another African American, who came to Interior as an assistant solicitor. Foreman, Weaver, and Hastie helped integrate Interior, which had been segregated since the Wilson administration. Foreman also pressured the CCC to hire black supervisors in the work camps. After the CCC refused, Foreman obtained an order from Secretary of the Interior Harold

---

[29] Thomas A. Krueger, *And Promises to Keep: The Southern Conference for Human Welfare, 1938–1948* (Nashville: Vanderbilt University Press, 1967), 105.

Mary McLeod Bethune, photo
by Carl Van Vechten, 1949.
Library of Congress.

Ickes requiring them to do so. The PWA (Public Works Administration), under Interior's supervision, allocated funds on a nondiscriminatory basis. Weaver and Hastie were instrumental in finding ways to enforce this policy.

Other African Americans participated in the New Deal through an extension of a system of "negro advisers." These included a network of younger black professionals trained in elite institutions. Hastie graduated from Amherst and Harvard Law School; Weaver attended Harvard. Beginning in 1933, "Negro advisers," such as Eugene Kinkle Jones in Commerce, were appointed in other cabinet positions. Later, other "negro advisers" included Henry Hunt in the FSA (Farm Security Administration), Mary McLeod Bethune in the NYA (National Youth Administration), and Ira De A. Reid in the Social Security Administration. By 1936, these midlevel black appointees constituted an informal "Black Cabinet" representing African American interests in the New Deal.

Federal agencies differed in their racial policies. The AAA and NRA (sarcastically called "Negroes Ruined Again" or "Negro Removal Act") both were known for observing segregationist practices, as were the CCC and TVA. The CCC, under the direction of Tennessean Robert Fechner, insisted on the segregation of its work camps. The agency, moreover, discouraged black participation, and participants during the first year were 95 percent white. The NRA codes of the early 1930s preserved a "racial differential"—lower wages for black workers. Essentially, federal officials looked the other way. The NRA also specifically excluded farmworkers and domestics, occupations in which three-quarters of black workers were employed. The AAA benefited landowners and disadvantaged sharecroppers and tenants. Gunnar Myrdal later estimated that 200,000 blacks were thrown off the land as a result of New Deal agricultural policies. Secretary of Agriculture Henry A. Wallace had no black advisers; the department's 52,000 employees included only 1,100 African Americans.

Under the programs of the Home Owners Loan Corporation (HOLC) and the Federal Housing Administration (FHA), government-sponsored financing encouraged the use of restrictive housing practices disadvantaging African Americans. Public-housing projects begun during the 1930s were segregated, but the Interior Department under Ickes integrated federal cafeterias. Relief went to large numbers of southern blacks—more than a quarter of all black families were on relief in 1935— but it was distributed in higher amounts to whites. However, the NYA and WPA were more aggressively experimental. The NYA, under director Aubrey Williams, established state-level supervisors of Negro affairs to increase the involvement of black students.

The failure of federal antilynching legislation suggests the limitations of civil rights advances during the 1930s. After lynch mobs murdered twenty-one people during the decade, a campaign led by the Association of Southern Women for the Prevention of Lynching, under the leadership of Texan Jessie Daniel Ames, pushed federal intervention. In addition, the NAACP made antilynching legislation a top priority and lobbied hard for it in Congress. In 1934, a bill sponsored by New York senator Robert Wagner and Colorado senator Edward P. Costigan proposed federal enforcement against lynching laws and state officials who did not prosecute it. After the bill failed because of a Senate filibuster in 1935, two years later antilynching legislation passed the House but stalled in the Senate. In 1937–1938, another southern filibuster in the Senate effectively killed antilynching legislation. Notably, Roosevelt refused to involve himself in the fight for fear of alienating southern white support in Congress. Eleanor Roosevelt, in contrast, favored a federal antilynching law, becoming what one historian calls the "administration's moral compass."[30] At the same time, despite moving cautiously, FDR communicated a sense of empathy with many African Americans.

A critical ingredient of change in chipping away at the system of white supremacy was the federal court system—and a series of decisions that began, though haltingly so, during the 1930s. In much of the South, the white primary system excluded African Americans from voting and officeholding. The Supreme Court, in decisions in 1927 and 1932, struck down legislation in Texas that authorized the white primary under the party's control as a private organization. The NAACP mounted a broad legal challenge to segregation and during the 1930s began to build a case against Jim Crow education. In the *Gaines* decision, the court in 1938 ruled that an applicant to the University of Missouri Law School deserved access to state-supported education. Activist Pauli Murray hailed the decision as "the first major breach in the solid wall of segregation since *Plessy*."[31] Law schools across the South hurriedly established all-black law schools to meet the terms of the decision or provided tuition grants to out-of-state schools. Under pressure, southern state legislatures began an effort to equalize state funding for black and white schools.

The 1930s were a pivotal decade in the history of the South. New policies that expanded federal intervention in public policy resulted from the Depression, and the New Deal restructured traditional roles in industry and agriculture. But federal intervention ultimately subverted the status quo. Farm policies accentuated the breakdown of the plantation system, which by the end of the 1930s was on its way out. The end of the plantation meant the accelerating departure of poor, largely African American rural people, many of whom migrated to northern cities. At the same time, other policies undermined traditionally low-wage policies in industry, while still others laid the basis for a subsequent challenge to white supremacy.

[30] Keith M. Finley, *Delaying the Dream: Southern Senators and the Fight against Civil Rights, 1938–1965* (Baton Rouge: Louisiana State University Press, 2008), 17.
[31] Sullivan, *Days of Hope*, 100–101.

20

WORLD WAR II

WORLD WAR II RESULTED in an unprecedented mobilization of human and economic resources into a war footing. Millions joined the military, participated in training camps around the country, and were shipped overseas to fight. The South housed
new military facilities, attracting federal investment and also thousands of outsiders
with their first exposure to the region. At home, the war boom spawned the growth of
industry, as well as changes in agriculture, in the super-heated economy. An acute
labor shortage, along with accelerated mobility and migration of people around the
South and the country, ended the Great Depression's problem of unemployment.
Opportunities for employment opened up for women, who gained access to occupations that were previously all-male. World War II also brought new roles for blacks in
the South, further eroding the stability of white supremacy. The struggle against
fascism abroad, in defense of global democracy, seemed incongruous set against the
Jim Crow practices still prevailing in the South. In many ways, World War II set the
stage for a future revolution in civil rights and an end to white supremacy. Thousands
of African Americans received military training and went abroad to fight for their
country. At home, meanwhile, using the courts and the political system, African
Americans laid the basis for a wide-ranging challenge to segregation.

WARTIME BOOM

The wartime military buildup created a boom economy, and the heated demand for
labor, goods, and services transformed the country, the South included. In contrast
to the Depression, which threw thousands of people out of work, the war called millions of men and women to arms, while employing still more millions in war-related

labor. As a result of wartime dislocation and economic boom, people migrated as they never had before; about three million southerners moved at least once during the war. In effect, the wartime experience turned southerners loose to new experiences at home and abroad.

The military forces that composed part of the buildup were mobilized in training facilities, many of which were located in the South. About $4.75 billion was poured into the construction of military camps in the South, more than a third of what was spent nationally. Overall, the South contained 41 percent of the nation's training camps and two-thirds of its military bases. The camps transformed isolated rural areas and small towns almost overnight, housing four to five million trainees. For many, it was their first exposure to the South. A trainee described a "vast sea of tents and one story buildings standing on light brown sticky clay, vegetation sparse, weather sultry and air of utter strangeness."[1] Camp Blanding, located outside the small north-central Florida town of Starke, was constructed in September 1940 after authorities purchased a 55,000-acre tract and quickly erected housing, roads, and railroads. The camp held 60,000 military trainees, becoming the fifth-largest city in Florida. Elsewhere, the pattern was the same, as the military mobilization gravitated to southern locations. Wherever the training camps were located, millions of dollars in federal funds followed. Across the region, infrastructure projects such as roads and airports were carried out as part of this massive mobilization. Overall, the military mobilization displaced southerners: the federal government purchased 710,000 acres of land for camps and production facilities, resulting in the dislocation of 25,000 people.[2]

During the war, the South also housed camp facilities for growing numbers of German and Italian prisoners of war (POWs). Some 244,000 prisoners were kept in camps in the South by the end of the war, and Texas alone held 80,000 POWs. They worked mostly as agricultural laborers, filling demand created by the departure of millions of rural migrants. The presence of POWs in the South illustrated the contradictions of Jim Crow: POWs rode in the front of streetcars, African Americans in the rear. As well, POWs attended USO concerts and shows in the South, while black soldiers were barred from these events.

The war brought on an economic boom. While wages grew by 40 percent between 1939 and 1942, by the end of the war employment in manufacturing had grown by 50 percent. Soon, wage levels expanded beyond the minimum wage of 40 cents per hour established by the Fair Labor Standards Act, increasing by 139 percent between 1940 and 1943. About a quarter of the southern workforce worked for the public sector by 1945. Unemployment sharply decreased from 626,000 in 1940 to 80,000 four years later. The manufacturing base of the South—in textiles, mining, oil, and steel—operated at full capacity. The war boom came in response to massive federal spending, $4.5 billion in the South. In Birmingham, the steel industry

---

[1] Norrell, *Dixie's War*, 8–9.
[2] Norrell, *Dixie's War*, 16.

revived during the war, employing 50,000 workers. Bauxite, a critical war supply, was mass-produced in Arkansas. More than half the aluminum produced in the United States came from plants in North Carolina and Tennessee.

Ordnance operations took place on a massive scale, with plants located across the South. At Childersburg, Alabama, 25,000 workers were engaged in the production of TNT and smokeless powder. The Holston Ordnance Works, located in Kingsport, Tennessee, manufactured the powerful explosive RDX. The oil industry, vital to the war effort, greatly expanded traffic and refining in the Gulf. During the war, Houston emerged as the center of the petrochemical industry. Texas accounted for more than a quarter of federal expenditures in the South with its aircraft, refineries, and petrochemical industry. A new oil pipeline known as the Big Inch connected Longview, Texas, with Phoenixville, Pennsylvania. Finished in a year, the pipeline extended 1,400 miles and transported 335,000 barrels of oil a day to northeastern refineries, avoiding the German submarines that were prowling the American coast. Synthetic rubber, a vital supply, was produced in great quantities in Texas.

New industries sprang up in the South in response to the mobilization around the production of aircraft, tanks, ships, and ordnance. In Dallas–Fort Worth and Atlanta-Marietta, new airframe plants sprang up. In Dallas–Fort Worth, Lockheed, North American Aviation, and Consolidated Vultee Aircraft hired thousands of workers. Bell Aircraft manufactured B-29s in Georgia factories for use in the air war against the Japanese. Perhaps the most significant wartime industry in the South was shipbuilding. In Pascagoula, Mississippi, the Ingalls shipyard constructed seamless hull barges and cargo ships, using steel from Birmingham for their bottoms. The town's population skyrocketed from 4,000 to 30,000 during the war; the number of workers employed at the Ingalls shipyard was larger than the entire population prior to the war. To the east, Panama City, Florida, grew from 12,000 to 55,000 people because of its military installations and shipyards.

Eastern Tennessee became the scene of another massive expansion of military plants with the establishment of the Oak Ridge plant in 1942. Part of the top-secret

Eleanor Roosevelt visiting Oak Ridge. *National Archives.*

"V" home campaign, Washington, DC, October 1942.   *National Archives.*

Manhattan Project, a crash program to develop nuclear weapons, the new town was located in a seventeen-mile-long valley in the Tennessee mountains. The army quietly acquired about 60,000 acres of land—often despite the unwillingness of local residents. Population of the new town grew exponentially, from 3,000 in 1942 to nearly 75,000 three years later, with thousands employed in the project's work. Military authorities strictly guarded the facility, providing housing for workers on the grounds.

During the war, Norfolk rapidly expanded as a shipbuilding center. The Newport News Shipbuilding and Dry Dock Company turned out Liberty Ships to transport supplies and troops to Europe. Nearby, the Norfolk Shipyard produced battleships. Over 150,000 workers flocked to the Hampton Roads area to take jobs in war industries. The Norfolk area was also an important staging and embarkation area, as supplies and men passed through there en route to Europe. Along with New York and San Francisco, Norfolk served as the most important port of embarkation, as 1.7 million servicemen and women passed through en route to war.

In Mobile, the Alabama Dry Dock and Shipbuilding Company constructed cargo ships, while the Gulf Shipbuilding Corporation built destroyers. The city increased in population to 200,000 from a prewar figure of 115,000—one of the fastest-growing cities in the United States. Many residents lived in temporary and sometimes squalid housing. Novelist John Dos Passos described Mobile as "trampled and battered" as if it had been "taken by storm."[3] New Orleans produced thousands of landing craft that would be used in the invasion of Europe, along with patrol boats and coastal freighters. Andrew Jackson Higgins, originally from Nebraska, developed an amphibious landing craft based on one he had devised for the Louisiana waterways. Higgins also established a bus system that transported workers to the plant; the routes totaled seven hundred miles, to plants employing twelve thousand people.

Like many other employers, Higgins hired significant numbers of female workers. In November 1942, the company started to hire and train women. According to the

African American factory workers working on the pilot compartment of an aircraft, May 1942. *National Archives.*

company bulletin, women were being slowly introduced "in order not to disturb production" and to "accustom the men on the job." The bulletin also stated that "woman's most honored place is in keeping the home fires burning, upon which the world depends." Women were employed at Higgins "with no intention of replacing men on a permanent basis, but to *relieve a man only for the duration* and then return to her home." Women were advised about appropriate dress, and the right amount of makeup.

As was true in the rest of the United States, the war opened up new work opportunities for southern women. Many of them took all-male jobs, such as riveting and welding. These new roles undermined existing taboos and stereotypes about gender. Lena Porrier Legnon recalled how she left rural Louisiana to take up work in New Orleans as a welder. Women, she said, were "better than men welders. Neater welders." Legnon led an independent life, much freer than she had experienced in rural Louisiana. When the war ended, she continued her welding work.[4]

The war boom drew people away from their homes, encouraging an unprecedented migration. About a fifth of the rural southern population, about two million whites and blacks, left their homes during the war, while urban areas grew by about 30 percent. In Appalachian areas, outmigration accelerated, as between 20 and 30 percent of its inhabitants moved during the 1940s. In Arkansas, 677,000 people were employed in agricultural work in 1940; by 1944, only 292,000 remained. Much of this migration went northward: about 100,000 people moved to Michigan because of jobs in defense plants. Rural migrants flocked to the war centers in the South, overwhelming existing housing and spurring rising rents. Residents of the southern boomtowns regarded the rural migrants suspiciously, blaming them for a perceived breakdown in the social and moral order.

The presence of a large number of unattached males created a demand for sex workers, as wartime dislocation aggravated social problems. The military attempted to eradicate prostitution. The May Act of 1941 made prostitution a federal crime and empowered the War Department to crack down if local authorities proved ineffective. In 1943, federal authorities imposed control over twelve counties surrounding Fort Bragg, near Fayetteville, North Carolina, when it appeared that locals could no longer handle the situation. At the same time, a similar lockdown

[4] Pete Daniel, *Lost Revolutions. The South in the 1950s* (Chapel Hill: University of North Carolina Press, 2000), 17.

A. Philip Randolph, 1963. *Library of Congress.*

was imposed on twenty-seven counties near Camp Forrest, Tennessee.

In early 1943, *Washington Post* reporter Agnes E. Meyer toured twenty-seven different communities across the country. Seven were in the South. Her account revealed a society that was turned upside down. Orange, a "sleepy little town" in 1940 in East Texas, underwent a boom as its population grew from 7,500 to 35,000 because of the presence of three shipyards, which built destroyers and destroyer escorts, and a naval training station. Meyer told how the schools of the community were overwhelmed with migrants and their children. Many moved from what was known as "Deep East Texas," a country in a "primitive existence." Coming from a "thicket . . . in cabins whose only ventilation comes through the door or through the chinks between the logs," the migrants had little understanding of gas stoves or flush toilets. For women, work in the shipyards represented the "first break they have had in the old routine of cooking, dishwashing, and child-bearing."[5]

Two weeks later, visiting Wilmington, North Carolina, Meyer found another community in upheaval. With a shipyard employing 20,000 workers and three major military bases, Wilmington saw its population swell to 120,000 from a prewar population of 33,000. Under rationing, shortages of food and other supplies became acute. Standing in line for her morning coffee for thirty minutes, Meyer skipped dinners at local cafeterias because "the meals were not worth the effort it takes to get them." The Wilmington shipyard, a subsidiary of the Newport News Shipbuilding and Dry Dock Company, constructed Victory ships, vessels used for cargo supplying the war effort abroad. A third of the workforce was black, employed in skilled occupations as riggers, drillers, shipwrights, and riveters. Workers came from local farms, and the shipyard's managers reported that, during the past month, two hundred had left work to return home to work on the farm.[6]

AFRICAN AMERICANS AND THE WAR

Black leaders realized that World War II offered a chance for racial progress at home. After the defense building began, A. Philip Randolph, president of the Brotherhood of Sleeping Car Porters, led an effort to ensure that black workers received equal treatment in war industries and to integrate the military. When Randolph in July 1941 threatened to organize the March on Washington, composed of 75,000 to 100,000 African Americans, to protest unequal use of federal funds in defense

[5] Agnes E. Meyer, *Journey through Chaos* (New York: Harcourt, Brace, 1944), 170–171.
[6] Meyer, *Journey through Chaos*, 222–229.

Black woman working at bomber factory near Nashville, February 1943. *Library of Congress.*

industries, President Roosevelt responded by issuing Executive Order 8802. Although this measure preserved segregation in the military, it banned discrimination in defense work and established the Fair Employment Practices Committee (FEPC) to oversee the order.

Roosevelt's executive order was far from perfect. The FEPC lacked the power to compel employers, relying instead on publicity and moral suasion. Employers and unions accustomed to excluding black workers realized that they could ignore the FEPC. Southern segregationists, exaggerating the FEPC's powers, tried to undermine it. The FEPC, claimed Gov. Frank Dixon of Alabama, wanted to "break down the principle of segregation of races, to force Negroes and white people to work together, intermingle with each other, and even to bring about the situation where white employees will have to work under Negroes."[7] Despite its deficiencies, the FEPC represented a milestone in federal civil rights policy. Both the Public Works Administration (PWA) and the Works Progress Administration (WPA) operated under nondiscrimination orders, the first time that federal policies had extended so widely and with such impact. Moreover, the establishment of the FEPC marked the first time that a federal agency attempted to enforce racial equality in the workplace.

Continuing from World War I and the 1920s, the black exodus from the South only briefly slowed during the Depression. During the 1930s, nearly half a million more African Americans migrated from the South than moved in. Black migration was a long-term trend, with about 1.6 million leaving in the 1940s, followed by 1.4 million in the 1950s, and another million during the 1960s. In the Mississippi delta, it was estimated that a tenth of the rural black population departed during the war years. The black population of California surged during the war years, increasing from 124,306 in 1940 to 337,866 a decade later—a larger black migration into the state than in all previous decades combined.

In the military, African Americans continued to experience Jim Crow, as the armed forces remained segregated throughout the war. In the army, they served in

_____
[7] Frederickson, *Dixiecrat Revolt*, 34.

segregated units, while the navy refused to admit African Americans as anything but mess men until June 1942. Thereafter, they continued to confine black seamen to menial positions. African Americans were excluded entirely from the marines. During the war, pressure mounted nonetheless against segregation in the military. In 1939, black veterans from World War I organized the Committee on the Participation of Negroes in National Defense Programs, and this group pressed for integration. The case against segregation was especially telling because war propaganda emphasized the worldwide struggle against fascism and racism. Could America "expect Negroes to be valiant defenders in time of war," said legal educator and activist Charles Houston, "when it ignored them in time of peace?"[8]

Change came only slowly, however. The army rejected large numbers of black draftees because they could not read or write, but the military accepted more white illiterates. In the army, black soldiers usually had white officers and were often confined to service positions. Indeed, of 450,000 black army members, only 100,000 served in combat units. In many ways, African Americans' military experience resembled their marginalization two decades earlier, during World War I. There were important differences, new ways in which blacks began to make inroads. Civil rights leaders campaigned to train more black pilots. In the army air corps, about a thousand black pilots were trained at the Tuskegee Army Air Field, in Alabama. The pilots were organized into two units, the 332nd Fighter Group and the 477th Bombardment Group, though only the 332nd saw action in Italy and Germany. Unlike white pilots, who trained across the country, the black pilots were confined to one base, and they became known as the Tuskegee Airmen. Predictably, they experienced discrimination on the base, though they conducted a sit-in protest that resulted in the integration of the mess hall and the abandonment of Jim Crow signs.

The military experience of black troops was mixed, to say the least. A northern black recruit observed that the "white civilians hate us, and we in turn despise them."[9] Four-fifths of them were trained in camps in the South, which were segregated, in communities deeply suspicious of African Americans under arms. Black soldiers were subjected to discrimination, harassment, violence, and even murder from southern whites, while white military police treated black soldiers harshly. One black soldier stationed at Camp Livingston, Louisiana, complained in January 1944 that the camp was a "hell hole" and that German POWs "here have more rights and freedom" than African American soldiers.[10]

Uncertainty and tensions led to an upsurge of racial violence both in civilian and military settings. In 1940, NAACP worker Elbert Williams, a Tennessee activist, was

[8] Sullivan, *Days of Hope*, 135.
[9] Numan V. Bartley, *The New South, 1945–1980* (Baton Rouge: Louisiana State University Press, 1995), 8.
[10] James Pritchett to James Evans, January 12, 1944, in *Taps for a Jim Crow Army: Letters from Black Soldiers in World War II*, ed. Phillip McGuire (Lexington: University Press of Kentucky, 1993), 23.

lynched after he led a voter registration drive. During the same year, two fourteen-year-old black boys, Charles Lang and Ernest Green, were lynched in Shubuta, Mississippi, for frightening a white girl. Black troops and white military policemen shot at each other in 1944 for two hours at Brookley Field in Mobile, while similar mutinies erupted among other black troops. Black servicemen and servicewomen complained of assault and raids into their camps by white soldiers; black women reported instances of sexual assault.[11]

As whites periodically attempted to restore racial authority, very often blacks fought back. In Wilmington, North Carolina, when a black serviceman was refused service in a bar, black soldiers and civilians rioted. Other outbreaks of violence occurred. Outside Fort Bragg, in 1941, white military policemen and black soldiers fought it out, resulting in two deaths. In 1942, black soldiers at Alexandria, Louisiana, objected to their segregation to a small section of the town for recreational activities. After a white policeman attempted to arrest a black soldier, a fight broke out between soldiers and authorities. In several army camps in Mississippi and Georgia, mutinies erupted by black soldiers unhappy about conditions and racial discrimination by the army and the local community.

Black officers also frequently resisted white supremacy. The Tuskegee Airmen were outspoken critics of white supremacy in part because they had greater status as officers. Outside a Waterboro, South Carolina, airbase, black airmen were refused service. In response, they told the owner to "go to hell," showed their revolvers, and issued a "Heil Hitler" to the shocked white onlookers. Some of the same black airmen from Waterboro were able to obtain service in a white cafeteria in a Washington, DC, airport, effectively integrating the facility. Protests also erupted among black officers at Selfridge Field near Detroit when they attempted to integrate the officers' club.

Similarly energized, some four thousand black women served in the armed forces during the war. Outside the military, the war elevated expectations and opportunities for black women to move up occupationally and professionally. The military

African American US Army nurses arriving at Greenock, Scotland. *Public domain.*

[11] Rollins W. James Jr. to P. L. Prattis, in *Taps for a Jim Crow Army*, ed. McGuire, 25–26.

severely limited the numbers of African Americans, and the National Association of Colored Graduate Nurses (NACGN) became an advocacy group for opening access to military nursing for black women. The NACGN president, Mabel Keaton Staupers, pressured the army to increase the number of black nurses from 56 to 160 by 1943. The War Department implemented a new policy in 1945 under which nurses were drafted without regard to race.

For African Americans, the war raised expectations about change; for whites, it accentuated fears that their social system was disintegrating. "We are living in the midst of perhaps the greatest revolution within human experience," wrote a black organizer in South Carolina. "Nothing, no nation, will be as it was before when the peace comes.... There is no such thing as the status quo."[12] The war spurred civil rights organizations' rapid expansion. The Southern Negro Youth Conference (SNYC), emerging from the National Negro Congress, provided a forum for younger black leadership after its creation in 1937. During the war years, the group expanded operations. Cooperating with the Congress of Industrial Organizations (CIO), the SNYC sponsored labor schools in Richmond, Hampton, New Orleans, and Birmingham. It also organized voter education drives by holding "citizenship" schools at various locations in the South. In 1944, the group ran an ambitious voter registration drive in Montgomery, Alabama.

The NAACP, meanwhile, accelerated its legal attack on segregation. In the case of *Steele v. Louisville & Nashville Railroad Co.* (1944), the Supreme Court ruled that railroad brotherhoods, which long excluded blacks and negotiated union contracts disadvantaging minorities, had a "duty of fair representation" that compelled them to fairly represent African American workers. The NAACP scored an even more significant victory in the *Smith v. Allwright* (1944) case, in which the Supreme Court struck down the white primary in Texas. This case culminated from years of litigation. After 1935,

Ella Baker. *Library of Congress.*

the NAACP recruited black attorneys to its newly organized Legal Defense Fund, with Howard University law school dean Charles Houston and attorney Thurgood Marshall assembling a new legal team of mostly black lawyers. The NAACP made the campaign against the white primary into a grassroots effort in Texas, which rallied support and money for the legal challenge. The Supreme Court, issuing its decision in April 1944, rejected the Texas law permitting political parties, as private organizations, to exclude black voters. Ruling for the majority, Justice Stanley F. Reed declared that, as a constitutional democracy, the United States possessed an "organic law" that granted "to all citizens a right to participate in the choice of elected officials without restriction by any state because of race." The "opportunity for choice" should not be nullified "by a state through casting its electoral process in a form which permits a private organization to practice racial discrimination in the election." By controlling qualifications for voting in a primary, "the state makes the action of the party the action of the state."[13]

While the NAACP slowly constructed a legal case against segregation during the war years, it also expanded its membership. The organization attracted a mass following and launched ambitious drives to expand voter registration. Field secretary Ella Baker played a key role. Born in Littleton, North Carolina, Baker moved to Harlem during the late 1920s. During the New Deal, she served as national director of the Young Negro Cooperative League, based in New York City. Under the New Deal, Baker participated in the Workers Education Project of the WPA by teaching African and labor history, as well as consumer education. During the war years, Baker practiced community-based activism and grassroots organization as director of branches for the NAACP. She successfully expanded the local chapters by regularly touring black communities across the South. Baker's effort focused on constructing "centers of sustained and dynamic leadership" that would empower local communities to become part of a national movement.[14] During the war years, the NAACP's local chapters increased their membership to nearly 400,000. "I am seeing so much and meeting so many people . . . that I could write a book," wrote an NAACP fieldworker. There was a "gold mine" of recruiting possibilities during wartime; black people were poised to challenge the status quo.[15]

The *Smith v. Allwright* case provided a huge boost in momentum for the NAACP. One Virginia activist described it as "the beginning of a complete revolution in our thinking on the right of suffrage."[16] The case emboldened voting-rights advocates about the potential of federal protection for black enfranchisement. In Mississippi, in 1944 the Mississippi Progressive Voters League conducted voter education and voter registration efforts in the state. When Sen. Theodore Bilbo urged the suppression of black voting during his reelection campaign in 1946, the Mississippi Progressive Voters League demanded an investigation. The Senate dispatched a five-member investigating committee to hold hearings, at which a large number of African Americans testified. Across the South, the NAACP conducted citizenship schools, while other African Americans organized voter leagues to promote voter registration. By the late 1940s and early 1950s, with the southern black electorate increased in communities such as Winston-Salem and Greensboro, North Carolina, black candidates were elected to city councils.

[13] *Smith v. Allwright* 131 F.2d 593.
[14] Patricia Sullivan, "Movement Building during the World War II Era: The NAACP's Legal Insurgency in the South," in *Fog of War: The Second World War and the Civil Rights Movement*, ed. Kevin M. Kruse and Stephen Tuck (New York: Oxford University Press, 2012), 76.
[15] Sullivan, "Movement Building," 71.
[16] Sullivan, "Movement Building," 75.

The war marked a turning point in the position of African Americans in the South and the United States. As historian Steven F. Lawson writes: "The World War II era furnished the staging ground for the black revolution. It revitalized black solidarity, tested innovative protest tactics, and moved the federal government closer to the side of racial equality." The end of conflict brought a renewed determination by returning black veterans. "Our people are not coming back with the idea of just taking up where they left off," wrote one black veteran. "We are going to have the things that are rightfully due us or else, which is a very large order, but we have proven beyond all things that we are people and not just servants of the white man."[17]

WHAT THE NEGRO WANTS

In January 1942, James G. Thompson, a twenty-six-year-old black cafeteria worker in Kansas, wrote to the editor of the *Pittsburgh Courier*, then the largest black newspaper in the country. "Like all true Americans," he wrote, his "greatest desire" was a victory over the "forces of evil." As an "American of dark complexion," however, he wondered whether he should "sacrifice my life to live half American." Instead, he believed that he deserved "full citizenship rights in exchange for the sacrificing of my life." Would America become a "true and pure democracy" once the war ended? Or would "colored Americans suffer still the indignities that been heaped upon them in the past?" The symbol of victory was "V." He suggested that there should be a "double V"—the first V for a triumph against "our enemies from without," the second V for "victory over our enemies from within." Those perpetuating "these ugly prejudices" were also "seeking to destroy our democratic form of government just as surely as Axis forces."[18]

In subsequent issues, the *Courier* adopted the Double V as a symbol for its war objectives—victory abroad against fascism, along with victory at home against racism. Although the campaign moved no further than the pages of the newspaper, it epitomized the momentum that the civil rights movement acquired during the war years. In many ways, the war accelerated change. The legal campaign against segregation made important strides, while at the same time the military experiences of millions of African Americans created a class of people impatient with the slow pace of change at home.

African Americans benefited from the war economy, though less than white workers. Employment for black workers remained especially limited during the initial buildup in 1940–1941. But, by 1942, the growing labor shortage forced employers to turn to black workers. On the West Coast the bulk of black migrants during the war went to California and its cities. Employed in the massive shipyards surrounding

---

[17] Steven F. Lawson, *Running for Freedom: Civil Rights and Black Politics in America since 1941*, 3d ed. (Malden, MA: Wiley-Blackwell, 2009), 25, 35.

[18] Patrick S. Washburn, "The Pittsburgh *Courier's* Double V Campaign in 1942," *American Journalism* 3, no. 2 (1986): 73–86.

San Francisco, the black population in the Bay Area grew by nearly 800 percent during the war years. Detroit's war production plants attracted 550,000 migrants from the South—500,000 whites and 50,000 blacks. White workers in southern plants often objected to working with African Americans. The opponents of the integrationist CIO, including the rival American Federation of Labor (AFL) and the hiring companies, fanned racial animosity. The AFL union in Mobile denounced the CIO as the "nigger union." In Beaumont, Texas, the Baytown Humble Oil Company distributed leaflets announcing that a "vote for the CIO is a vote for absolute equality between the white and colored races on every job in Baytown refinery from labor gang to department head."[19] In May 1943, after twelve black workers were hired as welders, 20,000 white workers went on strike at the Alabama Dry Dock and Shipbuilding Company in Mobile. The conflict was resolved only after the company set up separate workplaces for white and black workers.

Black migrants seeking work in northern cities also experienced racial hostility. In Detroit, thousands of rural southern blacks were drawn to the city's booming automobile industry, which was in full wartime mobilization. White residents feared the consequences of the onrush of black migrants. In 1940, Clark Foreman became director of the Division of Defense Housing, which was responsible for providing housing for workers in defense industries. In late 1941, Foreman approved the Sojourner Truth housing project in Detroit, which was for African Americans but was situated in a traditionally Polish neighborhood. An outcry resulted, focusing on keeping black residents from living in the all-white neighborhood; whites in the neighborhood objected to the project and rioted in a melee that caused forty injuries and two hundred arrests. The result was that Foreman's order was reversed, and he was fired from his position. In early 1943, when black workers were promoted to skilled jobs at the Packard plant, 25,000 white workers left their jobs in another "hate strike." Later, in June 1943, Detroit erupted in the worst race riot during World War II, with twenty-five black people massacred by roving white mobs.

When the Swedish sociologist Gunnar Myrdal published an intensive study of the status of race relations in 1944, titled *An American Dilemma*, he predicted a "redefinition of the Negro's status in America as a result of this War."[20] The first comprehensive social-scientific examination of the problem of race, Myrdal's study explored black as well as white attitudes. He found that the problem of race was, for black people, "all-important." Black males rarely spoke to whites without a "consciousness of this problem." Black leaders were expected to be race leaders, and "this expectancy is entrenched in all institutions in American society, including universities, learned societies and foundations." The "Negro genius," he wrote, was "imprisoned in the Negro problem." The black masses were even more imprisoned by race, "enclosed behind the walls of segregation and discrimination more acutely than

[19] Norrell, *Dixie's War*, 38.
[20] Gunnar Myrdal, *An American Dilemma: The Negro Problem and Modern Democracy* (New York: Harper & Brothers, 1944), 997.

might be expected." Like the black intelligentsia, they were "imprisoned in the Negro problem."[21]

The war years, Myrdal asserted, witnessed rising impatience with the continued humiliation of segregation. The war was of "tremendous importance to the Negro in all respects." For black people, their "strategic position" had become enhanced "not only because of the desperate scarcity of labor but also because of a revitalization of the Democratic creed." African Americans, Myrdal observed, approached the war with a spirit of a "new determination" not to let the status quo continue. The war, they realized, offered a huge opportunity. If the Negro "fails now to get into new lines of work when labor is scarce, it means that he has missed the best opportunity he is going to have for years."[22]

African American assertiveness thus grew during the war. "I am afraid for my people," a black preacher told Myrdal. "They have grown restless. They are not happy. They no longer laugh. There is a new policy among them—something strange, perhaps terrible."[23] The war, said southern sociologist Howard W. Odum, saw the emergence of a "a new Negro of great force and vitality which makes compromise well-nigh impossible." Black people had "changed tremendously" in the coming of age of their "magnificent" leadership class. Younger African Americans, "sensing the epochal spiritual change and racial attitudes and led by Negro leadership of the North and South," were more willing to "experiment with every type of equal opportunity." "It was as if some universal message had come through to the great mass of Negroes," observed Odum, "urging them to dream new dreams and to protest against the old order. It was as if there were pathos and tragedy in their misunderstanding, of the main tenets of a bitter Negro leadership, and as if many of the northern Negro leaders of limited mentality had confused them with the idea that any sort of work or courtesy or cheerfulness was an index of subservience to the white man. In all of this, whether it was pathos and tragedy or admirable idealism and noble effort, the net result was a new Negro."[24]

When black sociologist Charles S. Johnson surveyed race relations in 1944, he described "accelerated social changes" that were "wholesome, even if their temporary racial effects are bad." The war had undermined the traditional underpinnings of racial segregation. Black people, due to increased contact with the world outside the segregated South, were unwilling to tolerate segregation. A "great majority of southern Negroes" were "becoming increasingly dissatisfied with the present pattern of race relations and want a change." At the same time, a "great majority of southern whites" seemed "unable to contemplate the possibility of change in any fundamental sense." The war brought this contradiction into sharp focus. A "cataclysmic national event," Johnson wrote, the war loosened "many traditions from their deep moorings,

[21] Myrdal, *An American Dilemma*, 28–29.
[22] Myrdal, *An American Dilemma*, 409.
[23] Myrdal, *An American Dilemma*, 1013.
[24] Howard W. Odum, "The Way of the South," in *Special Issue: In Search of the Regional Balance of America*, *Social Forces* 23, no. 3 (March 1945): 261.

whether these traditions are economic, religious, racial or romantic." War production drew black people off the land, taking them out of the labor market as manual laborers and domestics.

Johnson noted "points of racial tension" appearing in the South during wartime. Between March and December 1943, he noted 111 racial incidents in the South that arose from conflicts over employment, public transportation, crime and police, black servicemen and military police, racial etiquette, and other challenges to the status quo. The "most frequent contact" between whites and blacks occurred in segregated transportation. The war heightened congestion, crowding, and shortages of transportation facilities. The lack of experienced drivers and conductors made matters worse. The "flexible and frequently undeterminable limits of racial segregation on public carriers" undermined customary patterns of segregation and highlighted "highly volatile issues of personal status in racial situations." Johnson believed that the war had let the genie out of the bottle: "What conclusions," he asked, should be drawn from "these currents of change?" The solution, he believed, lay in seeking "some acceptable methods of revising the racial attitudes and beliefs of the white South, and overcoming the educational and cultural lag in both the Negro groups and certain elements of the white population."[25]

A year before the war ended, in 1944, the African American historian Rayford Logan assembled a group of fourteen black intellectuals and asked them to describe the future of race in America. The director of the University of North Carolina Press, William T. Couch, encouraged Logan to publish a volume containing these essays. Couch was liberally minded, which meant that he believed in the alleviation of rather than ending apartheid. When Logan delivered the manuscript, which was titled *What the Negro Wants*, Couch was shocked. The volume included a range of opinions, from conservative to radical, from its black contributors. But even the conservatives agreed that segregation needed to end immediately. Couch wrote Logan that the essays suggested that what black people wanted was "far removed from what they ought to want." The "complete abolition of segregation" was not feasible, he warned, and if this was what the Negro wanted, "he needs, and needs most urgently, . . . to revise his wants." The book was published only after Logan threatened to sue Couch and after he inserted a publisher's introduction disclaiming responsibility.[26]

The volume included essays by W. E. B. Du Bois, Roy Wilkins, Gordon B. Hancock, Mary McCleod Bethune, and Langston Hughes. One of the contributors, Doxey Wilkerson, professor of education at Howard University, joined the Communist Party and organized protests against segregation in the District of Columbia. Logan provided the lead essay. Black people, he wrote, were disappointed that the war had not brought greater progress. Their expectations raised,

[25] Charles S. Johnson, "The Present Status of Race Relations in the South," *Social Forces* 23, no. 1 (October 1944): 27–32.
[26] Kenneth Robert Janken, introduction to *What the Negro Wants*, ed. Logan (Notre Dame, IN: Notre Dame University Press, 2001), xix. Originally published in 1944.

they feared that the end of the war would bring a reversion to old patterns of white supremacy. White liberals—such as Couch—had "warned us to keep quiet." But most African Americans remembered what "public lethargy" yielded. "If they can not assert their rights at the very time that they are risking their lives in the name of the very rights which they are asking," he wrote, "when will they receive consideration?" The end of white supremacy could come in a liberal democracy, he believed. A "lumbering, blundering democracy will eventually overcome its enemies at home just as today it is crushing them abroad."[27]

LABOR, CIVIL RIGHTS, AND THE POLITICS OF WAR

Labor unions, which made significant inroads in organizing during the New Deal, enjoyed even-greater federal protections during the war in order to maximize military production. As the end of the war approached, both unions and management prepared for conflict. While unions wanted to solidify their gains, management wanted to roll them back and to uproot unions. During the war years, liberals were hopeful about the southern political environment. In 1944, Lister Hill of Alabama and Claude Pepper were elected to the Senate on a progressive coalition, as was Lyndon Johnson of Texas in 1948. Southern governors such as Georgia's Ellis Arnall, who defeated Eugene Talmadge in the primary of 1942, "Big Jim" Folsom of Alabama, elected in 1946, and W. Kerr Scott of North Carolina, elected in 1948, all were politicians who, though segregationist, favored expanded governmental services in education, health, and roads. Disdaining the racial demagoguery of previous generations of southern politicians, the success of these white progressives seemed to indicate changes in the political system.

The war had solidified and extended the progressive leftist coalition of the late 1930s, even while it experienced concerted attack. Politically mobilized women, along with journalists and editors and other reformers, joined forces with civil rights leaders. The Southern Conference for Human Welfare (SCHW), based in Birmingham, advanced an agenda of labor and civil rights reform, becoming the main umbrella under which the southern progressive Left sustained itself during the 1940s. The SCHW took the lead in pursuing national legislation to abolish the poll tax, which, according to some estimates, disfranchised ten million potential voters.[28] The SCHW expanded significantly after its founding in 1938, especially during the war, and by late 1946 it had over 10,000 members, along with active state chapters in six southern states. With the CIO's financial backing, the SCHW recruited new members, cementing a biracial coalition and expanding voter registration. Meanwhile, the organization published a monthly, the *Southern Patriot*, devoted to the "complete and utter mobilization of all the people, Negro as well as

---

[27] Logan, ed., *What the Negro Wants*, 9, 30.
[28] Keith M. Finley, *Delaying the Dream: Southern Senators and the Fight against Civil Rights, 1938–1965* (Baton Rouge: Louisiana State University Press, 2008), 59.

white, and resources for the winning of this war." The SCHW also maintained a presence in Washington and New York City. With the end of the war, the SCHW officially disavowed segregation as "fundamentally undemocratic, un-American and unChristian." Its message offered a class analysis: racial discrimination reflected poverty and an oppressive class structure. [29]

The war unquestionably spawned a new African American activism. In 1942, the Congress of Racial Equality (CORE) was organized in Chicago, seeking an end to segregation by using direct-action, nonviolent protest. During the war, CORE staged protests in northern cities. In the South, the same spirit of militancy also affected African Americans. In October 1942, black leaders convened a meeting in Durham, North Carolina, and declared their opposition to white supremacy. The Durham group combined with the Commission on Interracial Cooperation (CIC) to form the Southern Regional Council (SRC), which was created in February 1944. Despite black membership and participation, the SRC was a predominantly white organization. Many of the white moderates associated with it remained conflicted about whether the time was right to end segregation. A proposed merger between the SRC and the SCHW failed because of the former organization's perceived conservatism on racial issues. The strongest African American organization, and the SCHW's most important black ally, was the NAACP, whose membership grew by six times during wartime, with more than 300,000 members by 1945. Notably, 15,000 of the NAACP members during the war were black soldiers.

Labor activism reached a peak of success during World War II. In 1943, the CIO Political Action Committee (CIO-PAC) became the union's main political organization that brought together a network of grassroots labor organizers, liberals, and civil rights advocates. Organized in support of FDR's reelection campaign in 1944, CIO-PAC promoted voter education and registration in the South and targeted black and female voters. Notably, the CIO-PAC was biracial and included African Americans in leadership. The fruit of the CIO-PAC's efforts was impressive, as an estimated 600,000 African Americans were registered to vote in 1946. CIO leader Sidney Hillman also created the National Citizens Political Action Committee (NCPAC) as an organization that sought support outside the union. These groups became the strongest advocates of extending the New Deal by seeking racial and economic democracy.

These efforts, mostly by northern and southern whites, were matched by a growing political mobilization by African Americans. In the immediate postwar years, the CIO-PAC and allies such as the SNYC, the SCHW, and the NAACP expanded their efforts in the South. Black activists Ella Baker, E. D. Nixon, and Rosa Parks coordinated efforts in voter registration and education in regional meetings of the NAACP branches. The results were notable, with about 900,000 black voters registered by 1950. On the heels of the *Smith v. Allwright* case, in 1944 two black leaders

[29] Krueger, *And Promises to Keep*, 107. See also John Egerton, *Speak Now against the Day: The Generation before the Civil Rights Movement in the South* (New York: A. A. Knopf, 1994).

of extraordinary energy and bold imagination, John McCray and Osceola McKaine, led the South Carolina Progressive Democratic Party (PDP) in support of FDR's reelection. McKaine worked as one of this group's field organizers. A World War I veteran (where he was an officer), McKaine remained in Belgium after the war, owning a supper club in Ghent. When the Germans invaded Belgium, he returned to South Carolina and began organizing. Active in the NAACP's Sumter branch, McKaine helped mount a statewide campaign to equalize black teachers' salaries. McKaine also helped organize a march of black veterans in Birmingham, Alabama, protesting their disfranchisement by attempting to register to vote.

In 1944, the PDP sent a slate of delegates to the Democratic National Convention in Chicago, unsuccessfully challenging the all-white South Carolina delegation. Eventually claiming 45,000 members, the PDP worked in alliance with the NAACP to register thousands of new voters. In 1944, McKaine mounted a campaign for the US Senate, the first time a black candidate ran for that office in the twentieth century. The PDP challenge served to illustrate the contradictions in the Democratic Party, in its growing northern liberal wing and the continuing presence of its white-supremacist southern wing.

The war years witnessed steady expansion for organized labor in the South. Under the protection of the National War Labor Board, unions recruited new members without encountering the usual harassment. In addition, the board issued equal-pay-for-equal-work regulations that diminished racial wage differentials. Trade unions under the AFL grew in a variety of industries, and the CIO enjoyed membership increases in oil, rubber, and automobiles. The war production plants became unionized across the South. Gadsden, Alabama, for example, had been an antiunion bastion prior to the war. By 1945, a sixth of its population belonged to CIO unions. Even the antiunion citadel, the cotton textile industry, saw a large increase in union participation.[30]

In 1940, founder and longtime CIO president John L. Lewis called organizing the South "one of the unfinished jobs ahead of labor in America."[31] Lewis rightly realized that the low-wage, nonunion economy threatened labor organizations outside the South, as firms sought to relocate south because of more-favorable conditions. Four years later, in 1944, CIO president Philip Murray said that organizing southern workers was a "civil rights program" that involved liberating southern workers from "economic and political bondage" and eliminating "all types of racial and other forms of discrimination."[32] Murray later added that organizing the South was the "most important drive of its kind ever undertaken by any labor organization in the history of this country."[33]

The union, by war's end, had 400,000 southern members, but these were concentrated in federally regulated and national steel, rubber, and automobile industries.

[30] Marshall, *Labor in the South*, 227–229.
[31] Bartley, *The New South*, 39.
[32] Sullivan, *Days of Hope*, 207.
[33] Marshall, *Labor in the South*, 254.

Traditionally southern industries such as cotton textiles, tobacco, and lumber remained mostly nonunion. Despite the gains of the war years, the cotton textile industry remained only 20 percent organized in 1946. Other industries similarly remained nonunion. Once the war ended, the CIO inaugurated a new campaign, Operation Dixie, to organize the southern workforce. The CIO established headquarters for a Southern Organizing Committee (SOC) in Atlanta, with steelworkers' organizer Van A. Bittner in charge and 250 fieldworkers, mostly native southerners and war veterans. The Textile Workers Union of America (TWUA), a CIO union, spent $4 million and dispatched its own large organizing force to southern mills. Lucy Randolph Mason, a CIO veteran, ran a community relations staff.

Operation Dixie enjoyed the support of the SCHW and other white progressives. The unionization campaign suffered from significant internal tensions. National CIO officials, unlike local organizers, expressed less enthusiasm for civil rights and less willingness to connect civil rights and unionism. The CIO had become a more institutionalized organization during the war, with more of a stake attached to the processes of governmental regulation. The union encountered resentment of some white workers and returning white veterans, who feared that black union members were threatening their jobs.

As a result of the threat posed by the Soviet Union abroad, organizations associated with the Communist Party came under suspicion. The CIO felt intense pressure to disavow its old connections with the Left. When a rally in Harlem supported Operation Dixie, the head of the CIO's SOC, Bittner, disavowed the group. Bittner had little interest in the supporters of Socialists and Communists, he said, and "that goes for the Southern Conference for Human Welfare and other organizations living off the CIO."[34] Fear of subversion included those groups that had allied themselves with the Communists in a Popular Front alliance. Soon after the war, the issue of loyalty split the New Deal progressive coalition, as many civil rights groups were tarred with charges of disloyalty. Beginning in May 1946, the AFL conducted a membership drive, which, it claimed, would be "an operation primarily by Southerners for Southerners." AFL organizers made the wild charge that CIO unions were "devoted followers of Moscow" and that its leadership had "openly followed the Communist line and is following that line today." AFL president William Green even suggested that employers should "grow and cooperate with us or fight for your life against Communist forces."[35]

Within the CIO there was strong support, especially among its leadership, for cutting all ties with Communist and Popular Front organizations in order to inoculate themselves against charges of disloyalty. On the other hand, many members of the progressive coalition believed that anticommunism was a phony issue devised to sow divisions. Anticommunism, said Clark Foreman, sought to "divide us, to make us attack each other instead of getting on with the job of democracy."[36]

[34] Krueger, *And Promises to Keep*, 140.
[35] Marshall, *Labor in the South*, 247.
[36] Bartley, *The New South*, 45, 47.

Weakened by internal divisions, the CIO encountered powerful opposition in the South. Local power structures remained hostile to efforts by organizers to unionize the workforce and threaten the low-wage economy. Local law enforcement, Myrdal wrote, often acted as "agents of the planter and other white employers." Stetson Kennedy described an alliance between "so-called public officials and law officers with anti-union employers" that was "everywhere apparent."[37] Lucy Randolph Mason recalled how southern communities "violently resisted" unions. In Alabama, one resident opposed the union because the visiting organizer was a "foreigner." When told that the organizer was from a neighboring county, he responded: "I knew he was a foreigner—and he was, born outside of this county."[38]

The CIO was thus seriously fractured when Operation Dixie began in 1946. Split between national advocates of Operation Dixie and local advocates of the CIO-PAC coalitionist approach, the CIO's leadership rejected an alliance with the SCHW and froze them out of participation in the campaign. Nonetheless, initially Operation Dixie seemed to yield results. In 1947, in elections supervised by the National Labor Relations Board (NLRB), 66,000 workers voted for CIO membership and 53,000 for AFL membership. The CIO continued to gain as it expelled Communist unions and reclaimed them. Infighting over charges of communism affected a strike by Local 22 in Winston-Salem, where five thousand black tobacco workers struck against the large R. J. Reynolds Tobacco Company factory. After the local press and the anti-Communist congressional committee, the House Un-American Activities Committee (HUAC), charged Communist influence, the SOC withdrew support from the strike. Even after Local 22 won concessions, the CIO supported another union backed by United Transport Services of America, but, in an NLRB election, a plurality voted for "no-union" with the split pro-union vote.

The suicidal purge in the tobacco industry was duplicated in mines, mills, and smelters. Often, attacks on Communists' unions meant attacks on black-controlled unions. Facing infighting within the union and the bitter opposition of the AFL and conservative unions, Operation Dixie stalled and, by early 1947, had failed. On top of that failure came an assault by congressional conservatives. In 1943, Congress enacted the Smith-Connally Act, which permitted the government to seize mines and industries threatened by strikes during wartime and banned the use of union funds in political campaigns. Congress's enactment of the Taft-Hartley Act in June 1947 limited the NLRB's power to intervene, prohibited secondary boycotts by unions, and allowed states to regulate right-to-work legislation. The latter provision enabled antiunion legislatures in the South to prohibit closed shops and undermine union membership. By 1949, even a CIO official was admitting that "we are gradually being liquidated in the South."[39]

---

[37] Stetson Kennedy, *Southern Exposure: Making the South Safe for Democracy* (Garden City, NY: Doubleday, 1946), 295.

[38] Mason, *To Win These Rights* , 19–20.

[39] Marshall, *Labor in the South*, 265; Robert Rodgers Korstad, *Civil Rights Unionism: Tobacco Workers and the Struggle for Democracy in the Mid-Twentieth-Century South* (Chapel Hill: University of North Carolina Press, 2003).

Operation Dixie's failure was matched by the defeat of the progressive political coalition during the late 1940s. In a sense, that coalition's last gasp was the
third-party candidacy of Henry Wallace for the presidency in 1948. Serving as
Roosevelt's vice president in 1941–1945, Wallace was displaced from the ticket in
1944 because conservatives in the Democratic Party saw him as tilted toward the
party's left wing. Harry Truman, nominated as vice president in 1944, became
president upon Roosevelt's death in April 1945. Soon, Wallace became estranged
and critical of Truman's Cold War policies of confrontation with the Soviet
Union. Favoring accommodation with the Soviets, Wallace also vocally opposed
Truman's anticommunism.

The anti-Communist attack on the Left took its toll, however. The SCHW, the
most important of the progressive civil rights organizations, suffered from charges
of disloyalty. Anti-Communists had long suspected the organization as a Communist-front organization, despite the group's claims to the contrary. In 1939, Frank
Porter Graham, SCHW president, investigated these charges and, along with Clark
Foreman, banned Communist participation in leadership positions. Yet, there were
doubtless Communists in the organization, and probably some in leadership
positions.

In 1947, HUAC published a report that was strongly critical of the SCHW.
The organization, the report claimed, sought to attract southern liberals "on the
basis of its seeming interest in the problems of the South." Many "well-inten-
tioned" people had been misled, the report charged. The SCHW had been "used
in devious ways" by Communists because they dominated leadership positions
and "pulled the strings." The report cited numerous instances of Communist
membership, which was true, but then went on to assert a subversive intent on the
organization, which was untrue. The report further smeared liberals who associated with Communists in a popular front through guilt-by-association tactics.
The HUAC report, for example, charged that Frank Graham was not a Communist but was "one of those liberals who show a predilection for affiliation to various
Communist-front organizations." HUAC further contended that the organization's administrators, including Foreman and James Dombrowski, were Communist dupes. "The common bond among its supporters," it concluded, was a "certain
degree of sympathy for the Soviet Union and/or the Communist Party rather than
any primary interest in human welfare in the South." The organization's professed
goals served as a smokescreen for subversion.[40]

In 1948, Wallace ran as the presidential candidate of the Progressive Party on a
platform of accommodation with the Soviet Union and labor and racial justice at
home. His candidacy enjoyed the full support of the southern Left, including the
SCHW. In 1947, Branson Price replaced Dombrowski as administrator of the
Southern Conference, and the organization became more aggressively opposed to

[40] Committee on Un-American Activities, 80th Cong. 1st session, report no. 592, *Report on the
Southern Conference for Human Welfare.*

Truman. During the fall of 1947 and 1948, the SCHW sponsored two tours of the South by Wallace, where he spoke to racially integrated audiences in eight cities. In August 1948, Wallace encountered a hostile reception. In North Carolina, touring Durham, Greensboro, and Hickory, he was hit by eggs and tomatoes and was shouted down. The liberal North Carolina press criticized Wallace. The *Raleigh News and Observer* described him as a "stooge if not the spearhead of those who talk[ed] much about democracy as cloak for their own disloyalty."[41]

Wallace went down to a decisive defeat in the presidential election of 1948, punctuating the demise of the southern Left. In the aftermath of the presidential election, the SCHW suspended operations. While Operation Dixie exposed differences within the labor movement, it also indicated the impact that anticommunism was having. At the same time, southern white opinion reacted sharply to the prospect of the demise of Jim Crow, in a spectrum ranging from Dixiecrats to a moderate segregationism that favored gradualism and a go-slow approach.

The World War II era brought profound changes in the South, nowhere more apparent in the destabilization of white supremacy, which had been in place since the 1890s. The war boom, though ending the Depression and resulting in full employment, spurred unprecedented migration and displacement of ordinary people. Millions of young men who served abroad returned home to a different world, but they also brought with them life-changing experiences. The 1940s thus inaugurated several decades of intense change that continued to transform the South.

[41] Sullivan, *Days of Hope*, 263–264.

PART SIX

THE CIVIL RIGHTS REVOLUTION

21

THE 1950s

AFTER THE LATE 1940s, the South, much like the rest of the country, experienced the benefits of a period of sustained growth. Beginning during the 1950s and lasting into the 1970s, the South witnessed rising incomes and an expanding middle class. Postwar residents were exposed to new media, different ways of communicating, and other ways of thinking and living. As was true in the rest of the country, significant cultural changes arrived during the 1950s in music, radio and television, and sports programs, and these influences tended to narrow differences between the South and the rest of the country. Most of this new prosperity occurred in cities, but it also reshaped the patterns of rural living. The plantation system, or what was left of it, disappeared, replaced by a less labor-intensive, more capital-intensive modernized agriculture. Rural southerners continued to leave the land in large numbers, depopulating the countryside, in order to move to urban communities both in the North and the South.

These changes reflected the extent to which the South underwent an economic transformation during the generation after World War II. In many respects, this transformation was an extension of trends begun during the 1930s and 1940s. Mobility and migration continued during the postwar years, as cities and especially suburbs grew. As in the rest of the country, this demographic change reflected unprecedented economic prosperity. Per capita income grew significantly, narrowing differences with the rest of the country, with most of the higher-paying jobs located in towns and cities.

THE TRANSFORMATION OF THE PLANTATION SOUTH

In 1961, historian Thomas D. Clark wrote a highly personalized account of the then-modern South. Born in rural Mississippi in 1902, Clark described the changes affecting his native state. Growing up in the cotton country near the Pearl River, he recalled how he had hauled thousands of feet of lumber and crossties; he remembered "every mudhole, rutted hillside, and rickety bridge [that] had to be negotiated according to its own bit of treachery." During Clark's boyhood, the five miles of road from his home to market were "dotted with cabins and cottonfields." The land included more blacks than whites; "new cabins appeared with the regularity of common law marriages." All along the road lay evidence of the consequences of rural poverty.

This world, Clark reported, had largely disappeared by the early 1960s. "Clusters of oaks and cedars and insect-damaged fruit trees droop over the crumbling mounds that we once called homeplaces." Cabins once housing black sharecroppers had "long ago melted into the ground, but more important the ebony faces which once crowded doors and windows to stare at passers-by have moved 'up North some place' or now live in town." The cotton fields had vanished, replaced by stands of lumber or herds of Angus or Hereford cattle. Mule barns gave way to tractor sheds; cotton houses, to cattle feed bins. Once southerners possessed a "fierce attachment to the soil" with an "affection only a step removed from motherhood itself." Clark remembered that most of his people "knew where every fertile spot of loam lay blanketed in mulch in the woods." Their existence was defined and marked by "homey landmarks." Now tractors and mechanization had "destroyed the laborious pace by which men moved about the land; tractors have leveled the ancient boundaries of fields." Most country folk no longer possessed a "deep love for the soil."[1]

Nowhere were these changes that Clark described more apparent than in the cotton South. One indictor came in the number of cotton gins, which declined from 32,000 in 1900 to 2,880 in 1973. The massive Delta and Pine Land Company's plantations, which used 1,200 workers and cultivated 16,000 acres in the Mississippi delta during the 1930s, grew only 7,200 acres of cotton in 1969 and employed 510 workers.

Tractor Operator on the Aldridge Plantation near Leland Mississippi, June 1937, photograph by Dorothea Lange. *Library of Congress.*

---

[1] Thomas D. Clark, *The Emerging South* (New York: Oxford University Press, 1961), 1–7.

Most of the acreage was devoted to soybeans and other new cash crops.[2] With much of the production of the crop moving westward, Arizona and California emerged as major players. In 1960, when Southern Tenant Farmers Union (STFU) founder H. L. Mitchell visited the Arkansas delta, formerly cotton growing, he found conditions "radically changed." Many fewer people lived in the countryside. Few jobs on the farms remained except for work as a tractor driver, and machines did most of the fieldwork. The old Cotton South was transformed.[3]

An even more significant trend was a transition from cotton to other crops. In 1930, 46 percent of southern agricultural income came from cotton. By 1960, that had declined to 18 percent. An especially popular alternative to cotton was soybeans, in a transition that occurred during the war and the generation after. In 1940, nine southern states in the cotton belt grew 7.6 million bales of cotton, while they harvested 5.4 million bushels of soybeans. In 1975, that trend continued: these same states produced about 3 million bales of cotton and 523 million bushels of soybeans.[4] Lumbering remained important, as well. In the early 1960s, 40 percent of the region was growing trees, and loblolly forest replaced cotton fields for rapidly harvested pulpwood. Southern timber constituted 39 percent of the national lumber supply and 56 percent of its pulpwood. Paper mills grew into a significant part of the South's post-1945 economy, and the region produced a majority of the nation's paper.

The collapse of plantation agriculture dated from the New Deal, rooted in the Agricultural Adjustment Administration (AAA) policies that sought to eliminate low-wage, labor-intensive farming. The elimination of sharecroppers and tenants, the most glaring examples of rural poverty, became a goal of federal agricultural policy. But these policies, rather than affecting country people equally, were shaped by existing factors of race and class. The poorest farmers, and the most marginalized, were African Americans. They possessed the least access to resources and received the least benefit from federal policies. The AAA and its successor agencies in the US Department of Agriculture had few dealings with marginal farmers and instead focused on capitalized enterprises as the future of southern agriculture. The collapse of the plantation system also reflected technological changes in agriculture. During and after World War II, a capital-intensive agriculture meant mechanization and the "green revolution"—highly capitalized and productive agriculture that relied on machines, fertilizers, engineered seeds, and pesticides.

With the departure of the rural poor, mechanization more than took up the slack. Row tractors continued to replace mules as the most important and most productive form of mechanization. In Alabama, the numbers of tractors doubled between 1939 and 1945 and then nearly quadrupled five years later. In Mississippi, which had 5,542 tractors in 1932, that number had grown to 81,621 in 1954. Correspondingly, the mule

[2] Schulman, *From Cotton Belt to Sunbelt*, 153–156.
[3] Pete Daniel, *Breaking the Land: The Transformation of Cotton, Tobacco, and Rice Cultures since 1880* (Urbana: University of Illinois Press, 1985), 239.
[4] Harry D. Fornari, "The Big Change: Cotton to Soybeans," *Agricultural History* 53, no. 1 (January 1979): 245.

population declined precipitously. Mississippi, which had 358,000 mules in 1930, could claim only 200,000 in 1958. In eleven southern states, the population of mules and horses declined by 293,000 between 1954 and 1957.[5]

Tractors reduced the need for human labor, making a large agricultural proletariat obsolete. They also applied large quantities of chemical fertilizers and pesticides. There were other important innovations as well. In 1942, International Harvester began producing a small number of mechanical cotton pickers, though wartime production remained limited. The mechanization of cotton picking depended on new approaches to planting, fertilization, and the massive use of pesticides. In addition, different varieties of cotton were developed that were more adapted to mechanical picking. Cotton-picking machinery became more refined and sophisticated over time, and the introduction of the spindle picker and stripper harvesters became more common during the 1950s. By the mid-1950s, about half the cotton crop was harvested by machine, and by the 1960s mechanization had completely taken over.

Government-sponsored chemicals greatly expanded in popularity. During World War I, the emphasis on developing chemical weapons in the War Department's Chemical Warfare Service also resulted in the introduction of new chemicals, and means of application, in agriculture. The development of air warfare also spilled over into agriculture, as military surplus biplanes were used as crop dusters. Chemicals were introduced with little regard for their effect on humans, and government agencies often hid the true effects of chemicals such as calcium arsenate, used to kill boll weevils but containing the highly toxic ingredient of arsenic.

World War II brought another infusion of military research into chemicals that were used in farming. The most popular of these was dichloro-diphenyl-trichloroethane (DDT), used to kill insects, and 2,4-D (dioxin), used to kill weeds. Thoroughly toxic (and potentially cancer causing) to humans and animals, these chemicals left residues potentially remaining for centuries; these residues appeared in the food chain—in meats, dairy products, and vegetables. Both of these highly toxic chemicals were regarded, when first developed, as something next to miraculous. They were used freely in the postwar South to eradicate insects and weeds with little consideration about their environmental impact.

This remaking of southern agriculture accelerated the departure of African Americans from the rural South, with important consequences. Whereas 34 percent of the total southern population was black in 1900, this portion had declined to 21 percent by 1960. The black exodus had an especially important impact in the Deep South. African Americans made up a majority of the population in South Carolina and Mississippi in 1910. In contrast, six decades later, blacks were minorities in both states. Meanwhile, in states such as Illinois, with a million former southerners living in the state in 1970, and Michigan, with 800,000, migration transformed urban centers.

<hr>

[5] Clark, *The Emerging South*, 61–62.

A little-known dimension of the Great Migration was the departure of southern-born Latinos, the great majority of whom left Texas. More American Latinos lived in Texas—some 456,000 in 1920—than in any other state; known as Tejanos, by the late 1930s they joined the exodus out of the South. Attracted to job opportunities during and after World War II, Tejanos settled in northern and midwestern cities. Nearly a half million Latinos born in the South lived elsewhere in 1970, with a large portion drawn to California, which became the center of the Latino population in the United States. Until the 1980s, southern-born Latinos tended to outnumber foreign-born immigrants.

The post–World War II diaspora also included white southerners. Rural whites departed farms, leaving as the cheap-labor economy collapsed. Millions of Appalachian whites moved north to industrial states such as Ohio. "Okies" left Oklahoma and other southern Plains states for California. During the 1930s, about 100,000 people moved from Oklahoma to California, while the states of the southern Plains—including Oklahoma, Arkansas, and Texas—witnessed an exodus totaling 350,000. "Okies" and "Arkies" stood out culturally and economically. They settled in agricultural towns in the San Joaquin Valley in California; they were poor and had different accents, different culture, and different dress. California regarded Okies suspiciously, and some communities even segregated Okies and black people in separate seating in theaters. As a result of this large migration both by whites and blacks, California counted 12 percent of its population in 1970 as southern born.

The transition from rural to urban living was not easy. Harry Crews, a novelist and the son of a sharecropper, moved from Bacon County, Georgia, to Jacksonville, Florida, during the 1940s. His family lived in the Springfield section of the city, which housed many Bacon County migrants. Sharing his neighbors' displacement, he remembered that they "loved it and hated it at the same time, loved it because it was hope, hated it because it was not home." While rural homes were spaced apart, congestion and the "odor of combustion" characterized city living. "They felt like animals in a pen," Crews recalled, which was "no way for a man to live."[6]

Occurring over four decades, the demise of the plantation was not confined to the 1950s, but during that decade the nature and significance of this change began to come into focus. This change meant that the South would be less rural, more urban, and—perhaps—less constrained by traditional hierarchies of race and class. People living in cities were exposed to different influences; southern immigrants outside the region acquired different perspectives. These social, economic, and cultural changes coincided with the onset of the civil rights revolution and the remaking of the southern political system. White supremacy, a bedrock of the social system along with the plantation, now came under attack.

---

[6] Daniel, *Lost Revolutions*, 39.

REVOLT OF THE DIXIECRATS

During the late 1930s an anti–New Deal coalition coalesced, composed of southern Democrats and northern Republicans. In the South, conservatives remained uneasy about federal intervention. The New Deal had greatly aggravated racial unrest, they believed, and they watched helplessly as biracial organizations such as the Congress of Industrial Organizations (CIO) grew and as African Americans began to develop a concerted challenge to segregation. Whites' suspicions of expanded federal power only grew during the 1940s. Conservatives endorsed the expansion of federal largesse in war industries and military mobilization, but they continued to oppose the New Deal's legacy. As former governor Leon Phillips of Oklahoma declared, the New Deal undermined the Constitution and destroyed individual initiative "through regimentation" while it allowed "labor racketeers" too-much political power.[7] Southern conservatives favored abolishing the National Youth Administration because it was perceived as excessively liberal on race. They opposed federal anti-poll-tax legislation and filibustered the bill in 1944 when it came before the Senate. They succeeded in gutting Roosevelt's proposal to permit black soldiers to vote in 1944, something that Texas representative Hatton W. Summers denounced as extending the "stranglehold of this great Federal bureaucracy upon the throats of the States."[8] Southerners opposed the Fair Employment Practices Committee (FEPC), which Mississippi senator Theodore G. Bilbo described as "nothing but a plot to put niggers to work next to your daughters."[9] In 1945, the conservative coalition succeeded in reducing the FEPC's budget by half and ordering its dissolution.

Southern conservatives especially feared the subversion of southern educational institutions. Attacking the state university system of Georgia for harboring integrationists, segregationist Eugene Talmadge declared that he wanted to kill "the snake before coils of racial equality suffocated the body of our educational institutions." Subsequently, segregationists suspected that any program of federalization in education—especially direct federal aid to public schools—masked plans to invade and control southern education. "Camouflaged education help," warned one newspaper editor in Mississippi, meant "Hitlerized totalitarian rule" and "social equality."[10]

While southern conservatives feared the prospect of integration, northern Democrats became more liberal on these very same issues. With growing African American constituencies, they supported greater federal involvement in civil rights. As early as the war years, southern conservative Democrats keenly felt their political isolation. New Deal policies, said Gov. Sam Houston Jones of Louisiana, had "continued to kick an already prostrate South in the face." Former governor Leon C. Phillips of

---

[7] Grantham, *The South in Modern America*, 184.
[8] Grantham, *The South in Modern America*, 182.
[9] Grantham, *The South in Modern America*, 195.
[10] Jason Morgan Ward, *Defending White Democracy: The Making of a Segregationist Movement & the Remaking of Racial Politics, 1936–1965* (Chapel Hill: University of North Carolina Press, 2011), 123–124.

Oklahoma declared that he would join the Republican Party. The New Deal, he claimed, had tried to "destroy individual initiative . . . through regimentation," while "labor racketeers" became dominant "bosses" under federal protection. Others agreed with an Alabama Democrat who objected to Roosevelt's position on the "racial issue" and for interfering in "our racial problems in the South."[11]

Southern conservatives challenged FDR's renomination in 1944. Gov. Frank Dixon of Alabama unsuccessfully tried to organize anti-Roosevelt support at the Southern Governors Conference in Tallahassee. Anti–New Deal conservatives captured control of Democratic conventions in Texas and Mississippi. Southern conservatives blocked Henry Wallace's renomination as vice president in 1944 because of their fears about his support for civil rights and labor. These conservatives feared northern invasion and encirclement. In 1947, Maryland segregationist Charles Wallace Collins published his *Whither Solid South?*, which became a basic text for white supremacists. The FEPC, Collins wrote, was waging a "nation-wide attack on the segregation of the Negroes from the whites in industrial employment and in work done under Government contracts." "Stripped of its non-essentials," he claimed, "the whole FEPC program is a movement to abolish separation of the Negroes and the whites in the South."

Collins urged southern Democrats to reconsider their blind partisan loyalty. "No people," he wrote, "have ever given to a political party such love, faith and sustained devotion." But with "dark clouds" on the horizon and "strange doctrines" abroad, it was time to reexamine long-standing political assumptions. The New Deal made the Democrats into "a labor party of the left-wing variety" and "one of the chief supporters of manhood suffrage for the Negro and the abolition of segregation." Collins favored a political realignment into liberal and conservative parties as a solution to protect southern white interests and to save the United States from federal tyranny.[12]

While southern conservatives dug in their heels, increasingly assertive African Americans demanded change. Civil rights organizations made a well-organized effort to challenge disfranchisement, resulting in increasing voter registration across the South—before the onset of more aggressive federal intervention that came in the late 1950s and 1960s. Although states such as Alabama and Mississippi witnessed declines in black registered voters, others recorded major increases. In Arkansas, for example, the percentage of African Americans registered to vote grew from 1.5 percent to 27 percent between 1940 and 1952. During the same period, black registration increased from 5.7 percent to 33 percent in Florida, from 3 percent to 23 percent in Georgia, from 0.5 percent to 25 percent in Louisiana, and from 6.5 percent to 27 percent in Tennessee. Much of this increase involved efforts in the urban South, where disfranchisement began to fray around the edges.

11 Grantham, *The South in Modern America*, 183–184.
12 Charles Wallace Collins, *Whither Solid South? A Study in Politics and Race Relations* (New Orleans: Pelican, 1947).

When returning black veterans expressed impatience with the status quo, they often encountered hostility and violence. In February 1946, a two-day riot erupted in Columbia, Tennessee, when a black veteran got into an altercation with a white radio repairman. The same month, another returning black veteran, Isaac Woodard, was arrested, beaten, and blinded by a South Carolina sheriff when he and a bus driver got into a verbal battle. In addition, a twenty-five-year-old black man, Willie Earle, was lynched in Greenville, South Carolina, when he was accused of assaulting a white taxicab driver. In July 1946, a white mob murdered two black men and their wives. These cases, especially the Woodard case, indicated simmering white hostility, and they also aroused national public opinion about racial violence.

In response to the postwar racial violence, Harry Truman organized a national commission, the President's Committee on Civil Rights. Its report, *To Secure These Rights*, was issued in October 1947. It called for an end to discrimination and white supremacy in voting, education, and public accommodations. "The time for action," the report declared, "is now." Action meant federal intervention. The report recommended strengthening the civil rights division in the Justice Department, federal measures to prevent lynching, banning segregation in interstate travel, creating a new federal civil rights commission, revitalizing the FEPC, and establishing a standing joint committee on civil rights in Congress.[13] Truman endorsed these recommendations, making federal involvement in civil rights a part of his presidency. For the first time, a president committed himself to protect civil rights. "Throughout our history," Truman declared in a message to Congress in February 1948, "men and women of all colors and creeds, of all races and religions, have come to this country to escape tyranny and discrimination." Americans were obliged to "correct the remaining imperfections in our practice of democracy." In July 1948, Truman went further by issuing an executive order desegregating the armed forces.[14]

One of the fifteen members of Truman's civil rights committee, famed southern liberal Frank Porter Graham, agonized about whether to support federal intervention. In the end, he and the other southern member, M. E. Tilley, wrote a minority dissent that appeared in the *Report*. "A minority of the committee," it read, "favors the elimination of segregation as an ultimate goal but opposes the imposition of a federal sanction." Graham and Tilley disagreed that the "abolition of segregation be made a requirement, until the people of the States involved have themselves abolished the provisions in their State constitutions and laws which now require segregation." The dissenters preferred ending segregation gradually—through improved education and religious training about human brotherhood. While the "ultimate goal" of Christianity was to "make everyone equal, regardless of race and color," Graham explained in an interview, "this is something that cannot be brought about by federal legislation." Ending white supremacy would be a slow, gradual process. He favored a program, he wrote, that had a "chance of possible achievement."[15]

The prospect of federal intervention further polarized southern white opinion. L. Mendel Rivers, a white congressman from South Carolina, denounced *To Secure These Rights* as a "brazen and monumental insult to the Democratic South and the southern way of life for both white and colored."[16] Other southern conservatives threatened to bolt the Democratic Party over Truman's civil rights positions. Mississippi's James Eastland refused to support a presidential candidate who wanted to "destroy our social institutions."[17] Democrats under Truman had made southerners "illegitimate children at a family reunion," complained another Mississippian. A South Carolina Democrat described how the white South had become the "red-haired stepchild in national Democratic Party affairs."[18]

When the Democratic convention adopted a civil rights plank in July 1948, the alienation of southern conservatives became complete. At the convention, the delegations from Mississippi and Alabama stormed out. At Birmingham, Alabama, the States' Rights Democratic Party—the so-called Dixiecrats—nominated South Carolina governor Strom Thurmond and Mississippi governor Fielding Wright for president and vice president, respectively. Warning that Truman's civil rights program would "lead to a police state," Thurmond declared that there were "not enough troops in the Army to force the southern people to break down segregation and admit the Negro race into our theaters, into our swimming pools, and into our homes."[19]

Strom Thurmond, 1961.
Library of Congress.

Born in 1902 in Edgefield, South Carolina, Strom Thurmond was elected to the state senate and became a state judge. Serving in Europe in World War II, Thurmond was elected governor of South Carolina in 1946. Thurmond's positions on race were ambiguous. In 1925, he had an affair with a young sixteen-year-old black housekeeper, with whom he fathered a child. For years, he supported and frequently met his daughter, Essie May Washington, but his paternity was kept a secret until after his death in 2003. Thurmond's first impulses were to seek compromise, to persuade Truman to back down by proposing at the

[15] Jake Wade, statement, 1948; Frank Porter Graham to James Dombrowski, November 16, 1948, Papers of Frank Porter Graham, Southern Historical Collection, Wilson Library, University of North Carolina, folders 2118B, 2116A.

[16] Frederickson, *Dixiecrat Revolt*, 65.

[17] Frederickson, *Dixiecrat Revolt*, 70.

[18] Kari Frederickson, "'As a Man, I Am Interested in States' Rights': Gender, Race, and the Family in the Dixiecrat Party, 1948–1950," in *Jumpin' Jim Crow: Southern Politics from Civil War to Civil Rights*, ed. Jane Dailey, Glenda Elizabeth Gilmore, and Bryant Simon (Princeton, NJ: Princeton University Press, 2000), 265.

[19] Frederickson, *Dixiecrat Revolt*, 140.

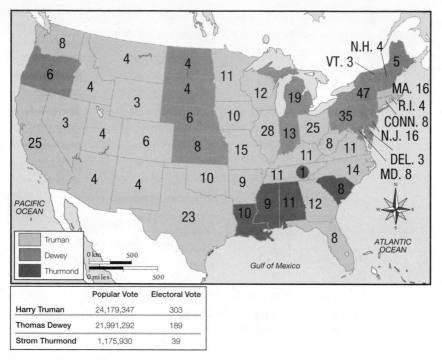

	Popular Vote	Electoral Vote
Harry Truman	24,179,347	303
Thomas Dewey	21,991,292	189
Strom Thurmond	1,175,930	39

MAP 21.1 The Presidential Election of 1948

southern governors' conference in February 1948 a negotiating committee that might seek a compromise.

Truman had no interest in negotiating, and events moved inexorably toward conflict. Thurmond had not been a racial demagogue—he prosecuted the murderers of Willie Earle—but when Truman's intervention on civil rights occurred in 1948, he emerged as one of the loudest of the postwar segregationists. Thurmond and others organized a states'-rights conference in Jackson, Mississippi, where Thurmond denounced the FEPC as interfering with employers' rights. Segregation, he said, was "essential to the protection of the racial integrity and purity of the white and Negro races alike." The Jackson conference agreed that the states'-rights delegates to the Democratic National Convention in Philadelphia would repudiate Truman's civil rights proposal. If the national party endorsed federal intervention, the southern conservatives promised to bolt the Democratic National Convention and reconvene in Birmingham.[20]

Dixiecrats, as they were popularly called, urged the recapture of state Democratic organizations in southern states, using a sharpened white supremacist message. They often warned of the consequences of federal intervention for southern society. "Organized mongrel minorities" now controlled the national government, said Eastland, who wanted to "Harlemize the country." This openly racist rhetoric

[20] Frederickson, *Dixecrat Revolt*, 106.

was clothed in a language of local control and state sovereignty. By the late 1940s, southern segregationists had already developed a defensive strategy in which they claimed that the constitutional issue of federal intervention, not race, was the key defining issue. The Dixiecrat message, in addition, was tied to a larger conservative message that opposed labor unions and favored the perpetuation of a low-wage economy.[21]

In the presidential election of 1948, the Dixiecrat ticket of Thurmond and Wright carried only four states—Alabama, Mississippi, South Carolina, and Louisiana. Outside of these states, the party's support was weak. In North Carolina, Thurmond carried only about 9 percent of the vote; in Tennessee, 13 percent; and in Florida, 10 percent. The Dixiecrats carried four Deep South states because they succeeded in making Thurmond the candidate of the main Democratic Party on the ballot; that strategy failed elsewhere. Rather than a permanent party, Dixiecrats saw themselves as a lobbying group that was attempting the takeover of the Democratic Party. Its focus was on Democratic Party leadership, writes a recent political historian, "and on obtaining a place on the ballot, rather than on appealing to and mobilizing voters." Constructing an "institutional structure and a mass base for a permanent political party was not part of the Dixiecrats' future plans."[22]

The Dixiecrats' brief existence marked an important chapter in the political history of the South. Although the organization dissolved soon after the presidential election, the divisions in the Democratic Party—and the coalescence of a conservative, anti-civil-rights bloc—persisted. Opposition to liberalism and federal intervention on civil rights, if anything, subsequently grew, infused with the powerful social and cultural force of anticommunism. Two years after the Dixiecrat defeat in 1948, conservatives asserted their power in two primary elections for seats held by prominent southern liberals, Florida's Claude Pepper and North Carolina's Frank Porter Graham. A staunch New Deal Democrat who was elected to the Senate in 1936, Pepper strongly supported Truman in 1948 despite Pepper's opposition to his civil rights positions. Rep. George Smathers, who successfully portrayed Pepper as "Red Pepper" because of his alleged Communist sympathies, mounted a primary challenge. Smathers claimed that Pepper had been "an apologist for Stalin, an associate of fellow travelers and a sponsor for Communist front organizations." Pepper lost by 60,000 votes.[23]

In North Carolina, Gov. W. Kerr Scott appointed Graham to fill the unexpired term of J. Melville Broughton in March 1949. Raleigh attorney and conservative Willis Smith challenged Graham. Although Graham won the first primary, in the runoff in June 1950 (North Carolina required that candidates win a majority of primary voters) Smith carried the election by the narrow margin of 20,000 votes. His

[21] Bartley, *The New South*, 82–83.

[22] Michael Perman, *Pursuit of Unity: A Political History of the American South* (Chapel Hill: University of North Carolina Press, 2009), 268.

[23] James C. Clark, *Red Pepper and Gorgeous George: Claude Pepper's Epic Defeat in the 1950 Democratic Primary* (Gainesville: University Press of Florida, 2011).

Lillian Smith, 1944. *Library of Congress.*

campaign against Graham was tinged with anti-Communist and racial themes. Graham was accused of being "soft" on Communists and of associating with subversives in organizations such as the Southern Conference for Human Welfare. He was also criticized for sponsoring an African American student from North Carolina admitted to West Point. One Smith ad declared: "WHITE PEOPLE WAKE UP!" "Do you want Negroes working beside you, your wife and your daughters in your mills and factories? Negroes eating beside you in public eating places? Negroes riding beside you, your wife and your daughters in buses, cabs, and trains. Negroes sleeping in the same hotels and rooming houses?"[24]

The Dixiecrat revolt and its aftermath suggested a larger backlash. In *Killers of the Dream*, author Lillian Smith described white southerners' fears about the end of segregation. Born in Florida, Smith grew up in Clayton, Georgia, in a privileged white family of nine children. For much of her life she ran Laurel Falls Camp in northern Georgia, and it became a magnet for experimentation in the arts and drama. After the late 1930s, Smith became a vocal critic of her home region's racial practices. Her first novel, *Strange Fruit* (1944), portrayed the consequences of an interracial love affair; the book so shocked readers that many states banned its sale. *Strange Fruit* nonetheless sold 200,000 copies and became a powerful indictment of the Jim Crow South. In 1949, Smith published *Killers of the Dream*, an extended semiautobiographical essay that explored how segregation and racism shaped her life.

Killers of the Dream described the psyche of southern whites, how they rationalized segregation and incorporated it into their worldview. In the late 1940s, she sensed a closing of the ranks. Segregation, she wrote, had become "so hypnotic a thing that it binds a whole people together, good, bad, strong, weak, ignorant and learned, sensitive, obtuse, psychotic and sane, making them one as only a common worship or a deeply shared fear can do." The sanctity of segregation had "taken on the terrors of taboo and the sanctity of religion" as southern whites united "in common worship and common fear of one idea." White supremacy had "woven itself around fantasies at levels difficult for the mind to touch, until it is part of each man's internal defense system, embedded like steel in his psychic fortifications."[25]

The Dixiecrat revolt suggested the shape of what Smith called the "internal defense system" that southern whites collectively assembled in defense of the racial status quo. Yet, white supremacy would experience challenges from several

fronts in the 1950s. Not least important was the growing role of the federal government, whose powers had increased during the New Deal. The full fruit of a
judicial revolution would have a major impact in further eroding the stability of
the Jim Crow system.

POPULAR CULTURE IN THE 1950S

Along with attacks on civil rights activists, the Cold War South experienced a
major cultural transformation. The diaspora of millions of displaced southerners,
formerly rural and now urban, suddenly enjoyed access to new forms of media in
commercialized music, movies, television, and sports. In each instance, southern
folk culture became a commodity reflecting rural roots but also became nationally,
and even internationally, marketed. The impact of the southern diaspora on popular culture became especially evident in stock-car racing and music.

In the postwar era, stock-car racing emerged as a new sport that originated in the
South but eventually commanded a national audience. Owning an automobile, and
making it a visible symbol of position and status in society, had long been part of
American culture. However, fast cars and racing emerged after World War II, when
car ownership became more accessible to more people. During the Prohibition era,
fast drivers moved bootleg liquor, or moonshine, across rural communities. These
drivers, called "trippers," became known for their racing abilities. In much of the
mid-twentieth-century South, trippers became folk heroes.

According to one estimate, four counties in Georgia, Virginia, and North
Carolina each accounted for about a half-million gallons of moonshine produced
during the 1930s through the 1950s—by far the most important industry in these
areas. "If they wadn't making it, they's selling the stuff to make it with," said one
resident of Wilkes County, North Carolina, "or they's hauling it. In some kind of
way about every family [in Wilkes County] was involved in the moonshine
business."[26] During Prohibition, moonshine producers found a market in the
urban Piedmont. Remote terrain and access to a new highway system, along with
the availability of automobiles, encouraged moonshining.

Having automobiles became a symbol of masculine power; driving and auto
tinkering were infused into the Piedmont rural culture. NASCAR legend Richard
Petty remembered growing up in Level Cross, in Piedmont North Carolina: "There
was always a car in the front yard or the side yard," he recalled, "or wherever there
was a shade tree to work under. And it was always apart, in one stage or the other,
being modified to make it run faster."[27] Street racing, done informally, developed
into a popular sport among young working-class men. The folk celebrity of drivers
translated into the popularity of stock-car racing. Racing events, at first held in

[26] Daniel S. Pierce, *Real NASCAR: White Lightning, Red Clay, and Big Bill France* (Chapel Hill:
University of North Carolina Press, 2010), 18.
[27] Pierce, *Real NASCAR*, 26.

backwoods locations, became scenes of release and escape from the workdays of ordinary southerners. Those attending, remembered one reporter, were "good folks, low-income people who worked on cars or used machinery, farmers and a lot of rural people, people who worked with their hands."[28]

From 1903 to 1935, Florida became a center of a new industry with races and speed trials at Ormond Beach and Daytona. Stock-car racing, which used automobiles that were retrofitted for racing, emerged as a popular new sport with a fanatical following during and after World War II. William Henry Getty France—"Big Bill" France—was a mechanic and driver who moved to Daytona Beach in 1934. France, who had become fascinated with driving in the 1920s, staged races at Daytona during the late 1930s that eventually attracted 12,000 fans. A national stock-car racing champion in 1940, he successfully combined the business of racing with popular automobile culture. France drew from drivers and mechanics associated with the bootlegging industry, with promoter-entrepreneurs assembling the races and housing growing crowds, often at fairgrounds facilities. He also marketed stock-car races outside Florida to the Piedmont South, where the first successful race occurred at Atlanta's Lakewood Speedway in November 1938. By World War II, France's operation moved north to Salisbury, Greensboro, and Charlotte, North Carolina, as well as Spartanburg, South Carolina. High Point, North Carolina, opened a speedway in 1941. Racers such as Joe Littlejohn, Roy Hall, Lloyd Seay, Harley Taylor, and Bob and Fonty Flock attracted a mass following.

At a meeting in the Streamline Hotel in Daytona Beach in December 1947, France laid out a future strategy for the industry. Rejected by the larger American Automobile Association (AAA), France wanted to form his own business. The new organization, at the suggestion of Red Vogt, was named the National Association for Stock Car Auto Racing (NASCAR). These "stock" cars were "common men in common cars"—and appealed to ordinary people interested in racing. The cars were modeled on the moonshiner cars that evaded federal revenue agents during the Prohibition era.

New speedways were constructed in 1947 in North Wilkesboro, North Carolina, and Martinsville, Virginia, both towns near moonshining counties of northwestern North Carolina and southwestern Virginia. Bootleggers became partners with France in running the speedways. "From the success of races held during the past 12 months," France announced in May 1947, "the people evidently want stock car racing."[29] The burgeoning industry became so successful that it led to even more ambitious marketing plans. The sport solidified its foothold in the Piedmont areas, expanding to mill towns such as Reidsville, Lexington, and Wadesboro, North Carolina, as well as Augusta, Georgia. Charlotte constructed a new speedway that became one of the most popular sites on the tour.

---

[28] Daniel, *Lost Revolutions*, 96.
[29] Pierce, *Real NASCAR*, p. 91.

France ran NASCAR with an iron hand, fending off competing races by banning his drivers from participating. He also instituted a system in which drivers accumulated points for races and could compete for a championship with financial rewards. The points system provided cash incentives for the drivers and heightened fan interest in the sport. NASCAR continued to grow in popularity under France's business model. New superspeedways that were more than 1.5 miles long further solidified the industry. In 1959, the newest of these superspeedways—constructed and owned by France—opened at Daytona, the sport's most modern facility, which was equipped with "tri-oval" designs that maximized speed and fan excitement. The Daytona track hosted the Daytona 500, which became one of the most popular racing events in the sport and a regular event in an evolving Grand National tour.

Other superspeedways followed Daytona's opening in 1959. In 1960, new tracks modeled on Daytona opened in Charlotte, Atlanta, and Hanford, California, the latter the location of the short-lived Marchbanks Speedway (which closed a year after opening). In 1965, a new North Carolina Motor Speedway opened in Rockingham, and the Grand National competition extended from the Carolinas to Florida. During the 1950s and 1960s, not only was the Grand National competition located in southern superspeedways, but nearly three-quarters of the drivers hailed from the South.[30]

In 1959, in a photo finish that took three days to determine the winner, Lee Petty became the event's first champion at the inaugural race at the Daytona 500 before 41,000 fans. Born in 1914 in the northern North Carolina Piedmont town of Randleman, Petty became one of the most successful race-car drivers—and the founder of a family dynasty. A car mechanic, at the age of thirty-five Petty participated in the first NASCAR race on June 14, 1959, at the Charlotte fairgrounds. In the 1950s, he won three Grand National championships, along with fifty-four races overall. Lee Petty today ranks fifth overall for races won in the sport. Petty,

Lee Petty, at Palm Beach, Florida. *State Archives of Florida.*

[30] Scott Beekman, *NASCAR Nation: A History of Stock Car Racing in the United States* (Santa Barbara, CA: Praeger, 2010), 74.

meanwhile, created a family business around racing, establishing shops in Level Cross, North Carolina. Although he gave up racing in 1960, Petty Enterprises remained prominent in the sport, and his sons Richard and Maurice and grandson Kyle all became stars in their own right. Richard Petty made his racing debut in July 1958, racing against his ferociously competitive father. (When Richard beat his father in a race at Atlanta's Lakewood Speedway in 1959, Lee protested the victory and won on appeal.) Richard won his first race in 1960, his first championship in 1964, and seven overall championships before he retired in the early 1990s. His two hundred career racing victories made him the most successful driver in NASCAR history.

After the late 1950s, France pushed to convert the red-clay tracks of the Piedmont to asphalt, and dirt tracks entirely disappeared from the circuit by the early 1970s. Older drivers resisted the change from red clay to asphalt, but those who survived the transition were gradually replaced by younger drivers during the 1960s. NASCAR was not the only example of the growing importance of the sports entertainment industry. As elsewhere, in the South college and professional athletics became fantastically popular, beginning in the post–World War II period. Yet, stock-car driving provides a clear example of how southern culture went national.

POPULAR AND YOUTH CULTURE

Migration to cities brought change and dissemination of folk and popular culture with roots in the South. Perhaps the most important of these cultural changes occurred in music, where the dynamic, adaptive fusion of white and African American folk musical traditions emerged in musical genres such as jazz, the blues, rock and roll, and country music. The locales for popular, commercialized music lay in cities housing the thousands of migrants who left the rural South in the twentieth century. In some instances, popular music spoke directly to their feelings of loneliness and alienation. In the blues, music reflected African Americans' experiences of oppression as they moved from rural deprivation to urban poverty. While becoming commercially successful, popular music was also culturally subversive. Very often it crossed racial lines by blending white and black folk traditions. In many instances, the public performance of this new music violated taboos about sexuality, encouraging new cultural attitudes. Music also came to embody a new, emerging youth culture of the 1950s, a rebelliousness that emanated from the South.

Decades earlier, during the mid-1920s, commercial entrepreneurs discovered potential in the production and sale of southern music. Producer Ralph Peer was an early pioneer in the recording industry. Born in Kansas City, Missouri, Peer worked at his father's store selling gramophones and records. In 1910, he began a career in music recording. Rather accidentally, Peer, who toured the southern hinterlands in search of talent, discovered the appeal of southern rural white music when he recorded Fiddlin' John Carson's "The Little Old Log Cabin in the Lane" and "The Old

Hen Cackled and the Rooster's Going to Crow." Both songs soon became hits. Peer created and promoted a new genre—"hillbilly" music—which came to characterize the diverse styles of the music of southern rural whites. Peer subsequently promoted the recordings of white artists such as Jimmie Rodgers, of Bristol, Tennessee, and the Carter Family, of the southwestern Virginia Appalachians. Rodgers, who became known as the "Father of Country Music," was by far the most popular country music artist until his death in 1933.

Hillbilly music represents what one historian calls the "single greatest contribution to American popular music" by southern whites.[31] Hillbilly artists drew on rich traditions in religious music, the main wellspring of vernacular music in the South. These musical traditions included African American spirituals, white Protestant hymns, and nineteenth-century shape-note hymnals. By the early twentieth century, a large amount of gospel music was readily available because of the spread of revivalism to big cities. Publishers issued editions of cheap hymnals available for conventions and singing schools. By the 1920s and 1930s, white hillbilly musicians, drawing on gospel music, began to record and broadcast their music. Declining record prices, and competition from radio broadcasting, created an ever-expanding market for commercially produced music.

Concentrated in Piedmont cities such as Charlotte, Richmond, and Atlanta, the hillbilly music industry became an urban phenomenon. Urban areas provided venues for performers, who drew on popular minstrels, medicine shows, and vaudeville acts. Beginning in the 1920s, recordings on 78 rpm vinyl became available; radio shows featuring local musicians further expanded the market. Radio stations such as WBAP in Fort Worth, WSB in Atlanta, and WSM in Nashville featured country music. The "barn dance" format also became popular among southern radio stations, extending the popularity of country music.

The most popular of the barn dance shows, the Grand Ole Opry, first broadcast in November 1925. It was the creation of entrepreneur George Hay, who came to Nashville and pitched the idea of a music show to the owners of WSM, the radio station owned by the National Life and Accident Insurance Company. Expanding the program from one featuring amateur unknowns to more-established artists, Hay cultivated the program's emphasis on southern rustic traditions. Among the most successful of the Opry performers was Roy Acuff, a Tennessean who tried out baseball and then joined a traveling medicine show. Performing on radio, Acuff organized his Crazy Tennesseans as a backup to his vocals and produced hits such as "The Great Speckled Bird" and "Wabash Cannonball." In 1938, Acuff joined the Opry as a regular artist, changing the name of his group to the Smoky Mountain Boys. Acuff was notably entrepreneurial, and in 1942 he organized Acuff-Rose Music, which helped establish Nashville as a center of the emerging country music industry.

[31]   Patrick Huber, *Linthead Stomp: The Creation of Country Music in the Piedmont South* (Chapel Hill: University of North Carolina Press, 2008), 21.

Another act appearing on the Opry, the Monroe Brothers, pioneered a new "bluegrass" style that emphasized the hillbilly string band, especially mandolin, fiddle, and banjo. In 1939, Bill Monroe and his Blue Grass Boys appeared on the show. His music fused elements of gospel, hillbilly, blues, and jazz to provide a fast beat, with frequent vocal harmonies. Bluegrass attracted an audience in the urban South, with its nostalgic recollection of rural living. Two members of the Blue Grass Boys, banjoist Earl Scruggs and guitarist Lester Flatt, later organized their own group, the Foggy Mountain Boys and, later, Flatt and Scruggs. Bluegrass artists such as Scruggs pioneered a new method of three-finger banjo picking. Along with the Scruggs and Flatt fast-moving style, the duo, joined by Chubby Wise on fiddle and Howard Watts on bass, sang unique harmonies.

Radio broadcasting offered new opportunities for female performers, especially vocalists. The Carter Family's popularity paved the way in the late 1920s for female vocalists such as Maybelle Carter and Sara Carter, both of whom sang with male performer A. P. Carter. Most female vocalists achieved success through radio, less so through recording, often combining singing with comedy. Notably, Minnie Pearl, born Sarah Ophelia Colley in rural Tennessee in 1912, became one of the more popular entertainers on the Grand Ole Opry by providing a comedy satire of southern rural culture. Myrtle Cooper, later known as Lulu Belle, born in the North Carolina mountains, became a regular performer on the National Barn Dance on WLS in Chicago and combined with her husband, Scott Wiseman, to produce an act known as Lulu Belle and Scotty.

World War II set the stage for important changes in the music industry. The exposure of southerners to the rest of the country, labor and population mobility, and the expansion of the armed forces in training camps all contributed. During the postwar years, bluegrass grew further with new artists such as North Carolinians Ralph Stanley and Doc Watson. At the same time, honky-tonk became a popular genre. Importing the style of western swing, honky-tonk appealed to southern urban audiences. Its lyrics emphasized displacement and alienation, loss of values, alcoholism, and betrayal in love relationships. Unlike many of the hillbilly performers, honky-tonk communicated acceptance of the urban-industrial world, but it also included a longing for a lost past. Nashville became a center of the honky-tonk sound with the popularity of Webb Pierce, Ernest Tubb, Lefty Frizzell, and Hank Williams.

Although honky-tonk emphasized themes of failed masculinity, it also featured female artists. Kitty Wells, born Ethel Muriel Deason in Nashville, became one of the most popular country performers of the 1950s. Her single "It Wasn't God Who Made Honky Tonk Angels" in 1952 established her as a top-ten artist, followed by "Release Me" two years later. Over the next two decades she remained

Kitty Wells. *Library of Congress.*

Juke joint, Belle Glade, Florida, February 1941. *Library of Congress.*

prominent. In 1956, Wells became the first female country artist to release an LP, with *Kitty Wells' Country Hit Parade.* Other female honky-tonk performers emerged during the 1950s, including Charline Arthur, Jean Shepard, and Texas Ruby.

Black music also expressed alienation, sorrow, and loss, while emphasizing perseverance despite hardship. Blues arose out of the experiences of migration from the rural South to southern cities and to the North. The audience for the blues developed in an informal network of juke joints, spread across the rural South, attracting workers from plantations and turpentine camps. In 1934, black folklorist Zora Neale Hurston described juke joints as "musically speaking . . . the most important place in America." In its "smelly, shoddy confines has been born the secular music known as blues, and on blues has been founded jazz."[32] The Great Migration spawned significant cultural change. This blues, and its dissemination to a listening audience, took shape in Chicago, which became a center of white promoters such as Lester Melrose and arrangers such as black performer Jelly Roll Morton. Artists such as Aaron "T-Bone" Walker, Eddie Durham, and Charlie Christian crafted a distinctive sound that relied on a new instrument, the electric guitar, while including horns, piano, bass, and drums.

Alan Lomax, playing guitar at the Mountain Music Festival, Asheville, North Carolina, late 1930s. *Library of Congress.*

African American music expanded significantly during World War II. McKinley Morganfield, later known as Muddy Waters, exemplifies one of the most important new blues artists with roots in the Deep South who were based in the urban North. Born in the heart of the delta, Waters grew up and worked in nearby Clarksdale, Mississippi. The famed ethnomusicologist

[32] Zora Neale Hurston, "Characteristics of Negro Expression" (1934), in *Sweat*, ed. Cheryl Wall (New Brunswick, NJ: Rutgers University Press, 1997), 66.

Alan Lomax, who traveled throughout the South collecting the music of the rural South in the 1930s and 1940s, recorded Waters in August 1941. Waters moved to Chicago in 1943 to launch a career with the growing blues industry. In Chicago's South Side, Muddy Waters joined other well-known acts such as Sunnyland Slim, Eddie Boyd, and Blue Smitty. In other cities, such as Detroit, Mississippian John Lee Hooker became an established recording star in the late 1940s.

Waters at first recorded for Columbia Records, which never released his music. Instead, Chess Records, which was founded by Polish immigrants (and brothers) Phil and Leonard Chess, produced and distributed Waters's early music. In 1947, Leonard bought a share of Aristocrat Records; three years later, he and his brother obtained full control, renaming the company Chess Records. Chess recorded and released a new sound that embodied the electric blues of Chicago. The company was tied to entrepreneurs in Memphis, where white record producer Sam Phillips promoted artists at his label, Sun Records. These artists offered what became known as rhythm and blues (R&B), a fusion of rural music with jazz traditions to create a new sound that relied on electric guitars, piano, bass, drums, and saxophones. Using the faster rhythms of boogie-woogie, swing, and jump blues popular in the 1930s and 1940s, R&B attracted a young, largely black audience. In the late 1940s, this became known as "race music," and from 1945 to 1949 *Billboard* magazine established the category of "race records," which substituted for the 1942–1945 listing of the "Harlem hit parade." In 1949, *Billboard* began a listing for rhythm and blues. In addition, R&B began to attract major labels such as RCA Victor.

A native of Alabama, Phillips worked as a radio DJ in Muscle Shoals's WLAY-AM. Like a growing number of post–World War II radio stations, WLAY broadcast to white and black audiences, specializing in rhythm and blues. Phillips moved to Memphis, opening a recording business and eventually producing under the Sun Records label. Among the best-known bluesmen recorded at Sun were Howlin' Wolf and B. B. King. Born on a plantation in rural Mississippi, Riley B. King, later called B. B. King, played in gospel bands in Mississippi, eventually moving to Memphis and working as a DJ on Memphis's WDIA, which began broadcasting in 1947 and became the first station in the country to play exclusively black music.

Phillips helped Howlin' Wolf obtain a contract with Chess, and his music became part of the Chicago R&B sound. Born Chester Arthur Burnett in West Point, Mississippi, Howlin' Wolf was a large man at six feet six inches tall and nearly 300 pounds of bulk. "A Robert Johnson may have possessed more lyrical insight, a Muddy Waters more dignity, and a B. B. King certainly more technical expertise," writes one critic, "but no one could match him for the singular ability to rock the house down to the foundation while simultaneously scaring its patrons out of its wits."[33] Another Mississippian émigré to Chicago, Ella Otha Bates—later known as

[33] Howlin' Wolf: Biography by Cub Koda; available at http://www.allmusic.com/artist/howlin-wolf-mn0000276085/biography.

Bo Diddley—adopted a distinctive beat that became influential for the next generation of musicians.

R&B, originally depending on an African American following, attracted a
growing white audience, despite fears about "race music." During the early 1950s,
the black music of R&B became the white music of rock and roll. In 1951, Ike Turner
and the Kings of Rhythm recorded "Rocket 88," which some claim to be the first
rock and roll hit. "Rocket 88" became one of the most popular crossover recordings,
and it opened up the way for white musicians to perform R&B songs and rhythms.
Bill Haley, a white artist, covered "Rocket 88" in 1951, and it became a hit among
young white listeners. Three years later, Haley covered black artist Big Joe Turner's
"Shake, Rattle and Roll," which became an anthem of the new rock and roll. Some
black artists, such as New Orleans's Fats Domino, appealed to white audiences
under the rock-and-roll moniker. Sam Phillips also promoted other white artists
such as Jerry Lee Lewis and Elvis Presley. Lewis, a pianist and singer from rural
Louisiana, was raised in traditions of white rural music. In 1956, he began recording
with Sun Records in Memphis.

The popularity of "race music," and its transfiguration into white rock and roll,
suggested larger tensions gripping the South of the 1950s. If music could cross racial
lines—especially the highly sexualized rhythms of the new postwar popular
music—what did that mean for white supremacy? The sudden popularity of black
R&B and white rock and roll became a subversive element, indicating a new youth
culture of rebellion, an impatience with the old social, racial, and gender hierarchies of the past.

SOUTHERN MUSIC GOES NATIONAL

The 1950s proved crucial for the nationalization of country music. The raw, emotional
sound of honky-tonk music, which emphasized alienation and loss, fused with pop
music. The result was a "soft" variation of honky-tonk more attuned and adapted to a
wider audience. Nashville became the most important center of the new country music
industry—and one of the leading record production centers outside Los Angeles and
New York City. During the 1950s and 1960s, producers and record companies such as
RCA, Decca, and Columbia Records, all locating in that city, developed a new style—
called the Nashville Sound—which appealed to the traditional sentimentality of Tin
Pan Alley, whose lyrics dominated popular songwriting during the first half of the
twentieth century. The honky-tonk genre, which relied on steel guitar, fiddles, and nasal
singing, was replaced by a pop style that included more-crooning vocals, different or-
chestration in the use of string sections, and background vocals. Country music became
more mainstream and national through the spread of radio stations devoted to that
format. In 1958, the Country Music Association (CMA) united broadcasters seeking a
wider, more national audience. Headquartered in Nashville, the CMA aggressively
marketed country music as a national cultural product, sponsoring all-country-music
radio stations around the country. In 1967, there were 328 such stations, with another

2,000 including country music in their broadcasting. The CMA encouraged the standardization of playlists and the promotions of designated stars in the industry.

Important figures in the Nashville Sound included Owen Bradley, Jim Denny, and Chet Atkins. Bradley, a Tennessee native, worked as a producer for Decca and began recording in a Quonset hut in Nashville in the 1950s, employing his own session musicians (who were known as the Nashville A Team). Denny, another Tennessean, worked as manager of the Grand Ole Opry and then became a successful agent, talent scout, and producer. By the 1960s, Denny's talent agency was instrumental in signing and booking country singers and helping to solidify Nashville as a center of the modern music industry. Atkins, born in 1924 in Union County, in eastern Tennessee, worked as a guitarist and fiddler and then became a DJ in Cincinnati, Springfield (Missouri), and Nashville. In 1950, Atkins came to Nashville as a guitarist for Mother Maybelle and the Carter Sisters, appearing at the Grand Ole Opry. Atkins signed a contract with RCA to record in Nashville and became known as a skillful practitioner of the three-finger style of guitar picking. Able to find session musicians for record producers, Atkins worked on the production side of the business through his close association, beginning in 1952, with RCA's Steven Sholes, who had moved to Nashville seven years earlier to head RCA's country music division. Sholes enjoyed a long career at RCA, which included signing artists such as Eddy Arnold, Hank Locklin, Jim Reeves, and Elvis Presley. In 1957, Atkins took over Sholes's operation after RCA constructed its own recording studio in Nashville, and in 1968 Atkins became a vice president with the company.

Atkins cultivated and sponsored a country-pop style that preserved country traditions but also expanded its appeal. He was successful in remaking a number of artists into performers in this new, more homogenized musical style. The first true hits of the Nashville Sound appeared after 1956, initially with Ferlin Husky's "Gone." A native Missourian who was a honky-tonk singer in the early 1950s, Husky altered his style, adopting a softer country-pop style with strings and vocal backups. "Gone," which sold a million copies, was followed by other hits over the next fifteen years. Texan Jim Reeves may have been the first official Nashville Sound artist when he released "Four Walls" in 1957. Unlike the music of Reeves's earlier career, "Four Walls," which was produced by Chet Atkins, was a softer song originally written for a female vocalist. Notably, the song included strings and background singers. Other successful artists under Atkins's tutelage included Don Gibson, who recorded his hits, "Lonesome Me," "I Can't Stop Loving You," and "Blue Blue Day" in 1958.

Female vocalists occupied a prominent place in the Nashville Sound. Born Virginia Patterson Hensley in Winchester, Virginia, in 1932, Patsy Cline developed into a major star in the late 1950s. Appearing on Arthur Godfrey's television talent search, Cline recorded her first hit for Decca in 1958, "Walking after Midnight." Two years later, she joined the Grand Ole Opry and recorded "I Fall to Pieces," a megahit that featured Decca's efforts to promote Cline as a national pop star. Cline, who died in a plane crash in 1963, represented the first female country star to become a pop sensation.

The homogenization of the Nashville Sound, aided by record producers such as Bradley and Atkins, resulted in greater concentration of the country music industry. During the 1960s and 1970s this strategy paid off, as country music became featured on radio and television broadcasting. Female vocalists such as Loretta Lynn, Tammy Wynette, and Dolly Parton succeeded in crafting a following from recordings and frequent television appearances. In 1969, television networks broadcast country shows such as the *Johnny Cash Show* (ABC), *Hee Haw* (CBS), and *Glen Campbell's Goodtime Hour* (CBS). *Hee Haw*, featuring comedy and country music, parodied southern rural life and included hayseeds and country bumpkins, but also other musical guests. Cash, an Arkansas native who emerged on the scene in 1955 with his "Folsom Prison Blues," was an artist of considerable talent whose melodies and lyrics often concerned themes of loss and alienation. His television show, early on featuring Bob Dylan (who collaborated with Cash in 1969 on Dylan's album *Nashville Skyline*), also had a pop emphasis. Campbell, another Arkansas native, produced hits such as "Gentle on My Mind" (1966), "By the Time I Get to Phoenix" (1967), and "Galveston" (1969). *Glen Campbell's Goodtime Hour* became a television success that survived four seasons.

With roots in the southern folk traditions, commercialized music became even more nationalized with the emergence in the mid-1950s of rock and roll. This new, hard-driving musical genre appealed to an emerging post-1945 youth culture. It fused two of the most powerful forms of southern popular music: African American blues and the rural white traditions of country music. Among the earliest rock-and-roll musicians were African Americans Little Richard, Fats Domino, and Chuck Berry. These black artists crossed racial barriers, and their success also encouraged white musicians to imitate their style.

White and black musicians in the 1940s and 1950s already borrowed heavily from each other in melodies, instrumentation, and vocals. Country musicians often used blues chords and rhythms; they also employed the faster beats of the African American boogie-woogie of the 1930s and 1940s. Crossover white artists covered black R&B melodies, harmonies, and chords, but they also relied on hillbilly traditions of country music. New forms of music such as rockabilly—fusing country music with R&B—targeted white teenagers and was, as one music historian writes, essentially "a music performed by white people for white audiences."[34]

Musical impresario Sam Phillips was said to have commented that any white musician able to adopt black R&B styles would become a rich man. In Elvis Presley, Phillips and Sun Records "discovered" this white artist, the most successful and one of the earliest rockabilly performers. Born in Tupelo, Mississippi, Presley moved to Memphis at age thirteen. Six years later, he began working with Phillips to record new music that brought together country and R&B. Presley's early successful singles included "That's All Right, Mama," a blues song, and the country song "Blue Moon on

[34] Bill C. Malone and Jocelyn R. Neal, *Country Music U.S.A.*, 3d rev. ed. (Austin: University of Texas Press, 2010), 247.

Kentucky." Presley's sensual and frenetic style created a new, national appeal among a developing youth market for music suggesting rebellion and escape. In 1956, Presley shed his southern identification when he signed with RCA and became one of the first stars of the rock-and-roll industry. In that year, he released his first LP record, *Elvis Presley*. The cuts on this album were covers that he remade into sensational hits, including Carl Perkins's "Blue Suede Shoes" and Little Richard's "Tutti-Frutti."

Rockabilly provided new opportunities for other white performers, many of whom Sam Phillips discovered, developed, and promoted. Carl Perkins, born in Tiptonville, Tennessee, released Phillips-produced hits such as "Blue Suede Shoes," "Honey Don't," and "Boppin' the Blues" in 1956. "All my friends are boppin' the blues," Perkins sang, "it must be going 'round.... I love you baby, but I must be rhythm bound." Other rockabilly artists whom Phillips developed included Johnny Cash, Jerry Lee Lewis, Roy Orbison, and Conway Twitty. Growing up in Ferriday, Louisiana, Lewis issued his first hit in 1957 with "Whole Lotta Shakin' Goin' On."

The line dividing rockabilly from rock and roll was thin; most early rock performers were white artists who migrated from the rockabilly format. Memphis became an early center of this musical style, which to some extent defied the mild conventions of the Nashville Sound. With Sun Records hosting the earliest performers, soon larger labels signed performers such as Buddy Holly and the Everly Brothers. While Presley signed with RCA in 1956, Johnny Cash moved to Columbia in 1958 and Roy Orbison jumped to Monument Records in 1961.

As was true elsewhere in America, the South's seeming stability during the 1950s disguised a brewing turmoil. Economic changes brought demographic and social changes, as southerners left the land and increasingly became city dwellers. Prosperity raised the incomes of southerners, especially whites, and elevated them into an expanding middle class. The economic transformation also heightened expectations among African Americans in the aftermath of World War II about the impending demise of Jim Crow. But the death of segregation came slowly. White resistance to changing the racial status quo stiffened, even while black activists were organizing a final challenge.

22

THE SECOND RECONSTRUCTION

〜

DURING THE 1950s, pressure was mounting on several fronts to force conflict between African Americans, who were no longer willing to accept the status quo, and white segregationists, who refused to change the system. The *Brown v. Board of Education* decision (1954) ended the constitutional basis for segregation, but white supremacy was not easily defeated as resistance among southern whites coalesced and progress stalled. The logjam broke up after 1960. Along with federal intervention through the courts, presidency, and Congress, the mobilization of a grassroots, nonviolent mass movement emerged during the late 1950s. This mass movement sought to demonstrate the immorality of white supremacy, to rally public opinion, and to force effective federal intervention. A constellation of forces upended public segregation, voter suppression, and legally sanctioned school segregation in a phenomenon known as the Second Reconstruction.

THE BROWN DECISION AND THE COLD WAR SOUTH

On May 17, 1954, the US Supreme Court handed down one of the most important decisions in its history in the *Brown v. Board of Education* case. Representing the culmination of decades of litigation by the NAACP's Legal Defense and Educational Fund, Inc., *Brown* was actually five cases brought against segregated schools in Kansas, South Carolina, Virginia, Delaware, and Washington, DC. The court was asked to consider the constitutionality of the *Plessy* case, which permitted state-required segregation if facilities were deemed "equal." In reality, segregated schools were obviously not equal, and the crux of the NAACP's case hinged on demonstrating that segregation was not only unequal but also harmful to black children. The litigants employed expert witnesses who argued from sociological, psychological, and historical perspectives. Segregation, they contended, was a conscious act of state policy that had harmful effects. In public schools, said Chief Justice Earl Warren, who wrote the opinion, *Plessy*'s doctrine of "separate but equal" had no place. "Separate educational facilities," said Warren, were "inherently unequal" and therefore violated the equal protection clause of the Fourteenth Amendment. Segregation had had a harmful effect on black children, an effect that was enhanced because the law placed a stamp of inferiority upon them. "A sense of inferiority," according to the decision, shaped "the motivation of a child to learn."[1]

Black southerners exulted in the *Brown* decision, which they saw as a breakthrough in the fight against segregation. The decision itself was ambiguous. Addressing the difficult question of how to implement desegregation, the Supreme Court provided no easy answers and, in a second ruling in May 1955, declared that segregation should be ended "with all deliberate speed" and that federal district courts should oversee the process. Predictably, despite the sweeping and unqualified nature of the ruling, without clear enforcement, southern schools integrated haltingly. In states of the Upper and Border South, integration occurred more quickly. In Kentucky, for example, more than half of black students attending public schools did so with whites by 1964. The same figure was 28 percent in Oklahoma in the same year. These developments were anomalous, however. In Tennessee and North Carolina, fewer than 3 percent of black students attended integrated schools a decade after *Brown*. As late as 1963, no black children attended schools with whites in South Carolina, Alabama, and Mississippi.[2]

While whites in *Brown*'s aftermath solidified their opposition to desegregation, southern blacks experienced heightened expectations. World War II had permanently altered the demographic, economic, and political conditions in the South in its relationship to the rest of the country. The departure of a large portion of the South's black population served as a referendum on Jim Crow, while it also nationalized the issue of race in modern America. The political balance of power seemed to be shifting with the position of the national Democratic Party, which was now permanently committed to a program of civil rights protections. And the Supreme Court had issued a ruling striking down the legal basis of Jim Crow.

Nonetheless, the pace of change through the legal and political system was slow. The *Brown* decision appeared to be ignored and stonewalled. The federal government, despite rhetoric, proceeded haltingly. In this setting, black leadership embraced a strategy of direct action. Based on the principle of nonviolence, direct action depended on at least two conditions to succeed. It depended, ultimately, on the ability to provoke the federal government to action. Second, this strategy depended on the mass mobilization of black people. Never before had so ambitious a

[1] *Brown v. Board of Education*, 347 U.S. 483 (1954).
[2] Michael J. Klarman, "How Brown Changed Race Relations: The Backlash Thesis," *Journal of American History* 81, no. 1 (June 1994): 84.

mobilization been envisioned. Although there was significant participation in this movement by whites, its most notable feature was that it represented a courageous uprising by African Americans, young and old, who were determined to overthrow the most-obnoxious manifestations of white supremacy.

Coinciding with acute white fears about the end of the racial system, fears of Communist subversion merged with fears of the end of Jim Crow. During the 1940s, those most concerned with preserving the racial order believed that civil rights advocates were connected to a worldwide Communist conspiracy. In part, this reflected the context of the 1930s. During that decade, the Communists, unqualified opponents of segregation, mounted an ambitious campaign to organize southern blacks. Many southern whites assailed the Popular Front strategy of activists during the New Deal, in which liberals sometimes made common cause with Communists. The Popular Front tainted a broad number of left-wing labor and civil rights organizers.

Rather than hardened subversives, southern Communists became attracted to the party mostly because of its uncompromising opposition to white supremacy. African Americans found the party's message of racial egalitarianism appealing, as did some southern whites. In 1928, the Sixth World Congress of the Communist International declared Deep South African Americans an oppressed nation, announcing the beginning of a campaign to recruit black Communists. After 1929, Communists led efforts to organize black sharecroppers into a union to resist white oppression, culminating in a racial massacre on July 15, 1931, at Camp Hill, Alabama. African Americans such as Al Murphy, born an Alabama sharecropper, became a Communist in 1930. Working in Birmingham, he successfully recruited new African American members, using an antiracist and interracial message in which Communists challenged white supremacy. Murphy recruited Hosea Hudson, an African American from rural Georgia who moved to Birmingham to work in the steel mills. Inspired by the Communists' campaign on behalf of the Scottsboro Boys, Hudson joined the party in September 1931, after hearing recruiters make the case that Scottsboro, he remembered, was "part of the whole frame-up of the Negro people in the South—jim crow, frame-up, lynching, all that was part of the system." Communists made an appeal that connected class oppression with racial oppression, and it made sense to many African Americans.[3]

Junius Scales, son of a prominent family in Greensboro, North Carolina, joined the Communist Party because of his opposition to racism and racial segregation. Communists, he believed in the 1930s, were the only national organization favoring racial equality. White liberals were "most courageous," he recalled, "and they often took moral stances which expressed the true conscience of their time and place." But they did not directly confront the evil of segregation. "What caused them to

[3] Nell Irvin Painter, ed., *The Narrative of Hosea Hudson: His Life as a Negro Communist in the South* (Cambridge, MA: Harvard University Press, 1979), 87.

temporize and waver on issues involving Negro rights," he wrote, "was the vested interest and depth, scope, and sheer virulence of the bigotry they opposed."[4]

Segregationists associated any force for change with the subversive influence of international communism. After the *Brown* decision, even the Supreme Court came under suspicion. The Independent American (IA) organization, a New Orleans segregationist group, provided "Pro-Red Batting Averages of Members of the Supreme Court," with top scores going to liberal justices Hugo Black, William Douglas, William Brennan, and Earl Warren. The court, claimed the group, was steadily moving "toward establishment of the Communist Conspiracy in the United States as a legal political entity." How many "more of these decisions," it asked, "must we take before we admit the apparent fondness of the Court majority for the Communist cause?"[5]

In 1939, when Scales was nineteen years old, he joined the Communist Party in Chapel Hill, where he was a student at the University of North Carolina. After serving in World War II, Scales returned to North Carolina, becoming the party's state chairman. By then, state and federal authorities were vigorously prosecuting the Communist Party leadership under the anticommunist Alien Registration Act of 1940. Inveterate anti–New Dealer and segregationist Howard Smith, congressman from Virginia, proposed this legislation, known as the Smith Act. While the law required resident aliens to register, it also criminalized any speech advocating or teaching the violent overthrow of the US government. In 1951, Scales went underground. Three years later, he was arrested and tried and convicted for membership in the party. He served fifteen months in federal prison before President John F. Kennedy commuted his sentence on Christmas Eve 1962.

There were a small number of Communists in the South, though they never offered any real threat. With few Communists to pursue, anticommunists looked for a larger group of "sympathizers." They painted in broad strokes, involving a widespread effort to suppress the civil rights movement. As early as the late 1940s, anticommunists focused on civil rights activists for their alleged "subversion." Along with the House Un-American Activities Committee (HUAC), the Senate sponsored standing antisubversion committees with broad investigatory powers. With sympathetic support from the FBI, which became an important source of information about alleged subversion, from 1951 to 1977 the fierce segregationist Sen. James Eastland of Mississippi chaired the Senate Internal Security Subcommittee (SISS). Eastland claimed that black civil rights activists were "dupes" of white Communists. African Americans blindly followed Communists, he claimed, and "do not realize this, or do not stop to think of it."[6]

In other instances, southern state legislatures authorized the creation of "little HUACs" to investigate alleged subversion. The Florida Legislative Investigation

---

[4] Daniel, *Lost Revolutions*, 24.

[5] George Lewis, *The White South and the Red Menace: Segregationists, Anticommunism, and Massive Resistance, 1945–1965* (Gainesville: University Press of Florida, 2004), 54.

[6] Sarah Hart Brown, "Redressing Southern 'Subversion': The Case of Senator Eastland and the Louisiana Lawyer," *Louisiana History* 43, no. 3 (2002): 298.

Florida state senator Charley Johns discussing plans to screen-out homosexuals, 1963. *State Archives of Florida.*

Committee—known as the Johns Committee because state senator Charley Johns was its chair—investigated civil rights organizations such as the NAACP and the Southern Christian Leadership Conference (SCLC). Coming up with little evidence of subversion, in 1961 the Johns Committee turned its attention against alleged homosexuals in schools and universities, including the University of Florida. Georgia and South Carolina also created "little HUACs" that focused on civil rights organizations, while in 1956 Mississippi created a State Sovereignty Commission with sweeping investigatory and intelligence-gathering powers—including spying and secret funding for local segregationists. States also suppressed activists in the name of anticommunism by using state sedition laws. In 1954, Carl Braden, along with his wife, Anne, a journalist in Louisville, purchased a home in a white neighborhood and transferred the deed to Andrew Wade, an African American. After the house was bombed, Braden was charged with sedition under a Kentucky law enacted in 1920 but never used. Convicted, he was sentenced to fifteen years but served eight months, after the US Supreme Court declared the law unconstitutional in April 1956.

MASSIVE RESISTANCE

The *Brown* decision coalesced a reaction among southern whites against the challenge to segregation. White segregationist sentiment had been brewing for about a decade. During the late 1930s and 1940s, there appeared some hope that the South was ripe for change. The New Deal brought forth political leadership that emphasized economic development and class over the old shibboleths of race. But the chaotic atmosphere of the war, followed by the turmoil of the postwar years, caused southern whites to rally around a defense of segregation.

At first, however, the white reaction to *Brown* was reluctant acceptance. The day after the decision, Ben Smith, the superintendent of the Greensboro, North Carolina, public schools, made a momentous announcement. As the second-largest city in North Carolina, Greensboro enjoyed a reputation for moderation and paternalism on issues of race. It was inconceivable, Smith said, that citizens would attempt to defy the law of the land. The Greensboro school board, agreeing with Smith's declaration, voted six to one in support of abiding by the *Brown* decision. Similarly, in Virginia, the governor urged "cool heads, calm study, and sound judgment," while the state attorney general believed that the commonwealth's leaders would "realistically endeavor to work out some rational adjustment." Elsewhere, in Arkansas and Alabama, the governors announced a cooperative stance.[7]

Obstruction and opposition followed these initially hopeful signs of white cooperation. Most states began a studied and deliberate campaign against public-school integration, ranging from complete opposition in the Deep South to the establishment of complex rules in North Carolina and Virginia that enabled communities to avoid compliance. During the three years after *Brown*, white opinion coalesced against desegregation, inaugurating what broadly has become known as "massive resistance." In part, this change reflected the attitudes of the federal courts and the presidency. Both branches proceeded cautiously. The Dwight D. Eisenhower administration worked to desegregate public accommodations in the city of Washington, where it also pressured local bus and utility companies to hire black workers. At the same time, the administration pressed for school integration in Washington and for more-complete desegregation of military bases. Eisenhower also supported the Civil Rights Act of 1957—the first federal civil rights act in eighty-two years—which created a Civil Rights Commission along with a Civil Rights Division in the US Department of Justice.

But Eisenhower remained largely silent about the tumultuous changes, including the *Brown* decision and rising African American protest. Much of this calculation was political, as Eisenhower courted southern whites and sought to avoid alienating them by appearing too favorable toward civil rights. Eisenhower and the Republican Party saw potential in cultivating the white South, and during the 1950s suburban voters began to vote Republican. In the face of white hostility, the Eisenhower administration remained lukewarm about enforcing school integration. Although Eisenhower appointed Earl Warren as chief justice of the Supreme Court, he had grave doubts about judicial activism and refused to take a forthright stance of support concerning *Brown*. In the 1956 Republican platform, Eisenhower agreed only to a statement of acceptance rather than support of school desegregation.

After southern schools appealed to the court for relief, on May 31, 1955, the court issued a second ruling, *Brown II*, detailing an implementation plan. The court punted in the decision, remanding "necessary and proper" enforcement to federal

7 Richard Kluger, *Simple Justice: The History of and Black America's Struggle for Equality* (New York: A. A. Knopf, 1975), 713–714; Ronald L. Heinemann, *Harry Byrd of Virginia* (Charlottesville: University Press of Virginia, 1996), 326–327; Benjamin Muse, *Virginia's Massive Resistance* (Bloomington: Indiana University Press, 1961), 5; and Joseph J. Thorndike, "'The Sometimes Sordid Level of Race and Segregation': James J. Kilpatrick and the Virginia Campaign against *Brown*," in *The Moderates' Dilemma: Massive Resistance to School Desegregation in Virginia*, ed. Matthew D. Lassiter and Andrew B. Lewis (Charlottesville: University Press of Virginia, 1998), 53.

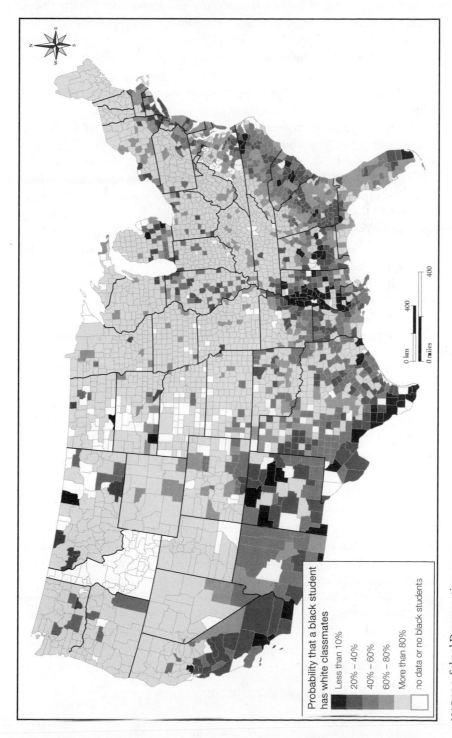

Probability that a black student
has white classmates

Less than 10%
20% – 40%
40% – 60%
60% – 80%
More than 80%
no data or no black students

0 km   400
0 miles   400

MAP 22.1   School Desegregation, 2000

district courts to establish public education on a "racially nondiscriminatory basis." In a key phrase, the Supreme Court instructed district courts to implement the decision "with all deliberate speed."[8] The court's instructions in *Brown II* stalled the momentum of *Brown I* and emboldened white opponents of desegregation. Without clearly articulated guidelines directing the district courts—which often contained segregationist judges—an opening existed to evade desegregation through delay and obstruction.

Southern segregationists dominated congressional delegations and provided a united front against *Brown*. Already, white opponents combined constitutionalism with a defense of the racial status quo. Since the New Deal, southern whites had become increasingly alarmed about the expansion of national power, fearing that it meant an end to their racial practices. These fears became realized in the *Brown* decision. White southerners claimed the constitutional high ground, charging violation of states' rights and local control at the expense of national control. In addition, conservatives fused hostility to the federal government and even anticommunism with a defense of Jim Crow.

On March 12, 1956, a group of congressmen—nineteen senators and seventy-seven members of the House—signed the Southern Manifesto. Only five senators from the former Confederacy—including newly elected Texas senator Lyndon B. Johnson—refused to participate. The Southern Manifesto stressed constitutional objections to federal intervention. Taking the lead was Georgia's senior senator, Walter George, chair of an ad hoc committee to draft the document. An opponent of the New Deal, George extended his critique of expanding federal power. The Supreme Court's "unwarranted decision" had substituted "naked power for established law" and was a "clear abuse of judicial power." In the South, claimed the manifesto, the *Brown* decision created "chaos and confusion" and undermined the "amicable relations between the white and Negro races that have been created through 90 years of patient effort by the good people of both races." "Hatred and suspicion" had replaced "friendship and understanding." The group announced its determination to seek "all lawful means to bring about a reversal of this decision, which is contrary to the Constitution."[9]

Massive resistance had its popularizers: southern journalists who adopted the cause. John Temple Graves II, an Alabama newspaperman and publicist, conducted a speaking tour across the South urging opposition to desegregation. Opponents of *Brown* fought a "constitutional cold war" against federal domination.[10] In 1957, the young North Carolina journalist Jesse Helms declared that desegregation should not take place at "the points of bayonets." A federal takeover of education, he wrote, matched Karl Marx's predictions: government-required integration was socialism. "The cackles you hear" had "a Russian accent," he claimed.[11]

---

[8] US Supreme Court 349 U.S. 294, *Brown v. Board of Education Topeka*.
[9] Finley, *Delaying the Dream*, 146.
[10] Ward, *Defending White Democracy*, 146.
[11] "We Aren't Solving Anything," *Tarheel Banker*, 36, no. 5 (November 1957): 32.

Perhaps the most insistent critic of the *Brown* decision was James J. Kilpatrick, Oklahoma native and editorial writer for the *Richmond News-Leader*. After the Supreme Court's ruling, Kilpatrick fashioned a constitutional defense of segregation. Arguing that the court had acted unconstitutionally, he maintained—reviving the nullification argument of the early nineteenth century—that states had the right to "interpose" between the federal government and its citizens. Recalling Thomas Jefferson's and James Madison's Kentucky and Virginia Resolutions, Kilpatrick argued that there were times "when the Federal government might usurp powers not granted it." In those times, states could "declare their inherent right—inherent in the nature of our Union—to judge for themselves not merely of the infraction, but of the mode and measure of redress."[12]

In the mid-1950s, southern state legislatures adopted measures designed to delay desegregation of schools. In North Carolina, known for its racial moderation, Gov. William B. Umstead appointed a special advisory committee in August 1954 composed of three black and twelve white members, with state senator Thomas Pearsall serving as chair. This committee, and one succeeding it in 1956, determined that desegregation was impossible. Its recommendations, known as the Pearsall Plan, would permit students to attend an integrated school. But the Pearsall Plan also empowered local communities to close schools threatened with integration and to establish segregated, state-supported private academies. The North Carolina legislature enacted these recommendations in July 1956, followed by a popular referendum during the following autumn that was adopted overwhelmingly.

Like North Carolina's Pearsall Committee, Virginia's Gray Commission proposed alternatives to integration that included school closings and public support for all-white private schools. Virginia's senator Harry F. Byrd, who controlled state politics with an iron hand, announced a policy of "massive resistance" on February 25, 1956. Massive resistance meant measures, which the Virginia legislature adopted in 1958, to obstruct desegregation. In thirteen new laws that became known as the Stanley Plan (named for Gov. Thomas B. Stanley), the Virginia legislature in September 1956 provided legal sanction for communities to close their schools and subsidize all-white schools rather than integrate under court order. Virginia's plan went further: while North Carolina permitted some urban communities to desegregate, Virginia's law cut off state aid to districts that educated black and white pupils together. Byrd's massive resistance defied federal authority because one of the five cases brought together in the *Brown* decision concerned the schools in Prince Edward County, Virginia.

After much of the Stanley Plan was struck down by the federal courts in 1958–1959, the legislature repealed compulsory education and returned authority over the schools to local school boards. Charlottesville, Norfolk, and Prince Edward County closed their schools. With the national spotlight focused on Virginia, the publicity was unfavorable. Noted CBS correspondent Edward R. Murrow broadcast a special series titled

---

[12] *Richmond News Leader*, Nov. 21, 1955; William P. Hustwit, *James J. Kilpatrick: Salesman for Segregation* (Chapel Hill: University of North Carolina Press, 2013).

The Lost Class of '59, which depicted the ill effects of the school closings on the children in Prince Edward County. Adverse publicity prompted authorities, including Gov. Lindsay Almond Jr., to break with the Byrd Machine and urge schools to reopen everywhere but Prince Edward. There, local authorities established the Prince Edward Academy as a publicly supported segregated academy, and the public school remained closed until 1964. Prince Edward, as newspaperman Jonathan Daniels put it, had participated in "secession from civilization."[13] In the end, the Supreme Court in that year ruled that the closings were illegal.

Other evidence suggested widespread white opposition to integration during the 1950s. The Ku Klux Klan enjoyed a revival as a terror organization intimidating black civil rights activists. The KKK was especially active in the Deep South, but it existed in most of the former Confederate states. A more respectable organization was the White Citizens' Council, first organized in Greenwood, Mississippi, on July 11, 1954, and, after 1956, reorganized into the Citizens' Councils of America. The citizens' councils represented more-affluent southern whites—planters, bankers, businessmen, attorneys, ministers, and physicians—who rallied in opposition to *Brown*. This organization spread across the Deep South especially, eventually claiming 60,000 members and serving as a segregationist pressure group that often used its economic power against civil rights groups. The organization remained most powerful in Mississippi, where it dominated politics. Although publicly rejecting violence, the citizens' councils effectively encouraged it. The organization mounted local efforts to slow or even reverse black voter registration. These campaigns partially succeeded in blunting the progress in voting rights achieved during the 1930s and 1940s.

In Alabama, the government attempted to expel the NAACP in 1956 by using the state's foreign-corporation qualification law, which required that foreign enterprises register with the state and provide their membership list. When the NAACP refused, the state obtained an injunction banning the group from operating in the state. Only after the US Supreme Court ruled in its favor, in *NAACP v. Alabama*, were its operations resumed.[14] Other southern states enacted legislation designed to intimidate the NAACP. In South Carolina, members of the organization were prohibited from state employment. For much of the 1950s, these efforts succeeded in tying up the NAACP and crippling it as an effective civil rights organization. Much of white opposition enjoyed the active support of state governments. In March 1956, the Mississippi legislature established the Mississippi Sovereignty Commission. Awarded ample powers, the commission was charged with protecting state sovereignty from "encroachment thereon by the Federal Government or any branch, department or agency thereof." It engaged in a variety of activities,

---

[13]   David R. Goldfield, *Promised Land: The South since 1945* (Arlington Heights, IL: Harlan Davidson, 1987), 71.

[14]   *NAACP v. Alabama ex. Rel. Patterson*, 357 U.S. 449 (1958).

such as public-speaking campaigns and public relations, but also conducted surveillance of civil rights leaders.[15]

White opposition to *Brown* did not blunt rising expectations among African Americans. The kidnapping and brutal murder of fourteen-year-old Emmett Till in August 1955 crystallized their revulsion against white violence and reaffirmed their grim determination to push forward. Till, who grew up in Chicago, was visiting relatives in the Mississippi delta when he was accused of speaking suggestively to the wife of a white grocer in Money, Mississippi. Roy Bryant, the grocer, conspired with his half brother, J. W. Milam, to abduct Emmett. Although they intended to pistol whip him, Till's defiant attitude prompted them to beat him brutally, to execute him with a shot to the head, and to dump his body in the Tallahatchie River. After Till was reported missing, his badly mangled and partially decomposed body was found three days after the murder.

Till's murder caused a sensation, attracting national and even international attention. Transporting his body for a funeral in Chicago, his family conducted an open-casket service that exposed the horrors of Till's death to a national audience. Black-owned publications such as the *Chicago Defender* and *Jet* publicized the murder and funeral to rally public opinion against southern violence. Till's killing, said the *Defender*, was "an outrage to all decent American citizens, white, and colored, and dramatically points out to the world the ugliest aspects of life in our Democracy."[16] The trial of Bryant and Milam, conducted in LeFlore County Courthouse, attracted national media coverage. Emmett's mother attended, as did one of three African Americans serving in Congress, Charles C. Diggs Jr. In addition, black witnesses, including Till's granduncle, Moses Wright, testified—at personal risk—for the prosecution and identified Bryant and Milam as the perpetrators. Despite a preponderance of evidence against them, Bryant and Milam were acquitted by the all-male, all-white jury after it deliberated only sixty-seven minutes.

The aftermath of Till's murder solidified the opinion of Mississippi whites, who regarded the efforts of the NAACP and the national media to publicize the case as further evidence of northern interference. The national furor, according to the *Greenwood* (Mississippi) *Morning Star*, resulted from "outside agitators" who had spurred a "growing resentment against those who seek to use the affair to create strife and ill feeling." These "outside agitators" were "inspired by Communists or by persons," it added, "who have become unwitting victims of the Communist plan to stir up trouble where possible."[17] Many African Americans saw Till's murder—one of thousands of instances of racial violence occurring in the South since the 1880s— as confirming the need for more-radical measures against white supremacy. By 1955, civil rights leaders, writes one historian, had come to realize that "the continued

---

[15] Sovereignty Commission Online; available at http://mdah.state.ms.us/arrec/digital_archives/sovcom/scagencycasehistory.php.

[16] *Chicago Defender*, September 10, 1955, in *The Lynching of Emmett Till: A Documentary Narrative*, ed. Christopher Metress (Charlottesville: University Press of Virginia, 2002), 25

[17] *Greenwood Morning Star*, September 6, 1955, in *Emmett Till*, ed. Metress, 27–28.

passive acceptance of evil could only perpetuate its existence." This event "cauterized almost all Negroes and prepared them for more radical departures," declared the black-run magazine *Ebony*.[18]

THE MONTGOMERY BUS BOYCOTT

World War II permanently altered the demographic, economic, and political conditions in the South in its relationship to the rest of the country. The departure of a portion of the South's black population became a referendum on Jim Crow, but it also nationalized the issue of race in modern America. The political balance of power seemed to be shifting with the position of the national Democratic Party, now committed to a program of civil rights. Nonetheless, the pace of change through the legal and political system was slow. The *Brown* decision was stonewalled. The federal government, despite rhetoric, proceeded haltingly. In this setting, black leadership embraced a strategy of direct action. Based on a principle of nonviolence, direct action depended on at least two conditions to succeed: first, its ability to provoke federal intervention; second, its ability to mobilize black people. Never before had so ambitious a mobilization been envisioned. Although there was significant participation in this movement by whites, its most notable feature was that it represented a courageous uprising by African Americans, young and old, who were determined to overthrow the most-obnoxious manifestations of white supremacy.

With the NAACP finding it increasingly difficult to operate in the South, other approaches emerged, including nonviolent protest. The first significant site of mass protest was Montgomery, Alabama. The capital of Alabama and the first capital of the Confederacy, Montgomery was seemingly a citadel of segregation. Actually, it was the scene of previous organizing efforts by black activists. Nearly 8 percent of the black electorate was registered to vote in the city, a higher proportion than anywhere else in the state, though the city was slightly less than two-fifths black in 1955. The humiliating segregation of public accommodations remained a symbol of white supremacy. Particularly obnoxious were local ordinances requiring that black passengers board buses by the rear door and be barred from sitting in the front ten seats in the whites-only section of the bus. Black riders could sit in the next two rows—a "no man's land"—only if no whites wanted those seats. If the bus filled up, blacks were required to relinquish their seats to white riders. Bus drivers enforced these practices, often summoning police. There were numerous complaints about abusive bus drivers, who harassed black riders or refused to pick them up. African Americans responded vociferously, and, during the 1940s, a number protested and were arrested.

In March 1955, fifteen-year-old Claudette Colvin was handcuffed and arrested—to the general outrage of the black community—for refusing to give up her seat to a

---

[18] Quoted in Stephen J. Whitfield, *A Death in the Delta: The Story of Emmett Till* (Baltimore: Johns Hopkins University Press, 1992), 89.

Rosa Parks, during arrest in Montgomery, Alabama. *Library of Congress.*

white person. Months later, on December 1, 1955, a Montgomery seamstress, Rosa Parks, refused to relinquish her seat to a white passenger and was arrested and fined. Parks's arrest was not accidental. Parks was active in the local NAACP chapter, serving as its secretary since 1943 and as advisor to the chapter's youth auxiliary. In July 1955, she participated in an interracial conference at the Highlander School in Tennessee.

Parks's stature rallied the black community. Word of her arrest "traveled like wildfire into every black home," according to a contemporary; local civil rights activists rallied to her cause.[19] Along with the local NAACP chapter and its head, E. D. Nixon, who also served as an official in A. Phillip Randolph's Brotherhood of Sleeping Car Porters, other local black groups such as the Women's Political Council (WPC) and the Citizens Steering Committee came together. Women suffered especially from the humiliation of segregated buses. The WPC's Jo Ann Robinson, who taught English at the all-black Alabama State College, helped mobilize black women. Three-quarters of the bus riders were African Americans, a WPC mimeographed statement read, "yet we are arrested, or have to stand over empty seats."

The organization called for a one-day boycott, asking "every Negro to stay off the buses."[20] Expanding to a general boycott of the bus system, the emerging mass movement attracted widespread support, especially from black churches. A boycott was announced on December 4, 1955, and about 40,000 black riders refused to board buses the next day. The boycott supporters formed a new group, the Montgomery Improvement Association (MIA), and elected the twenty-six-year-old pastor Martin Luther King Jr. as president.

[19] Jo Ann Gibson Robinson, *The Montgomery Bus Boycott and the Women Who Started It*, ed. David J. Garrow (Knoxville: University of Tennessee Press, 1987), 44.

[20] Robinson, *The Montgomery Bus Boycott*, 46.

A recent arrival to Montgomery, King was the son of a prominent Atlanta minister, enjoying a privileged existence among that city's black bourgeoisie. Graduating
from Morehouse College in Atlanta at the age of nineteen, King attended Crozier
Theological Seminary in Chester, Pennsylvania. He pursued a doctoral degree at
Boston University and in 1954 was called to the Dexter Avenue Baptist Church in
Montgomery, at the age of twenty-five. Having concentrated mainly on his pastoral
duties, the young minister was suddenly vaulted to leadership of a major social movement. His speech to the MIA on December 5, 1955, with thousands packing the Holt
Street Baptist Church, rallied the movement. Black people, he said, had been "intimidated and humiliated and impressed—oppressed—because of the sheer fact that
they were Negroes." Rosa Parks was not just "one of the finest Negro citizens . . . but
one of the finest citizens in Montgomery." Black people, he said, were simply "tired of
being trampled over by the iron feet of oppression."[21]

During the bus boycott, activist Bayard Rustin became a key strategic adviser for
King; the two men formed a partnership in fashioning a mass movement. Born in West
Chester, Pennsylvania, Rustin grew up a Quaker and was a lifelong pacifist; he was im-
prisoned during 1944–1946 because he claimed conscientious-objector status. In 1941,
Rustin worked as youth organizer on A. Philip Randolph's March on Washington.
During the war years, he participated in the Fellowship of Reconciliation (FOR) and
participated in the founding of the Congress of Racial Equality (CORE), which spun
off as a separate organization in 1942. After 1946, Rustin worked as a field organizer for
CORE, pursuing a direct-action strategy of challenging segregation at the local level. In
1947, after the Supreme Court outlawed segregation in interstate travel, CORE planned
a Journey of Reconciliation. An early harbinger of the later (and more famous) Freedom
Rides, this direct-action event involved training in nonviolence. Eight whites and eight
blacks traveled through North Carolina, Virginia, Tennessee, and Kentucky riding
buses and trains. Rustin was arrested in North Carolina and spent twenty-two days on
the chain gang.

Rustin first visited Montgomery in February 1956, a few months after the boycott began. He was immediately impressed with the movement's energy. "As I
watched the people walk away," he wrote after one meeting of the MIA, "I had a
feeling that no force on earth can stop this movement. It has all the elements to
touch the hearts of men."[22] Rustin and King formed an unusual partnership. Rustin
had some baggage: not only had he flirted with communism during the 1930s, he was
also gay. Later, both his Communist past and his sexuality would be used against
him. During the mid-1950s, Rustin mentored King in the philosophy and strategy of
nonviolence. He advocated pacifism and peaceful nonviolence, modeled on
Mahatma Gandhi's strategy to undermine British rule in India. "The glorious

[21] King's speech to the MIA, December 5, 1955; available at http://mlk-kpp01.stanford.edu/
   index.php/encyclopedia/documentsentry/mia_mass_meeting_at_holt_street_baptist_
   church/.
[22] Rustin, Bayard (1910–1987); available at http://mlk-kpp01.stanford.edu/index.php/encyclopedia/
   encyclopedia/enc_rustin_bayard_1910_1987/.

thing," Rustin later wrote, was that King "came to a profoundly deep understanding of nonviolence through the struggle itself, and through reading and discussions which he had in the process of carrying on the protest."[23]

King was recruited to serve as the movement's public face, a leader of what soon became a mass, cross-class social movement. The boycott succeeded in mobilizing the black community, which rallied in support, while women led the effort at crippling the bus system. Women also served as the backbone of church meetings and staffed the day-to-day work that kept the boycott machinery moving. As maids and other service workers, black women were visible in walking to their jobs, carpooling in vehicles provided by the MIA, and even getting picked up by their white female employers, whose homes could not function without their presence. The MIA at first called for better treatment of black people on the buses, but after the city rejected negotiations, demanded integration of the buses. The boycott lasted for more than a year, and over time black leaders escalated their goals, from simply improving the segregated bus system to abolishing it altogether. King was joined by members of other black churches in Montgomery and across Alabama, who helped mobilize black people behind the movement. Despite arrests of black leaders and the dynamiting of King's home, the movement persisted, using Gandhian nonviolence, as King later wrote, as the "guiding light of our technique."[24]

The Montgomery Bus Boycott ended on November 13, 1956, when the Supreme Court ruled that segregation of public buses was illegal and unconstitutional. King later wrote that "rational explanation" did not adequately account for what happened in Montgomery. There was something "suprarational" about the movement, which fashioned "a harmony out of the discords of the universe." Combating "mountains of evil," Montgomery became a "proving ground for the struggle and triumph of freedom and justice in America." The Alabama capital was transformed from the Cradle of the Confederacy into the Cradle of Freedom and Justice.[25]

KING AND THE SCLC

In the wake of the Montgomery Bus Boycott, King and his supporters considered the way forward. In late 1956, Rustin urged King to fashion a new group with "ties to masses of people so that their action projects are backed by broad participation of people."[26] King envisioned a network of black churches spearheading a new, grassroots movement. In January 1957, he organized the Southern Negro Leaders Conference on

[23] John D'Emilio, *Lost Prophet: The Life and Times of Bayard Rustin* (Chicago: University of Chicago Press, 2004), 230–231.

[24] From *Ebony*, July 1959; available at http://mlk-kpp01.stanford.edu/index.php/encyclopedia/documentsentry/590701_my_trip_to_the_land_of_gandhi/.

[25] Martin Luther King Jr., *Stride toward Freedom: The Montgomery Story* (New York: Harper & Brothers, 1958), 69–70.

[26] Clayborne Carson, Stewart Burns, and Susan Carson, eds., *The Papers of Martin Luther King, Jr.*, vol. 3, *Birth of a New Age, December 1955–December 1956* (Berkeley: University of California Press, 1997), 493.

Transportation and Nonviolent Integration at a meeting at Ebenezer Baptist, his father's church in Atlanta. Subsequently, the organization became known as the Southern Christian Leadership Conference. King was elected its first president on February 14, 1957.

The SCLC assembled a group of sixty black ministers willing to participate in the civil rights movement. The new group drew veteran organizers such as Ella Baker, who became the organization's only staff member (and only woman among male ministers) in a small headquarters in Atlanta. Drawing on the resources of black churches mobilized during the Montgomery Bus Boycott, the SCLC included other Alabama black clergy such as Ralph David Abernathy of Montgomery, Joseph Lowery of Mobile, and Fred Shuttlesworth of Birmingham, as well as others outside the state, such as C. K. Steele of Tallahassee, T. J. Jemison of Baton Rouge, and A. L. Davis Jr. of New Orleans. Adopting the strategy of direct-action protest, the SCLC advocated nonviolence as a guiding principle. Rather than an organization with a mass following, it served as a coordinating group that interacted with local groups, such as Shuttlesworth's Birmingham-based Alabama Christian Movement for Human Rights. Primarily appealing to urban African American churches, the SCLC enjoyed some economic and political independence from white pressure.

King's influence in the organization was crucial, though he received advice from Rustin, along with white activists Harris Wofford and Stanley Levison. Born and raised in New York City but with grandparents in the South, Wofford had become intensely interested in race issues. He attended Howard Law School for a year, before transferring to Yale Law School. Like Rustin, he was an advocate of Gandhian nonviolence. When the Montgomery Bus Boycott showed the possibilities of mass organizing, he introduced himself to King. In 1957, after the boycott, Wofford raised foundation support for King to travel to India to study nonviolent political philosophy. Levison served as a close friend and key adviser to King, especially concerning the movement's financial logistics. Long involved in civil rights and labor causes, during the 1930s Levison participated in leftist causes. Attending law school but never practicing the law, he earned a fortune in the real-estate business. Levison devoted much of his wealth, and the wealth of others, to support victims of McCarthyite persecutions during the 1950s. Although some of the people whom he supported were Communists, Levison's leftist connections did not bother King.

Much of King's work, as a media star, publicized the plight of southern blacks before a national audience. Logging hundreds of thousands of miles of travel and speaking as often as four times a week, he was on the road constantly. Relying on King's charismatic leadership, the SCLC combined national pressure-group politics with local organizing. When Congress debated a new civil rights bill in 1957, King organized a national push for its passage. In February, the organization called for President Eisenhower's support. Despite several bombings of Montgomery black churches associated with the civil rights movement in early 1957, including Ralph Abernathy's First Baptist Church, there was little response from Washington. "Lawlessness" had become a "deeply disturbing feature" of life in the South,

King and other black leaders wrote in a telegram to Eisenhower. Presidential leadership was essential; "morality, like charity, begins at home," and "drastic and remedial action" was necessary. The telegram urged the president to speak out about violence in the South and to visit the region, to organize a White House conference on civil rights, and to exercise leadership to begin "democracy at home" during the Cold War era. If nothing were done, the telegram promised a "pilgrimage of prayer" in Washington to call attention to efforts to achieve "freedom and first class citizenship."[27]

Working with A. Philip Randolph, NCAAP president Roy Wilkins, and Harlem congressman Adam Clayton Powell, King organized a Pilgrimage of Prayer. It convened at the steps of the Lincoln Memorial on May 17, 1957, the third anniversary of the *Brown* decision. Although turnout was disappointing, the Pilgrimage provided a forum for King to urge federal involvement. Washington leadership, he said, possessed "a high blood pressure of words and an anemia of deeds." King emphasized the need for nonviolence, meeting "hate with love" and "physical force with soul force."[28] The Pilgrimage exposed King to Washington politics but had a limited effect. Eisenhower kept his distance, avoiding mention of the civil rights issue.

In September 1957, Eisenhower was forced into action when a crisis erupted in Little Rock, Arkansas. Its school board attempted to desegregate Central High School by admitting a handful of black students. But hardline opposition by the local Citizens' Council inflamed matters. On September 4, as Central High prepared to open, Gov. Orville Faubus ordered National Guard units to block the admission of nine African American students, despite a federal court order requiring integration. Meanwhile, crowds outside the high school threatened the students and grew angrier by the day. When the deadlock continued and threatened to spiral out of control, Eisenhower was forced to intervene. After Faubus initially agreed to permit the students to enroll but then withdrew National Guard protection, Eisenhower federalized the National Guard and dispatched paratroopers. On September 25, after the Little Rock Nine finally took their place in Central High, Faubus announced that the state was now "occupied territory." The crisis gradually subsided, though the black students were subject to continued abuse and intimidation.

Although the Civil Rights Act of 1957 strengthened federal protection of voting rights, southern white elections officials continued to suppress most of the black vote. King believed that local action would prompt change. He also became involved during the late 1950s in more grassroots efforts at voting rights. In 1958, King launched a Crusade for Citizenship planned for twenty-one southern cities and designed to rally opinion behind black voting. After the enactment of the

---

[27] King to Eisenhower, February 14, 1957; available at http://mlk-kpp01.stanford.edu/index.php/encyclopedia/documentsentry/to_dwight_d_eisenhower/.

[28] "Give Us the Ballot," address at the Prayer Pilgrimage for Freedom, Washington, DC, May 17, 1957; available at http://mlk-kpp01.stanford.edu/index.php/encyclopedia/documentsentry/doc_give_us_the_ballot_address_at_the_prayer_pilgrimage_for_freedom/.

101st Airborne escorts African American students integrating Central High School, Little Rock, Arkansas. *National Archives.*

Civil Rights Act of 1957, the organization sought to increase voter registration through a direct-action, mass-movement campaign. "The time has come to broaden the struggle for Negroes to register and vote," it declared, "for the simple reason that until this happens we cannot really influence the legislative branch of government."[29]

The key figure in this effort, Ella Baker, was a veteran of campaigns for voter registration for the NAACP beginning in the 1940s. Less an inspirational speaker than an organizer, Baker was a genius in grassroots operations. Rustin and Levison favored using her to coordinate the effort, and King relented, despite his doubts about her as a female and nonminister. No fan of charismatic leadership, Baker had little regard for self-important ministers and probably little tolerance for King's sexism. Baker rescued the ill-organized Crusade for Citizenship and then began organizing a more deeply rooted campaign for voter registration. In the end, during two years, the campaign fell far short of its goals of registering three million new black voters; about 200,000 joined the voting rolls. Matters appeared to have reached a dead end by the election of a new president, John F. Kennedy, in November 1960.

STUDENT REBELLION AND SNCC

On February 1, 1960, a group of four black students, freshmen at the all-black North Carolina A&T State College, challenged one of the cherished taboos in the Jim Crow South. The students lived near each other, in the same dormitory, and were enrolled in a college algebra class together. Carefully following the unfolding developments in the civil rights movement, they frequently discussed current events. Some of the students internalized a new spirit of restiveness. One of them, Joseph McNeil, was from Wilmington, where local African Americans boycotted a

[29] Steven F. Lawson, *Running for Freedom: Civil Rights and Black Politics in America since 1941,* 3d ed., (New YOrk: McGraw-Hill, 2009), 75.

Pepsi-Cola bottling company because of its discriminatory practices. "Why don't we do something like that in Greensboro?" one of them asked. After a spontaneous "bull session," they decided to seek service at the lunch counter of the Woolworth's store in downtown Greensboro.[30] When the students arrived at Woolworth's, they were refused service. Feeling an "intense sense of pride" along with a "bit of trepidation," they remained at their seats until the store closed.[31] The next day, about thirty students appeared and stayed for two hours; the day after, those numbers doubled. By the end of the week, hundreds of other students from A&T and Bennett College, a local black women's college, joined in daily protests, attracting the attention of the national news media. The sit-in movement had begun.

A critical ingredient in the civil rights movement was the thousands of black students drawn to protest. Products of the Baby Boom, these students were better off than their parents. They enjoyed greater freedoms on campuses, which were to some extent insulated from retaliation from the white power structure. In Greensboro, where white city fathers considered themselves racially enlightened, the city elected its first black city council member in 1951. The city nonetheless remained thoroughly segregated, and the bustling downtown excluded African Americans or subjected them to humiliating Jim Crow regulations.

Black students in Greensboro and elsewhere had grown impatient with the slow pace of change after the *Brown* decision. Many belonged to NAACP Youth Councils, which were more committed to direct-action protests than were the leaders of their parent organization. Sit-ins and direct-action protest became a way to express their frustration. "I felt as though I had gained my manhood," Franklin McCain, one of the Greensboro protesters, later explained.[32] During February 1960, sit-ins at Woolworth's and other national chain stores—which were more susceptible to protest and adverse media—occurred across North Carolina towns and cities. On February 10, 1960, a sit-in occurred in Hampton, Virginia—the first protest outside North Carolina—and by the end of the month the movement had spread to a number of southern cities. By the end of March, sit-ins had taken place in sixty cities. Once the movement expanded from Greensboro, student leaders emerged. The early sit-ins were spontaneous, but the movement acquired greater planning and strategy. The sit-ins were loosely based on a nonviolent strategy of protest, and among the most important organizations promoting that philosophy was CORE. The students' nonviolent resistance undergirded the movement, which drew inspiration from King's tactics and his Gandhian philosophy of social change.

During the spring of 1960, the black student movement emerged most powerfully in Nashville, where students from Fisk University organized an ambitious

---

[30] Interview with Robert T. Patterson, July 17, 1979, Civil Rights Greensboro, University of North Carolina Library; available at http://library.uncg.edu/dp/crg/oralHistItem .aspx?i=565.

[31] Interview with Joseph McNeil, October 14, 1979; available at http://library.uncg.edu/dp/crg/ oralHistItem.aspx?i=555.

[32] Lawson, *Running for Freedom*, 78.

effort to desegregate the city's downtown despite white opposition. Out of the Nashville movement came leaders such as ministers James Lawson and John Lewis and students Diane Nash and Marion Barry. Nash, originally from Chicago, was, along with Barry, a Fisk student. Lewis was a seminary student at the American Baptist Theological Seminary in Nashville, while Lawson was a divinity student at Vanderbilt who also worked for CORE and advocated nonviolent resistance. An Ohio native, Lawson was imprisoned for refusing to serve in the military during the Korean War, and then he spent three years as a Methodist missionary in India, where he studied nonviolence. He led workshops in Nashville in the late 1950s that offered training in nonviolence. These leaders crafted a protest strategy based on community empowerment and nonviolent resistance.

At a two-day conference on April 16–18, 1960, at Shaw University in Raleigh, North Carolina, the Student Nonviolent Coordinating Committee (SNCC) was founded. One hundred twenty student activists from twelve states and fifty-six colleges attended the meeting, which represented other organizations such as CORE, the Fellowship of Reconciliation, Students for a Democratic Society, and the National Student Association. Ella Baker was a key figure. Impatient with King's charismatic leadership, which depended so much on one person and top-down leadership, she favored a "group-centered leadership" that sought to empower people

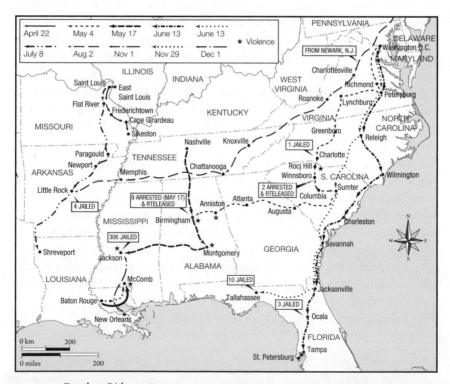

MAP 22.2 Freedom Rides, 1961

from below. Baker advocated, she later said, a social movement that drew on "people who are interested not in being leaders as much as in developing leadership among other people."[33]

In 1961, working in alliance with CORE, SNCC led the Freedom Rides, in which white and black students and adults rode buses in the South in order to desegregate buses and bus stations. SNCC leaders John Lewis and Henry Thomas participated in the first Freedom Ride, which left Washington in May 1961 and traveled through Virginia, the Carolinas, Georgia, and Alabama. The group encountered the worst white violence in Anniston, Alabama, where a mob burned a bus and beat the Freedom Riders, and in Birmingham and Montgomery, where an angry white mob assaulted them. Without a bus driver willing to risk further mob violence, the first Freedom Ride ended.

SNCC responded by recruiting a new group of volunteers. As the buses moved from Alabama to Mississippi, mass arrests took place in Jackson, the Mississippi capital. By the summer of 1961, volunteers poured into Jackson, where over three hundred protesters were arrested and jailed. Many of the protesters were white students. The protests were conducted with strict observance of nonviolent principles, and the escalating violence—and the coverage by the national media—appalled national public opinion. The John F. Kennedy administration, though reluctant to alienate southern supporters, attempted to intervene and mediate. Then, in October 1961, the Interstate Commerce Commission (ICC) issued a new directive ending segregation in interstate transportation.

TOWARD A CIVIL RIGHTS ACT

Black students' protest raised the stakes substantially. SNCC extended its activities across the Deep South, emphasizing voter registration. In selected locales student activists also campaigned to end segregation. During the fall of 1961, SNCC began the Albany movement. The largest city (about 60,000 people) in southwestern Georgia, Albany was targeted because segregation was so firmly entrenched. The movement began after Freedom Riders arrived in Albany and were arrested. Protesters, organized by SNCC and supported by students from the all-black Albany State College, staged a sit-in at a bus station, testing compliance with the ICC ban on segregated facilities. In 1961, W. G. Anderson, an osteopath, became president of an expanded SNCC-sponsored community coalition known as the Albany movement, composed of black ministers, women's clubs, and the local NAACP. SNCC organizers and former Freedom Riders Charles Sherrod and Cordell Reagon, working in local churches in nighttime workshops, fashioned a movement that sought to desegregate public accommodations, parks, hospitals, and libraries.

[33] Clayborne Carson, *In Struggle: SNCC and the Black Awakening of the 1960s* (Cambridge, MA: Harvard University Press, 1981), 20.

A main tool in the Albany movement was mass arrests. In December 1961, when activists tried to integrate the train station, scores were arrested. After protests at their trial, hundreds of arrests followed, and the jails were soon full with about five hundred protesters. In a mass meeting, local civil rights and community groups formally organized the Albany movement. On December 15, 1961, King arrived on the scene at the request of local organizers and was arrested. City officials then agreed to abide by the ICC desegregation orders. King was released, and some momentum in the movement was lost. After Albany officials stalled further, the movement reemerged in the spring and summer of 1962.

The Albany campaign tested out new strategies of mass protest. SNCC and SCLC organizers mounted protests in order to invite arrest, just as the Freedom Riders and their supporters had done. The jails became filled with arrested protesters. But the Albany movement encountered a formidable opponent in Sheriff Laurie Pritchett. Born in Griffin, Georgia, Pritchett was educated at Auburn and South Georgia College before receiving training at the FBI National Academy. He ensured that his police operated without excessive violence and brutality. Fully aware of the adverse effects of bad publicity in the national media, Pritchett also developed a plan for mass arrests that used the jails of three neighboring counties. As one SNCC worker put it, "We were naïve enough to think we could fill up the jails. . . . We ran out of people before [Chief Pritchett] ran out of jails." By early August 1962, the Albany movement had stalled.[34]

Despite the setback at Albany, the movement learned important lessons. SNCC activists sought community mobilization; that necessitated alliances with other civil rights organizations and community groups. African Americans in southern communities responded enthusiastically to protest movements; achieving a mass mobilization seemed critical. SNCC pursued a strategy that insisted on community empowerment. Although King and the SCLC possessed a certain star power

James Meredith attempting to integrate Ole Miss, September 1962. *Library of Congress.*

---

[34] Carson, *In Struggle*, 61.

that attracted media attention, much of the grassroots organizing reflected SNCC community-based work.

Notably, freedom songs of the culture associated with the movement emerged, reflecting African American musical traditions. The Freedom Singers, led by activist Bernice Johnson, came from Albany and became nationally known. Songs from the Albany movement became a standard feature of SNCC's new emphasis on community-wide mobilization. "When I opened my mouth and began to sing," recalled Johnson, "there was a force and power within myself I had never heard before." The music "released a kind of power and required a level of concentrated energy that I did not know I had."[35] Freedom songs bound people together and gave them the courage to face the opposition of hostile police and surly white crowds.

The conflict over segregation spread to southern public universities, many of which continued to obstruct desegregation. In September 1962, when James Meredith attempted to become the first African American admitted to the University of Mississippi, the campus exploded into violence. Only after Gov. Ross Barnett refused to provide for Meredith's safety did Kennedy, like Eisenhower before him, reluctantly respond by sending in military forces. Seeking to encourage civil rights activities that would avoid the hostile results of confrontational demonstrations, in 1961 the Kennedy administration began the Voter Education Project (VEP), a collaboration between the Justice Department and activists. The Southern Regional Council hired black attorney Wiley Branton to work on the VEP. SNCC had already sent Robert P. Moses, a New York City school teacher, to run efforts at voter registration. Moses conducted an all-out effort involving community groups in Mississippi. At great danger, SNCC fieldworkers encouraged rural African Americans to attempt to register to vote. In Greenwood, Mississippi, SNCC led an effort to mobilize the community around voter registration. SNCC organizers encountered white intimidation and violence in February and March 1963. Activists responded with marches and direct-action protests. In Greenwood, the Justice Department intervened behind the scenes but was hesitant to inflame white passions. Although the Greenwood movement failed to change things, it succeeded in mobilizing Mississippi blacks. Out of SNCC's efforts, the Council of Federated Organizations (COFO) coordinated the Mississippi movement.

In the spring of 1963, meanwhile, SCLC made Birmingham, Alabama, known as an impregnable fortress of segregation, into a test of the new mass-mobilization strategy. Birmingham pastor Fred Shuttlesworth led the campaign. A former truck driver and pastor of the Bethel Baptist Church, Shuttlesworth was a founding member of the SCLC. He led the Alabama Christian Movement for Human Rights (ACMHR), which came into existence after the Alabama legislature banned the NAACP in 1956. The fearless Shuttlesworth, unfazed by white terror tactics, survived two bombing attempts. Attempting to enroll his children in a white school, he

---

[35] Clayborne Carson, "SNCC and the Albany Movement," *Journal of Southwest Georgia History* 2 (1984): 18.

was attacked with brass knuckles and chains. By 1963, according to his own estimate, he had been arrested forty times.

A hard-nosed, noisy white supremacist, Eugene "Bull" Connor served as Birmingham's commissioner of public safety—a perfect foil to the nonviolent SCLC. Shuttlesworth summoned King, and they organized protest tactics of boycotts, sit-ins, and marches through the downtown to dramatize the evil of segregation. By April 1963, the ACMHR/SCLC alliance sought the desegregation of stores and lunch counters, the adoption of nondiscriminatory hiring practices by downtown businesses and city departments, the desegregation of city parks and playgrounds, and the establishment of a timetable for school desegregation. The movement pushed things along with sit-ins at various downtown establishments, along with marches, both of which resulted in arrests. In addition, Connor used attack dogs to break up the crowd, a strategy that backfired because of adverse media attention.

The SCLC hoped to obtain media exposure and federal intervention. "We wanted confrontation, nonviolent confrontation, to see if it would work," Shuttlesworth remembered. "We were trying to launch a systematic, wholehearted battle against segregation, which would set the pace for the nation."[36] SCLC organizer Wyatt T. Walker called this approach Project C—the "C" standing for confrontation.[37] Bull Connor responded by suppressing five weeks of street demonstrations with police dogs and fire hoses. With Connor filling the jails with black demonstrators, the SCLC recruited children, some as young as eight, and teenagers to join the marches. King faced criticism for this, but the kids clearly understood that they were fighting for their parents' and their own freedom. In addition, white supremacist groups conducted a bombing campaign, including an attack on King's hotel and the homes of civil rights supporters. The city became known, as "Bombingham" because of the extent of violence. On September 15, 1963, the bombing of the Sixteenth Street Baptist Church, a protest center, resulted in the deaths of four young black children.

During the Birmingham demonstrations, on April 12, 1963, King was arrested for breaking the Alabama state law prohibiting mass demonstrations. In response, eight white religious leaders published a statement in the *Birmingham News* criticizing King's strategy as "unwise and untimely." In response, King composed what became known as the "Letter from Birmingham Jail," first circulated by mimeograph and then published in *Ebony*. A year later, he included the letter as part of his memoir of the Birmingham demonstrations, titled *Why We Can't Wait*. While white clergy were calling for moderation, in his letter King pointed out that the time for patience had ended. "You deplore the demonstrations that are presently taking place in Birmingham," he wrote. "But I am sorry that your statement did not express a similar concern for the conditions that brought the demonstrations into

---

[36] Shuttlesworth obituary, *New York Times*, October 5, 2011.
[37] Glenn T. Eskew, *But for Birmingham: The Local and National Movements in the Civil Rights Struggle* (Chapel Hill: University of North Carolina Press, 1997), 228.

being." Although it was unfortunate that mass demonstrations had occurred, he declared, it was "even more unfortunate that the white power structure of this city left the Negro community with no other alternative."[38]

In the midst of the crisis in Birmingham, Kennedy dispatched Burke Marshall, head of the Justice Department's Civil Rights Division, to mediate. Robert Kennedy had appointed Marshall, who had virtually no experience in civil rights law, because he was seen as less threatening to white supremacists. Nonetheless, Marshall became the administration's point person during the African American mass movements of the early 1960s. King wrote in *Why We Can't Wait* that Marshall "did an invaluable job of opening channels of communication between our leadership and the top people in the economic power structure" during negotiations between Birmingham whites and blacks. Marshall helped broker a compromise that desegregated restaurants and provided for the hiring of African Americans but retained the overall segregation of public accommodations.

Birmingham was part of a mass uprising occurring across the urban South against Jim Crow. The attacks in Birmingham, and the violence generally, received national media coverage, while protests spread throughout southern cities in the spring and summer of 1963. During these months, 930 protests erupted in 115 cities in eleven states. Prior to the fall of 1961, 3,600 protesters were arrested; in spring and summer 1963, more than 20,000 arrests occurred. Most of these protests were nonviolent, though the protesters were victims of white violence, with ten people killed and thirty-five bombings occurring.[39]

Under these circumstances, it became impossible for Kennedy not to respond. The president found little cooperation with Alabama officials and Gov. George Wallace, who had sent in state police against the demonstrators. After Wallace refused to permit the court-ordered admission of two black students to the University of Alabama, Kennedy dispatched national guardsmen to enforce the order. On June 11, 1963, Kennedy became the first president in American history to endorse strong federal intervention in civil rights. Recalling the hundredth anniversary of the Emancipation Proclamation, he declared that the heirs of American slaves were "not yet freed from the bonds of injustice. They are not yet freed from social and economic oppression." The "heart of the question," he said, was whether black people could "enjoy the full and free life which all of us enjoy." Delay no longer worked. The federal courts had already intervened, as had the presidency. Now what was required was congressional intervention and a strong civil rights act assuring the "elementary right" of equal access to public accommodations, education, and voting rights.[40]

---

[38] "Letter from Birmingham Jail"; available at https://kinginstitute.stanford.edu/king-papers/documents/letter-birmingham-jail.

[39] Carson, *In Struggle*, 90.

[40] Text of Kennedy speech, June 11, 1963; available at http://www.americanrhetoric.com/speeches/jfkcivilrights.htm.

Later that summer, in August 1963, King and his allies organized a March on Washington campaign, which brought 200,000 civil rights supporters to the National Mall. In 1941, A. Philip Randolph had planned a similar march but was dissuaded by FDR when the president promised to adopt antidiscrimination measures in federal employment. Now a second march, urged on by Randolph and organized by Bayard Rustin, involved diverse civil rights groups such as SNCC, NAACP, SCLC, and CORE. The march's main objective was to press for adoption of federal civil rights legislation. King's "I Have a Dream Speech" attracted the most attention, and in many ways the march represented a high point of the movement. Unhappy with the Kennedy administration, SNCC remained determined to keep the pressure up for further changes and a strong policy of federal intervention.

FREEDOM SUMMER

The Civil Rights Act was enacted in July 1964, about seven months after the assassination of John F. Kennedy. Notably, from the South only 7 of 104 congressmen and one of twenty-two senators voted in favor of the measure. The law was arguably the most consequential in American history. It required an immediate end to the most-obnoxious forms of public segregation in schools and accommodations. Committing federal intervention in local and state affairs to enforce this edict, the law prohibited state and local governments from prohibiting access to public facilities because of race, national origin, and religion, and it banned discrimination in public accommodations. Empowering the Justice Department to initiate suits to desegregate the public schools, the Civil Rights Act also denied funding to any government entity practicing discrimination. The law also outlawed discrimination in employment and created an Equal Employment Opportunity Commission to enforce it.

Where the Civil Rights Act was most lacking was in voting rights. Title I of the act, dealing with voting rights, provided little federal protection. Nor did it empower federal officials to assume a proactive stance in encouraging African American enfranchisement and officeholding. Again, SNCC pushed matters and forced further federal action. Since 1961, SNCC had organized voter registration efforts in the Deep South, including southwestern Georgia and central Mississippi, headed by Charles Sherrod and Robert Moses, respectively. SNCC's approach was democratic: they entered communities intent on empowering local leaders to develop leadership.

Predictably, SNCC met determined and often-violent resistance. They had little faith in the Kennedy administration's willingness to protect them. "If we are murdered in our attempts," declared Sherrod in January 1963, "our blood will be on your hands; you stand in the judgment of God and of our people."[41] During the next year, SNCC pushed things further in Mississippi, where perhaps the greatest danger of white violence existed. Just as Birmingham symbolized a citadel of urban segregation,

---

[41] Carson, *In Struggle*, 85.

Mississippi best represented a state most committed to maintaining white supremacy. Between 1961 and 1963, SNCC documented 150 instances of violence against
civil rights workers. Nearly all of these were perpetrated against black people, with
little government response. A key part of SNCC's strategy was to recruit northern
white student volunteers in their organizing activities. The presence of white activists
provided some degree of protection, on the theory that national public opinion and
the federal government would be less willing to accept violence against them.

In the fall of 1963, Allard Lowenstein, a white activist, recruited about one hundred students from campuses such as Yale and Stanford. Lowenstein and Robert
Moses then recruited more white students during the following summer of 1964.
Moses and other SNCC leaders believed that by forcing a crisis on Mississippi, national attention would lead to federal intervention to protect voting rights. The key
to change, according to Moses, was to have "white people working along side of you,
so then it changes the whole complexion of what you're doing, so it isn't Negro fighting white, it's a question of rational people against irrational people." John Lewis
maintained that SNCC's project would so aggravate things that the "Federal Government will have to take over the state."[42]

In an ambitious Summer Project—also known as Freedom Summer—SNCC
helped organize the Mississippi Freedom Democratic Party (MFDP) and launch freedom schools to teach black political consciousness. In late June 1964, three COFO
workers—two of whom were white—disappeared near Philadelphia, Mississippi.
President Lyndon Johnson ordered a massive federal dragnet that eventually produced
their bodies. The dragnet focused attention on the Philadelphia murders at the expense of white intimidation and violence elsewhere. "It's a shame that national concern
is aroused only after two white boys are missing," commented SNCC's Lewis.[43]

African American and White Mississippi Freedom Democratic Party Supporters
Demonstrating outside the 1964 Democratic National Convention, Atlantic City,
New Jersey, photograph by Warren K. Leffler. *Library of Congress.*

[42] Carson, *In Struggle,* 99.
[43] Carson, *In Struggle,* 115.

Having spent the summer in voter registration, MFDP held a statewide convention and elected a slate of delegates to send to the Democratic National Convention (DNC) meeting in August 1964 in Atlantic City, New Jersey. The MFDP asserted that they legitimately represented Mississippi Democrats. COFO leader Fannie Lou Hamer testified at the meeting of the DNC's credentials committee on August 22, 1964. Born in rural Mississippi to a family of twenty children, Hamer grew up in the oppression of sharecropping and white dominance in Sunflower County, Mississippi. She informed the credentials committee about her experiences. Badly beaten while organizing in Winona, Mississippi, in June 1963, Hamer played a key role in Freedom Summer. "All of this is on account of we want to register," she told the committee, "to become first-class citizens." If the MFDP was not seated, she declared, "I question America. Is this America, the land of the free and the home of the brave, where we have to sleep with our telephones off of the hooks because our lives be threatened daily, because we want to live as decent human beings, in America?"[44]

Lyndon Johnson, president after the assassination of Kennedy in November 1963, immediately made enactment of a new civil rights act a top priority. Because of his legislative abilities, the bill overcame southern opposition in Congress and became law in July 1964. The Atlantic City convention was scheduled to serve as a coronation event for Johnson and his reelection campaign; he did not want the MFDP to alienate southern white support. Johnson's forces forged a compromise in which two MFDP delegates, one black and one white (Aaron Henry and Ed King), were seated while the rest of the delegation was permitted to attend as nonvoting guests. The MFDP rejected the compromise and split the COFO coalition, convinced that Johnson had betrayed them. Meanwhile, the all-white delegation did little to prevent Republican candidate Barry Goldwater from carrying Mississippi in November 1964.

In the aftermath of Johnson's landslide victory in the presidential election, a large congressional coalition existed to push through the president's remaining civil rights agenda. Again, activists pushed things along at the local level. Alabama, like other Deep South states, had stiffly resisted registering African Americans, and only 23 percent of the black electorate was enfranchised.[45] In Selma, Alabama, SNCC had already been active in voter registration beginning in 1963, with the resulting creation of the Dallas County Voters League. After the SNCC campaign stalled, the SCLC entered the scene. King was at the height of his powers, having triumphed over Bull Connor and white supremacy in Birmingham and having received the Nobel Peace Prize in October 1964. Selma became what Birmingham had been two years earlier—another citadel of white oppression that could be publicized nationally to rally public opinion. On March 7, 1965, the SCLC and six

[44] Fannie Lou Hamer, testimony before DNC credentials committee, August 22, 1964; available at http://www.americanrhetoric.com/speeches/fannielouhamercredentialscommittee.htm.
[45] Lawson, *Running for Freedom*, 108.

Selma to Montgomery March, 1965. *Library of Congress.*

hundred protesters began a fifty-mile march from Selma to Montgomery, Alabama's capital. Outside Selma, as they attempted to cross the Alabama River on the Edmund Pettus Bridge, the marchers were brutally attacked by Alabama state troopers and Selma police. After the attack another march occurred a few weeks later, but the damage for white supremacists had been done. Public opinion overwhelmingly supported strong voting-rights legislation; one opinion poll measured support at 76 percent nationally.[46]

On March 15, 1965, Johnson proposed legislation, the Voting Rights Act, that suspended literacy tests and other disfranchising measures in seven targeted southern states with a long history of voting discrimination and gave the president, through the Justice Department, power to require prior approval of changes in voting in these states. Enacted in August 1965, the law enfranchised thousands of new black voters and made possible the most-significant changes in southern politics

Lyndon Johnson and civil rights leaders after the signing of the Voting Right Act. *Public domain.*

[46] Lawson, *Running for Freedom*, 118.

since Reconstruction. At the same time, it prompted the beginning of a massive defection of whites from the Democratic Party and the growth of a conservative Republican Party in the region and the nation.

Federal intervention in civil rights proved decisive in ending the segregation of public spaces in transportation and public accommodations and in reestablishing a right to vote among African Americans. The promise of the *Brown* decision to end segregation also gained momentum, though the details of how to accomplish it— and what it meant—continued to prove elusive. The accomplishments of the civil rights movement did not mean the end of racial oppression, however. Black poverty, crime, and discrimination continued, though the issue of how to rectify these evils became much more complex than ending the segregation of public accommodations. In addition, with the migration of millions of southern blacks to urban communities around the country, race had become a national issue, no longer something unique to the South.

23

SOUTHERN SUNBELT

IN THE EMERGING REPUBLICAN MAJORITY (1969), political strategist Kevin Phillips described how the election of Richard Nixon in 1968 anticipated a new political coalition. Phillips predicted that voters, rejecting New Deal liberalism and favoring limited government, would make the Republican Party into a majority for the next generation. Anchoring this coalition, Phillips contended, was the South, historically a bastion of Democratic control. Predicting the defection of rural voters to Republican ranks, he also saw a crucial role for what he called the "Sunbelt." "Devoid of Northeastern-type heavy industry, aggressively middle-class rather than stratified along European and Northeastern lines," Phillips wrote, the new cities of the Sunbelt "mushroomed as their Megalopolitan forebears began to stagnate and decay." From St. Petersburg retirees to the "air-conditioned affluence of Dallas," a new urban world connected people living in the urban South, Southern California, and Arizona.[1]

Mid-twentieth-century southerners were on the move, with millions of white and African American southerners departing rural communities and heading to cities. Rimmed by expanding suburbs, a southern Sunbelt emerged during the late twentieth century in cities such as Charlotte, Atlanta, Miami, Houston, and Dallas—communities much like cities such as Las Vegas, Phoenix, and Los Angeles. The rise of these communities reflected the decline of the traditional southern social system. The plantation system, dominating the southern economy for more than three centuries, all but disappeared, replaced by a highly mechanized, less labor-intensive agricultural system. A new, modernized transportation system spurred the further reach of market capitalism.

---

[1] Kevin Phillips, _The Emerging Republican Majority_ (New Rochelle, NY: Arlington House, 1969), 273–274.

Just as the South formed an important part of the emerging Sunbelt, it also proved crucial in the late-twentieth-century realignment of American politics. The civil rights movement, and the reaction of whites to it, created a ripple effect politically. The national Democratic Party, supporters of the Civil Rights and Voting Rights Acts, lost support among southern whites. In the aftermath of *Brown*, federal courts required school desegregation, further alienating white Democrats and driving the Republican resurgence. Race was not the only factor at work, however. The economic transformation of the South, the rise of suburbs, and the changing demographic landscape created a new dynamic in southern politics.

THE SUNBELT SOUTH

The Sunbelt South reflected narrowing regional differences. The long-standing disparity in per capita income in the South compared to the rest of the country shrank to 94 percent of the national average in 2000, as compared to 52 percent in 1930. Attracting migrants during the second half of the twentieth century, the South saw significant population changes. In 1980 about a fifth of southerners were born outside the region—the highest percentage since the end of the colonial era. The South's share of the national population grew from 24 percent in 1950 to 30 percent fifty years later. The growth of the postwar South was focused especially in urban centers, as the percentage of southerners living in cities grew from 37 percent in 1940 to 70 percent four decades later.

The rise of the Sunbelt South depended on an important technological innovation: the availability of air conditioning. Making hot southern summers cool

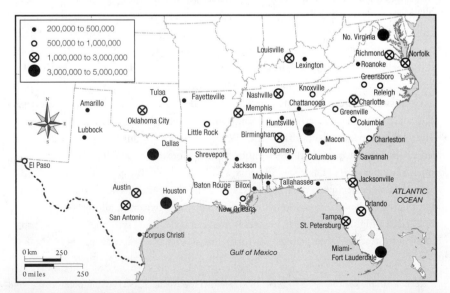

MAP 23.1 Metropolitan Centers in South, 2000

Sheet music celebrating air conditioning in Sarasota, Florida, 1949. *University of South Florida Library.*

proved indispensable in encouraging migration and economic development. First developed in the 1920s, air conditioning, except for in movie theaters, hotel ballrooms, banks, trains, and buses, remained mostly unavailable until after 1945. Until the 1980s, most southern homes lacked air conditioning—only 3 percent had it in 1950, rising to 18 percent in 1960. The number of air-conditioned homes thereafter accelerated, with two-fifths of new construction in 1960 having central air conditioning. By 1980, nearly three-quarters of southern residences were air-conditioned. "Can you see a Honeywell or Sperry or anyone else opening a big plant where their workers would have to spend their time mopping their brows and cursing mosquitos," quipped a southern columnist.[2] Metropolitan areas—Atlanta, Miami, Dallas, Nashville, and Charlotte—all came to depend on the ability to escape the South's hot summers.

As one historian writes: "General Electric has proved a more devastating invader than General Sherman. As long as air conditioning," he continues, "abetted by immigration, urbanization, and broad technological change, continues to make inroads, the South's distinctive character will continue to diminish, never to rise again."[3]

Along with Texas, Florida also experienced spectacular growth after 1940. Long sparsely populated, mid-twentieth-century Florida had large, unspoiled water resources and a rural and mostly dispersed population, with most people living in the northern third of the state. "I should think Florida was nine-tenths waters," wrote one visitor, "and the other tenth swamp."[4] During World War II, the infusion of federal funds and the location of training camps and bases spurred a long-lasting transformation. After the war, returning veterans relocated to Florida or later retired there. During the fifty years prior to 1980, Florida's population grew from around 1.5 million to 10 million, an increase of 564 percent. The state continued to grow during the next thirty years, and by 2010 nearly 19 million people lived in the state.

[2] Raymond Arsenault, "The End of the Long Hot Summer: The Air Conditioner and Southern Culture," *Journal of Southern History* 50, no. 4 (November 1984): 610–611, 619.

[3] Arsenault, "Long Hot Summer," 628.

[4] Raymond Arsenault and Gary R. Mormino, "From Dixie to Dreamland: Demographic and Cultural Change in Florida, 1880–1980," in *Shades of the Sunbelt: Essays on Ethnicity, Race and the Urban South,* ed. Randall M. Miller and George E. Pozzetta (Westport, CT: Greenwood, 1988), 163.

Much of this growth resulted from migration. Between 1950 and 2010, sixteen million people moved to Florida, making it, along with Texas and California, among the fastest-growing states in the Union. By 1980, more than two-thirds of Florida's residents were born outside the state. Most migrants settled in the state's southern two-thirds, with midwestern transplants populating the southwestern portion of the state and northeasterners moving to the southeastern part. Overall, by the end of the twentieth century, nine out of ten Floridians lived in urban communities—the most urban state in the Union except for California. During the 1980s, half of the twenty fastest-growing communities in the United States were in the state, including the metropolitan regions of Miami, Tampa–St. Pete, Orlando, and Jacksonville.

Visitors to Florida were attracted to the state's natural beauty and warm climate. During the late nineteenth century, glass-bottomed boats transported visitors down Florida's rivers. Beginning in the 1890s, a tourist industry emerged, with the construction of modern hotels such as the Ponce de Leon in St. Augustine. Miami Beach and its surrounding areas later became popular wintertime tourist destinations. The tourism industry fueled Florida's growth after 1945, as the warm weather and deliberately created cultural fantasy of palms, leisure, and perpetual sunshine became trademarks. The numbers of tourists visiting the state grew from 1 million in 1930 to 2.8 million ten years later. This number rose to 20 million in 1980, 40 million in 1990, and 87 million in 2011. The top tourist destination in the world, Florida's revenues from visitors grew from $32 billion in 1990 to $67 billion in 2011.[5] In addition, Florida saw increased numbers of longer-term "snowbirds" who resided in the state during cold-weather months. By 2003, a million snowbirds took up temporary residence in the state.

The biggest single boon to tourism, Disney World, first opened in 1971 in Orlando. Following the success of his Disneyland theme park in Southern California, entertainment impresario Walt Disney wanted to expand to an East Coast location. While Disneyland was located on eighty landlocked acres in Anaheim, California, Disney World would become its own community. Secretly assembling small parcels, Disney managed to purchase more than 27,000 acres of central Florida land, much of it orange groves. Disney gained extraordinary rights that essentially placed Disney World outside the control of local government, what one observer called "a sort of Vatican with Mouse ears: a city-state within the larger state of Florida."[6] Other Disney theme parks opened in the same tract of land—EPCOT in 1982, Disney/MGM Studios in 1989, Disney Animal Kingdom in 1998—drawing more tourists to central Florida. In addition, the Orlando area became home to non-Disney attractions such as Universal

[5] Raymond A. Mohl and Gary R. Mormino, "The Big Change in the Sunshine State: A Social History of Modern Florida," in *The New History of Florida*, ed. Michael Gannon (Gainesville: University Press of Florida, 1996), 436–437; available at http://www.stateofflorida.com/Portal/DesktopDefault.aspx?tabid=95.

[6] Gary R. Mormino, *Land of Sunshine, State of Dreams: A Social History of Modern Florida* (Gainesville: University Press of Florida, 2005), 103.

Florida Visitors Sampling Some
Florida Orange Juice at the
Highlands Hotel—Ocala, Florida,
1950. *State Archives of Florida.*

Studios and SeaWorld. By 2013, nearly fifty-nine million people visited the Orlando area.

The opening of Walt Disney World remade Orlando from an important midsize city into a major metropolitan area. The rise of the sleek Disney resorts eclipsed the family-run attractions that had dotted Florida's landscape since the 1930s. More visitors flew into Orlando International Airport, which by 2004 had become the busiest airport in the state. Central Florida underwent a decades-long land boom that transformed the largely rural counties of orange groves and cattle pastures into tract homes and shopping malls, ringed by interstate highways. By 2010, the Orlando area claimed a population of 2.1 million people, in an economy almost entirely dependent on tourism and visitors.

Many of the post-1945 migrants to Florida were retirees, arriving in droves because of the warm climate. Longer life spans and the existence of Social Security and pension funds enabled thousands of retirees to move to the state. Large tracts of new homes were constructed in the state, as well as retirement communities. Florida also claimed more mobile homes than any other state—some 760,000 in the 1990s. Florida retirees were concentrated in South Florida counties: Charlotte County, in southwestern Florida, counted about 35 percent of its population as senior in 2010. The median age of Floridians rose from eighteen in 1880 to thirty-six in 1990. At the same time, while only 2 percent of the state's residents were older than sixty-five in 1880, that percentage grew to 18 percent by 2012.[7] The retiree population grew by 70 percent during the 1970s and 40 percent during the 1980s. In 2000, of the ten cities nationally with the highest proportion of seniors, six were in Florida. Three million state residents collected Social Security checks in 1990.[8]

Beacon Hotel in Miami
Beach, Florida, 1959. *State
Archives of Florida.*

Florida, in the post-1945 era, was also on the leading edge of a new, multicultural South. In the early twentieth century, the state's population was overwhelmingly

7 Mohl and Mormino, "The Big Change," 423; available at http://quickfacts.census.gov/qfd/
   states/12000.html.
8 National Institute on Aging, "Dramatic Changes in U.S. Aging Highlighted in New Census,"
   March 9, 2006; available at http://www.nia.nih.gov/newsroom/2006/03/dramatic-changes-us-
   aging-highlighted-new-census-nih-report.

southern-born white and black. In the 1950s, an important new migration took place with the arrival of thousands of Jewish migrants to South Florida, many of them retirees. Miami became an important center of Jewish life, and the city ranked second only to New York City in the percentage of its population that was Jewish (almost 9 percent). The state became one of the leading recipients of Latin American immigrants; the percentage in the state that was Latino grew from less than 1 percent to 22.5 percent between 1945 and 2010. Like the rest of the South, Florida experienced the migration of rural African Americans to cities or outside the state, and the proportion of the state that was black declined from about 30 percent in 1930 to about 14 percent in 1990. But that percentage grew, reaching 17 percent statewide in 2010. Florida attracted black migrants; most African Americans leaving Georgia between 1880 and 1960 moved to Florida. Historically, black migrants from the Bahamas had composed a portion of South Florida's population. Other Caribbean migrants had been part of the populations of Miami, Key West, Tampa, and Jacksonville. The phenomenon also increased during the late twentieth century. Overall, the state's black population grew from 432,000 in 1930, to 1.3 million in 1980, and to about 3 million in 2010.

Miami became a center of nonwhite immigration, with 52 percent of Miami-Dade's population Latino in 2004. Until about 1960, the proportion of the city's population that was foreign born remained under about a tenth of the total. Then,

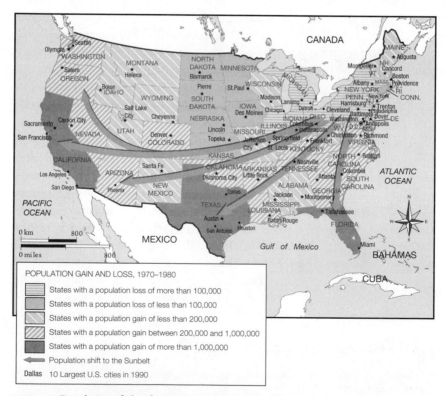

MAP 23.2 Population of Florida, 2000

between 1959 and the 1990s, about 1.2 million Cubans migrated to South Florida. After 1959, when Fidel Castro came to power as a result of the Cuban Revolution, hundreds of thousands of middle-class Cubans moved to South Florida. During the Cuban Missile Crisis, this first wave of immigration ended, but then a second wave occurred after 1965. Miami was transformed into a Cuban enclave with a Little Havana as its cultural center. Between April and October 1980, after Castro announced that he would permit departures, a third migration of 125,000 Cubans occurred, mostly working class and poorer. This was supplemented by the arrival of about 100,000 Haitian refugees during the 1970s and 1980s, along with another, fourth wave of Cuban immigrants arriving in a massive boatlift originating from the Cuban port of Mariel (the refugees became known as *Marielitos*). The *Marielito* exodus included 20,000 Cubans released from prison and mental hospitals. Later, in 1991–1994, in a fifth immigration wave, the *Balsero* (or rafter) crisis resulted in the arrival by makeshift rafts of 230,000 more Cubans.

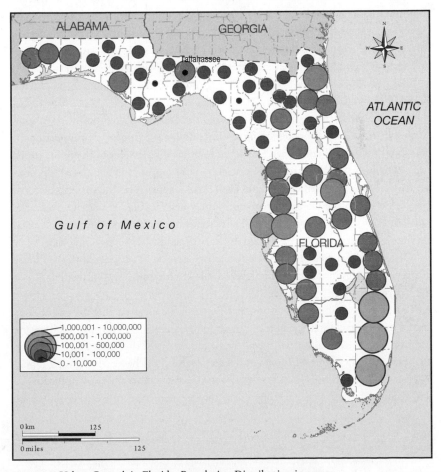

MAP 23.3 Urban Growth in Florida: Population Distribution in 2000

THE ROLE OF GOVERNMENT

The rise of the Sunbelt South resulted from public policies as well as market economic forces. World War II military expenditures stimulated southern economic development; after the war, federal dollars continued to pour in. After the war, federal expenditures became a significant force in the remaking of the South. "Our economy is no longer agricultural," novelist William Faulkner commented in 1956. "Our economy is the Federal Government."[9] A key part of federal investment came in defense installations and industries. During the 1950s alone, the proportion of defense dollars that was spent in the South increased from 7 percent to 15 percent of the national total. By 1980, this figure had grown to a quarter of the total.

Defense expenditures fueled modern southern economic growth, accounting for as much as a fifth of income growth in Mississippi, Florida, Georgia, Alabama, and Texas during the 1950s. Military spending generated a tenth of personal income in the South by 1955. The number of southern workers employed in defense industries was greater than that of the leading industries of synthetics, apparel, and textiles combined. Based in Marietta, Georgia, Lockheed became a major employer throughout Georgia, spending hundreds of millions of dollars and employing numerous workers in the aeronautics industry. Defense industries developed into the most important employer in four southern states by the 1970s, with large corporations such as Rockwell, Lockheed, McDonnell-Douglas, and General Dynamics employing thousands of southern workers.[10]

That federal defense expenditures favored the South reflected political realities. With southern congressmen enjoying seniority and occupying key committee chairmanships, millions of dollars were directed to home districts. From the 1940s to the 1970s, Democratic domination of southern politics meant long tenures, and powerful seniority, for key southern congressmen. Mississippi's John Stennis, first elected in 1947, served in the US Senate for forty-one years. During his last eight years, he was that body's most senior member. For eleven years, he chaired the Senate Armed Services Committee, where he steered military expenditures to his home state.

Other southern congressmen were equally successful. First elected to the House of Representatives in 1940, L. Mendel Rivers of Charleston, South Carolina, served the district for nearly three decades and was for many years chair of the House Armed Services Committee. From that position, he ensured that federal dollars flowed to his home district, including an air force base, a naval shipyard, a submarine training station, a naval hospital, and the headquarters of the Sixth Naval District, all located in Charleston. Military contractors such as Lockheed, McDonnell-Douglas, and General Electric all set up shop in the Charleston area. Rivers, according to one account, "transmogrified Charleston into a microcosm of military-industrial

---

[9] Schulman, *From Cotton Belt to Sunbelt* , 135.
[10] Schulman, *From Cotton Belt to Sunbelt*, 139–143; James C. Cobb, *The South and America since World War II* (New York: Oxford University Press, 2011), 62.

civilization." As much as a third of Charleston's income and half of its employment was defense related.[11]

Southerners tended to be the most promilitary region in the country, even during the antiwar era of the Vietnam War. Southerners in Congress ensured that federal defense dollars were spent in their home states. Congressmen such as South Carolina's James F. Byrnes and senators such as William Fulbright of Arkansas became important figures in foreign policy. Similarly, Rep. Carl Vinson of Georgia, who preceded Rivers as chair of the House Armed Services Committee, and Georgia senator Richard Russell were big supporters of the military who steered contracts to their states.

The national effort to improve missile technology resulted in federal funds benefiting southern communities. Huntsville, in northern Alabama, was a small textile town until World War II changed things. During the 1950s, Huntsville's population grew from 16,000 to 72,000, and, during the next decade, it doubled. The town's explosive growth reflected military expenditures. The US Army established its missile research program at Redstone Ordnance Plant at Huntsville in 1941. Eight years later, the Huntsville missile facility underwent a huge expansion. In 1950, German rocket scientists such as Werner von Braun, who had worked on Nazi ballistic technology during wartime, were relocated to Redstone as part of a new missile program. Huntsville's missile program was closely connected to the early space program. In 1960, the George Marshall Space Center was established in Huntsville, along with, a year later, the Huntsville Research Institute. The concentration of federally supported research facilities attracted new industry; both IBM and Rockwell established industrial parks in Huntsville in 1964–1965.

Many southern congressmen saw space technology as a tool to modernize the South into a high-tech region. The National Aeronautics and Space Administration (NASA), established in 1958, located five of nine important facilities in the South, including those in Cape Canaveral, Florida; the mission control center in

Mission Control on the first day of the Apollo 10 lunar orbit mission. *Public domain.*

[11] Schulman, *From Cotton Belt to Sunbelt,* 146.

Houston, Texas; the Michoud Assembly plant in New Orleans; and a testing plant in Bay St. Louis, Mississippi. In 1949, Congress created a long-range proving ground at Cape Canaveral, which became known two years later as the Florida Missile Test Range. After 1959, the 88,000-acre tract provided launching pads for the space program. This massive complex remade Broward County, attracting migrants along with federal investment in the area.

Houston benefited especially from federal largesse in the space program. The Manned Spacecraft Center (later the Lyndon B. Johnson Space Center), established in Houston in September 1961, was constructed on land provided by Rice University. The nerve center of manned flight, the space center proved crucial for Houston's growth, attracting twenty-nine new companies to the city within a year of its establishment. The arrival of the space center helped make Houston into an economic center of the Southern Sunbelt. During the 1960s and 1970s, Houston became an important metropolis and the center of the energy industry. During the oil boom of 1979, the city gained 79,000 jobs and 1,000 new inhabitants a week. Between 1971 and 1978, ninety-nine firms set up new operations in the city. Also buoyed by the oil and gas industry, Texas experienced rapid growth. During the first half of the 1970s, the state saw its nonfarm employment grow by more than Massachusetts, Michigan, Illinois, and Ohio combined.

The construction of a national interstate system provides yet another example of the way in which federal investment spurred change. In 1916 and 1922, federal highway acts provided appropriations to the states to build a numbered system of primary roads. Prior to the 1950s, however, county and state governments shouldered a large share of construction costs. Even as late as the 1940s, federal contributions were limited to a one-to-one basis. As early as the late 1930s a nationally integrated superhighway system was contemplated. Originally conceived in the 1930s, the Federal Highway Defense Act of 1956, championed by Texas senator Lyndon B. Johnson, created a new funding basis in which 90 percent of funds for the construction of a new interstate highway system came from the federal government. Spreading across the nation during the next thirty-five years, interstate highways especially benefited interior cities such as Atlanta, Charlotte, and Nashville, spurring suburbanization. At the same time, the spread of superhighways tore flourishing black neighborhoods apart, with negative economic and social consequences. The importance of the interstate system, most of which was constructed between the 1950s and 1990s, cannot be underestimated.

Federal subsidization of airport construction also benefited the South, spurring urbanization and growth of air-freight hubs. As was true elsewhere in the country, federal highways and airports encouraged urban sprawl, with economic activity spreading from the original urban core. Federal housing policies, such as urban renewal efforts and the razing of downtown residential and business districts, also encouraged the decline of the urban core. Cities added to urban and suburban sprawl by aggressive annexation campaigns. In Texas, the state legislature enacted legislation permitting widespread annexation by Houston, San Antonio, and Dallas. Similarly, Charlotte and Memphis extended their city limits by annexation. In 1967, Jacksonville, Florida, became the largest geographical city in the country by annexing most of the surrounding Duval County.

No better example of the changes affecting the Sunbelt South exists than the metropolis of Atlanta. The population within its city limits expanded from 270,000 in 1930 to a peak of 497,000 in 1970. Much of this resulted from aggressive annexation and the extension of city limits. Although annexation proved unpopular among the annexed sections because of higher taxes and congestion, popular opposition did not stop Atlanta's urban promoters. Metropolitan growth relied on an aggressive class of boosters, who promoted their cities and, controlling the local governments, pursued progrowth public policies. In 1951, city boosters persuaded the Georgia legislature to enact a "Plan of Improvement" that annexed more than eight square miles, increasing the size of the city by three times and incorporating 100,000 people within the city limits.

Atlanta solidified its position as the most important city of the post-1945 South by constructing highways that connected to major markets. The city also built the most ambitiously conceived airport in the Southeast, which by the 1970s established Atlanta as a key hub in the national air transportation system. By 2014, it ranked as the world's busiest airport, with nearly thirty million passengers using the facility annually. No one better exemplified this booster spirit—and that of other Sunbelt cities—than Mayor William B. Hartsfield. First elected in 1936, Hartsfield served six terms until his retirement in 1961, the longest-serving mayor in Atlanta's history. Centralizing power over municipal government by diminishing the traditional alderman and ward system of city government, Hartsfield established an alliance with local businessmen to promote Atlanta.

A relentless booster, Hartsfield also espoused racial moderation. He favored making Atlanta into a city "too busy to hate" by favoring gradualism. Civil rights protesters were dealt with by accommodation and compromise rather than confrontation. Hartsfield and other boosters realized that economic development in the mid-twentieth-century South depended on outside investors' confidence in racial stability. When a federal court ordered the desegregation of the city's golf courses in 1955, for example, Hartsfield enforced the edict during the Christmas holiday, when the public's attention would be diverted. In 1961, the city adopted a policy of token integration in its public schools rather than resist federal intervention. Atlanta's physical expansion ended by 1960, at least within its city limits. Urban growth, especially after 1970, became focused in suburbs springing up in surrounding counties. Meanwhile, "white flight" drained white residents from within city limits to nearby suburbs. Atlanta's population decreased, falling from 497,000 to 420,000 residents between 1970 and 2010, while the suburban population steadily increased from 715,000 in 1930 to 5.7 million in 2010.

State-run campaigns promoting economic development through outside investment and relocation of industry constituted another important form of public policy. These efforts involved simple salesmanship, but often they also required public subsidies through direct appropriations of state-guaranteed industrial bonds. By the early 1960s, nine states in the South operated industrial bonding programs. Increasingly popular, as well, was the use of tax exemptions for industries that relocated. In the mid-1960s, of the seven states using tax exemptions for industrial relocation, five were in the South. Very often boosters used other forms of state subsidies to stimulate outside investment, partnering with state-run development agencies. City- and county-level industrial-development organizations also worked hard, offering local incentives or seeking state ones. Development agencies by the 1960s were becoming slick, well-financed, and sophisticated operations. During the 1950s and 1960s, governors such as North Carolina's Luther Hodges, Florida's Leroy Collins, and South Carolina's Ernest Hollings served as salesmen for their states, traveling nationally and internationally. Often, industrial recruiters advertised the main advantages of the South in abundant land, favorable climate, looser state regulation, and, above all, cheap nonunion labor. "Our workers are Americans," announced a Louisville recruiter. "They talk and think American."[12]

Hodges, who became governor of North Carolina in 1955, successfully marshaled state resources, using the advantages of the state's public and private universities. Hodges's most lasting achievement was the creation of the Research Triangle Park (RTP) near Raleigh, North Carolina. Drawing on the ideas of a Greensboro contractor, Hodges established a Governor's Research Triangle Committee to help start a new, public-private enterprise to attract outside investors. In 1957, RTP acquired four thousand acres of pine forest near the Raleigh-Durham airport. Working with Winston-Salem banker and booster Archie Davis, Hodges arranged financing from philanthropists and corporate foundations to establish the research park as a nonprofit enterprise. The RTP Foundation sponsored the creation of the Research Triangle Institute in order to recruit technology-dependent industries. Hodges, university educators, and North Carolina industrialists worked hard to sell the RTP concept to outside investors.

The Research Triangle project eventually proved one of the most successful of the state-supported efforts at industrial recruitment. Three local universities—the University of North Carolina at Chapel Hill, North Carolina State College (later University), and Duke University—provided an attractive research infrastructure. The presence of the RTP also greatly enhanced and reinforced the universities' prestige, and in the 1970s the region became the most PhD-intensive of any in the country. RTP attracted new industry, making Raleigh-Durham into one of the fastest-growing regions of the late-twentieth-century South. By 1977, twenty-two research facilities were established in the park, including corporate giant IBM's manufacturing facility, established in the mid-1960s. Federal research offices also located in the park, including the Environmental Protection Agency's main research facility, which opened in 2001.

[12] James C. Cobb, *The Selling of the South: The Southern Crusade for Industrial Development, 1936–1990*, 2d ed. (Urbana: University of Illinois Press, 1993), 92.

As early as the 1950s, state industrial recruiters worked hard to lure foreign investors. Their efforts paid off. In the 1970s, the South was attracting about half of US foreign industrial investment, as overseas industrialists were drawn to the nonunion, low-tax, lenient regulatory environment. South Carolina garnered 40 percent of industrial investment from abroad by the late 1970s. Spartanburg, in the South Carolina upcountry, succeeded in attracting twenty-four foreign companies by the mid-1970s. In 1992, German automobile manufacturer BMW established a plant in Spartanburg, adding to the city's success at wooing other German firms.

Gov. Ernest Hollings, who was elected in 1958, became an avid industrial recruiter of overseas firms. In 1961, Hollings toured Europe in search of new investment, emphasizing to his audience his state's dynamic market, cheap and abundant labor, and superior transportation facilities. The governor expanded the state's development board, increasing staff from five to fifteen and doubling its budget. He also led an effort to expand the state's technical-education program through the community colleges, as part of an effort to upgrade the labor force. Hollings and state officials worked closely with local businessmen and boosters in a coordinated campaign to attract industry. During this period, the role of state governments grew also with the expansion of public universities, many of which expanded into much-larger, multicampus state systems. The growth of higher education received the support of southern political leaders such as Hodges and Hollings, who saw a connection between economic growth and expanded access to college-level education.

THE BREAKDOWN OF ONE-PARTY RULE

Since 1900, the southern Democratic Party had controlled elections and office-holding. Anyone possessing political ambitions at the state and local levels became a Democrat. Winning the party's nominating primary became tantamount to election; general elections were rarely competitive. Unlike the rest of the modern democratic world, wrote political scientist V. O. Key in 1949, the South had "no political parties—at least as we have defined them." Although general elections fostered the fiction of party competition, Key argued, the Democratic Party served as a "holding company for a congeries of transient squabbling factions, most of which fail by far to meet the standards of permanence, cohesiveness, and responsibility that characterize the political party."[13]

By the 1970s, this pattern was in flux. The Republican Party, writer Kirkpatrick Sale observed in 1976, was formed in the mid-nineteenth century "to transform the South." During the post-1945 era, Republicans abandoned these goals. Instead, now it was the case that the South had "transformed the Republican Party." In one of the "most far-reaching changes in any political party in recent times," Republicans no

[13] V. O. Key Jr., *Southern Politics in State and Nation* (New York: A. A. Knopf, 1949), 16.

longer relied on an industrial northeastern and midwestern political base. Instead, the party depended on the votes of southern whites.[14]

Two factors eventually eroded Democratic dominance. First, the civil rights era enfranchised large numbers of African American voters. A large majority voted Democratic mostly because of the national party's pro-civil-rights identification. With many white voters uneasy about the end of white supremacy, the reenfranchisement of African Americans led to defections of conservative Democrats to Republican ranks. Second, in a broad structural change, the rise of Sunbelt suburbs gradually upset the political equilibrium. Suburban voters, many of them northern urban immigrants, favored the low-tax, minimalist government policies of the modern Republican Party. Although there were significant signs of these changes, they did not become potent factors until the 1970s. In most southern states, Republican candidates were unable to win statewide elections until after 1972. Thereafter, the party infrastructure at the local level remained weak, preventing a full mobilization of Republican power until the 1980s and 1990s.

No single politician drew more on white backlash to the civil rights era than George Corley Wallace. Born in Clio, Alabama, in 1919, Wallace attended the University of Alabama, where he worked his way through college and then law school in part by boxing professionally (he had been a state Golden Gloves champion), working as a waiter, and driving a taxi. Serving in World War II, Wallace was elected state legislator and local judge. In 1958, he ran for the Democratic nomination for governor but lost to John Patterson, who made opposing integration the primary issue. Criticized for softness on the race issue, Wallace supposedly informed a campaign aide: "I was out-niggered, and I will never be out-niggered again." Running for governor again and winning in 1962, Wallace remade himself into an avid segregationist. "There's some people who've gone over the state and said, 'Well, George Wallace has talked too strong about segregation,'" he said in one speech. "Now let me ask you this: how in the name of common sense can you be too strong about it? You're either for it or you're against it. There's not any middle ground as I know of."[15]

Elected governor in 1962, Wallace announced in his inaugural address in January 1963 that he would support "segregation now, segregation tomorrow, segregation forever." Subsequently, Wallace fought federal efforts to integrate the University of Alabama, while he opposed civil rights activists in Birmingham, Selma, and Montgomery. In June 1963, in an act of pure political theater, Wallace blocked the entrance of two black students to the university. The "unwelcomed, unwanted, unwarranted and force-induced intrusion upon the campus of the University of Alabama," he announced, represented the "might of the Central Government" and a "frightful example of the oppression of the rights, privileges and sovereignty of this State by officers of the Federal Government." Wallace asserted

[14] Kirkpatrick Sale, *Power Shift: The Rise of the Southern Rim and Its Challenge to the Eastern Establishment* (New York: Vintage, 1976), 109.

[15] Wallace Quotes; available at http://www.pbs.org/wgbh/amex/wallace/sfeature/quotes.html.

that federal intervention was unconstitutional, "in violation of rights reserved to the State by the Constitution of the United States and the Constitution of the State of Alabama."[16]

Wallace's support for white supremacy had a constitutional basis: federal intervention, he contended, represented the excessive power of the national government. States' rights became the rallying cry for national opposition to civil rights intervention, but it also embraced wider fears about a large, intrusive government. Though Wallace's actions were symbolic, they made him into a national figure—a symbol of resistance to civil rights and the national liberal state. Within weeks of his stand in the schoolhouse door, he received 100,000 letters and telegrams of support, half originating from outside the South. A national audience opposed to the federalization of civil rights policy, it appeared, had now come into existence.

Wallace tied changes in civil rights with social disorder and rising crime. The source of social decline, he argued, lay with liberalism and left-wing elitists and subversives. The Civil Rights Act, he declared in one speech, meant that federal authorities would "destroy the homogeneous neighborhood and dictate who you shall sell your real estate to, who you shall rent a room to, who will be your lease tenant."[17] He informed the Senate Commerce Committee in July 1963 that the civil rights bill before Congress represented a "drift toward centralized socialist control and away from the free enterprise system." Martin Luther King Jr. and civil rights activists, he charged, participated in a larger Communist conspiracy.[18]

In 1964, Wallace took his critique to a national forum in a brief campaign for the Democratic nomination for president. On March 6, 1964, he entered the Wisconsin primary, in a mercurial challenge to incumbent president Lyndon Johnson. Ignoring Wallace, Johnson did not run in the primary, instead allowing surrogates to run as "favorite-son" candidates pledged to his candidacy. Eventually, however, the Wallace campaign in Wisconsin gained traction. Appealing to the working-class ethnic population of Milwaukee, which resented Democratic governor John Reynolds's support for an open-housing law, Wallace denounced civil rights legislation. He criticized the "destruction of property rights" and the "unnatural and unhealthy accumulation of power in the hands of an all-powerful central bureaucracy."[19] On April 1, 1964, he spoke before a wildly enthusiastic Milwaukee crowd, which interrupted him with standing ovations. Wallace promised to "shake the eyeteeth of leaders in both national parties." In Oshkosh, he told an audience "I do not come here to

[16] Wallace, speech, June 11, 1963; available at http://www.archives.state.al.us/govs_list/schooldoor .html.

[17] Gary Donaldson, *Liberalism's Last Hurrah: The Presidential Campaign of 1964* (Armonk, NY: M. E. Sharpe, 2003), 100–101.

[18] Dan T. Carter, *The Politics of Rage: George Wallace, the Origins of the New Conservatism, and the Transformation of American Politics* (Baton Rouge: Louisiana State University Press, 1995), 157–158.

[19] Carter, *Politics of Rage*, 205.

tell you how to handle your local affairs." "Your systems, traditions and ideals are for you to determine."

The results of the April 7, 1964, Wisconsin primary were devastating to mainstream Democrats: Wallace gained 264,000 votes, more than a third of Democratic votes.[20] Wallace followed this up with primary campaigns in Indiana, where he captured 30 percent, and Maryland, where he garnered 43 percent in the largest primary turnout in the history of the state. Wallace actually won a majority of white votes in Maryland. He was overheard by a reporter, saying "If it hadn't been for the nigger bloc vote, we'd have won it all."[21] After rioting in Jacksonville, Florida, in March 1964 and in New York City in July 1964, Wallace's appeals seemed to resonate with working-class white northerners. Because of winner-take-all Democratic primary rules, Wallace gained no delegates to the 1964 nomination. But he sent a powerful message about the power of backlash politics.

In the wake of Wallace's presidential campaign in 1964, Arizona senator Barry Goldwater, the Republican nominee for president, made himself into a vocal opponent of federal civil rights policy. Goldwater's bid for southern white votes followed inroads made by Dwight D. Eisenhower in his presidential campaigns during the 1950s, but the 1964 elections marked the Republican Party's most aggressive effort to win southern votes since Reconstruction. When the US Senate adopted the civil rights bill on June 19, 1964, Goldwater was one of six Republicans voting no. Days earlier, he supported an unsuccessful southern filibuster against the act, along with subsequent attempts to weaken the law by amendments. The law's sections prohibiting racial discrimination in public accommodations, Goldwater declared, would "force you to admit drunks, a known murderer or an insane person into your place of business." Fair employment meant the hiring of "incompetent" workers. The new civil rights bill, Goldwater announced in a Senate speech, was the "hallmark of the police state and a landmark in the destruction of a free society." The Senate had given way to "political demagoguery" and "sledgehammer politics."[22]

Goldwater won the Republican nomination as an insurgent opponent of the New Deal liberal state. To some extent, his nomination served as an ideologically driven conservative rebuke to the Republican moderate establishment. On September 15, Goldwater conducted a tour in southern states where he repeated a new Republican message. Although not overtly racial, he stressed support for state control of civil rights and a greatly reduced role for the national government—coded terms that gave succor to segregationists. Enthusiastic crowds of white supporters greeted him. "Federal power," Goldwater declared in Charlotte, "crushes the concurrent powers of the state in one field or another, until the states have no will, and finally no resources, moral or financial, of their own." Power ought to be shifted to

---

[20] Claude Sitton, "Wallace Presses Wisconsin Drive," *New York Times*, March 22, 1964.
[21] Donaldson, *Liberalism's Last Hurrah*, 143.
[22] Donaldson, *Liberalism's Last Hurrah*, 162; Robert Alan Goldberg, *Barry Goldwater* (New Haven, CT: Yale University Press, 1995), 196–197.

the state and local levels, he said in a speech in Montgomery, Alabama, "where they belong."[23]

Goldwater's candidacy stimulated defections from conservative Democrats. In September 1964, during a Goldwater visit, South Carolina senator Strom Thurmond announced in a speech televised statewide that he was switching his party registration to Republican. Democrats, Thurmond declared, had turned their backs "on the spiritual values and political principles which have brought us the blessings of freedom under God and a bountiful prosperity." Liberalism was leading the country toward a "socialistic dictatorship," he warned. The Goldwater campaign wanted to "return the National Government to its Constitutional role and our nation to its rightful place of strength and respect in the world."[24]

In the end, Goldwater suffered one of the largest electoral defeats in American history. President Lyndon B. Johnson won more than 61 percent of the popular vote and defeated Goldwater in the electoral college by 486 to 52. Goldwater won five Deep South states (South Carolina, Georgia, Alabama, Mississippi, and Louisiana), along with his home state of Arizona. Goldwater's strongest base was the South: he carried Mississippi with 87 percent of the vote and Alabama with 69 percent of the vote. White districts in such cities as Jackson, Mississippi, and Mobile, Alabama, went for Goldwater by close to 90 percent. Of the 507 counties that he won in the South, 233 had never before voted Republican. Seven new Deep South Republican congressmen were elected, with five of them coming from Alabama.

THE POST–CIVIL RIGHTS ERA

The "classic" civil rights movement, spanning the era from the *Brown* decision to the mid-1960s, ended segregation in public accommodations, transportation, and public facilities and reenfranchised thousands of African American voters. The Civil Rights Act ended Jim Crow segregation, declaring that all persons were "entitled to the full and equal enjoyment of the goods, services, facilities, and privileges, advantages, and accommodations of any place of public accommodation, . . . without discrimination or segregation on the ground of race, color, religion, or national origin." Hotels, restaurants, movie theaters—all of which, in the South, commonly provided racially separated facilities or excluded blacks entirely—were prohibited from segregating. According to Title VII of the law, equal employment—including the employment of women—also became law, leading to the eventual establishment of the Equal Employment Opportunity Commission (EEOC). Congress empowered the US attorney general to enforce the new law. At the same time, the law provided new measures to desegregate public schools.[25]

---

[23] Donaldson, *Liberalism's Last Hurrah*, 254.

[24] John H. Kessel, *The Goldwater Coalition: Republican Strategies in 1964* (Indianapolis, IN: Bobbs-Merrill, 1968), 195.

[25] Transcript of Civil Rights Act (1964), available at http://www.ourdocuments.gov/doc.php?flash=true&doc=97&page=transcript.

The Voting Rights Act, signed into law on August 6, 1965, was equally revolutionary. Section 2 prohibited any voting practices, such as literacy tests, that discriminated on the basis of race or ethnicity. The law also empowered federal registrars to oversee voter registration in counties and states with a poor voting record. Section 5 of the law required that those states and localities with a history of voter discrimination be subjected to "preclearance." Under this portion of the law, any changes in voting practices required the approval of the US Justice Department. Section 4(b) identified those communities under preclearance provisions. Although the Supreme Court's decision in *Shelby County v. Holder* (2013) struck down Section 4(b)—and effectively gutted Section 5—the Voting Rights Act ushered in a new period of African American enfranchisement.

The results of federal civil rights intervention were remarkable. In the space of months, the obnoxious Jim Crows signs and restrictions that had dominated southern life since the early twentieth century disappeared. Similarly, black voters flocked to the polls and registered and voted, especially in the Deep South. Between 1964 and 1968, the number of registered African American voters increased sharply from 6.7 percent to 59.4 percent in Mississippi and from 23 percent to 53 percent in Alabama. Much of the actual work of voter registration fell to civil rights activists, whose grassroots networks sought black voting and political power. During 1966–1968, the Southern Regional Council operated a second Voter Education Project, which sponsored more than two hundred voter registration drives.

The increased number of African American voters brought real changes. The number of black officeholders grew significantly during the years after the Voting Rights Act, with most of this growth occurring at the local and county levels, and in smaller towns. In the mid-1970s, about half of African American officeholders were elected at the municipal level—mostly occupying city council seats—but especially so in communities of less than 5,000 people. That number continued to grow, increasing to 7,480 elected officeholders for the South as a whole by 1991. In many Deep South communities with black majorities, local government included many more black officeholders. In Mississippi, for example, there were 117 black elected officeholders in 1971 —the greatest number of any state in the Union; this number grew to 548 by 1987.

Ten years after the *Brown* decision, progress on school desegregation stalled. The Civil Rights Act's Title IV required federal intervention to promote school desegregation. The law empowered the US commissioner of education and the Department of Health, Education, and Welfare (HEW) to require school boards to submit acceptable desegregation plans. The HEW-initiated proceedings threatened the cutoff of federal funds; school boards sought new plans that would preserve neighborhood schools. Pressure from the Supreme Court accelerated federal intervention. In 1968, the court considered "freedom-of-choice" plans, which had become a popular way for school boards to avoid more-drastic desegregation measures. Freedom-of-choice plans provided that parents could choose their schools without any restrictions based on race, but only if they petitioned the school board.

In practice, however, freedom-of-choice plans resulted in minimal school desegregation. Few white parents wanted to transfer their children to all-black schools;
the numbers of black students attending white schools remained small. As historian
James Cobb writes, freedom-of-choice plans were "geared much more toward keeping whites out of integrated classrooms than putting blacks into them."[26] In southeastern Virginia, in New Kent County, under the school board's freedom-of-choice
plan most black students attended the all-black George W. Watkins High School.
Calvin C. Green, the president of the local NAACP chapter, filed suit, and the case
was eventually decided in the Supreme Court in May 1968. Ruling that the New
Kent school system remained "dual" and therefore violated the *Brown* decision, the
court rejected the use of freedom-of-choice plans and told school boards that they
had an "affirmative duty" to desegregate meaningfully. Henceforth, school boards
were expected to "convert promptly to a system without a 'white' school and a
'Negro' school, but just schools."[27]

The *Green* decision was followed by two other important Supreme Court cases:
Alexander v. Holmes (1969) and *Swann v. Board of Education* (1971). Mississippi
school authorities sought a delay in implementing *Green*'s ambitious school desegregation imperative; Richard Nixon's HEW endorsed the plan. The NAACP sued,
demanding immediate desegregation. In October 1969, the Supreme Court, agreeing with the NAACP, refused to permit any further delay. "School districts must
immediately terminate dual school systems based on race," the court declared, "and
operate only unitary school systems."[28] With a court order requiring immediate—
and significant—school desegregation, HEW encouraged the use of busing to transport children across neighborhood lines. In Charlotte, district court judge James B.
McMillan rejected the school board's plan, and the *Swann v. Charlotte-Mecklenburg
Board of Education* case reached the Supreme Court in May 1971. "Nearly 17 years
ago this Court held, in explicit terms," Chief Justice Warren Burger wrote, "that
state-imposed segregation by race in public schools denies equal protection of the
laws." Now the time had come to fulfill *Brown*'s promise.[29]

The impact of the Civil Rights Act's Title IV, in combination with intervention
by the federal courts, led to radical restructuring. Especially in communities such as
Charlotte, in which more than 70 percent of the school population was white, integration occurred smoothly. In other communities possessing larger black school
populations, white parents became frightened by the prospect of majority-black
schools. In Mississippi, a widespread system of private "white flight" schools sprang
into existence that paralleled the largely black public schools. In suburban Atlanta,
thousands of white parents fled to the suburbs to escape incorporation into the integrated city school system. Atlanta's city population declined by a fifth during the

[26] Cobb, *The South and America since World War II*, 110.
[27] *Charles C. Green et al. v. County School Board of New Kent County*, 391 U.S. 430, 88 S.Ct. 1689,
    20 L.Ed.2d 716.
[28] *Alexander v. Holmes Board of Education*, 396 U.S. 19 (1969).
[29] *Swann v. Charlotte-Mecklenburg Board of Education*, 402 U.S. 1 (1971).

1970s, a phenomenon that white flight fueled. In Richmond, where 65 percent of the school population was black, white flight also swelled the surrounding suburbs.

THE SOUTHERN STRATEGY

Increasingly, conservative Democrats voted Republican in national elections, if they retained their party identification. Two-thirds of white southerners identified as Democratic in 1964. Four years later, that proportion had declined to about 50 percent. Before the mid-1960s, the election of statewide Republican candidates in the South was unheard of; thereafter, it became much more common. In 1966, a national reaction against Johnson's civil rights policies and his Great Society domestic programs led to Republican gains in congressional midterm elections. In the South, Republicans elected governors in Florida, Arkansas, Kentucky, and Oklahoma in 1966–1967. Howard Baker became the first Republican US senator since Reconstruction elected from Tennessee in 1966, and, within two years, there were six Republican senators and twenty-nine congressmen from southern districts.

The Republican resurgence formed the basis of Richard Nixon's "Southern Strategy." Its most important advocate was Strom Thurmond, along with his political operatives, staffers, and advisers. Harry Dent joined Thurmond's senatorial staff in the 1950s and helped persuade the South Carolina senator to defect to the Republican Party in 1964. Becoming South Carolina state Republican chairman in 1965, Dent was one of the most successful builders of a new southern Republican Party. One historian describes him as a "behind-the-scenes player who did the most to turn the South from a region that despised Republicans into a Republican bastion."[30] After Nixon's election to the presidency in 1968, Dent joined the White House as a political adviser, and he advocated a strategy to solidify Republican gains in the South. Dent later described the Southern Strategy as an attempt to solidify a conservative coalition by converting the South, long a Democratic bastion, into a key piece of a Republican majority. Some southerners saw the Southern Strategy, Dent wrote, as of "profound national significance" in its promise for the "salvation for America." This approach would help restore conservative policies at the national level, and "free enterprise [would] be preserved and individual freedoms in this country and around the world."[31]

In 1968, George Wallace again ran for the presidency, this time as an independent, third-party candidate. Appearing on the ballots of all fifty states, Wallace opposed excessive federal power and argued for a return to states' rights. He also capitalized on popular discontent during the 1960s with campus disruptions, the sexual revolution, a new secularism and a decline of Protestant religious authority, and a supposed lack of patriotism in supporting American involvement in the Vietnam War. A liberal elite had misled the country, Wallace charged, taking the country toward ruin. Wallace fashioned a populist crusade against what he called "intellectual snobs who don't

[30] Rick Perlstein, "The Southern Strategist," *New York Times Magazine*, December 30, 2007.
[31] Harry S. Dent, *The Prodigal South Returns to Power* (New York: John Wiley, 1978), 75.

Governor George Wallace Attempting to Block Integration at the University of Alabama, June 11, 1963, photograph by Warren K. Leffler. *Library of Congress.*

know the difference between smut and great literature." These "intellectual snobs" sent their children to private schools while forcing ordinary folk to be bused to far-away, integrated schools.[32]

In the end, despite opinion polls showing his support in the election as high as 21 percent, Wallace carried only the five Deep South states of Arkansas, Alabama, Mississippi, Georgia, and Louisiana during the presidential election of 1968, while Nixon carried seven southern states. Nonetheless, Wallace's candidacy made the election between Republican Richard Nixon and Democrat Hubert Humphrey much closer than it would have otherwise been. As a second choice, Wallace's voters likely favored Nixon, who continued to expand Republican strength in the South.

Ultimately, the Southern Strategy relied on race, but using coded language. Dent, claiming that the Southern Strategy was not based on racial appeals, later remembered in his 1978 memoirs that Republican campaigns in the South sought to defeat liberalism and to defend the "preservation of individual freedom, not only for Americans, but for people the world over." Southern conservatives, Dent wrote, were primarily concerned about higher taxes and federal intervention, rising crime, and a breakdown in morals.[33] Later in life, near his death in 2007, Dent would admit that he used race politically. "When I look back," he confessed, "my biggest regret now is anything I did that stood in the way of the rights of black people."[34]

Like Dent, Lee Atwater began work on Thurmond's staff and then rose to national importance as a Republican strategist. Atwater explained in an anonymous interview in 1981 about the changing importance of race (he was not identified until 2012, twenty-one years after his death in 1991). "You start out in 1954 by saying, 'Nigger, nigger, nigger,'" Atwater declared. "By 1968 you can't say 'nigger'—that hurts you, backfires." Instead, the Southern Strategy called for using "stuff like . . .

forced busing, states' rights, . . . [and] cutting taxes." These issues were "totally economic things," but their byproduct, Atwater admitted, was that "blacks get hurt
worse than whites. . . . 'We want to cut this,' is much more abstract than even the
busing thing, uh, and a hell of a lot more abstract than 'Nigger, nigger.'"[35]

In his *Emerging Republican Majority*, strategist Kevin Phillips saw the South as
instrumental to long-term Republican dominance. Phillips emphasized that the
emergence of a new set of "social" issues would galvanize voters; these issues were
rooted in fears of change. Race figured prominently, because the increasing presence
of African Americans and civil rights issues drove white voters around the country
away from the Democratic Party. Phillips favored expanding black reenfranchisement in order to motivate whites to vote Republican. Dent and Nixon, impressed by
Phillips's book, fastened on a political strategy favoring racial conservatism, which
would attract southern whites without alienating northern white voters.

Concerned about another challenge from Wallace in 1972, Nixon announced his
opposition to "forced busing," even while he was powerless to prevent court-ordered
desegregation that unfolded after 1969. "Let's just stop this hypocrisy," Nixon announced, "that the problem in our schools is only in the South."[36] He ordered HEW
to go slowly in enforcing school desegregation. "Do what the law requires and not
one bit more," Nixon wrote in a memo.[37] Yet, ironically, southern schools experienced
more integration under the Nixon administration than ever before.

Nixon also attempted to reshape the Supreme Court with the appointment of
conservative white southerners. In 1969, he nominated Clement F. Haynsworth Jr.,
a judge on the Fourth Circuit Court of Appeals, to the Supreme Court. Labor and
civil rights groups vigorously opposed the nomination because of Haynsworth's
record as a judge. After his nomination was defeated in the Senate, Nixon nominated another white southerner, G. Harrold Carswell, a federal district court judge
from Florida and an Eisenhower appointee. Carswell, with a past as a segregationist,
was also rejected by the Senate in April 1970.

The Southern Strategy yielded important results in continuing the expansion of
Republican support among southern white voters. Political change, drawing on white
backlash, also reflected the extensive changes that reshaped life in the South after
World War II. Economic change, stimulated by heavy federal expenditures in the
military sector, diversified the southern economy in a way that changed old patterns of
life. While millions left the region with the collapse of the plantation system, millions
more immigrated to the South, filling the growing Sunbelt urban centers. The region
became, to some degree, more American, as differences in income narrowed and as
southern culture became a dominant medium in entertainment, sports, and music.

[35] Rick Perlstein, "Exclusive: Lee Atwater's Infamous 1981 Interview on the Southern Strategy,"
     The Nation, November 13, 2012.
[36] Cobb, *The South and America since World War II*, 132.
[37] Carter, *From George Wallace to Newt Gingrich*, 45.

24

SOUTHERNIZING AMERICA

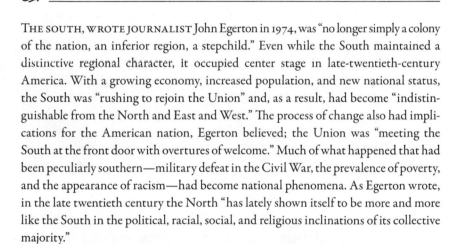

THE SOUTH, WROTE JOURNALIST John Egerton in 1974, was "no longer simply a colony of the nation, an inferior region, a stepchild." Even while the South maintained a distinctive regional character, it occupied center stage in late-twentieth-century America. With a growing economy, increased population, and new national status, the South was "rushing to rejoin the Union" and, as a result, had become "indistinguishable from the North and East and West." The process of change also had implications for the American nation, Egerton believed; the Union was "meeting the South at the front door with overtures of welcome." Much of what happened that had been peculiarly southern—military defeat in the Civil War, the prevalence of poverty, and the appearance of racism—had become national phenomena. As Egerton wrote, in the late twentieth century the North "has lately shown itself to be more and more like the South in the political, racial, social, and religious inclinations of its collective majority."

Writing about the same time, in 1976, Kirkpatrick Sale reached the same conclusion in his book *Power Shift*. He was not sanguine about how the balance of power seemed to have shifted "away from the Northeast and toward the Southern Rim." This newly empowered region included Southern California, Texas and the Southwest, and the South. There was now a "power base" whose influence rested on the "unsurpassed population migration that began to attract millions and millions of people" from the Northeast and Midwest. What had occurred in recent years amounted to an "authentic economic revolution that created the giant new postwar industries of defense, aerospace, technology, electronics, agribusiness, and oil-and-gas extraction." These developments depended on the unprecedented expansion of the federal state and the disposition of its largesse in public works, transportation

Talladega Superspeedway Race, Talladega, Alabama, 2010, photograph by Carol M.
Highsmith. *Library of Congress.*

systems, and defense-related industries. The economic, cultural, and political balance of power had shifted.[1]

THE RETAIL REVOLUTION AND THE NEW WORLD OF LABOR

The intersection between the South and the rest of the country found an important
manifestation. A new paradigm of corporate enterprise, consumerism, and labor
management first gestated in the South and then became a national phenomenon.
The South led the way in late-twentieth-century America in the emergence of mass-
market retailing and the development of new methods of labor management. Manufacturing and consumption became globalized, in a production and retail chain
extending from Asian factories to American consumers. Large, multibillion-dollar
corporations dominated retailing. Sales were largely conducted in big-box stores
selling consumer goods, electronics, clothing, and groceries. The workers at these
retail giants were mostly low paid and nonunion.

The most important retailer of the late twentieth century, Walmart, emerged from
the changes affecting the modern South. By 2014, Walmart employed 2.2 million
workers, operated 4,253 stores, recorded sales of $405 billion, and served 200 million
customers worldwide in North America, South America, Asia, and Europe. The third-
largest corporation and the largest retailer in the world, Walmart is the largest private
employer on the globe. If Walmart were a country, it would have the nineteenth-
largest economy in the world.

Walmart's founder, Sam Walton, was born in Oklahoma in 1918, moved with his
family to Columbia, Missouri, attended the University of Missouri, and then
worked in retailing for J. C. Penney Company. After serving in World War II,
Walton bought a Newport, Arkansas, Ben Franklin store, a franchise of the Butler

[1] Kirkpatrick Sale, *Power Shift: The Rise of the Southern Rim and Its Challenge to the Eastern
Establishment* (New York: Vintage, 1976), 6–7.

Brothers five-and-dime retail chain store. During the first half of the twentieth century, the Butler Brothers chain stores became a different sort of retailer. The stores spread across the small towns of America, distributing their wholesale inventory to local retail franchisers. Using a $20,000 loan from his father-in-law and $5,000 in savings to buy the store, Walton grew into a highly successful retailer by selling low-cost goods such as pots, pans, sheets, and tools.

Walton exploited his franchising relationship with Butler Brothers to open new Ben Franklin stores in small towns across Arkansas. In addition, he discovered that discount retailing worked successfully with high-volume sales. Small towns, lacking access to retail discounting, became a rich field for expansion. Walton tried to enlist Butler Brothers in the further spread of the existing retail model by reducing the frills in physical appearance and encouraging customer self-service. After Butler Brothers rebuffed him, he used cash from his wife's trust fund and, in 1962, opened his first Walmart Discount City in Rogers, Arkansas. Walton then expanded to small towns in Arkansas, Oklahoma, Missouri, and Louisiana. These stores drew on traditions of cooperative marketing and voluntarism by drawing in local partners to provide capital for expansion. By 1970, thirty-two Walmarts were in existence, and during the next two decades, Walmart underwent a new era of expansion.

Today, the corporation's world headquarters are located in Bentonville, in northwestern Arkansas. The town is a bustling community with an airport with direct flights to financial centers in New York, Los Angeles, and Chicago. Bentonville houses offices for five hundred of Walmart's vendors, with companies such as Proctor & Gamble, Levi Strauss, and Kraft Foods maintaining large offices in or near Bentonville. These vendors interact with a production supply system that depends on factories in southern China, where 80 percent of Walmart's cheap consumer items are manufactured. Walmart possesses a large presence in the Chinese city of Shenzhen, which serves as the center of manufacturing, containing hundreds of thousands of factory workers. In effect, Walmart has created a worldwide network that, as the largest retailer in the world, makes the corporation deeply involved in the manufacturing process.

Walmart, and other post-1945 southern enterprises, depended heavily on the lower cost structure of a nonunion workforce. In the post–New Deal era, southern legislatures led the way in reducing union power. A key figure during the 1940s was Texan Vance Muse. Organizing the Christian American Association as a conservative, anticommunist pressure group, Muse helped push through "anti-violence" laws in Texas that limited picketing and strikes at wartime plants in the state. During World War II, Mississippi, Florida, Arkansas, and Alabama adopted "antiviolence" legislation in the name of the war effort. In alliance with other groups such as the Fight for Free Enterprise, the Christian American Association pushed further, and in 1944 Florida and Arkansas enacted the first right-to-work laws. By 1947, fourteen states had enacted antiviolence laws, with the core support for it in the South.

Congress guaranteed such legislation in the Taft-Hartley Act in 1947, adopted over Harry S Truman's veto. The law was a turning point for organized labor, displacing the protective umbrella of federal power and limiting unions' increased membership achieved during the 1930s and 1940s. Reversing many of the protections gained by organized labor during the New Deal and World War II, Taft-Hartley also limited the ability of unions to engage in tactics such as wildcat strikes, jurisdictional strikes, and secondary boycotts, while it also prohibited closed shops, which required union membership at work places. The act's Section 14(b) further restricted unions' power by permitting states to enact right-to-work laws. These laws prohibited employers from requiring union membership for employment and enabled nonunion workers to enjoy the same benefits earned by union members—thus diminishing the attractiveness of union membership. Right-to-work laws became especially popular in the South, long an antiunion bastion. Between 1947 and 1954, every southern state but Oklahoma enacted right-to-work legislation. In 2013, eleven of the twenty-four states with these laws were in the South.

Limiting unions became an article of faith in post-1945 southern economic development. Walmart led the way in maintaining an antiunion environment in retailing, and in promoting a low-wage environment. When union operatives attempted to organize Walmart distribution centers in the 1970s, Sam Walton hired John Tate, a noted antiunion attorney with a long record of success in blocking union organizing. Walmart also became known for its "Union Prevention Index," which provided a measure of discontent among its workers, in an effort to avoid unionization. In addition, the Bentonville headquarters maintained a department of antiunion operatives whom they could deploy if needed.

NASCAR AND SOUTHERN SPORTS

The southernization of American life also affected culture. After 1960, NASCAR and stock-car racing became a huge entertainment industry with a truly national reach. Much as other elements of southern culture had gone national, stock-car racing provided another instance of how the southern experience became a national commodity. By the end of the twentieth century, the sport had become a national industry, highly commercialized and the second most popular sport in America. NASCAR attracted a national audience in major urban centers. Increasingly, fans were no longer working class but instead were college graduates of middle- or larger-income backgrounds. Advertising especially targeted women and young people. The fan base steadily increased, doubling in the 1990s and expanding at a rate of 10 percent per year.

The sport remained under the domination of Bill France, who served as NASCAR owner and pioneered the growth of the sport. During the 1970s, France turned over control of the business to his elder son, "Little Bill." He successfully expanded NASCAR's radio and television presence, as two networks, ABC and CBS, televised races in the 1970s, including flag-to-flag coverage. At the end of the decade, CBS obtained sole coverage rights, while in the late 1980s ESPN expanded its coverage. In 2007, national networks signed a $5 billion contract with NASCAR, assuring a steady flow of money and primetime audience for the sport.

In 2003, Bill Jr.'s son, Brian France, took over as CEO, running the company with his sister and brother. With NASCAR remaining a privately held company, the France family empire was worth billions of dollars. NASCAR adopted an openly conservative cast that celebrated its southern roots and emphasized the rugged individuals that were its star drivers. In 1969, France appointed southern conservative Democrat L. Mendel Rivers as NASCAR commissioner. France also enjoyed the strong support of Gov. George Wallace when NASCAR opened its Alabama International Motor Speedway in Talladega; France even chaired Wallace's 1972 presidential campaign in Florida.

Much of NASCAR's success depended on advertising; cars and drivers were decked out in ads. According to one account, races consist of "40 extremely mobile billboards [that] circle a track for three hours, driven by men in jumpsuits that make bowling apparel look sharp." NASCAR revenues had reached more than $3 billion a year by the first decade of the twenty-first century. Fans also bought more than $2 billion a year in merchandise.[2] The relationship between NASCAR and its sponsors began in 1970, when the sport began a three-decades-long relationship with R. J. Reynolds Tobacco. The Reynolds partnership reflected NASCAR's move away from its southern base and a conservative, working-class audience. Reynolds insisted on the sport's standardization, including the abandonment of remaining dirt tracks, a reduction of Grand National races to one per week, and the limitation of all tracks to under one hundred miles in length. Reynolds agreed to sponsor a new event, the Winston 500, which would be held at the new Talladega Superspeedway, which opened in Lincoln, Alabama, in 1969. In 1972, the chief prize in stock-car racing was renamed the Winston Cup in honor of the Reynolds cigarette brand, replacing the Grand National designation.

The sport was changing. After Congress banned cigarette advertising on television and radio, the company explored new media. In 2004, NASCAR dropped its association with the tobacco industry and instead adopted Nextel, a telecommunications company, as its chief sponsor, for an annual payment of $750 million. The Nextel Cup attracted huge audiences totaling 200,000 fans. As is true of other professional sports, the major drivers commanded large salaries and enriched themselves by lucrative endorsement deals.

NASCAR also promoted a star system of celebrity drivers, the most successful of whom was Richard Petty. In 1964, he earned $114,000, a fantastic salary for a driver in that era. Three years later, he won his second Grand National championship—the first driver to accomplish this feat—followed by a third championship in 1971. In that year, Petty became the first driver to earn $1 million; four years later, he earned $2 million. The peak of Petty's career and fame occurred during the 1970s. Retiring in 1992, Petty was inducted into the NASCAR Hall of Fame in 2001. The most important NASCAR star driver of the 1980s and 1990s, Dale Earnhardt, won seven

[2] Neal Thompson, *Driving with the Devil: Southern Moonshine, Detroit Wheels, and the Birth of NASCAR* (New York: Crown, 2006), 352–353.

Talladega Superspeedway Race, Talladega, Alabama, 2010, photograph by Carol M. Highsmith. *Library of Congress.*

championships during his career. Earnhardt, with a reputation for hotheadedness and intense competitiveness, was nicknamed Ironhead. Wrangler Jeans promoted Earnhardt in its "One Tough Customer" advertising campaign, portraying him as rough and tumble, independent, and confrontational—a sort of antihero. Earnhardt shared personal rivalries with other drivers, but none as intense as the one with driver Jeff Gordon. Beginning in 1994, Gordon—known as the Intimidator—won a series of races that challenged Earnhardt's supremacy, and the two racers competed to become the leading NASCAR driver. Because of his personality, Earnhardt attracted a popular following and became a major media star. Earnhardt's death from a crash and head injury in 2001 led to an outpouring of grief among his numerous fans, and also to changes in safety procedures for drivers.

SOUTHERN MUSIC

The popularity of NASCAR reflected the wider national expansion of southern culture, especially in music. After the 1940s, the most popular—and commercialized—forms of music included variations of white country music on the one hand, along with, on the other hand, African American blues, jazz, and rhythm and blues. Southern white music drew upon a rich rural heritage of gospel music instrumentation and vocals. During the 1950s, these musical forms entered the national cultural mainstream and over the next generation began to dominate commercially produced music.

Southern-roots music continued to shape the post-1945 revolution in popular music. In the late 1960s, country rock, which fused country music melodies and instruments with rock and roll, became popular. Another genre, southern rock, emerged in the mid-1970s, borrowing from country rock but employing southern themes and settings. The most-successful southern rock performers included the Allman Brothers Band, the Marshall Tucker Band, Wet Willie, ZZ Top, Lynyrd Skynyrd, and the Charlie Daniels Band. The Allman Brothers, from Jacksonville, successfully combined blues, jazz, country music, and improvisational rock. The group employed an instrumental format that included keyboards, bass, two guitars, and drums that other southern rock bands generally adopted. With lead vocalist Gregg Allman using a soul style, his brother Duane, a slide guitarist, used familiar blues chords. Guitarist Dickey Betts adopted a country style.

Some of the southern rock bands exalted regional values. Lynyrd Skynyrd's "Sweet Home Alabama" (1974) responded to Neil Young's "Southern Man (1970), in which Young had declared: "Southern change / gonna come at last / Now your crosses are burning fast." Although none of the band members were from Alabama, the song intoned a defense of southern differentness: "I hope Neil Young will remember / A Southern man don't need him around anyhow." At the same time, nonsoutherners adopted southern music styles, including Linda Ronstadt, Gram Parsons, and the Flying Burrito Brothers. Even British artists such as the Rolling Stones and Elton John adopted southern rock and blues rhythms as part of their acts.

A center of the diffusion of southern-based rock and roll was based in the studios and session musicians and producers located in Sheffield, Alabama. Beginning in 1969, the studio at 3614 Jackson Highway became headquarters of the Muscle Shoals Sound Rhythm Section. Including Barry Beckett on drums, Jimmy Johnson on guitar, and David Hood on bass, the studio provided backup and arrangement for a variety of artists looking for a southern-based sound. These included soul artists such as Aretha Franklin and Wilson Pickett, as well as British artists such as the Rolling Stones and Traffic. *Sticky Fingers*, the Stones' bestselling platinum album, featured "Brown Sugar," a tune heavily dependent on country melodies.

The emergence of the folk scene in the urban North after the late 1950s drew upon southern country music traditions, melodies, and rhythms. Folk music also relied on the heritage of protest music dating from the 1930s and 1940s South and Southwest. Florence Reece's "Which Side Are You On?" was composed during the 1930s in the strike-torn coal-mining region of Harlan County, in eastern Kentucky. Singer Woody Guthrie captured the music of Okie migrants, creating a lode of materials later covered by folk musicians. Pete Seeger, a northern musician, sang many of these protest songs to a devoted national audience.

Beginning in the 1970s, bluegrass enjoyed a revival that depended largely on a nonsouthern following. A number of virtuoso performers came out of the South during this era. Arthel "Doc" Watson, born in Deep Gap, in northwestern North Carolina, got his start in a band in which he played fiddle tunes on an electric guitar. In the 1960s, Watson joined the folk music revival with a distinctive, flat-picking acoustic guitar music. A guitarist virtuoso, Watson first played to a Greenwich Village audience in 1961 and regularly performed at the Newport Folk Festival during the 1960s. Other traditional country musicians and bluegrass artists, such as Earl Scruggs, Bill Monroe, and Merle Travis, developed a national following.

The nationalization of southern culture through music became an international phenomenon. African American music, in blues, jazz, and swing, already enjoyed European following during the 1920s. World War II and the Cold War brought further internationalization through the presence of American soldiers and the development of the Armed Forces Network (AFN), which by 1960 had over fifty million European listeners. Country performers regularly toured abroad, commanding a huge following. Rock and roll and country music became international idioms, with many artists adopting these styles who were not southern or even American. Country music artists exist in great numbers, for example in Asia, with the Grand Ole Opry enjoying popularity in Tokyo.

The South manifested itself in national culture in other ways. In literature and film, regional themes of race and sexuality were often depicted with unusual vividness. Authors such as Eudora Welty and Flannery O'Connor emphasized the gothic dimensions of southern life. On stage, Tennessee Williams's portrayal of dissipation and moral decay appeared vividly in *The Glass Menagerie* (1944), *A Streetcar Named Desire* (1947), and *Cat on a Hot Tin Roof* (1955). Williams used the setting of the South as the scene of sexual repression and conflict, presented to national and international audiences. Other representations of the South on film also explored themes of race and sexuality. *The Long Hot Summer* (1958), *The Defiant Ones* (1958), and *To Kill a Mockingbird* (1962) all were motion pictures that used the South to portray moral decay, repressed sexuality, and racial repression. *To Kill a Mockingbird*, published as a bestselling novel by Alabaman Harper Lee in 1960, charted issues of race and sexuality in a fictionalized small Alabama town. James Dickey's *Deliverance*, published as a novel in 1970 and made into a film two years later, explored the cultural conflict between the modern and traditional South in northern Georgia.

On matters of race, television networks proceeded more cautiously. Singer Nat King Cole hosted a variety show beginning in November 1956, though the show was canceled in 1957 after failing to find a national sponsor that didn't fear adverse southern white reaction. A much more appealing format was situation comedies that emphasized the rustic, hillbilly qualities of the South, generally scrubbed clean of mention of race or civil rights conflict. *No Time for Sergeants*, starring Andy Griffith, was anthologized in a television production in 1955. It depicted a southern yokel, Will Stockdale, drafted into the Air Force, expressing clueless contentment though able to triumph over seemingly smarter urban counterparts. *The Real McCoys*, which aired from 1957 to 1963, was another situation comedy about a family of West Virginians, also rubes, who moved to California. The *Andy Griffith Show*, broadcast between 1960 and 1968, was a situation comedy about a fictional town, its sheriff, and assorted characters—loosely based on Mt. Airy, North Carolina—that parodied small-town southern living. And *The Beverly Hillbillies*, on air from 1962 to 1971, satirized the sudden wealth of Arkansas rustics who discovered oil and moved to Beverly Hills, California. Like Andy Griffith, the main character, Jed Clampett (played by longtime actor Buddy Ebsen), played the serious straight man encircled by buffoons.

The South as a setting for rustics attempting to deal with the modern world, even while maintaining their core values, remained a part of television programming

Billy Graham, 1966. *Library of Congress.*

during the 1970s. The *Misadventures of Sheriff Lobo,* which ran from 1979 to 1981, was set in fictional Orly County, Georgia, and concerned a corrupt but ultimately morally good sheriff. *The Dukes of Hazard,* airing between 1979 and 1985, similarly portrayed southern life in satiric terms. Set in fictional Hazzard County, Georgia, the show was based on *Moonrunners* (1975), a movie about moonshining. *Dukes* was set in a stereotypical rural southern community filled with buffoons, corrupt local officials (including the local kingpin Boss Hogg), and fast-driving comic heroes. The popular TV series *Dallas,* which ran from 1978 to 1991, parodied southern cattle barons in a modern-day western format.

EVANGELICALISM AND CULTURAL POLITICS

In the late twentieth century, the South became the center of another cultural phenomenon of national political implications: the rapid spread of evangelical Christianity. Evangelicals were a diverse group, embracing a variety of beliefs and practices but holding in common the experience of becoming "born again." The most successful and popular evangelist in modern America, North Carolinian Billy Graham, captured a national and international audience. Born outside Charlotte, Graham studied at a bible college in Florida and graduated from Wheaton College near Chicago, the best fundamentalist college in America. Working with the national Youth for Christ organization, in the late 1940s Graham became a rising star. In late 1949, he led an eight-week crusade in Los Angeles that attracted 350,000 people, with 4,200 conversions. Graham established himself as a national figure and over the next half century regularly advised and counseled presidents. Dwight D. Eisenhower became the first president ever baptized in the White House, an event over which Graham officiated.

The fastest-growing groups of evangelicals were the Southern Baptist Convention (SBC) and Pentecostal denominations. The SBC grew from 4.5 million members in 1935 to nearly 16 million in 2011, with its greatest expansion occurring in the South. Much of its appeal lay in its insistence on biblical inerrancy—the belief that the Bible should be taken literally. Existing in a decentralized church structure, Southern Baptists spread rapidly during much of the twentieth century. The SBC experienced significant divisions over theology and politics, however. Conservatives insisted on biblical inerrancy and believed in political activism in support of conservative candidates who held "correct" views on gay rights, school prayer, abortion, and an anticommunist foreign policy. Moderates advocated the traditional Baptist belief in separation of church and state and noninvolvement in politics. In 1979, conservatives took control of the denomination, displacing moderates and beginning a new era of political activism. In 1980, the convention endorsed a statement opposing abortion; two years later, it supported school prayer—despite long-standing and historical Baptist opposition to state involvement in church affairs. Conservatives also purged moderates from SBC organizations, publications, and seminaries.

Pentecostal churches composed another rapidly expanding evangelical group. Composed of fifty-seven separate church groups, the largest of which are the Assemblies of God, the Church of God, and the Church of God in Christ, Pentecostalism arose after the Civil War from the northern-based holiness movement. It appealed especially to the working class and the dispossessed; the faith crossed racial lines. Pentecostals relied on individual conversion, like other evangelicals, but they also encouraged postconversion phenomena such as expressive worship, faith healing, and prophecy. Strong believers that the world was entering its last stages—an end time—these Christians favored preparing for Christ's return and the establishment of heaven on earth. Pentecostals also often spoke in tongues, a practice by which congregants, gripped by the Holy Spirit, uttered an unknown foreign language—much as the original Christians did. Dismissed by outsiders as a religion of "holy roller" fanatics, Pentecostalism became a vibrant faith with a powerful appeal to southerners.

In the late twentieth century, Pentecostalism moved toward middle-class respectability. Jim Bakker, a Pentecostal Minnesotan who moved to Charlotte, North Carolina, became a highly successful television broadcaster whose *PTL Club* was one of the most watched evangelical television programs of the 1970s and 1980s. Bakker's message was Pentecostal but also materialistic, celebrating the accumulation of wealth. Bakker was mostly apolitical, and, prior to the 1970s, most Pentecostals rejected political involvement. That changed as the same threats arousing other evangelicals—theological modernism, secularism, and what they saw as antifamily lifestyles—motivated many Pentecostals to support conservative activism.

A number of factors motivated a new political mobilization of southern evangelicals, but the unifying force involved fears about supposed increasing secularization and moral decline. In two rulings issued in 1962–1963, the US Supreme Court determined that state-sponsored prayers in schools were unconstitutional. Along with the court's decision in *Roe v. Wade* (1973), which struck down state restrictions on abortion, evangelicals became aroused. Other developments spurred the evangelical mobilization. In an important ruling, the Internal Revenue Service (IRS) revoked the tax-exempt status of Bob Jones University, in Greenville, South Carolina. Beginning in July 1970, the IRS revoked the nonprofit status of any private schools practicing racial discrimination—a policy affecting Christian schools across the South. Bob Jones University, founded in 1927, did not admit black students until 1971 and permitted unmarried black students beginning only in 1975. Once it admitted unmarried African Americans, Bob Jones University instituted new policies prohibiting interracial dating, which threatened expulsion for any students dating interracially. In January 1976, the IRS revoked the university's tax-exempt status. A Christian high school, the Goldsboro (North Carolina) Christian

Schools, which excluded black students entirely, also saw its tax-exempt status revoked. Bob Jones and Goldsboro Christian Schools sued, claiming that the First Amendment protected them. Federal authorities responded by contending that the IRS was obliged to withdraw any tax support of racial discrimination. In May 1983, the Supreme Court affirmed the IRS's power to deny tax-exempt status to private schools practicing racial discrimination.[3]

The Bob Jones case encompassed a decade-long conflict between federal authorities and Christian schools. Many of these schools were established as white-flight institutions, in response to court-ordered desegregation. The Bob Jones and Goldsboro cases, from evangelicals' perspective, reinforced fears that the federal government wanted to regulate the religious education of evangelicals, even in private schools. Although these fears proved unfounded, they were nonetheless real. North Carolina senator Jesse Helms led efforts to limit the IRS's authority in this case, and the US Senate actually enacted such a limitation, though it failed in the House of Representatives. The conflict with the IRS, as one conservative activist remembered, "scared the dickens" out of evangelicals and served as a "galvanizing, unifying issue."[4]

Evangelicals also worried over eroding family and moral values. They opposed expanding women's rights and especially the Equal Rights Amendment (ERA), which Congress adopted and submitted to the states for ratification in 1972. The amendment, containing only three sections and fifty-two words, stated that neither the federal government nor the states could abridge "equality of rights ... on account of sex." After a decade-long battle, anti-ERA forces eventually defeated ratification, but the battle lines over gender roles hardened. Except for Texas and Tennessee, no southern state ratified the amendment, and Tennessee later rescinded its approval. Evangelicals reasserted a view holding that men and women were biologically different. According to their scriptural interpretation, evangelicals insisted on the moral, economic, and political authority of men. Evangelicals rejected full gender equality, and in most of their denominations they maintained restrictions limiting women's power in church organizations.

The rise of gay rights as a civil rights issue during the 1970s, and its successes, also aroused evangelical opposition. In early 1977, Dade County, Florida—which encompasses Miami and Miami Beach—enacted a local ordinance prohibiting discrimination by schools in hiring teachers on the basis of sexual orientation. A popular, antigay movement, Save Our Children, ensued, led by former Miss Oklahoma Anita Bryant, favoring repeal of the law. Bryant's efforts resulted in 60,000 signatures on a petition placing repeal on the ballot. The Save Our Children campaign attracted support from around the country, and repeal of the Dade County ordinance passed by a 2-to-1 margin. Opposition to gay rights became a cornerstone issue for evangelicals' political mobilization.

---

[3] *Bob Jones University v. United States*, 461 U.S. 574 (1983).
[4] William A. Link, *Righteous Warrior: Jesse Helms and the Rise of Modern Conservatism* (New York: Macmillan, 2008), 179.

Jerry Falwell. *Library of Congress.*

A key figure in the political mobilization of southern evangelicals was Virginia Baptist preacher Jerry Falwell. In 1956, Falwell founded the Thomas Road Baptist Church in Lynchburg, Virginia. It eventually grew into a megachurch with over three thousand members. In 1967, Falwell moved into broadcasting with his *Old Time Gospel Hour*, which broadcast his Sunday morning services. The show eventually reached a large audience, appearing on 373 television stations while claiming a mailing list of 2.5 million people, a church membership of 18,000, a television and radio audience of 60 million, and annual fundraising revenues of $100 million. Falwell joined a growing number of conservative religious broadcasters during the 1970s and 1980s. Pat Robertson, the son of US Senator A. Willis Robertson, was born in Lexington, Virginia. In 1960, Robertson created the Christian Broadcasting Network (CBN), based in Norfolk, Virginia, which became a success by the late 1970s. Both Falwell and Robertson founded new evangelical universities: Falwell, Liberty Baptist College and Seminary (which became Liberty University in 1984) in Lynchburg; Robertson, Regents University in Norfolk.

Religious broadcasters such as Falwell and Robertson warned of moral decline; they demanded renewal and revival. Liberals were "attempting to secularize society," Falwell claimed, "purging society of God and religious heritage." America, he believed, was in trouble because of moral decay.[5] Robertson similarly asserted that "secular humanists" were attempting to control society through liberalized morality and secularization. Legalized abortion, the ERA, pornography, the absence of school prayer, and gay rights, evangelicals believed, served as indicators of decline. Evangelicals blamed liberalism and its supposed indifference to moral standards. "Our response to seventeen years of liberal insensitivity to pro-moral concerns," Falwell declared in 1979, "was not only to cry 'enough,' but also to stop crying and organize to do something about it." "Seventeen years of liberal insensitivity" referred to the Supreme Court's 1962 school prayer decision.[6]

Falwell continued as an uncompromising opponent of this "liberal insensitivity." He even maintained that the terrorist attacks on the World Trade Centers in New York City on September 11, 2001, represented God's vengeance on a nation that had strayed from its founding Christian principles. Appearing on Pat Robertson's TV show, Falwell said that God had protected America for most of its history. "Throwing God out successfully with the help of the federal court system, throwing God

[5] Erling Jorstad, *The New Christian Right, 1981–1988: Prospects for the Post-Reagan Decade* (Lewiston, NY: Edwin Mellen, 1987), 77.
[6] David Snowball, *Continuity and Change in the Rhetoric of the Moral Majority* (New York: Praeger, 1991), 2.

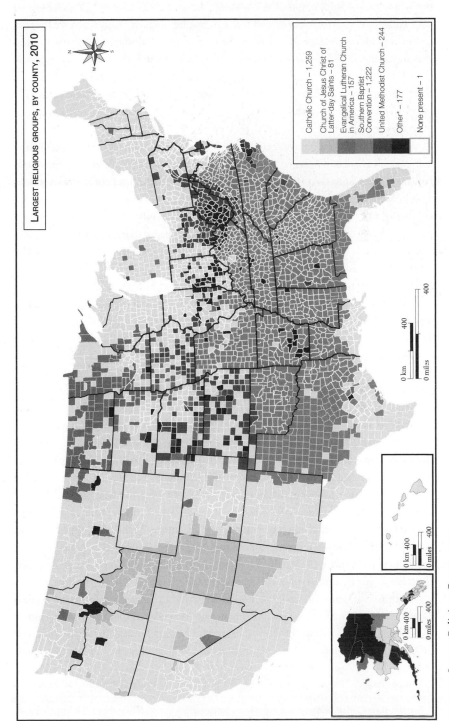

Largest religious groups, by county, 2010

Catholic Church – 1,259

Church of Jesus Christ of Latter-day Saints – 81

Evangelical Lutheran Church in America – 157

Southern Baptist Convention – 1,222

United Methodist Church – 244

Other* – 177

None present – 1

MAP 24.1 Largest Religious Groups, 2010

575

out of the public square, out of the schools," he said. "The abortionists have got to bear some burden for this because God will not be mocked. And when we destroy 40 million little innocent babies, we make God mad," he declared. "The pagans and the abortionists and the feminists and the gays and the lesbians who are actively trying to make that an alternative lifestyle, the ACLU, People for the American Way—all of them who have tried to secularize America," Falwell maintained. "I point the finger in their face and say 'you helped this happen.'" Robertson agreed with this assessment.[7]

Another successful televangelist with a conservative political message, Jimmy Swaggart, was born in Ferriday, Louisiana, in 1935, the first cousin of early rock-and-roller Jerry Lee Lewis. At the age of twenty, Swaggart became a Pentecostal minister and, beginning in 1960, began a radio ministry. In 1975, he expanded to television, capturing an ever-increasing audience, and by the early 1980s his shows appeared on 250 television stations. Swaggart reached a height of popularity in the mid-1980s. After he became involved in a scandal involving an association with prostitutes, the Assemblies of God, his denomination, defrocked him.

Much of Swaggart's message, like that of Falwell and Robertson, focused on moral decline and secularization. Secular humanism was the work of a liberal elite, "an insidious cabal blatantly working against God." Swaggart criticized feminists who "disregard the God of the Bible and laud that which is perverted." He opposed the teaching of evolution as "the garbage my children are being taught in the public schools, that we came from monkeys and disregarding God." He also described "every homosexual act" as "unnatural, not so much because it cuts across the individual's natural sexual orientation, or even infringes Old Testament Law, which it definitely does, but rather because it flies in the face of God's Creation Plan for human sexual expression."[8]

As the AIDS epidemic became a public-health crisis after the early 1980s, conservative Protestants often portrayed the disease as divine retribution for supposedly immoral behavior. The debate about AIDS meant a debate about tolerance of homosexuality. "Militant homosexuals" were threatening to "take over both political parties," Falwell declared in 1984. They were determined to persuade Americans that "the only sin is to feel guilt or shame—that Jesus Christ was gay—that the Bible endorsed lesbian and homosexual behavior—that there are no values." Gay activists wanted to "recruit" young people to homosexuality, Falwell claimed, and they had "their eyes on our schools . . . our churches . . . our government . . . and our precious children."[9]

· With his influence expanding through television broadcasting during the 1970s, Falwell ventured further into politics. He previously believed that the reformation of society was not the affair of churchmen. But these views changed: by the 1970s, Falwell believed that a "pro-moral" political position needed to be asserted, and he felt called to

[7] Marc Ambinder, "Falwell Suggests Gays to Blame for Attacks"; interview quoted at http://abcnews.go.com/Politics/story?id=121322.

[8] Jorstad, *New Christian Right*, 166–167; from Swaggart's website, November 2013, http://www.francesandfriends.com/homosexuals-born.

[9] Jorstad, *New Christian Right*, 87.

this role. In 1976, he sponsored "I Love America" events at state capitols, which energized a network of local evangelicals. A year later, Falwell allied with Anita Bryant in a "Clean Up America" campaign that opposed ERA ratification and gay rights.

In June 1979, Falwell helped organize a national evangelical-political organization, the Moral Majority. Established with the support of conservative activists and pastors of megachurches, the organization, with headquarters in Lynchburg, claimed millions of members. The Moral Majority was organized around a large network of Christian schools. Employing new methods of direct-mail advertising, the organization tapped into a national database of evangelicals that Falwell had already constructed, crafting a vision of decline and rejuvenation. In one document sent to supporters, the Moral Majority, describing the "moral decline of our nation," appealed to those "who are sick and tired of the way many amoral and secular humanists and other liberals are destroying the traditional family and the moral values on which our nation was built." The pamphlet urged a "return to moral sanity in these United States of America."[10]

The Moral Majority was loosely organized and decentralized, relying on state chapters operating more or less on their own. The group attracted media attention, but it was only one of various groups advocating a Christian Right agenda. Among the most important groups emerging during the late 1970s were national evangelical groups such as the Christian Voice and the Religious Roundtable. The Christian Voice, organized in 1978, was dominated by California evangelicals and focused its effort as a national lobbying organization based in northern Virginia. The Religious Roundtable came into existence in September 1979, created by Ed McAteer, a Southern Baptist activist. The group primarily provided a networking tool composed of evangelical ministers interested in political issues and mobilization of religious conservatives.

Southern conservative evangelicals achieved a peak of influence during the presidential election of 1980, when they played a prominent role in the election of Republican Ronald Reagan. On August 21, 1980, evangelicals and religious broadcasters sponsored a meeting in Dallas that served, according to one account, as a "marriage ceremony" between Southern Baptists and the Republican Party. With the Religious Roundtable sponsoring the event, the meeting included Falwell, Robertson, SBC president Bailey Smith, Charles Stanley, and Ed McAteer. Among the more prominent leaders was James Robison, a Texas religious broadcaster who opposed homosexuality and gay rights. Robison, who broadcast to ninety television stations, was described as "the angry young man of American revivalism." "A great army" was assembling, declared a meeting participant. "We are to fight a war," with the main weapon being religious faith. "This is our day," Falwell declared. "The liberals have blown it."[11]

Ronald Reagan, Republican presidential candidate in 1980, was an especially attractive candidate for evangelicals: though he was not evangelical himself, he spoke their language. Reagan's speech before the Dallas meeting of evangelicals announced a new political alliance. "I know you can't endorse me," he said, "but I want you to

[10] Snowball, *Continuity and Change*, 13.
[11] Kenneth A. Briggs, "Evangelicals Hear Plea: Politics Now," *New York Times*, August 24, 1980.

know that I endorse you and what you are doing." America should restore its mission, he said, by embracing "that old-time religion" and making itself into "that shining city upon a hill."[12] Reagan's election represented the new national power of another source of southern culture—Protestant evangelicalism.

Throughout the 1980s and 1990s, the South provided a political base of conservative Republicanism that relied on evangelical support. The Moral Majority had dissipated by the mid-1980s, replaced by new Christian Right organizations such as the Family Research Council and the American Coalition for Traditional Values, both of which emphasized an antigay agenda. In 1988, Pat Robertson unsuccessfully campaigned for the Republican nomination for president. After the election, Robertson's organization morphed into the Christian Coalition, which became a lobbying organization and pressure group pushing an evangelical agenda. Under the leadership of Christian Coalition executive director Ralph Reed, a smart political operative, the organization rallied evangelicals into even more active supporters of the Republican Party.

LATINOS IN THE NUEVO SOUTH

The South, according to a report by the Pew Charitable Trusts in 2005, served as a "magnet to young, male, foreign-born Latinos migrating in search of economic opportunities." This development was not unique to the South: the nation was becoming increasingly Latino, but, said the report, immigration was "playing out in that region with a greater intensity and across a larger variety of communities—rural, small towns, suburbs and big cities—than in any other part of the country." In this instance, as in many others in late-twentieth-century America, significant demographic change indicated the relationship between region and nation. "The South, different in so many ways for so much of its history, now offers lessons to the rest of the country."[13]

Latinos had composed a prominent part of the South since the founding of Florida, the acquisition of Louisiana, and the annexation of Texas. Mexican Americans in Texas, including the American-born *Tejanos* and more-recent immigrants, figured in the state's culture and politics. In the Southeast, a large portion, about three-quarters, of the Latino population lived in Florida. The migration of Cubans into South Florida and, more recently, of Puerto Ricans into central Florida brought significant changes to that state.

During the 1990s, the most important demographic change occurring in the South was the rise in the Latino population outside Florida and Texas. All told, the Hispanic population of the Southeast grew by 2.25 million during the 1990s. The spread of Latino culture throughout the South was a startling change in a region heretofore dominated mainly by white and black populations. Immigrants from Mexico and

12 Bruce Buursma, "A New Crusade . . . Right-Wing Christians Gird for Election Day," *Chicago Tribune*, August 31, 1980.
13 Rakesh Kochhar, Roberto Suro, and Sonya Tafoya, "The New Latino South: The Context and Consequences of Rapid Population Growth" (Washington, DC: Pew Hispanic Center, July 26, 2005); report available at http://pewhispanic.org/files/reports/50.pdf.

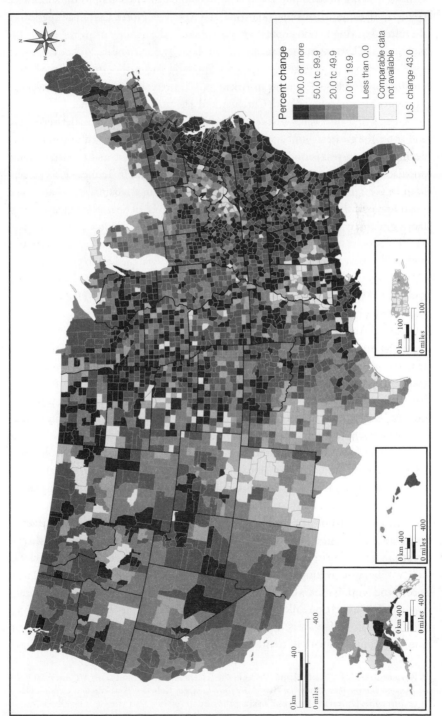

MAP 24.2 Increase in Latino Population, 2000–2010

Central America flooded into the area between the Carolinas and, to the southwest, Georgia, Alabama, Mississippi, Louisiana, and Arkansas. North Carolina experienced the fastest-growing Latino population of any state in the nation during the 1990s. The population of Latinos in the state grew from about 77,000 to nearly 638,000 between 1990 and 2007—an increase of 732 percent. Similarly, during the same years the Latino population grew by 656 percent in Arkansas, 580 percent in Georgia, 558 percent in Tennessee, 454 percent in South Carolina, and 406 percent in Alabama.

During the early twenty-first century, these trends only accelerated. Between 2000 and 2007, the greatest number of immigrants—10.3 million—arrived in this country during any seven-year period in American history. Between 2000 and 2008, the Latino population grew by 78 percent in South Carolina, 74 percent in Tennessee, 68 percent both in Georgia and North Carolina, and 62 percent in Alabama. Rural areas and small towns of the Southeast saw the sudden appearance of Spanish-language stores, radio stations, churches, and community groups. By 2004, in some parts of eastern North Carolina, a fifth of the population was Latino, while in other communities, such as Siler City, North Carolina, or Gainesville, Georgia, the Latino population was close to two-fifths of the total. "Life in the South used to be defined in shades of black and white," wrote an Alabama journalist. "But a growing wave of Hispanic immigrants is adding brown to that color scheme."[14]

Central American immigration was concentrated in particular counties and cities of the South. In Mecklenburg County, North Carolina, which includes the city of Charlotte, the Latino population grew from 7,000 in 1990 to about 45,000 in 2000, an increase of 570 percent. In the Raleigh-Durham area, Latinos increased by 1180 percent between 1980 and 2000, while in Atlanta during the same years the growth rate was 995 percent. These same trends also occurred outside large cities. The late 1990s brought an economic boom, with low unemployment, which made the South—expanding even more rapidly than other parts of the country—an attractive location for immigrants.

It was estimated that a majority of these immigrants, nearly two-thirds of them, were undocumented. North Carolina alone had 300,000 undocumented immigrants in 2000. Only a minority of immigrants spoke English. Latinos filled the demand for labor in a variety of occupations, including textiles, manufacturing, construction, and farm work. "If it weren't for immigrants, there wouldn't be an agriculture industry in North Carolina," said a North Carolina Farm Bureau official, "because picking tobacco is hot and hard, and harvesting Christmas trees is cold and hard. Farmers can't hire enough local people to do the work anymore."[15]

Latino immigration followed jobs that were created in the South, many of which existed outside urban areas. For the country as a whole, Latinos were the fastest-growing ethnic population in rural areas and small towns. Of the ten states with the

[14] Raymond A. Mohl, "Latinos and Blacks in the Recent American South," in *Migration and the Transformation of the Southern Workplace since 1945*, ed. Robert Cassanello and Colin J. Davis (Gainesville: University Press of Florida, 2009), 85.

[15] Rick Martinez, "Immigration Hits 'Critical Mass' in NC," *Carolina Journal Online*, December 12, 2005; available at www.carolinajournal.com/exclusives/display_exclusive.html?id=2983.

greatest increases in nonmetropolitan Latino population, seven were southern states. Gordon County, Georgia, was a mostly rural county in 2000, with 44,000 inhabitants. But during the 1990s it became a center of carpet and floor-covering manufacturing, with much of the factory workforce supplied by Latino immigrants. The overall Latino population during the 1990s grew rapidly, from 200 to 3,200. The new Latino South is also characterized—in contrast to the rest of Latino America—by the predominance of recent immigrants. Nationally, about 41 percent of the Latino population are foreign born, compared to 57 percent in six southern states. In thirty-six southern counties with the heaviest recent immigration, about two-thirds of Latinos were born outside the United States as of 2000. About half these immigrants to the South arrived during the late 1990s, a period of especially rapid growth.

Hispanic workers filled the ranks of labor in agriculture and forest products. Migrant workers found jobs around the region and eventually dominated that form of labor in orchards, tobacco fields, and Christmas tree farms. Among North Carolina Christmas tree growers, for example, about four-fifths of the labor force was Latino in 2001. The construction boom across the South during the 1990s and early twenty-first century relied on immigrant labor, which composed around a fifth of the workforce. Industry and manufacturing figured importantly in employment, though much of this was organized in low-cost settings outside cities. Carpet manufacturing became a significant employer of cheaper Latino labor. In Dalton, Georgia, 120 carpet factories sprang up, and these relied on Latino workers.

Another significant employer of Latino labor outside cities was the Southeast poultry industry. After the 1970s, American food tastes shifted away from red meat toward chicken as a lower-fat alternative. In the 1980s, per capita consumption of poultry, for the first time, exceeded that of beef, doubling between 1977 and 1999, while that of beef declined by nearly a third. Meanwhile, exports of poultry grew from 500 million pounds in 1987 to 6.5 billion pounds in 2002. Increases in production resulted in a steady decline in prices paid by consumers, as poultry prices dropped by about 50 percent in real dollars between 1960 and 1999.

In order to satisfy this growing market, poultry operations increasingly located in the rural and small-town South. While in 1963 the South produced half the chickens sold to Americans, by the first few years of the twenty-first century that proportion had grown to two-thirds. The warmer climate of the South made it ideal for large, industrial-style production of poultry, while access to cheaper grains also provided lower costs. Chickens in this setting are raised in large warehouses and, on the same location, are slaughtered, cut up, and packaged for distribution. These large operations required heavy capitalization, and the business became concentrated in a few big corporations. The large poultry operations also located in the South because of its traditional non-union practices and, increasingly, because of the availability of cheap Latino labor.

The rapid acceleration of immigration in the South led to a political backlash. In six states, legislatures enacted their own immigration laws designed to restrict the rights of undocumented workers. The Georgia legislature, for example, enacted legislation in 2006 that limited undocumented immigrants from obtaining driver's licenses, imposed new standards for documentation for employers, and restricted healthcare and educational benefits for illegal immigrants. Across the South, law enforcement officials stepped up efforts to apprehend undocumented workers in order to deport them. In North Carolina, the legislature in 2006 prohibited illegal immigrants from obtaining driver's licenses. The law of 2013 loosened these restrictions somewhat. Under this new law, the 325,000 undocumented immigrants in North Carolina would be able to obtain a driver's license if they had lived in the country for a year, but the law added a host of new restrictions. Modeled on a tough law in Arizona that the Supreme Court upheld in a 2013 decision, police were authorized to detain people if "reasonable suspicion" existed that they were undocumented. The law also made possessing a false driver's license a felony, while it tightened requirements for employers to confirm workers' identity status. The law was passed in July 2013 but was vetoed by Gov. Pat McCrory. The legislature then overrode the veto in September 2013.

Latino immigration into the South has coincided with the continuing immigration of nonsoutherners into the region. In the early twenty-first century, the South has become the fastest-growing area of the country. At the turn of the twentieth century, roughly 95 percent of people living in the South were born there. By 2010, that proportion declined, but it was most marked in states such as Florida (where a majority of residents were born outside the South), Virginia (with 60 percent southern-born), North Carolina (70 percent), South Carolina (75 percent), and Georgia (72 percent). Migration of nonsoutherners was least evident in states such as Mississippi and Louisiana (about 90 percent southern-born each). In Virginia, North Carolina, and Florida, migrants from the Northeast and West Coast outnumbered those from elsewhere in the South.

Domestic Migration and Immigration Felt Differently Across South

Domestic migration has driven the decline in the Southern-born share of the population in the Mid-Atlantic, while immigration has been a much bigger factor in Texas.

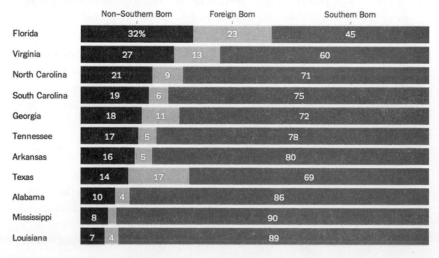

	Non-Southern Born	Foreign Born	Southern Born
Florida	32%	23	45
Virginia	27	13	60
North Carolina	21	9	71
South Carolina	19	6	75
Georgia	18	11	72
Tennessee	17	5	78
Arkansas	16	5	80
Texas	14	17	69
Alabama	10	4	86
Mississippi	8		90
Louisiana	7	4	89

Measuring Northeast and West Coast Migrants

Only in Florida, Virginia and North Carolina do Northeastern and West Coast migrants outnumber people from elsewhere in the South.

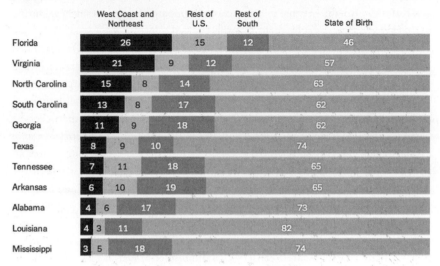

	West Coast and Northeast	Rest of U.S.	Rest of South	State of Birth
Florida	26	15	12	46
Virginia	21	9	12	57
North Carolina	15	8	14	63
South Carolina	13	8	17	62
Georgia	11	9	18	62
Texas	8	9	10	74
Tennessee	7	11	18	65
Arkansas	6	10	19	65
Alabama	4	6	17	73
Louisiana	4	3	11	82
Mississippi	3	5	18	74

The Rise of the New South

The share of the Southern population born outside the South has surged over the last century.

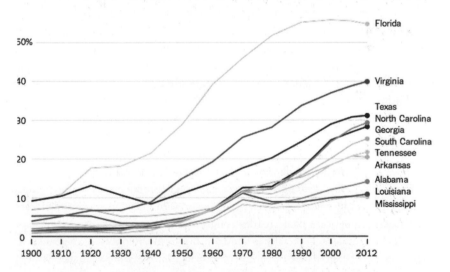

CONCLUSION: THE REPUBLICAN SOUTH

After the Goldwater presidential campaign of 1964, Republicans made deep inroads in national politics. After 1972, only southern Democrats Jimmy Carter and Bill Clinton stalled the Republican advance in the South. In 1976, Carter carried all of the region except Virginia. Four years later, however, Ronald Reagan's strong appeal to Christian evangelicals had major consequences; Carter won only his home state of Georgia and the Democratic bastion of West Virginia. Bill Clinton, a four-term Arkansas governor, carried Louisiana, Arkansas, Tennessee, Georgia, West Virginia, and Kentucky in 1992 en route to his successful campaign for the presidency. During his reelection campaign in 1996, Clinton carried Florida, Louisiana, Arkansas, Tennessee, Kentucky, and West Virginia. In 2008, Democrat Barack Obama, aided by African American turnout and white suburbanite voters, captured Florida, North Carolina, and Virginia. Four years later, in 2012, he won Florida and Virginia.

Despite these results, the Republican Party after 1984 began to establish regional political dominance. Statewide senatorial elections were either split between the parties or trended Republican. In addition, Republicans became competitive in state legislative races and in gubernatorial elections. Midterm elections of 1994, 2010, and 2014 became "wave" elections in which Republicans racked up major wins because of a larger white turnout. In 1990, there were eighty-three Democrats and forty-six Republicans among the South's congressmen. After the 1994 elections, Republicans controlled these seats by a 73–64 margin. In addition, Republicans after 1994 won a majority of governorships and US senator seats for the first time since Reconstruction. Particularly exposed were conservative and moderate Democrats, who suffered acute losses in 1994. Southern Democrats never reestablished themselves thereafter, especially in the Deep South, which by the 1990s became solidly Republican at local and state levels.

Much of the early twenty-first-century electorate was racialized: a majority of southern whites voted Republican, while most African Americans voted Democratic. In the aftermath of the Voting Rights Act, African Americans supported the creation of new congressional and legislative districts that would increase the number of black officeholders. By 2014, despite increases in the number of black congressmen, Democrats could not win a single majority-white congressional district in the South. Moreover, the electorate in certain southern states in particular was racially polarized. In Mississippi—the most polarized state in the nation—pollsters estimated that 89 percent of whites voted for the Republican presidential candidate in 2012, while 96 percent of blacks voted for Obama.

Thereafter, Republicans became increasingly successful in recruiting new candidates and attracting younger politicians to the party. Increasingly in control of state legislatures, Republicans could redraw congressional districts to the advantage of the party's candidates. Especially in the 2010 midterms, Republican donors spent large amounts of cash to capture control of state legislatures. They were successful in Virginia, North Carolina, Georgia, Florida, and Texas, Louisiana, and Tennessee, all of which emerged from the elections with large Republican majorities. The 2010 legislatures carved out congressional districts that gave them a partisan advantage. North Carolina's congressional delegation, for example, returned three Democrats and eleven Republicans, even though the overall vote was 44 percent for Democrats and 56 percent for Republicans.

In sweeps during 2010 and 2014, the party solidified its status in the region, which became nearly a one-party region. In 2014, there were US Senate elections in every southern state but Florida; Republicans' margin of victory in ten campaigns exceeded double digits. The GOP after 2014 controlled southern governorships, legislatures, and congressional delegations. Overall, Republicans won these elections by an average of 21 percent.

Especially in the Deep South, Democrats offered little competition. In Texas, the Republican candidate for governor, Greg Abbott, won 235 of the state's 254 counties. From 2010 to 2014, states that had been competitive came under Republican dominance. In 2010, North Carolina, which had experienced Democratic control, elected Republican majorities in both houses for the first time since 1868. Two years later, North Carolina voters elected only the third Republican governor since 1896. After the 2014 elections, Democrats held on to a majority only in the Kentucky House of Representatives. West Virginia, solidly Democratic prior to 2000, became a Republican bastion as coal miners and white voters migrated out of the Democratic Party. Republican candidates for US Senate won all of the state's fifty-five counties. In 2014 alone, Republicans won fifteen seats in legislative elections, capturing the House of Delegates and gaining enough seats to obtain a 17–17 tie in the state senate. All told, Republicans won sixty-four additional seats in ten southern legislatures in 2014. Democrats had a long-term minority status in the South.

The South of the early twenty-first century has become a region of contrasts. Across the region, migration into southern cities means a new influence for outsiders. Race is no longer a binary—the arrival of millions of Latinos has had profound social, cultural, economic, and political results. Southerners remained different from the rest of the country, but the differences narrowed in the later twentieth century. In part, those differences narrowed because the rest of the country became more southern. In culture, entertainment, politics, religion, and sports, Americans have become more southern, and the southern idiom has come to dominate national life.

INDEX

Index

IN-19

Quakers: late seventeenth-century North Carolina, 50, 52–53; eighteenth-century immigrants to southern backcountry, 105; Gabriel's Rebellion, 163; Virginia debate about gradual emancipation (1831–32), 167
Quasi-War with France, 143
Quebec, 103, 113
Queen Elizabeth, 20
Quejo, Pedro de, 13
Quincy, Josiah, 85
Quinipiassa, 92
Quitman, John, 226, 238
Quitrents, 30

R. J. Reynolds Tobacco Company, 329, 407, 413, 482, 567
Racial Integrity Act, 408–9
Railroads, 153–54, 157,160, 205; problems in the Confederacy, 262; growth after the Civil War, 322–27; standardization of time and rail gauge, 326; workers, 326; impact on agriculture and rural South, 334, 345–46
Rainey, Joseph H., 312
Raleigh News and Observer, 353, 484
Raleigh *State Chronicle*, 368
Raleigh, NC, 212, 346, 580
Raleigh, Sir Walter, 20
Randolph family, 77
Randolph-Macon College, 189
Randolph, A. Philip, 468, 523–24, 527–28, 536
Randolph, John, 144–45, 180, 183
Randolph, Thomas Jefferson, 167–68
Ranger, 52
Ransom, John Crowe, 415
Rappahannock Indians, 9
Rappahannock River, 3, 78
RCA Victor, 506–7, 510
RDX, 465
Readjusters, 343
Reagan, Ronald, 577–78, 583
Reagon, Cordell, 532
Real McCoys, 570
Reconstruction Acts, 306
Reconstruction Finance Corporation (RFC), 441
Reconstruction: uncertainty about emancipation, 295–96; persistence of slavery work regime and white brutality, 295, 299, 302; sexual abuse of women, 296, 314; labor contracts, 298–99, 303; Christianity, 299–300; reunification of black families after emancipation, 302; women, 302–3; self-reconstruction, 304–5; political mobilization of African Americans, 307; black officeholders, 311–12
Red River valley, 150
Red River, 92, 151
Red Shirts, 353
Red Stick War, 146, 214, 216
Redeemers, 342–43
Reece, Florence, 569; "Which Side Are You On?," 569
Reed flutes, 136
Reeves, Jim: "Four Walls," 508
Regents University, 574

Regulators, 109–12
Regulators. *See* Backcountry
Reidsville, NC, 417, 500
Religious Roundtable, 577
Report on the Economic Conditions of the South (1938), 455–56, 458–59
Research Triangle Park (RTP), 552
Resettlement Administration (RA), 445–46
Restoration, 50
Retirees, 544
Revels, Hiram, 312
Revenue Act of 1916, 390, 396
Revolt among the Sharecroppers, 453
Revolution, American: origins, 112–17; British enlist slaves, 118–21, 270; war in the South, 121–25; solidifies southern identity, 127; inspires egalitarianism, 163
Reynolds, John, 555
Reynolds, R. J., 329
Reynolds, William H., 288
Rhett, Robert Barnwell, 207–8, 227, 240, 259
Rhine valley, 104
Ribault, Jean, 14–15, 67
Rice University, 550
Rice: introduction to South Carolina, 56–57; cultivation and trade, 57–61, 88–90, 132–33; *Oryza sativa* (Asian rice), 58; *Oryza glaberrima* (West African rice), 59; Georgia, 59, 132–33; collapse of plantation system after Civil War, 331
Richardson, Colonel Richard, 122
Richmond and Danville Railroad, 325
Richmond College (later University of Richmond), 189
Richmond College, 170
Richmond County, VA, 48, 79
Richmond Enquirer, 182, 227
Richmond Examiner, 182
Richmond News-Leader, 519
Richmond Terminal system, 325
Richmond Whig, 182, 238
Richmond, VA, 79, 154, 163, 170, 262, 296 323; industrialization, 232–33; Civil War, 261, 266–68, 274; Bread Riot (1863), 264–66; Lincoln visits, 284; Confederate surrender, 284, 287; black militias, 313; post-Civil War status, 320, 322; Progressive Era, 377, 379; World War II, 472; hillbilly music, 503; school desegregation, 560
Ridge, Major, 217
Ridgeway, Robert, 182
Rivers, Eurith D., 457
Rivers, L. Mendel, 495, 548, 567
Roane, William Henry, 167
Roanoke Island, NC: Lost Colony, 20, 25; freedmen's colony, 287–88
Roanoke River, 4
Roanoke, VA, 320
Robertson, Pat, 574, 577–78
Robeson County, NC, 266
Robinson, James Harvey, 422
Robinson, Jo Ann, 523
Robinson, Joseph, 456
Robison, James, 577
Rochester, NY, 196

Swaggart, Jimmy, 576
Swamp Acts of 1849 and 1950, 435
Swann v. Board of Education (1971), 559
Syphillis, 95

Taft-Hartley Act (1947), 482, 565–66
Tallahassee, FL, 17, 93, 97
Tallahatchie River, 521
Tallapoosa River, 92, 99
Talmadge, Eugene, 450, 456, 478, 492
Tambourines, 136
Tampa Bay, FL, 13, 97
Tampa, FL, 324, 366, 431, 546
Tanensas, 98
Taney, Roger, 238–39
Tar River, 4
Tariffs: political issue, 205–10; 1828 (Tariff of
    Abominations), 205–6
Tarleton, Banastre, 124
Tate, Allen, 415
Tawasa, 98
Taylor, Harley, 500
Taylor, John, 132, 144
Taylor, Thomas, 165
Taylor, Zachary, 228–29
Tennessee River valley, 150, 260
Tennessee Supreme Court, 423
Tennessee Valley Authority (TVA), 444–45,
    456, 461
Tennessee: cotton, 149–50; population growth
    during cotton boom, 151, 157; slave exporting,
    155; voter turnout in antebellum era, 203;
    Indian Removal, 214–15; secession, 253, 256;
    Civil War, 260, 263, 266, 303; KKK, 313, 315;
    convict lease, 336
Tenth Calvary, 398
Tenure of Office Act, 306
Terhune, Mary Virginia (Marion Harland), 220
Terrell, Mary Church, 374–75
Terry, Alfred H., 277
Texarkana, AR, 429
Texas Idea, 373
Texas: cotton, 149–51, 334; "Gone to Texas," 151;
    Lone Star Republic and annexation, 224;
    secession, 252; Confederate surrender, 267;
    Reconstruction, 311; KKK, 315, 429
Textile mills, 317, 327, 329–31; mill paternalism,
    330; workers, 330–31; women workers, 373;
    World War I, 398; 1920s, 413; mill villages
    and paternalism, 416–17; rayon, 417; general
    strike (1934), 449
Textile Workers Organizing Committee
    (TWOC), 451
Thirteenth Amendment, 269, 290, 295–96,
    313, 335
Thirty Years a Slave (1897), 270
Thirty-Ninth Congress, 306
Thomas Road Baptist Church, 574
Thomas, Francis, 180
Thomas, Henry, 531
Thomas, Norman, 445, 452
Thompson, James G., 474
Thompson, John, 140
Thorimans, 91
Throuet, H., 180
Thruston, John, 81

Thruston, Thomasine, 81
Thurber, John, 56
Thurmond, Strom, 495–97, 557, 560–61
Tiffany, Louis C., 324
Tilden, Samuel, 341
Till, Emmett, 521
Tilley, M. E., 494
Tillman, Benjamin, 350, 352, 360
Timuca, 67, 96
Tin Pan Alley, 507
To Kill a Mockingbird (1962), 570
To Secure These Rights (1947), 494–95
Tobacco Road, 414, 445
Tobacco Workers International Union, 449
Tobacco: introduction in Chesapeake, 22, 32–33;
    culture, 33–38; grown in Spanish Caribbean,
    33; *Nicotiana rustica* variety, 33; *Nicotiana
    tabacum* variety, 33; boom in production in
    seventeenth century, 33; decline in eighteenth
    century, 76; export trade, 76–77, 79;
    factories, 232–33; post-Civil War
    manufacturing, 327–29; post-Civil War
    decline in farming, 331; Great Depression, 439
Tohomes, 95
Tojetti, Virgilio, 324
Tombigbee River, 95
Toningas, 91
Tories. *See* Loyalists
Tougaloo College, 311
Tourgée, Albion W., 308, 313
Tourism: Florida, 324, 544–45; Sandhills region,
    324–25; western North Carolina, 325
Towne, Laura M., 288
Townshend duties, 117
Townshend, Charles, 117
Tractors, 489–90
Tracy City, TN, 338
Traffic, 569
Trail of Tears, 217–18
Train robbers, 334
Transportation: river, 34–35, 76, 85, 152–53;
    upcountry farmers, 134; Transportation
    Revolution, 152–54; canals, 152, 205;
    steamboats, 152–53, 160; flatboats, 152;
    slave labor, 160; internal improvement,
    205, 209–10, 258
Travis, Joseph, 165, 167
Travis, Merle, 569
Treasurer, 27–28
Treaty of Fort Jackson, 146, 214
Treaty of Guadalupe Hildago, 225, 227
Treaty of New Echota, 217
Treaty of Paris (1783), 113, 124–25
Treaty of Paris (1783), 121
Tredegar Iron Works, 233, 262, 264
Trent River, 4
Trinity River, 151
Trion, GA, 450
Troubled Waters (1885), 375
Truman, Harry, 483–84, 494–96, 565
Tryon, William, 110–11
Tubb, Ernest, 504
Tuberculosis, 95
Tucker, George, 250
Tucker, Henry St. George, 163
Tucker, Sarah, 78